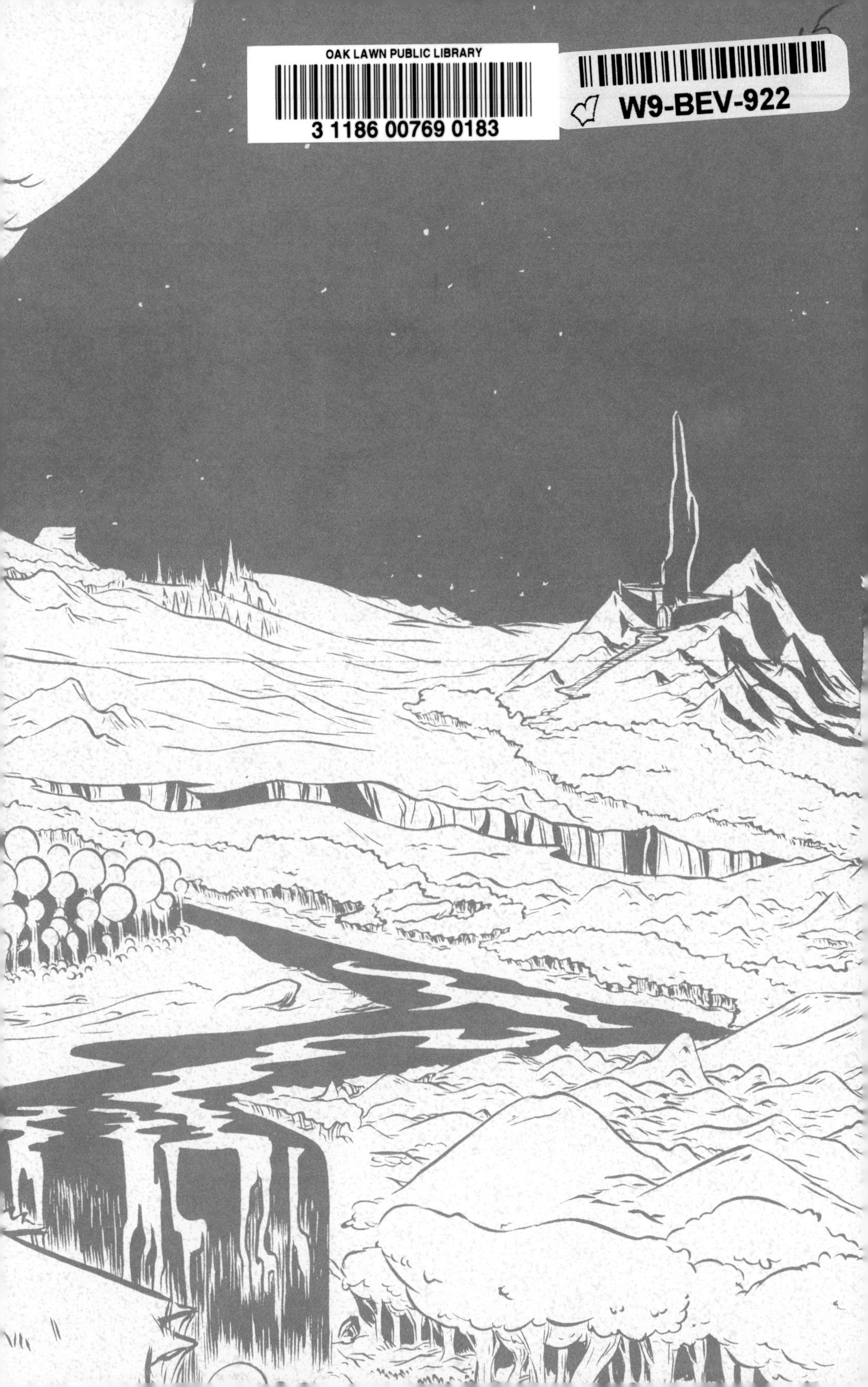

— THE RETURN OF —
KING DOUG

WRITTEN BY
GREG ERB & JASON OREMLAND

ILLUSTRATED BY
WOOK-JIN CLARK

LETTERED BY
DOUGLAS E. SHERWOOD

COVER COLORS BY
DAN JACKSON

DESIGNED BY
KEITH WOOD

EDITED BY
JAMES LUCAS JONES WITH JILL BEATON

PUBLISHED BY ONI PRESS, INC.

JOE NOZEMACK • PUBLISHER

JAMES LUCAS JONES • EDITOR IN CHIEF

RANDAL C. JARRELL • MANAGING EDITOR

CORY CASONI • MARKETING DIRECTOR

KEITH WOOD • ART DIRECTOR

JILL BEATON • ASSISTANT EDITOR

DOUGLAS E. SHERWOOD • PRODUCTION ASSISTANT

ONI PRESS, INC.
1305 SE MARTIN LUTHER KING JR. BLVD.
SUITE A
PORTLAND, OR 97214
USA

WWW.ONIPRESS.COM

FIRST EDITION: SEPTEMBER 2009
ISBN: 978-1-934964-15-6

1 3 5 7 9 10 8 6 4 2

PRINTED IN CHINA.

To my mom and dad – whose belief in me sometimes flew in the face of all reason.

– Greg Erb

This book is dedicated to my wife, son, brothers, and parents. If you didn't make the cut, try harder next time.

– Jason Oremland

To Mom and Dad

– Wook-Jin Clark

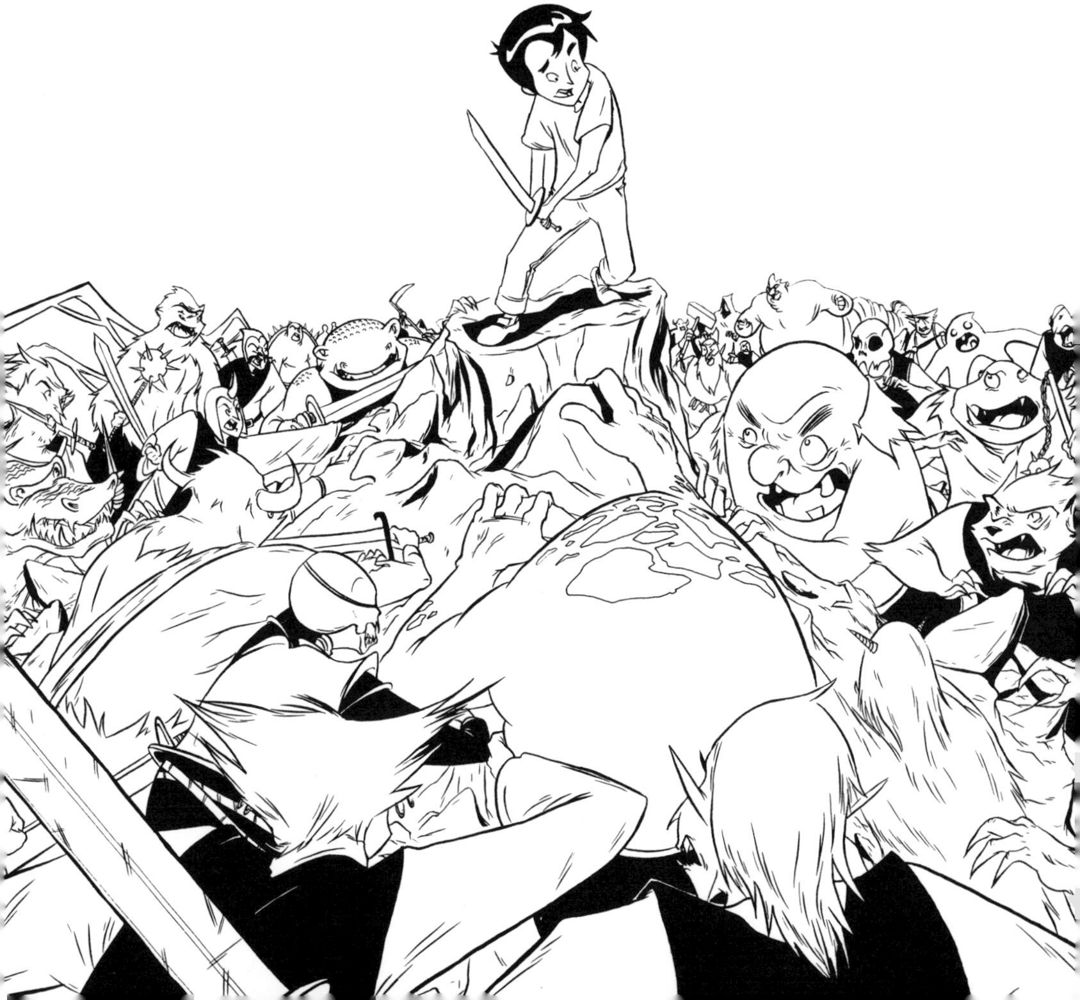

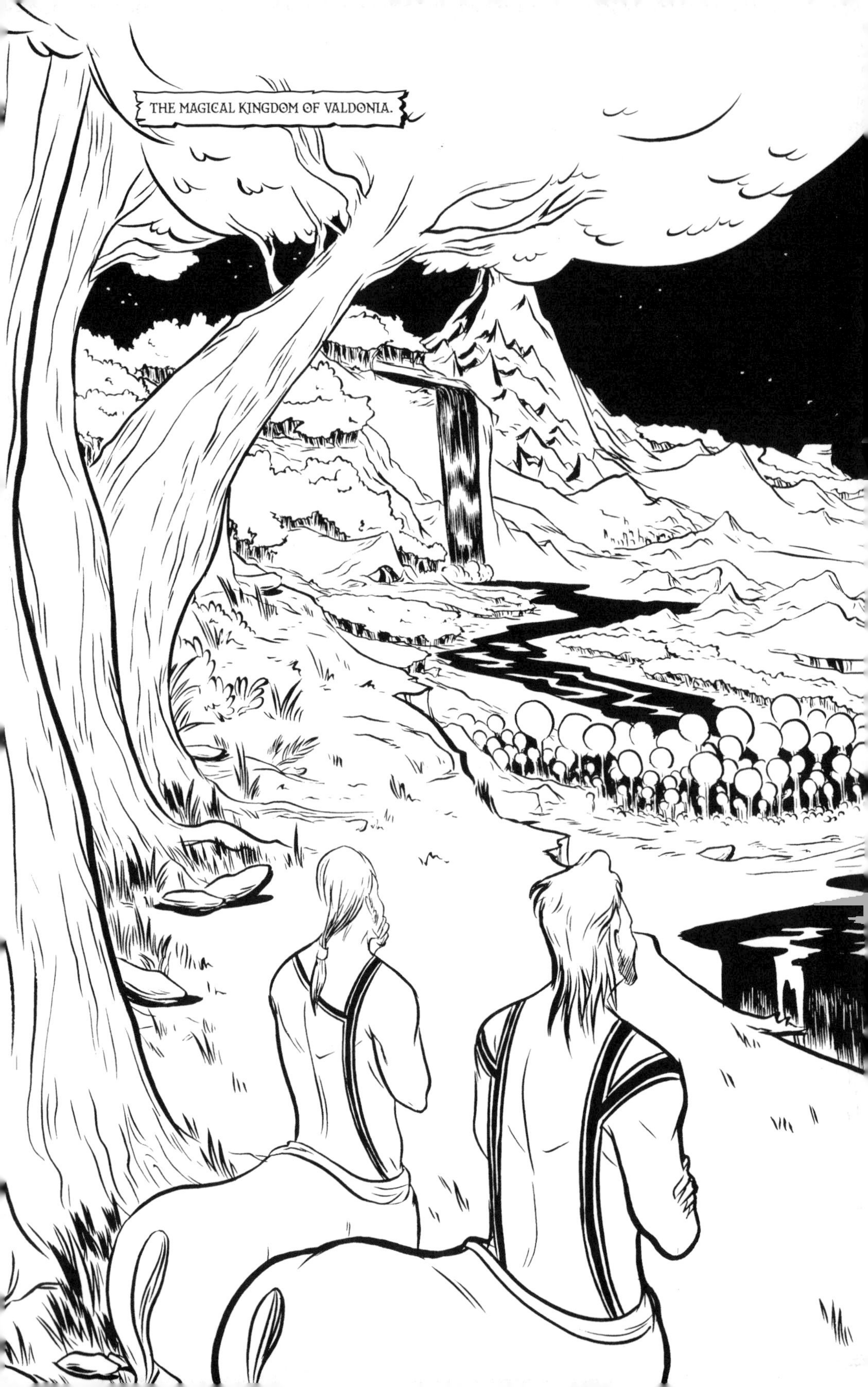
THE MAGICAL KINGDOM OF VALDONIA.

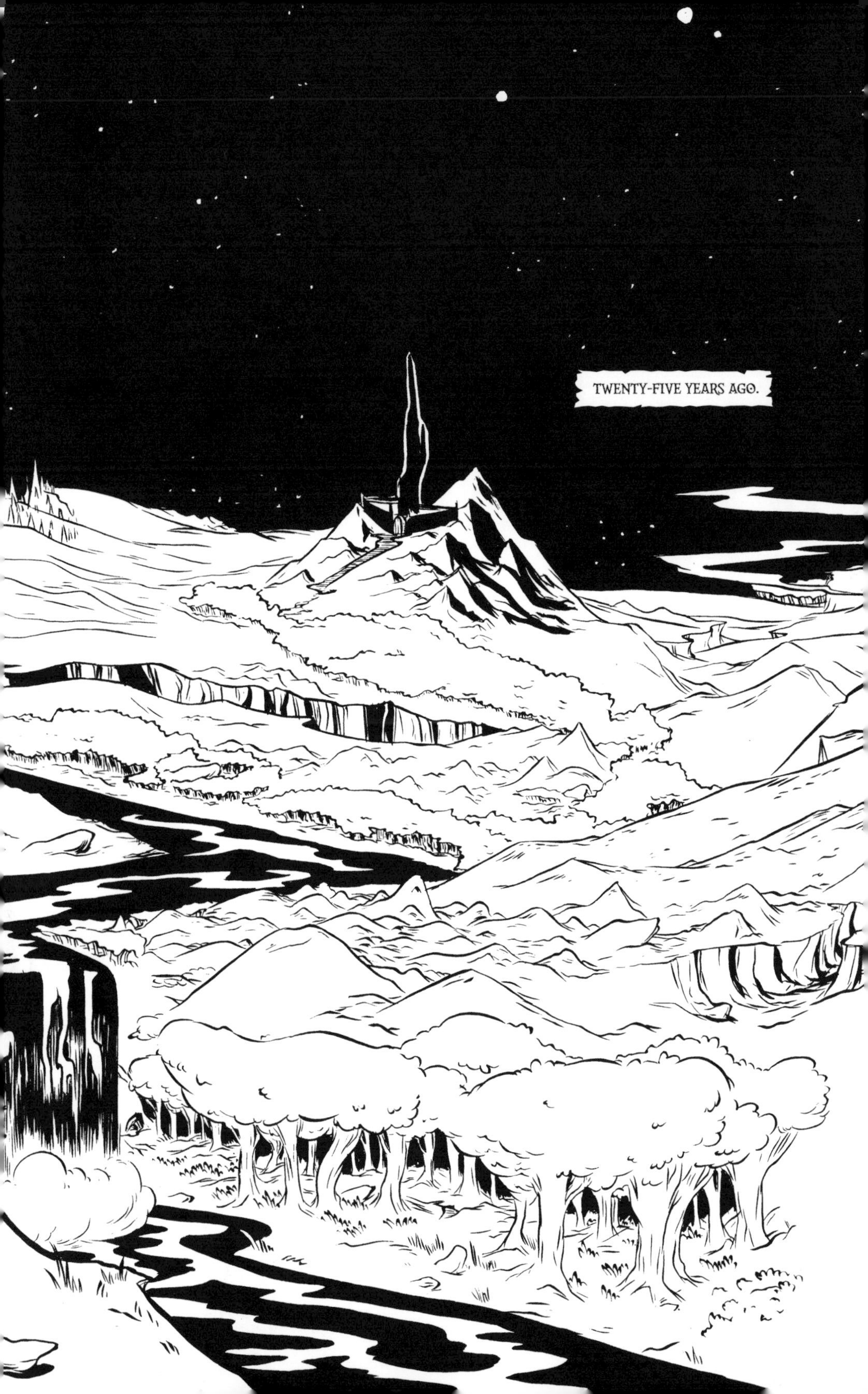
TWENTY-FIVE YEARS AGO.

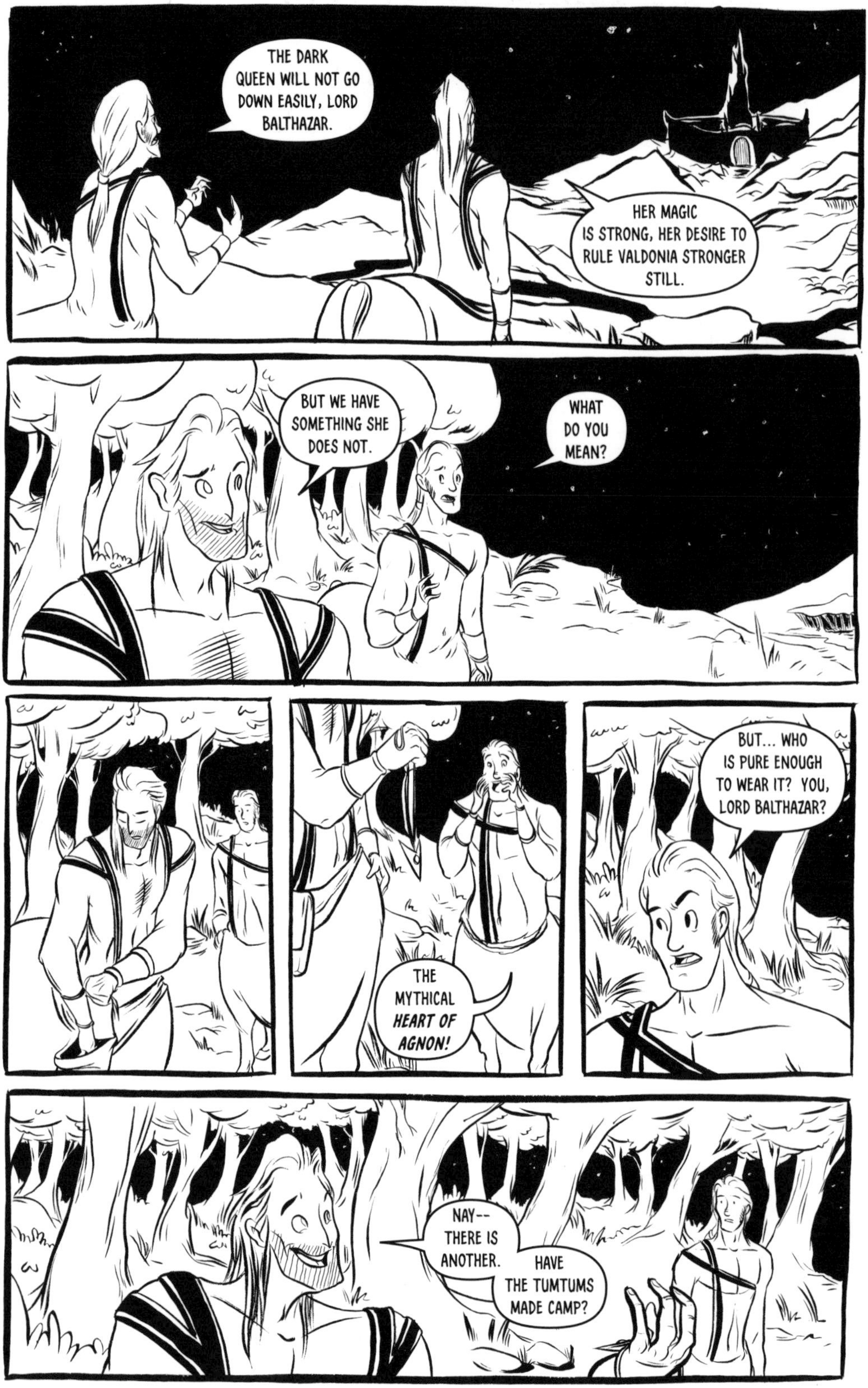
THE DARK QUEEN WILL NOT GO DOWN EASILY, LORD BALTHAZAR.
HER MAGIC IS STRONG, HER DESIRE TO RULE VALDONIA STRONGER STILL.
BUT WE HAVE SOMETHING SHE DOES NOT.
WHAT DO YOU MEAN?
THE MYTHICAL *HEART OF AGNON!*
BUT... WHO IS PURE ENOUGH TO WEAR IT? YOU, LORD BALTHAZAR?
NAY-- THERE IS ANOTHER.
HAVE THE TUMTUMS MADE CAMP?

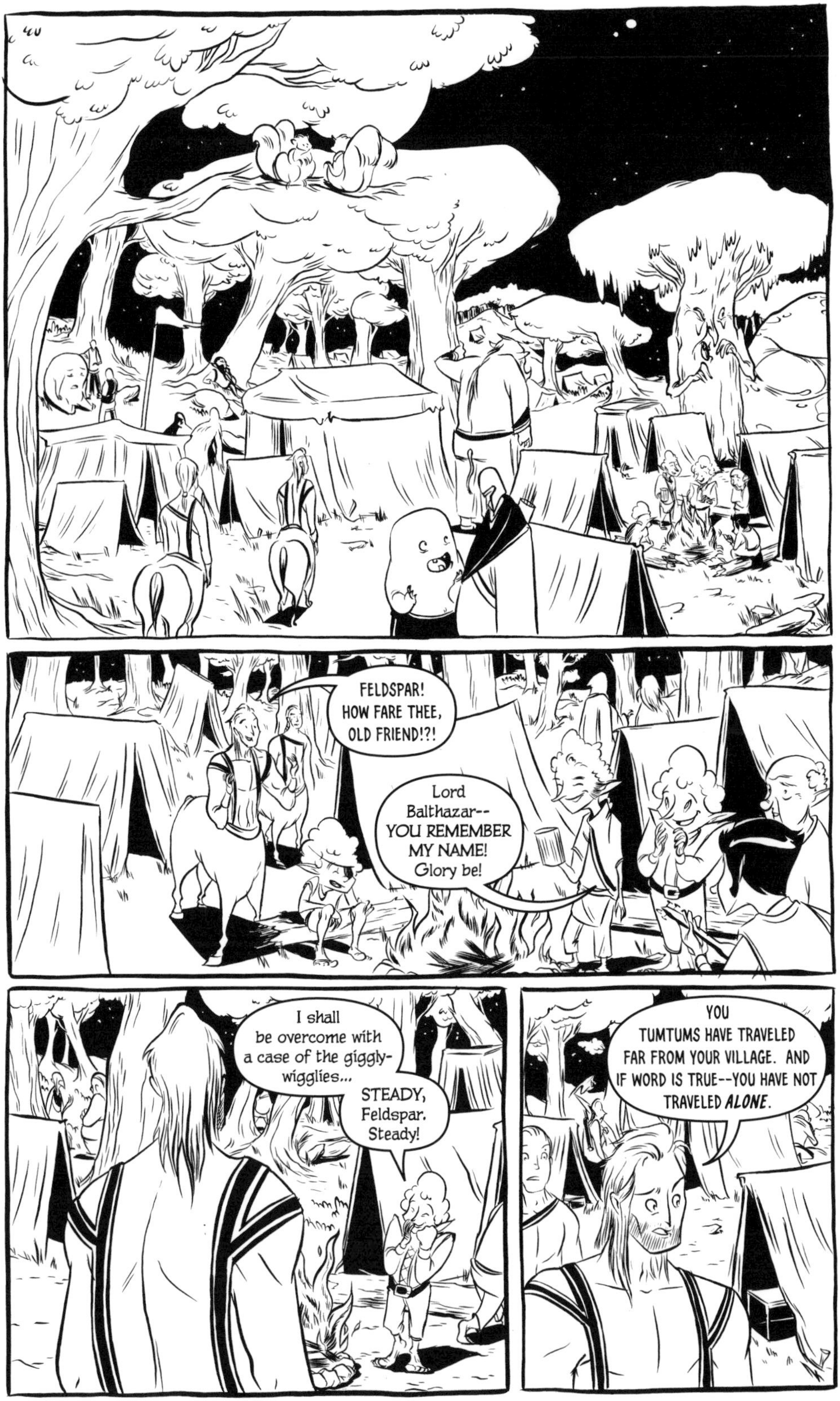
FELDSPAR! HOW FARE THEE, OLD FRIEND!?!
Lord Balthazar-- YOU REMEMBER MY NAME! Glory be!
I shall be overcome with a case of the giggly-wigglies...
STEADY, Feldspar. Steady!
YOU TUMTUMS HAVE TRAVELED FAR FROM YOUR VILLAGE. AND IF WORD IS TRUE--YOU HAVE NOT TRAVELED *ALONE*.

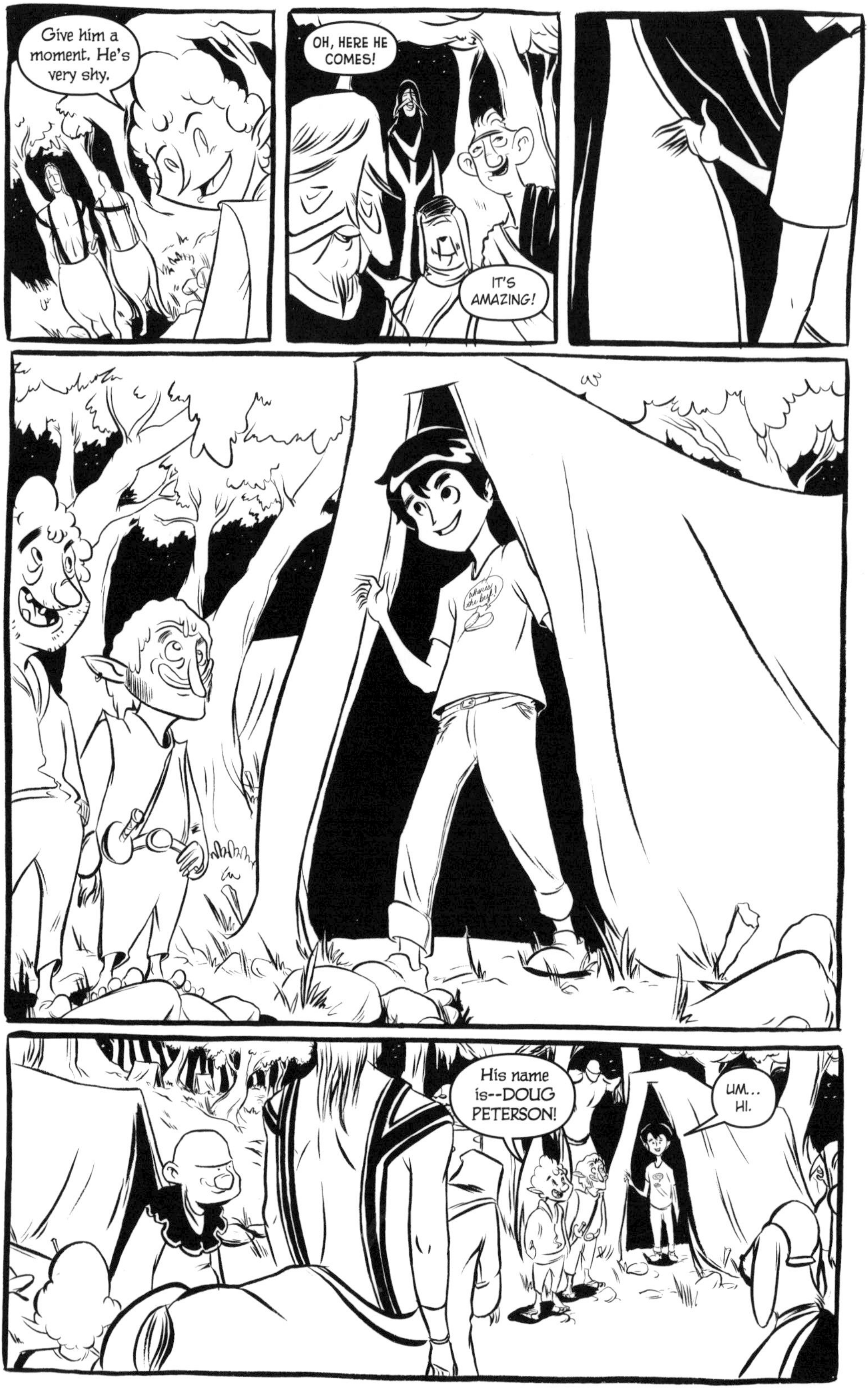
Give him a moment. He's very shy.
OH, HERE HE COMES!
IT'S AMAZING!
His name is--DOUG PETERSON!
UM... HI.

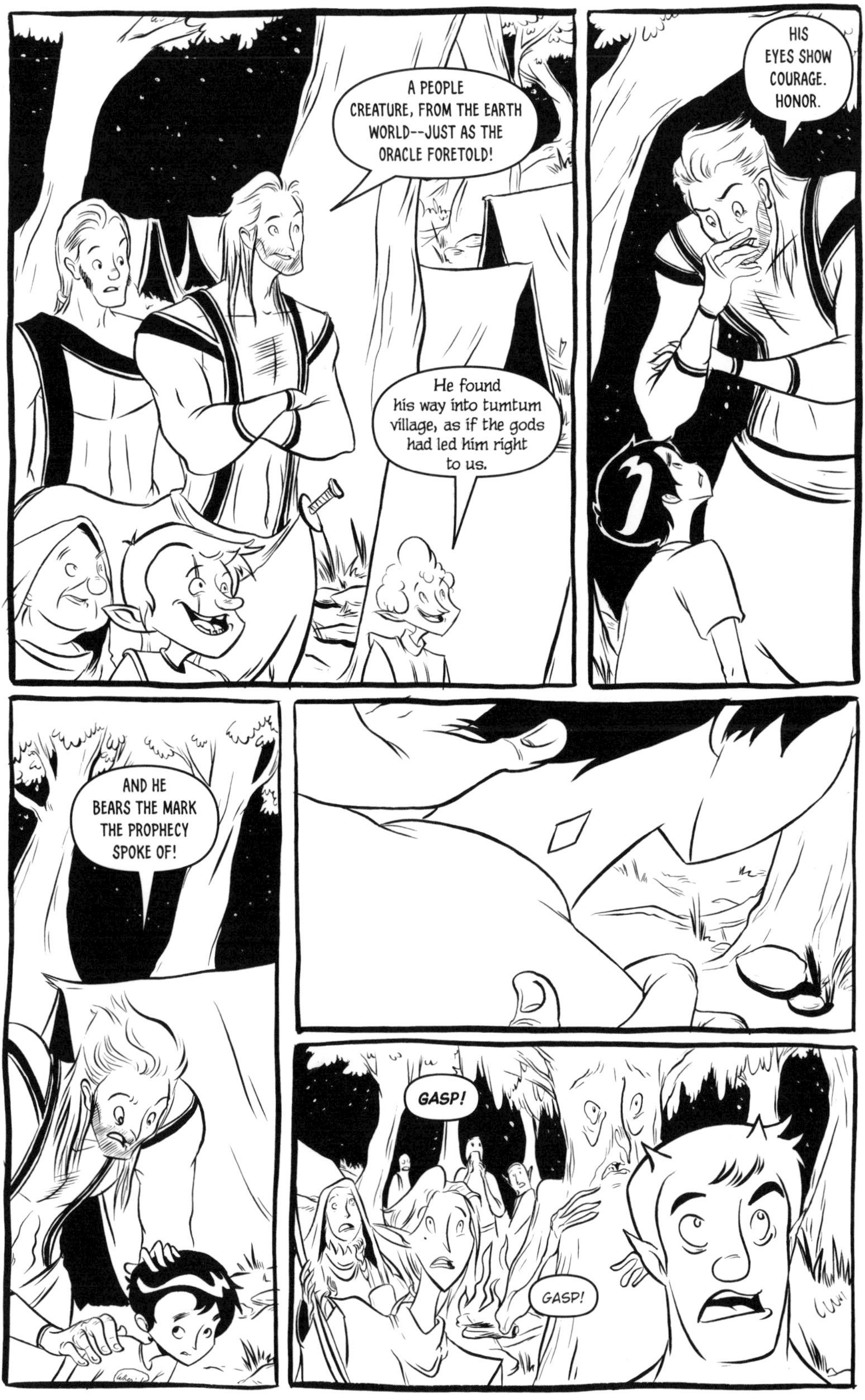
A PEOPLE CREATURE, FROM THE EARTH WORLD--JUST AS THE ORACLE FORETOLD!
He found his way into tumtum village, as if the gods had led him right to us.
HIS EYES SHOW COURAGE. HONOR.
AND HE BEARS THE MARK THE PROPHECY SPOKE OF!
GASP!
GASP!

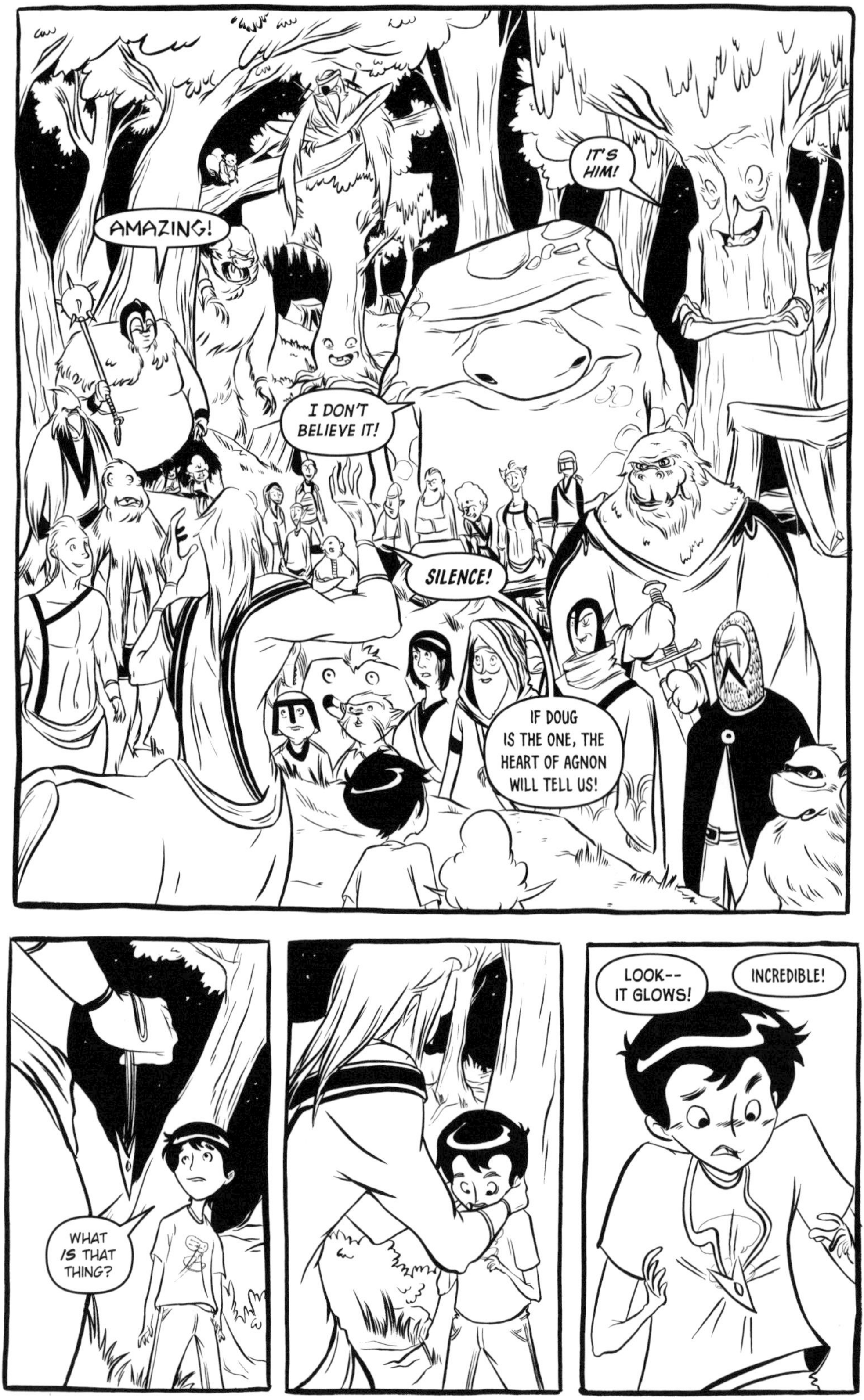
AMAZING!
IT'S HIM!
I DON'T BELIEVE IT!
SILENCE!
IF DOUG IS THE ONE, THE HEART OF AGNON WILL TELL US!
WHAT IS THAT THING?
LOOK-- IT GLOWS!
INCREDIBLE!

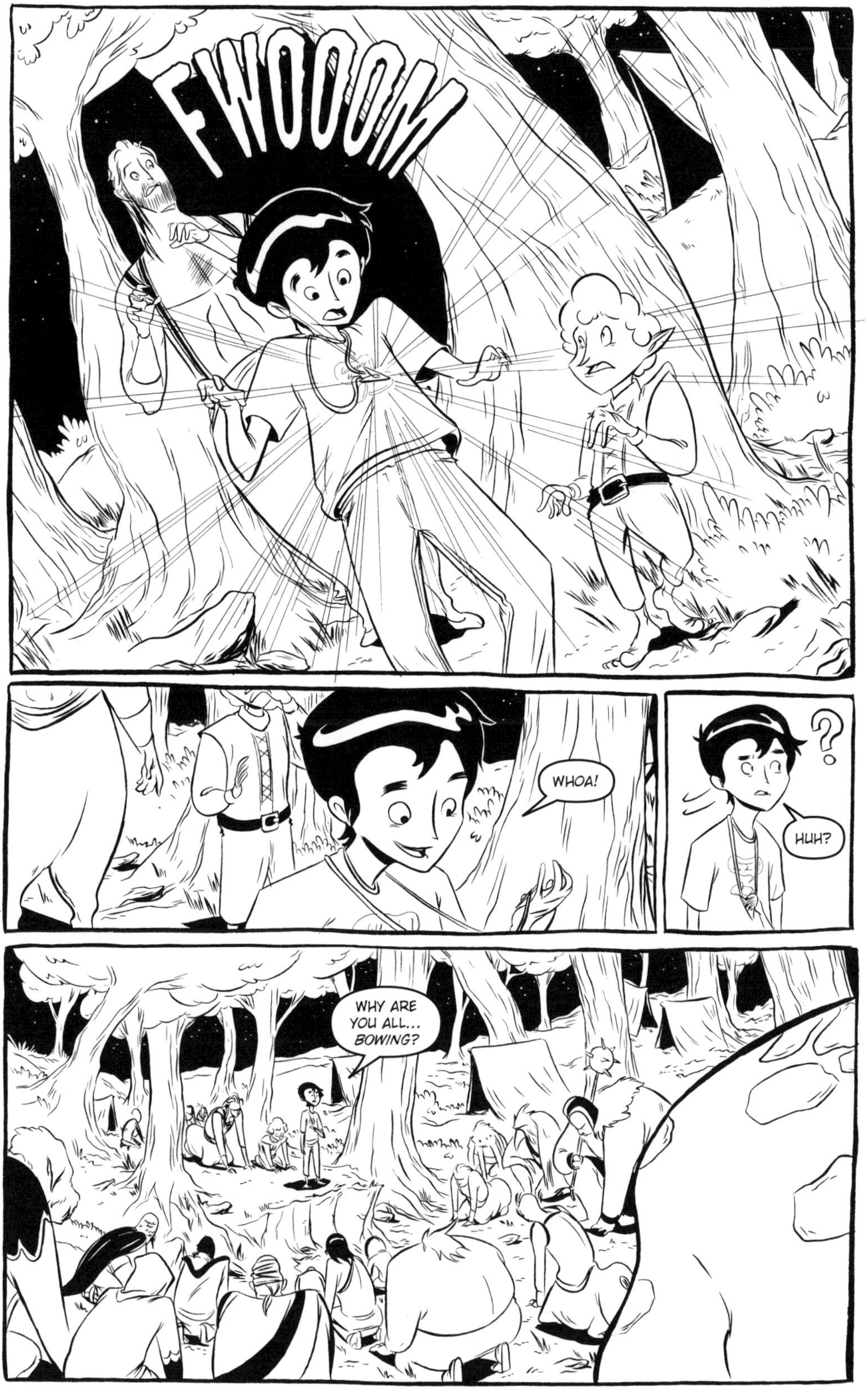
FWOOOM
WHOA!
?
HUH?
WHY ARE YOU ALL... *BOWING?*

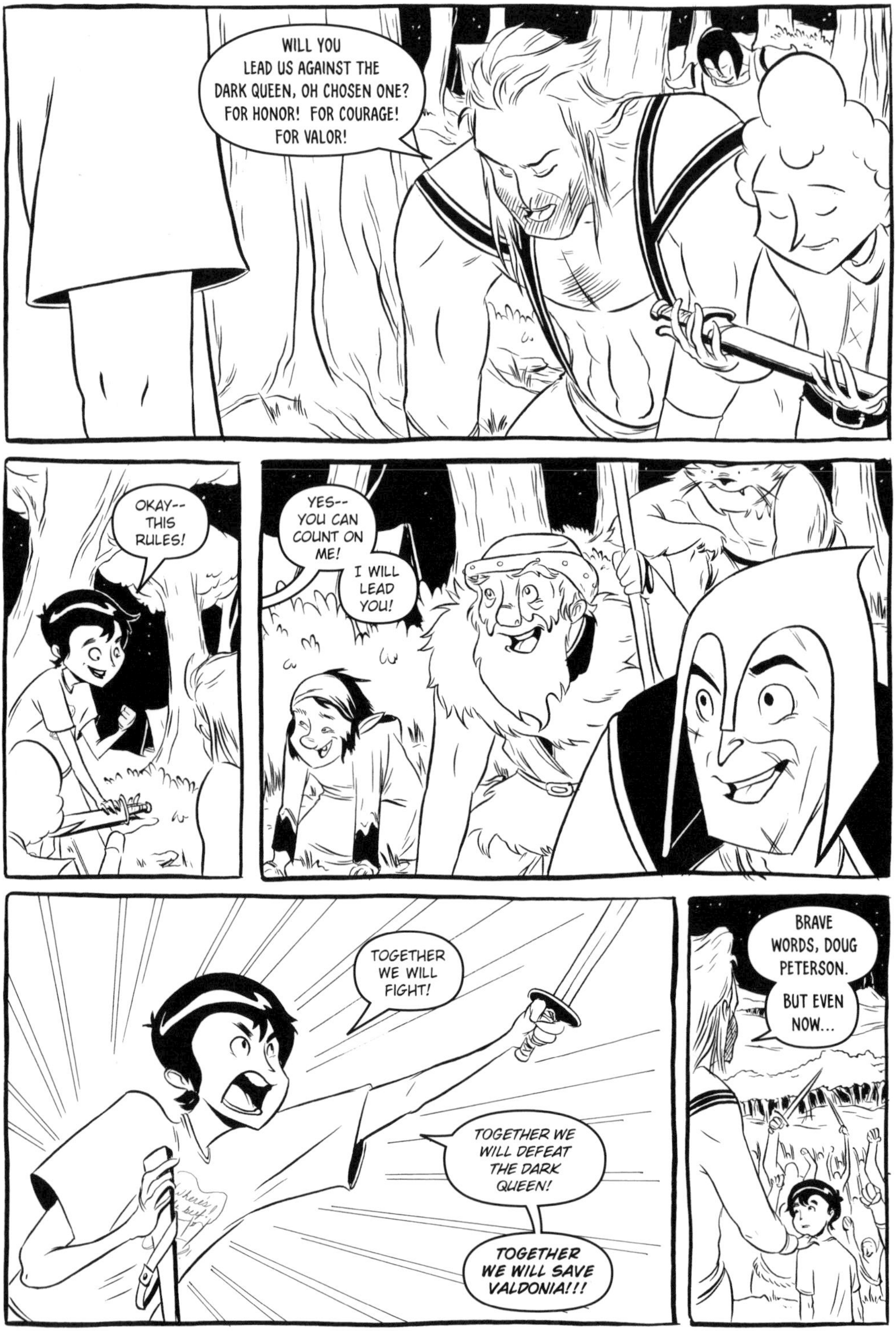
WILL YOU LEAD US AGAINST THE DARK QUEEN, OH CHOSEN ONE? FOR HONOR! FOR COURAGE! FOR VALOR!
OKAY-- THIS RULES!
YES-- YOU CAN COUNT ON ME!
I WILL LEAD YOU!
TOGETHER WE WILL FIGHT!
TOGETHER WE WILL DEFEAT THE DARK QUEEN!
TOGETHER WE WILL SAVE VALDONIA!!!
BRAVE WORDS, DOUG PETERSON.
BUT EVEN NOW...

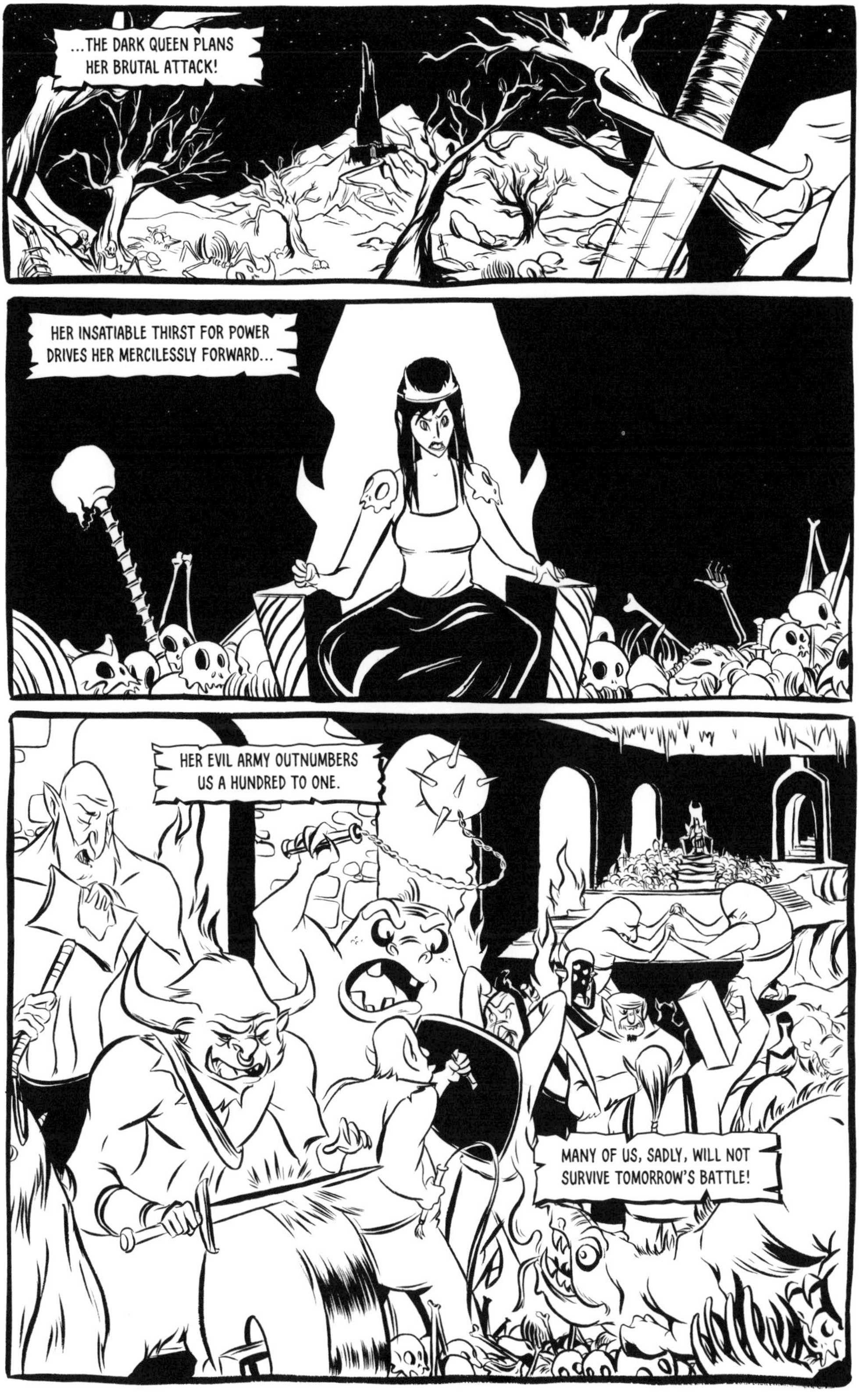
...THE DARK QUEEN PLANS HER BRUTAL ATTACK!
HER INSATIABLE THIRST FOR POWER DRIVES HER MERCILESSLY FORWARD...
HER EVIL ARMY OUTNUMBERS US A HUNDRED TO ONE.
MANY OF US, SADLY, WILL NOT SURVIVE TOMORROW'S BATTLE!

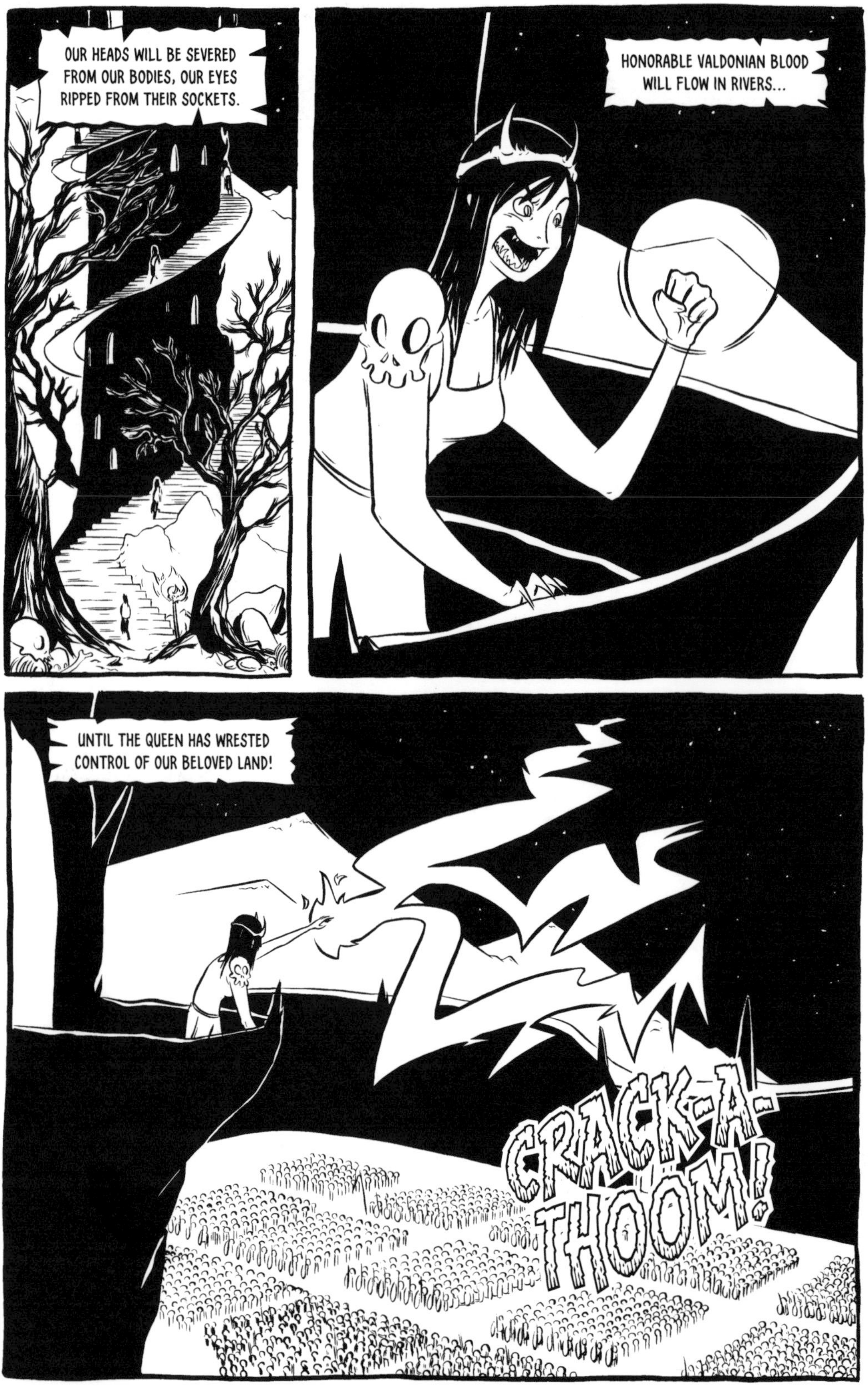
OUR HEADS WILL BE SEVERED FROM OUR BODIES, OUR EYES RIPPED FROM THEIR SOCKETS.
HONORABLE VALDONIAN BLOOD WILL FLOW IN RIVERS...
UNTIL THE QUEEN HAS WRESTED CONTROL OF OUR BELOVED LAND!
CRACK-A-THOOM!

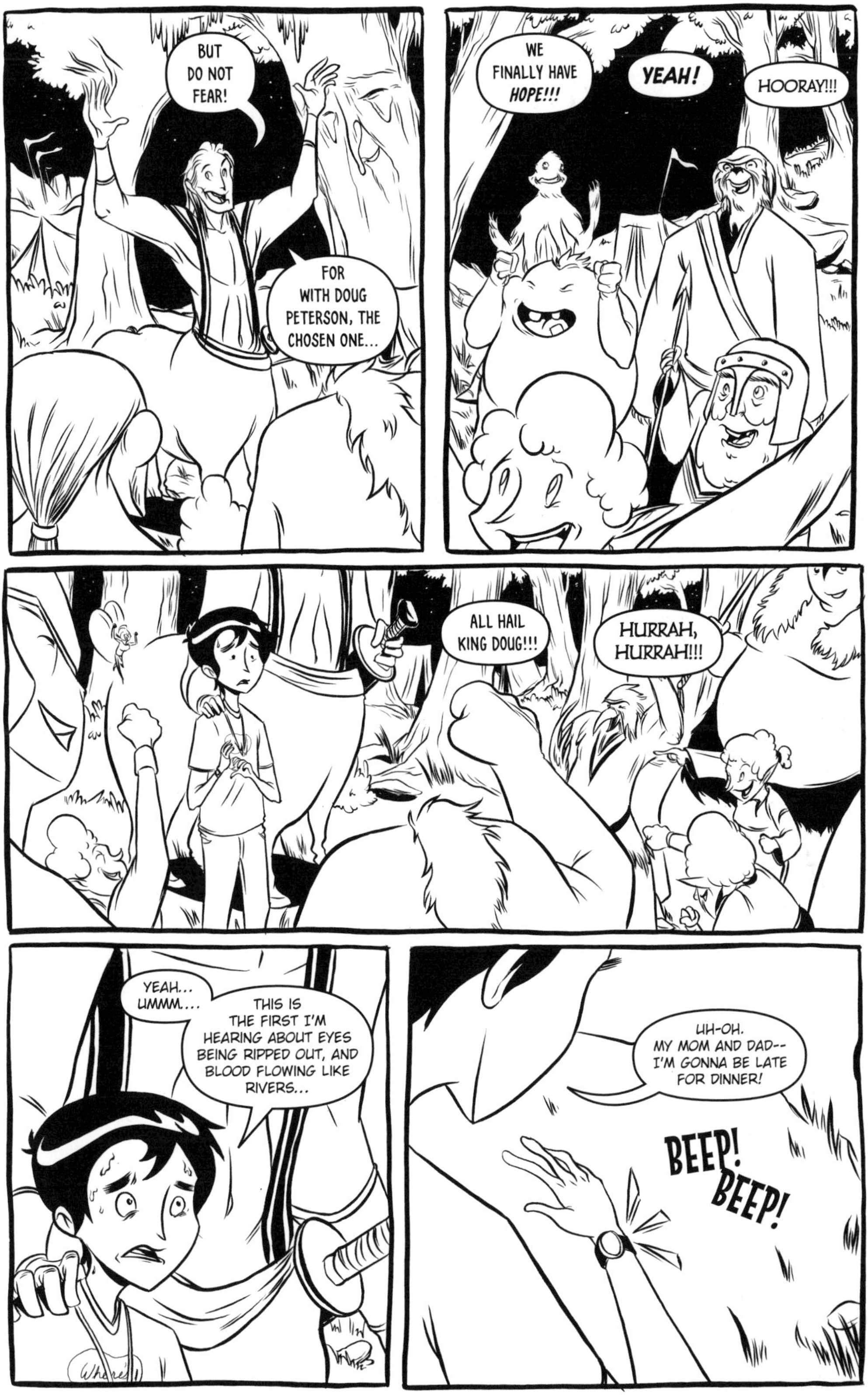
BUT DO NOT FEAR!
FOR WITH DOUG PETERSON, THE CHOSEN ONE...
WE FINALLY HAVE HOPE!!!
YEAH!
HOORAY!!!
ALL HAIL KING DOUG!!!
HURRAH, HURRAH!!!
YEAH... UMMM....
THIS IS THE FIRST I'M HEARING ABOUT EYES BEING RIPPED OUT, AND BLOOD FLOWING LIKE RIVERS...
UH-OH. MY MOM AND DAD-- I'M GONNA BE LATE FOR DINNER!
BEEP! BEEP!

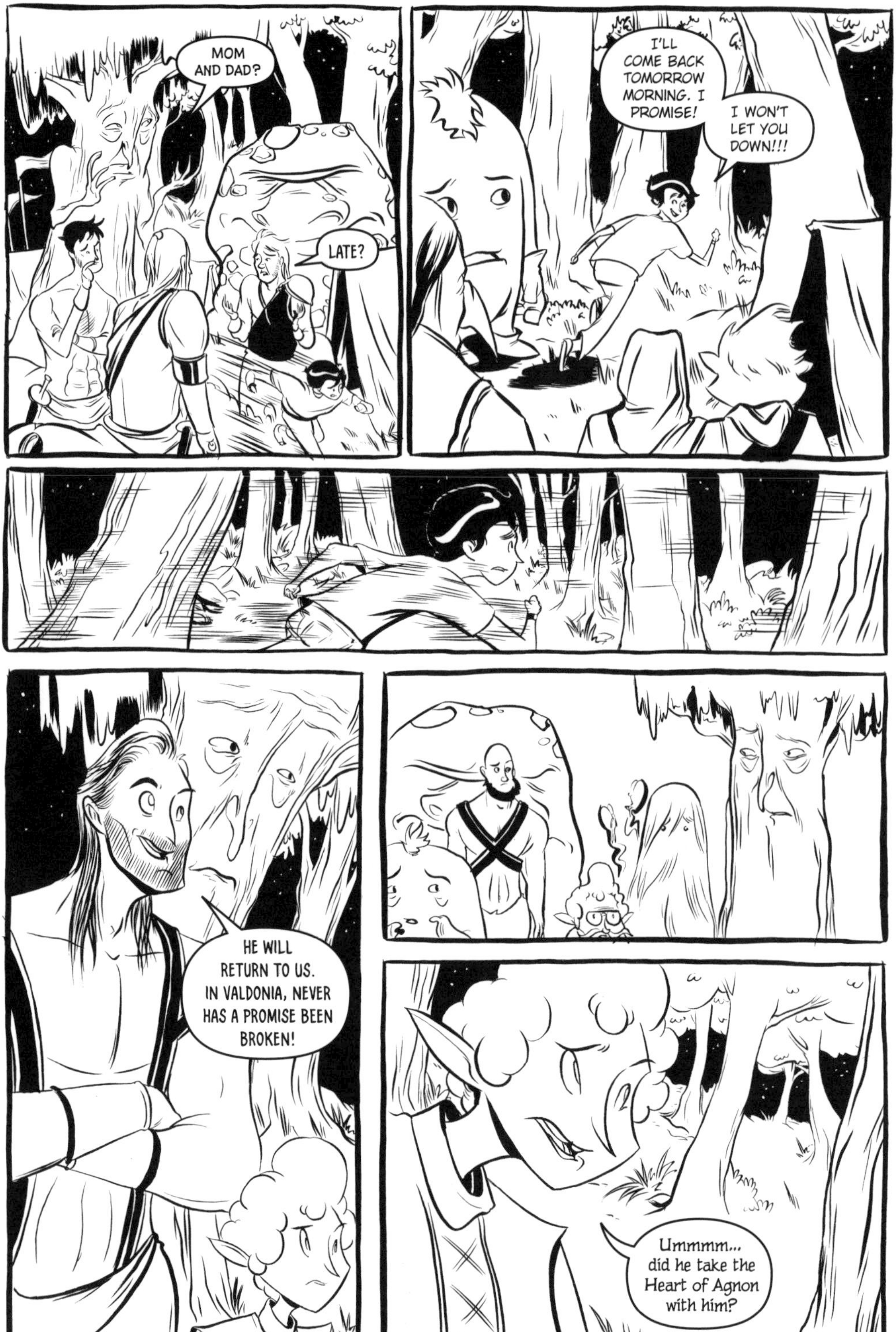
MOM AND DAD?
LATE?
I'LL COME BACK TOMORROW MORNING. I PROMISE!
I WON'T LET YOU DOWN!!!
HE WILL RETURN TO US. IN VALDONIA, NEVER HAS A PROMISE BEEN BROKEN!
Ummmm... did he take the Heart of Agnon with him?

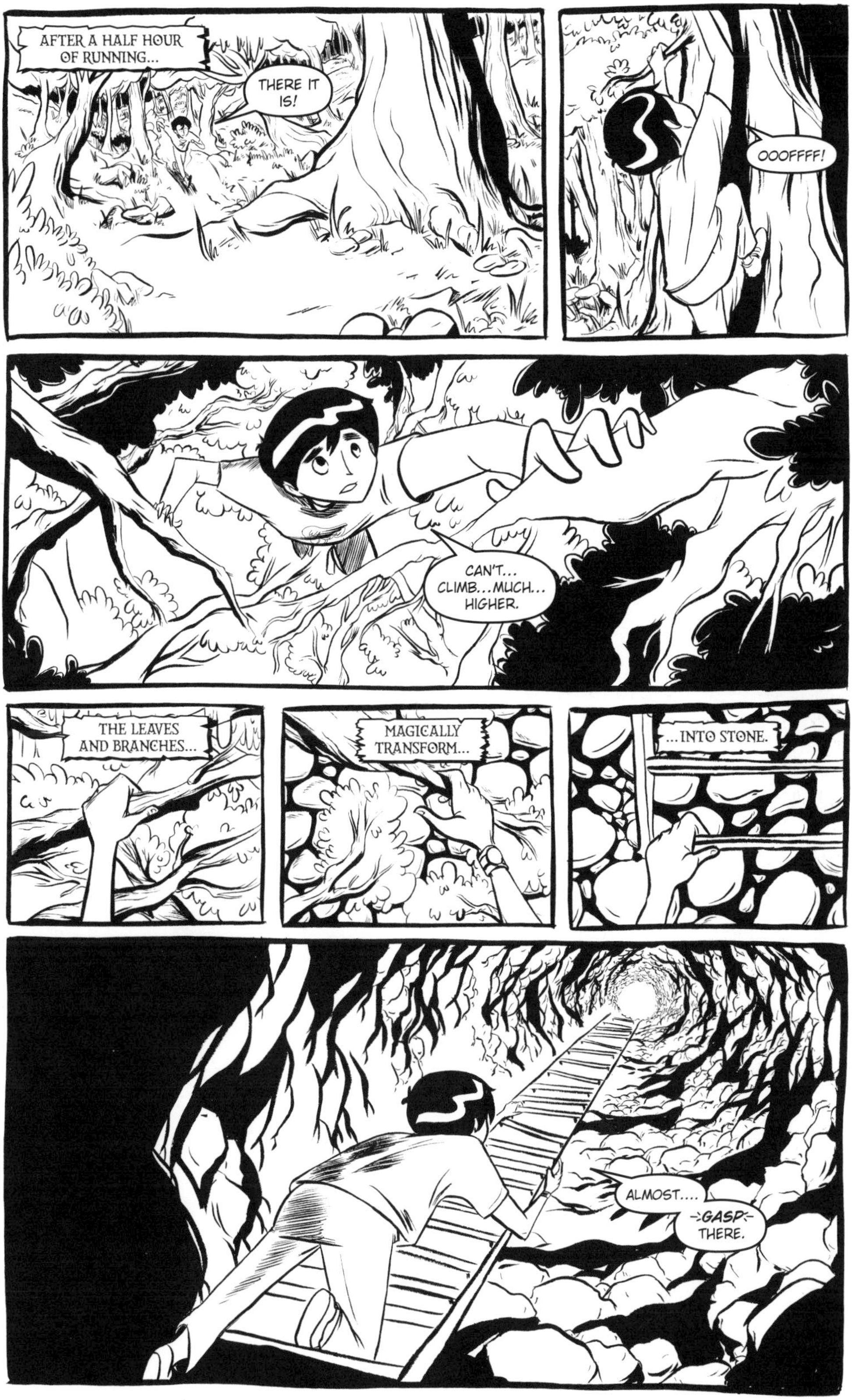

AFTER A HALF HOUR OF RUNNING...
THERE IT IS!
OOOFFFF!
CAN'T... CLIMB... MUCH... HIGHER.
THE LEAVES AND BRANCHES...
MAGICALLY TRANSFORM...
...INTO STONE.
ALMOST....
-GASP- THERE.

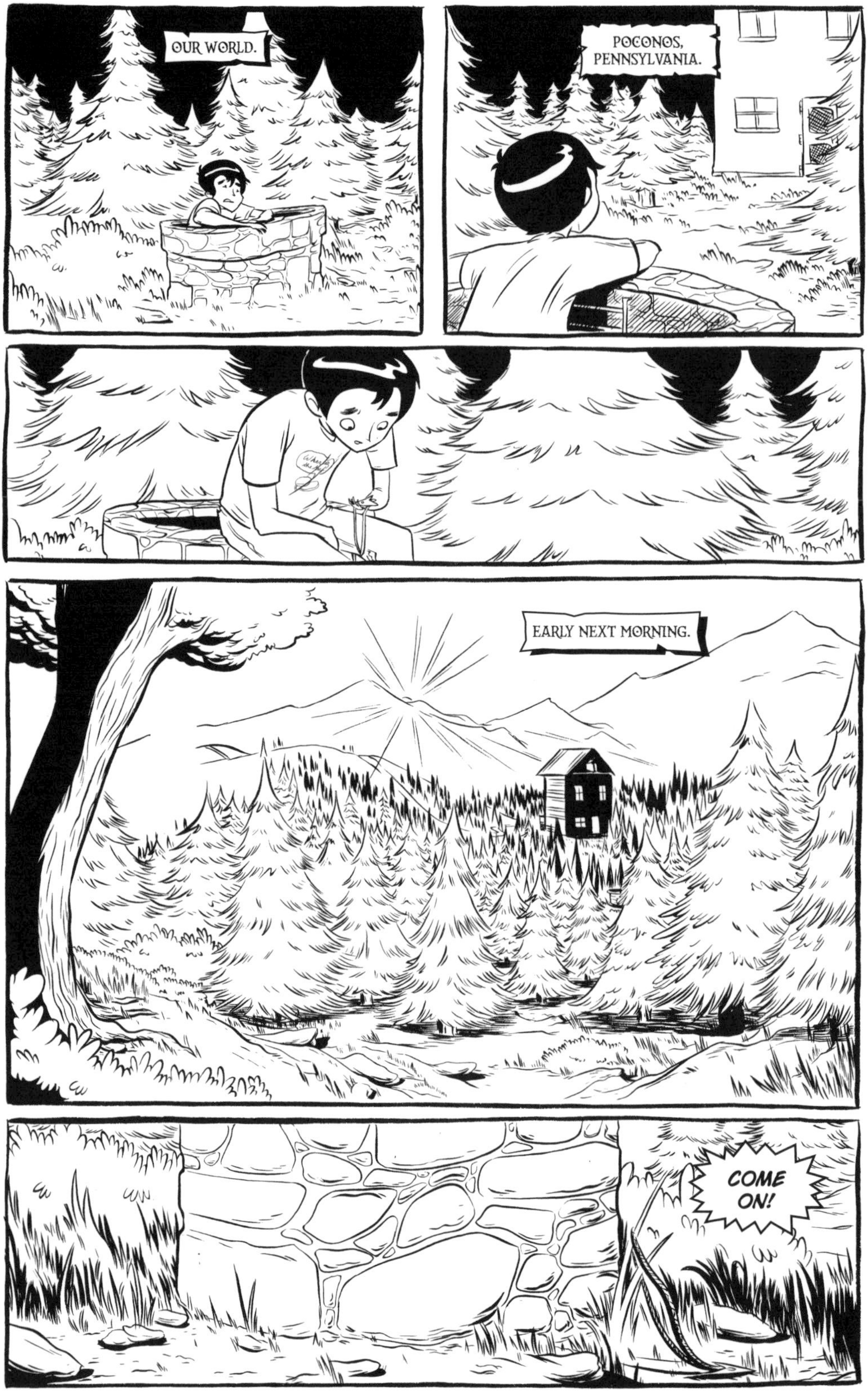
OUR WORLD.
POCONOS, PENNSYLVANIA.
EARLY NEXT MORNING.
COME ON!

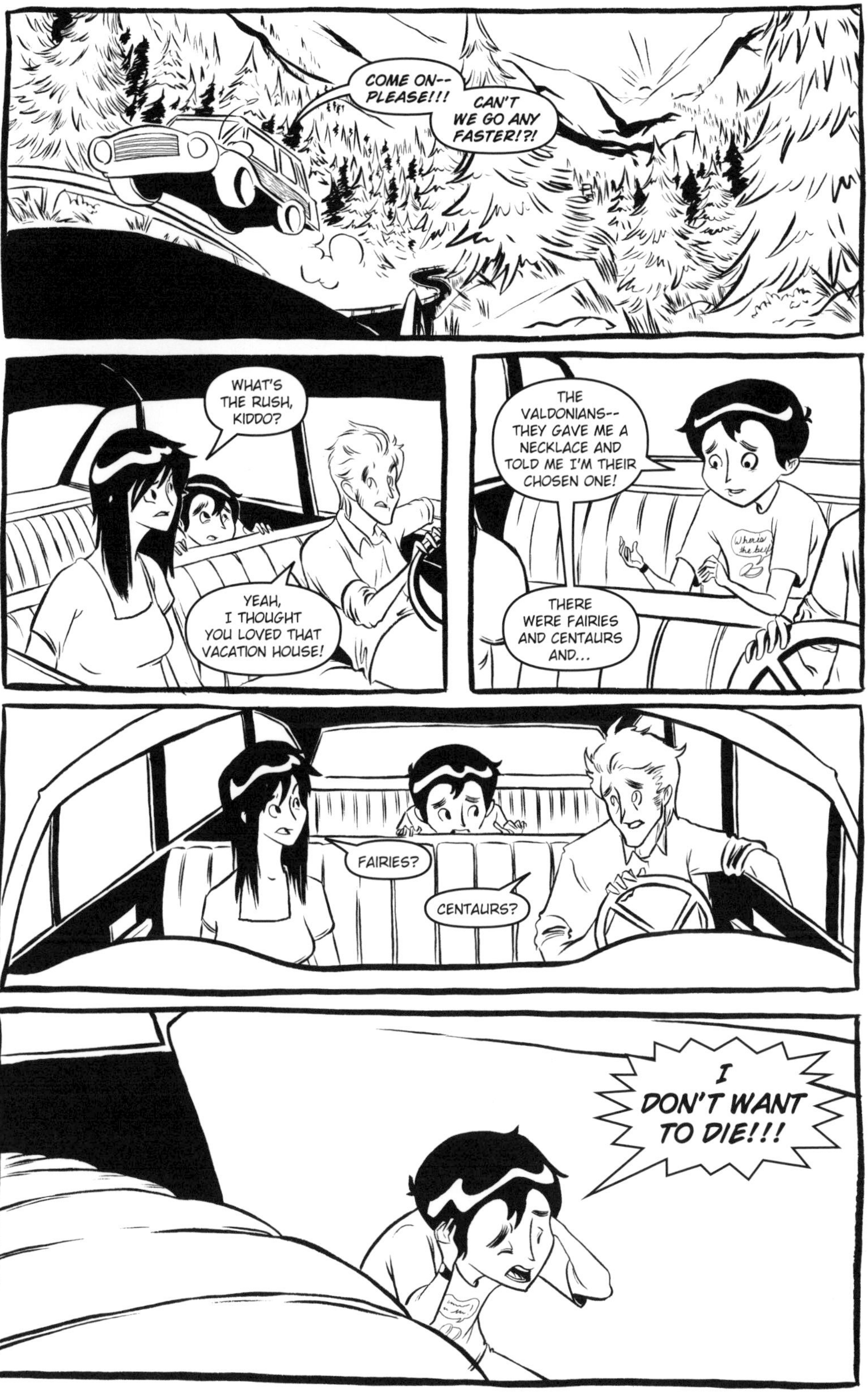
COME ON-- PLEASE!!!
CAN'T WE GO ANY FASTER!?!
WHAT'S THE RUSH, KIDDO?
YEAH, I THOUGHT YOU LOVED THAT VACATION HOUSE!
THE VALDONIANS-- THEY GAVE ME A NECKLACE AND TOLD ME I'M THEIR CHOSEN ONE!
THERE WERE FAIRIES AND CENTAURS AND...
FAIRIES?
CENTAURS?
I DON'T WANT TO DIE!!!

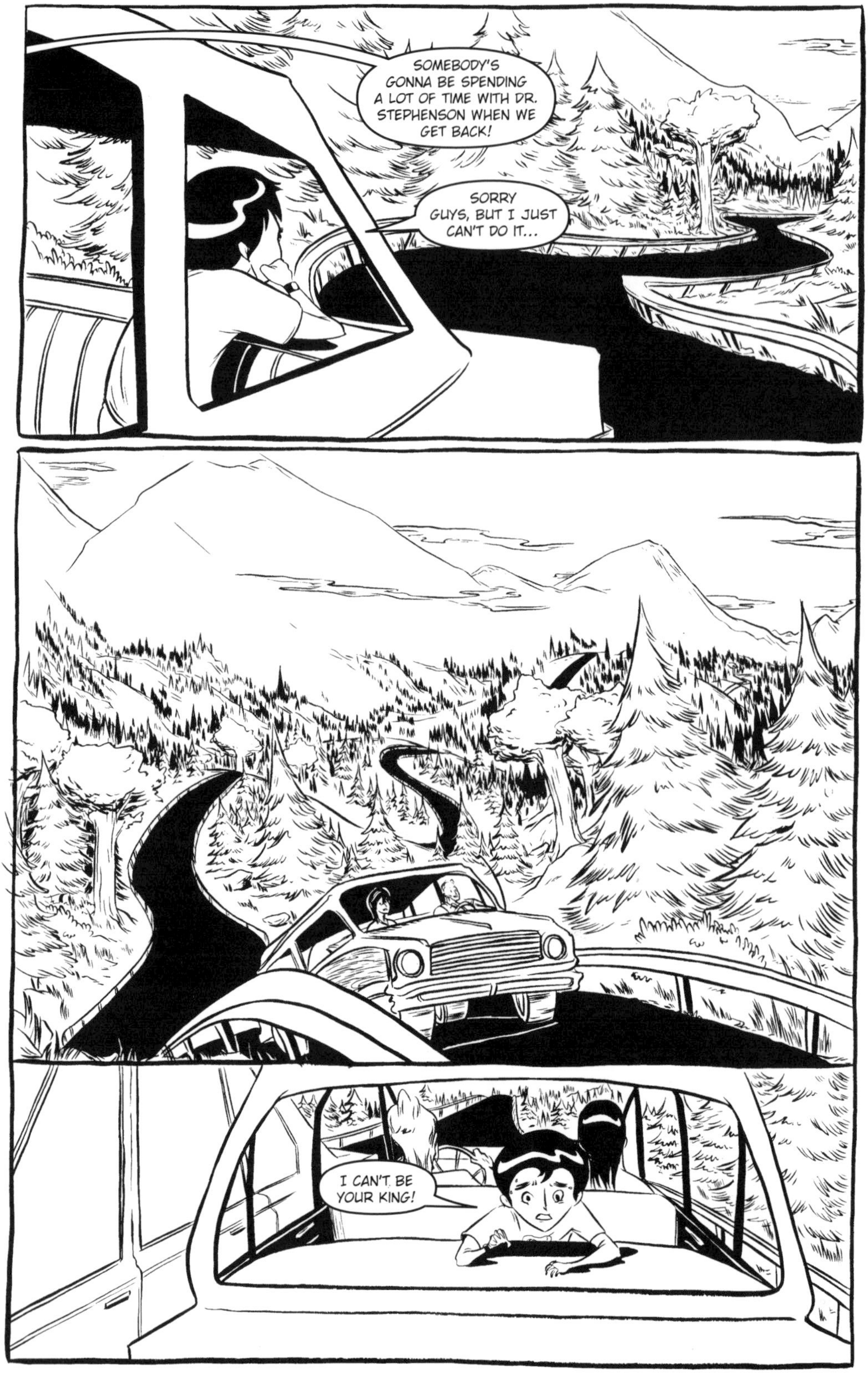
SOMEBODY'S GONNA BE SPENDING A LOT OF TIME WITH DR. STEPHENSON WHEN WE GET BACK!
SORRY GUYS, BUT I JUST CAN'T DO IT...
I CAN'T BE YOUR KING!

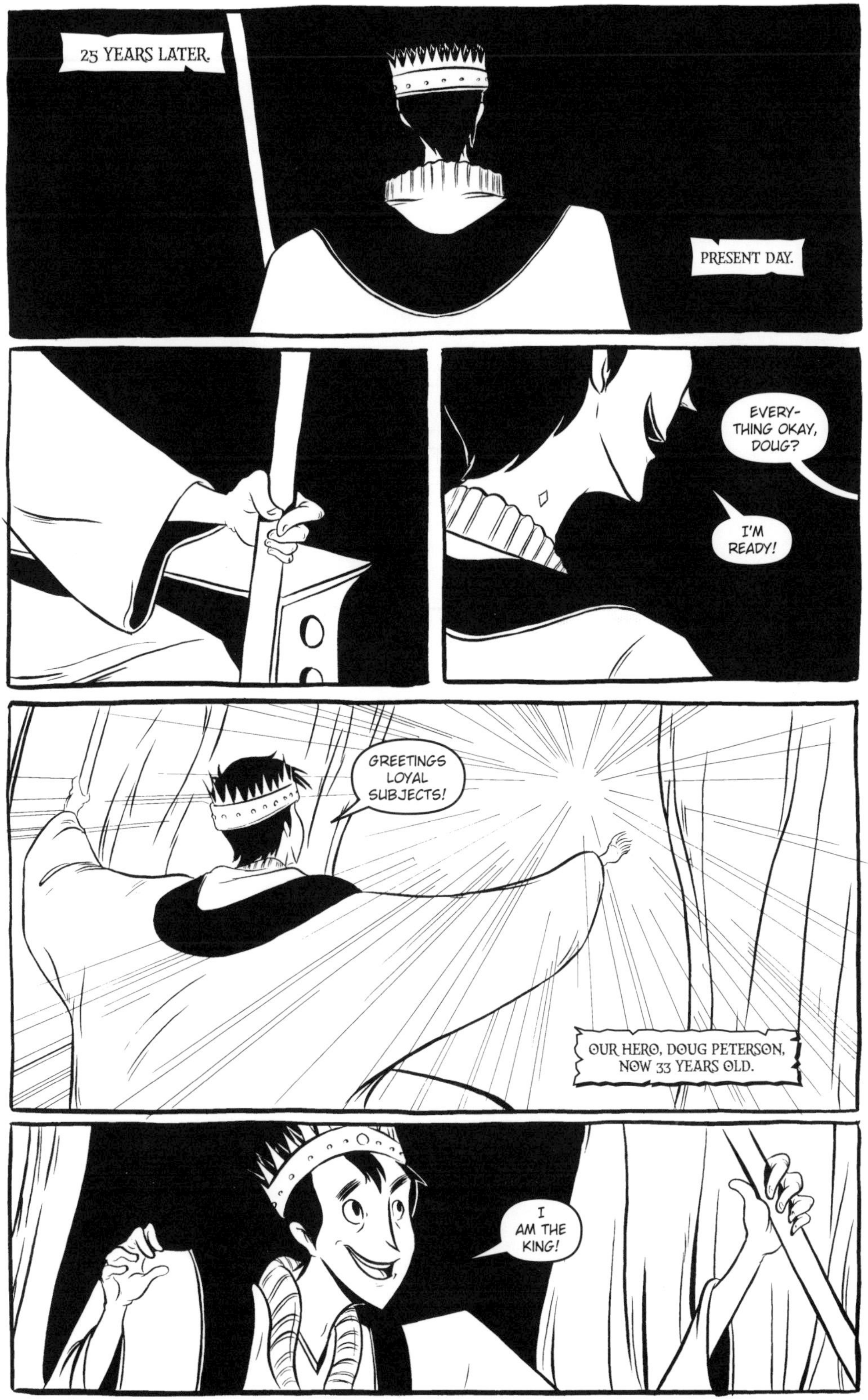
25 YEARS LATER.
PRESENT DAY.
EVERY-THING OKAY, DOUG?
I'M READY!
GREETINGS LOYAL SUBJECTS!
OUR HERO, DOUG PETERSON, NOW 33 YEARS OLD.
I AM THE KING!

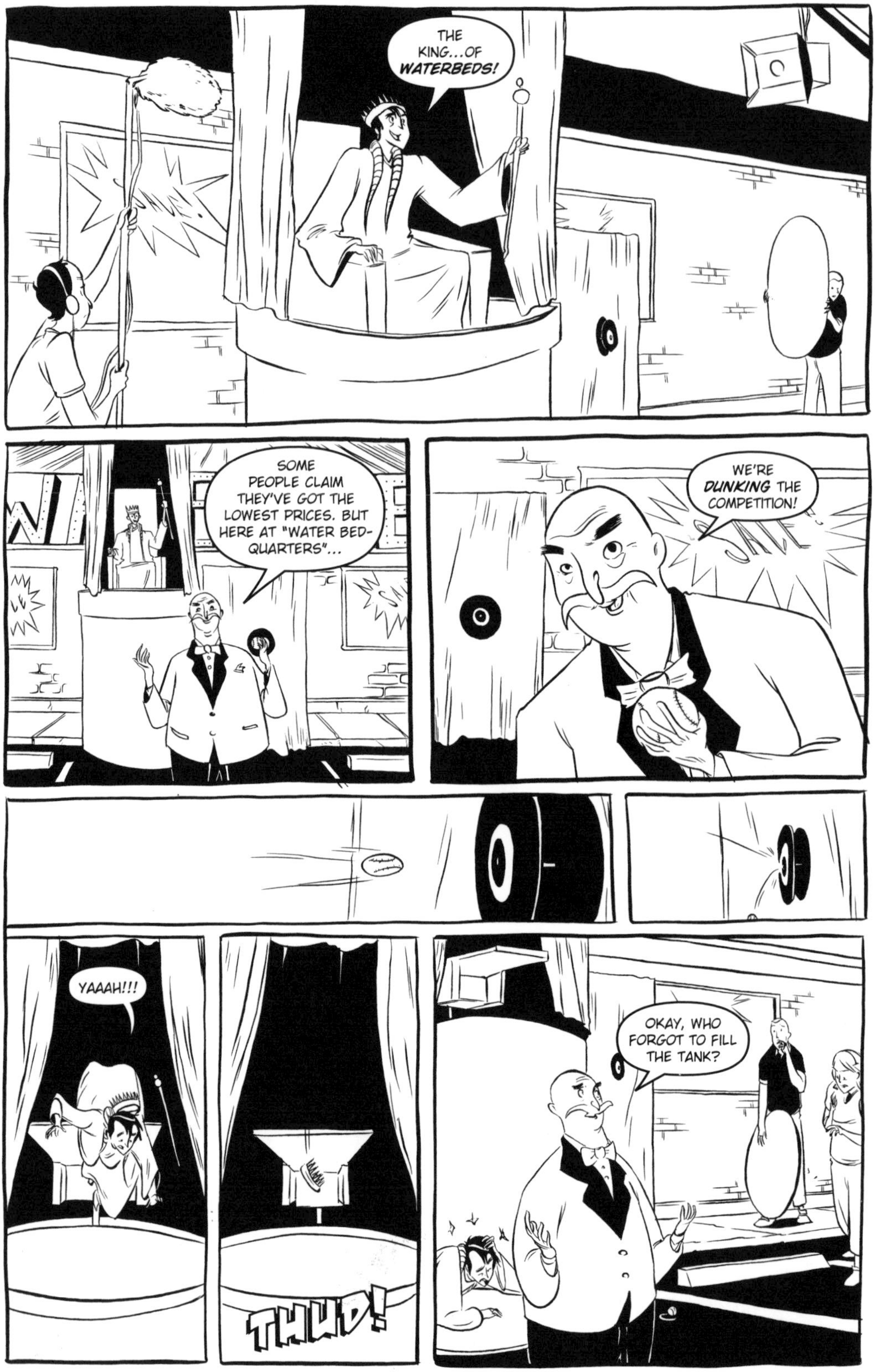
THE KING...OF **WATERBEDS!**
SOME PEOPLE CLAIM THEY'VE GOT THE LOWEST PRICES. BUT HERE AT "WATER BED-QUARTERS"...
WE'RE **DUNKING** THE COMPETITION!
YAAAH!!!
THUD!
OKAY, WHO FORGOT TO FILL THE TANK?

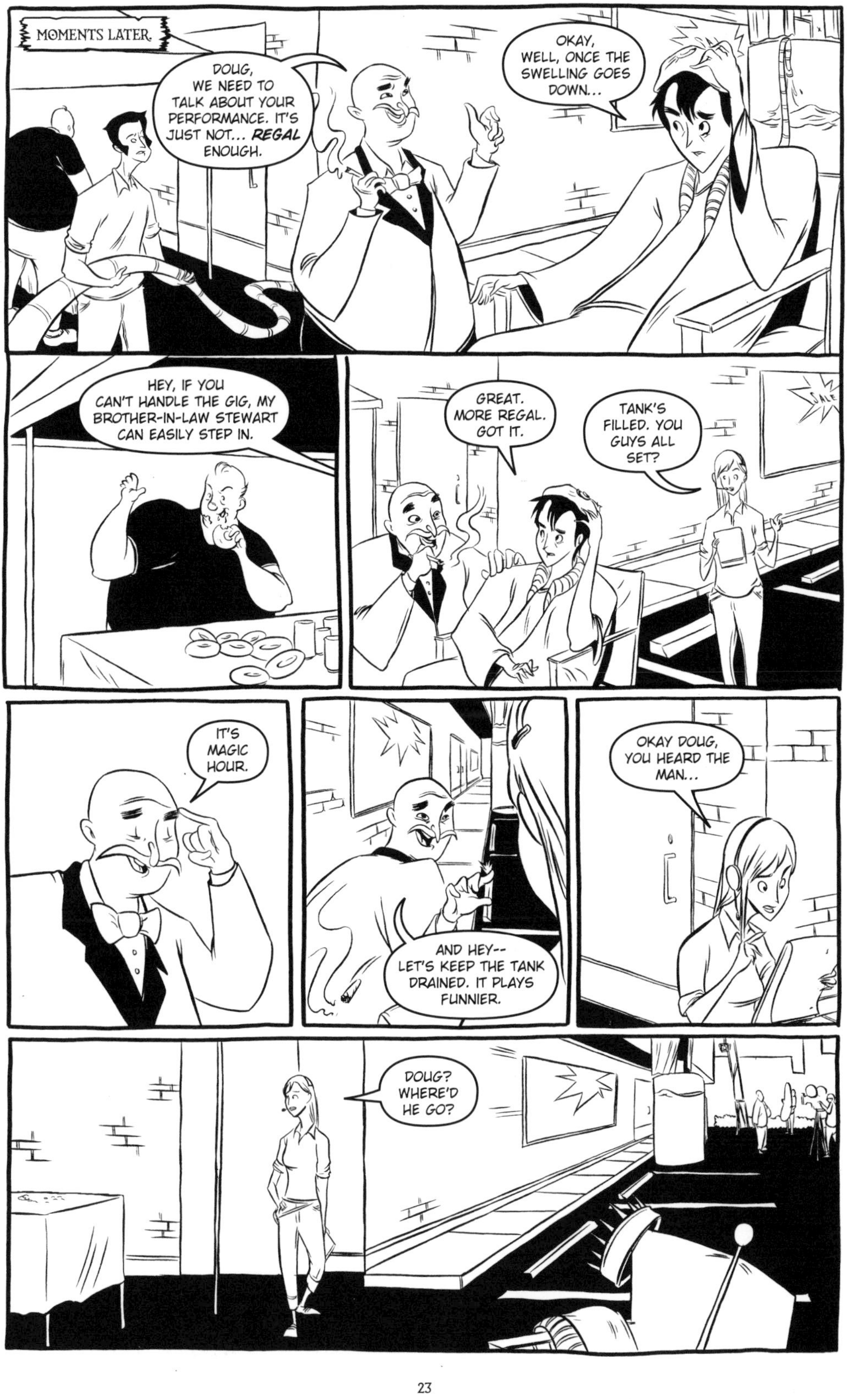
MOMENTS LATER.
DOUG, WE NEED TO TALK ABOUT YOUR PERFORMANCE. IT'S JUST NOT... **REGAL** ENOUGH.
OKAY, WELL, ONCE THE SWELLING GOES DOWN...
HEY, IF YOU CAN'T HANDLE THE GIG, MY BROTHER-IN-LAW STEWART CAN EASILY STEP IN.
GREAT. MORE REGAL. GOT IT.
TANK'S FILLED. YOU GUYS ALL SET?
IT'S MAGIC HOUR.
AND HEY-- LET'S KEEP THE TANK DRAINED. IT PLAYS FUNNIER.
OKAY DOUG, YOU HEARD THE MAN...
DOUG? WHERE'D HE GO?

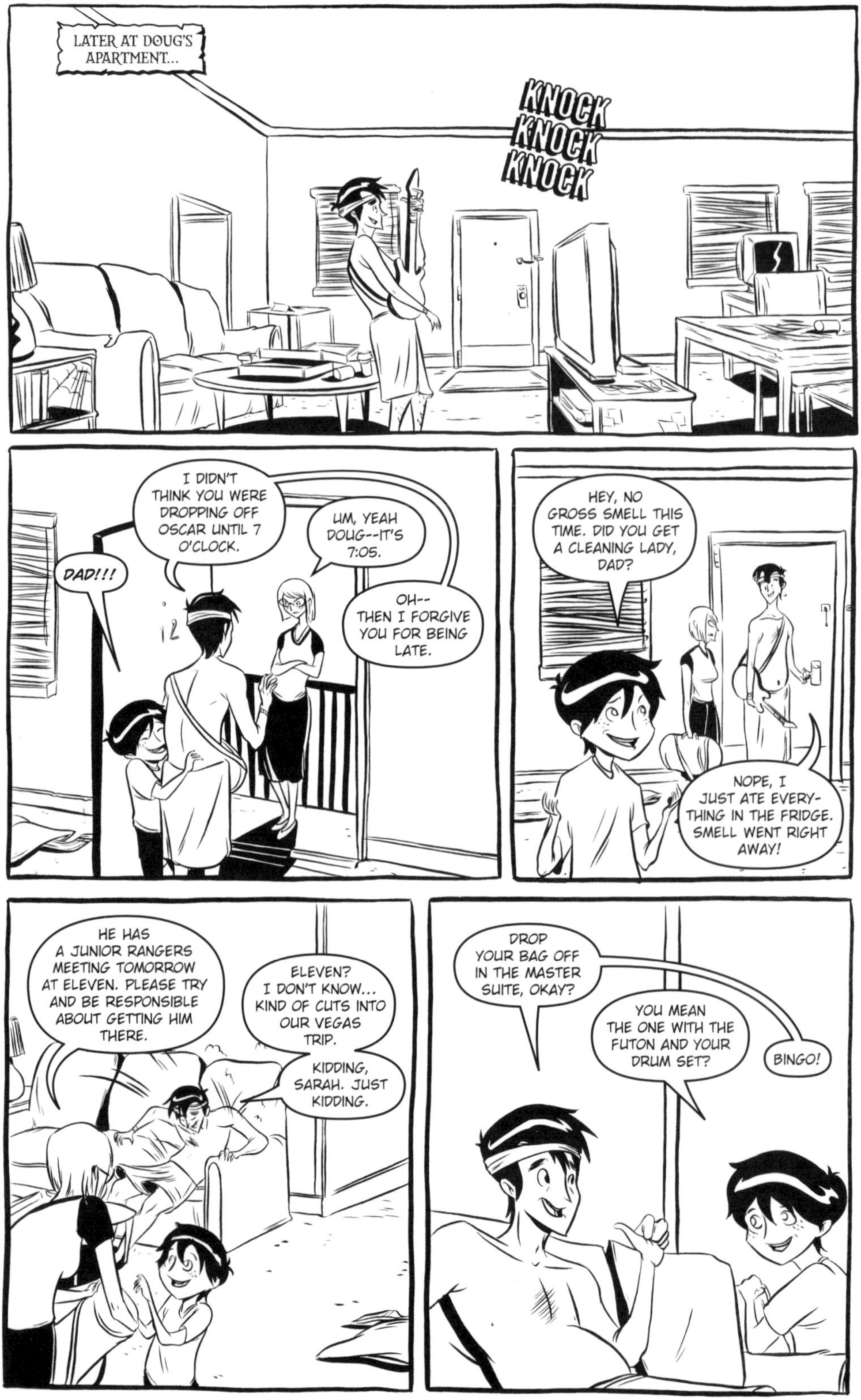
LATER AT DOUG'S APARTMENT...
KNOCK KNOCK KNOCK
DAD!!!
I DIDN'T THINK YOU WERE DROPPING OFF OSCAR UNTIL 7 O'CLOCK.
UM, YEAH DOUG--IT'S 7:05.
OH-- THEN I FORGIVE YOU FOR BEING LATE.
HEY, NO GROSS SMELL THIS TIME. DID YOU GET A CLEANING LADY, DAD?
NOPE, I JUST ATE EVERY-THING IN THE FRIDGE. SMELL WENT RIGHT AWAY!
HE HAS A JUNIOR RANGERS MEETING TOMORROW AT ELEVEN. PLEASE TRY AND BE RESPONSIBLE ABOUT GETTING HIM THERE.
ELEVEN? I DON'T KNOW... KIND OF CUTS INTO OUR VEGAS TRIP.
KIDDING, SARAH. JUST KIDDING.
DROP YOUR BAG OFF IN THE MASTER SUITE, OKAY?
YOU MEAN THE ONE WITH THE FUTON AND YOUR DRUM SET?
BINGO!

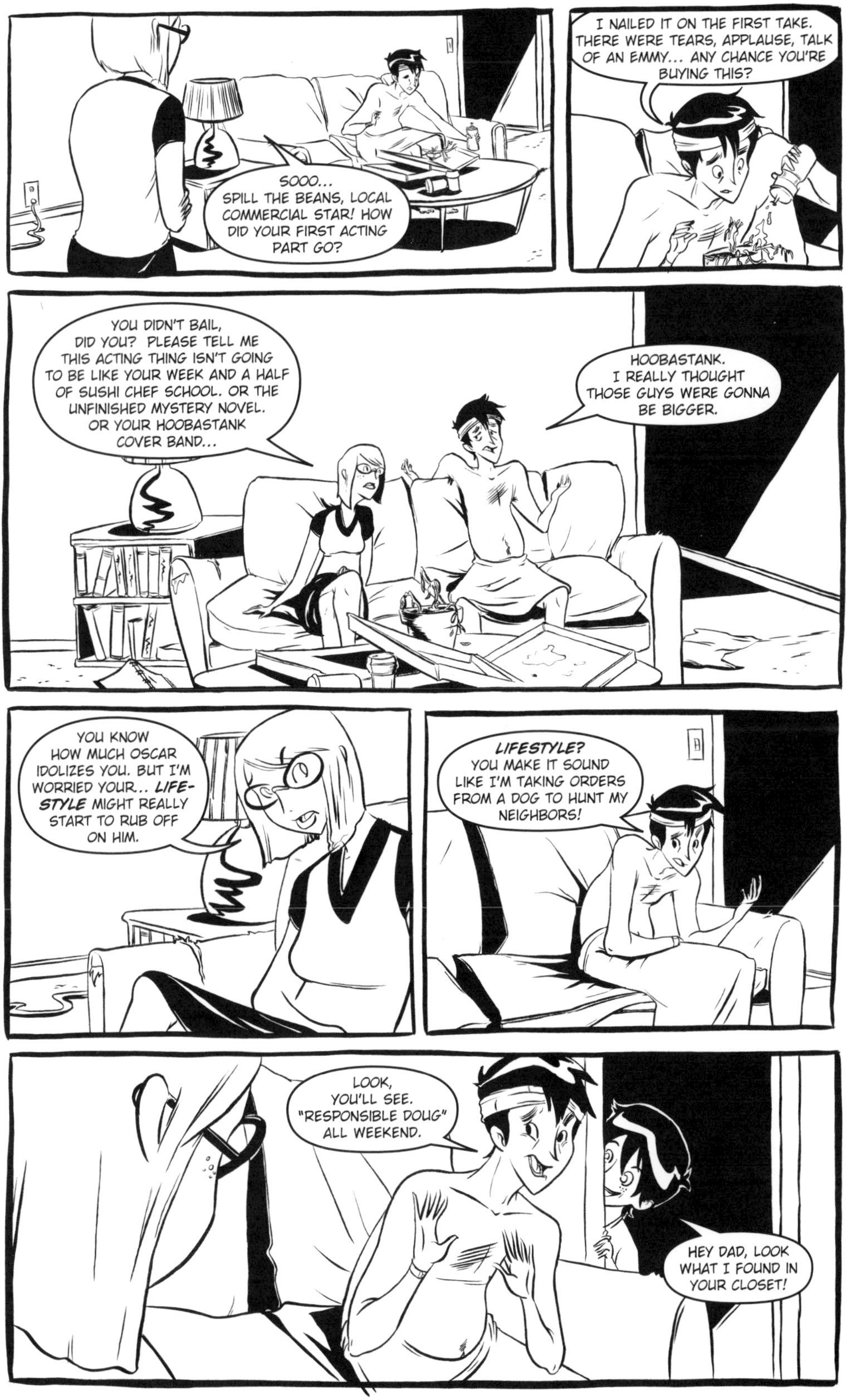
SOOO...
SPILL THE BEANS, LOCAL COMMERCIAL STAR! HOW DID YOUR FIRST ACTING PART GO?
I NAILED IT ON THE FIRST TAKE. THERE WERE TEARS, APPLAUSE, TALK OF AN EMMY... ANY CHANCE YOU'RE BUYING THIS?
YOU DIDN'T BAIL, DID YOU? PLEASE TELL ME THIS ACTING THING ISN'T GOING TO BE LIKE YOUR WEEK AND A HALF OF SUSHI CHEF SCHOOL. OR THE UNFINISHED MYSTERY NOVEL. OR YOUR HOOBASTANK COVER BAND...
HOOBASTANK. I REALLY THOUGHT THOSE GUYS WERE GONNA BE BIGGER.
YOU KNOW HOW MUCH OSCAR IDOLIZES YOU. BUT I'M WORRIED YOUR... ***LIFE-STYLE*** MIGHT REALLY START TO RUB OFF ON HIM.
LIFESTYLE? YOU MAKE IT SOUND LIKE I'M TAKING ORDERS FROM A DOG TO HUNT MY NEIGHBORS!
LOOK, YOU'LL SEE. "RESPONSIBLE DOUG" ALL WEEKEND.
HEY DAD, LOOK WHAT I FOUND IN YOUR CLOSET!

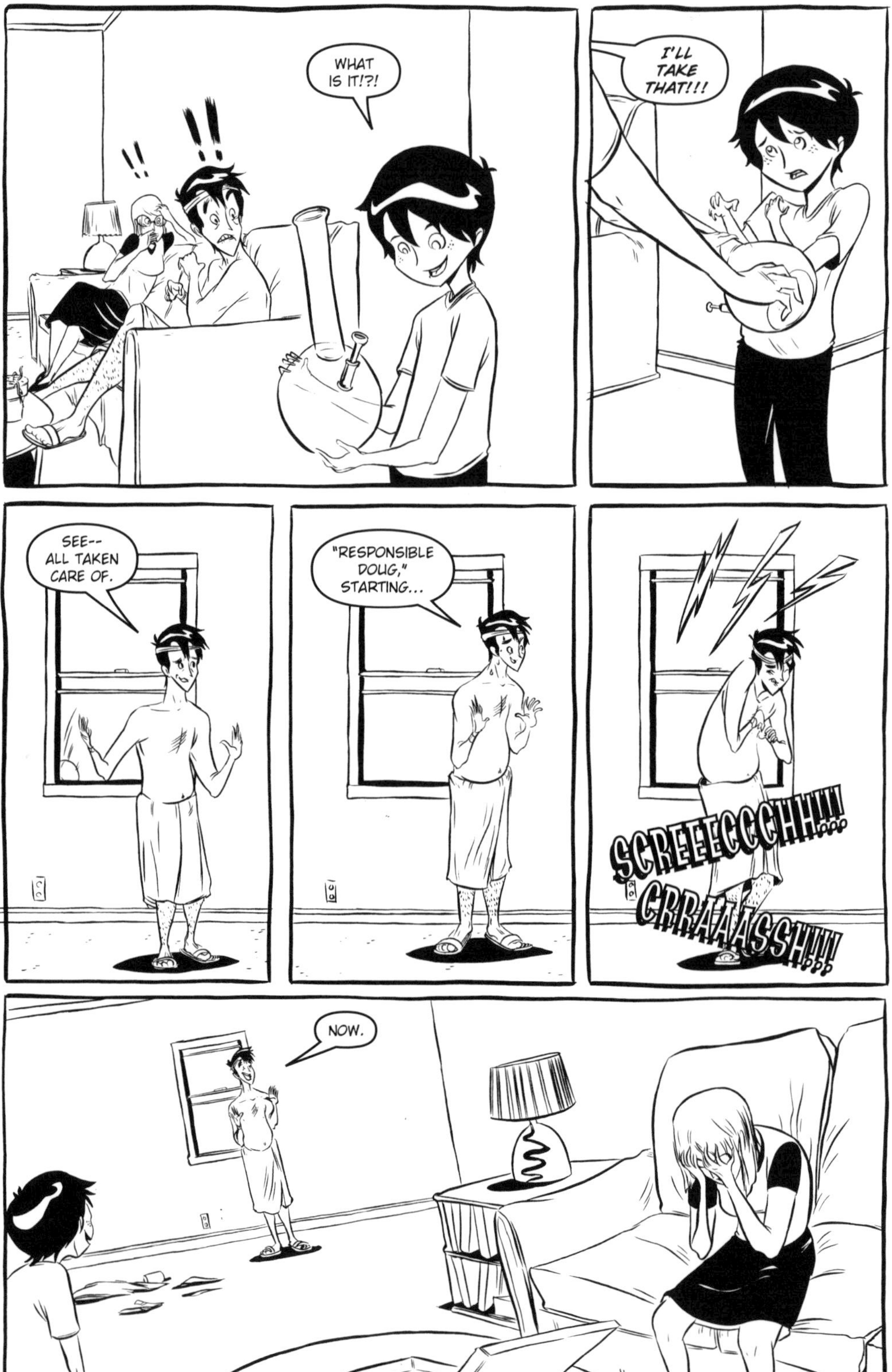
WHAT IS IT!?!
!!
!!
I'LL TAKE THAT!!!
SEE-- ALL TAKEN CARE OF.
"RESPONSIBLE DOUG," STARTING...
SCREEECCCHH!!!
CRRAAASSH!!!
NOW.

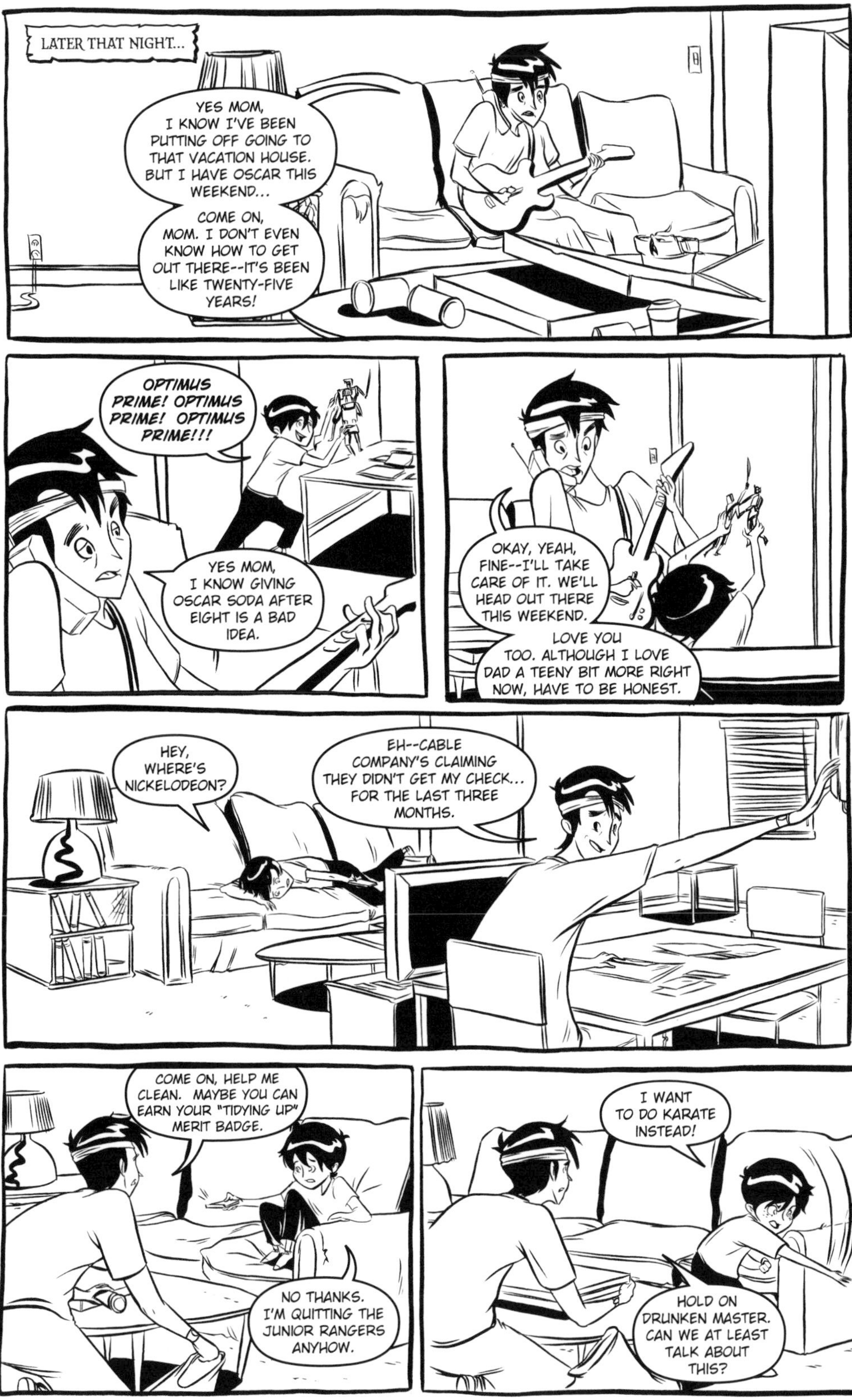
LATER THAT NIGHT...
YES MOM, I KNOW I'VE BEEN PUTTING OFF GOING TO THAT VACATION HOUSE. BUT I HAVE OSCAR THIS WEEKEND...
COME ON, MOM. I DON'T EVEN KNOW HOW TO GET OUT THERE--IT'S BEEN LIKE TWENTY-FIVE YEARS!
OPTIMUS PRIME! OPTIMUS PRIME! OPTIMUS PRIME!!!
YES MOM, I KNOW GIVING OSCAR SODA AFTER EIGHT IS A BAD IDEA.
OKAY, YEAH, FINE--I'LL TAKE CARE OF IT. WE'LL HEAD OUT THERE THIS WEEKEND.
LOVE YOU TOO. ALTHOUGH I LOVE DAD A TEENY BIT MORE RIGHT NOW, HAVE TO BE HONEST.
HEY, WHERE'S NICKELODEON?
EH--CABLE COMPANY'S CLAIMING THEY DIDN'T GET MY CHECK... FOR THE LAST THREE MONTHS.
COME ON, HELP ME CLEAN. MAYBE YOU CAN EARN YOUR "TIDYING UP" MERIT BADGE.
NO THANKS. I'M QUITTING THE JUNIOR RANGERS ANYHOW.
I WANT TO DO KARATE INSTEAD!
HOLD ON DRUNKEN MASTER. CAN WE AT LEAST TALK ABOUT THIS?

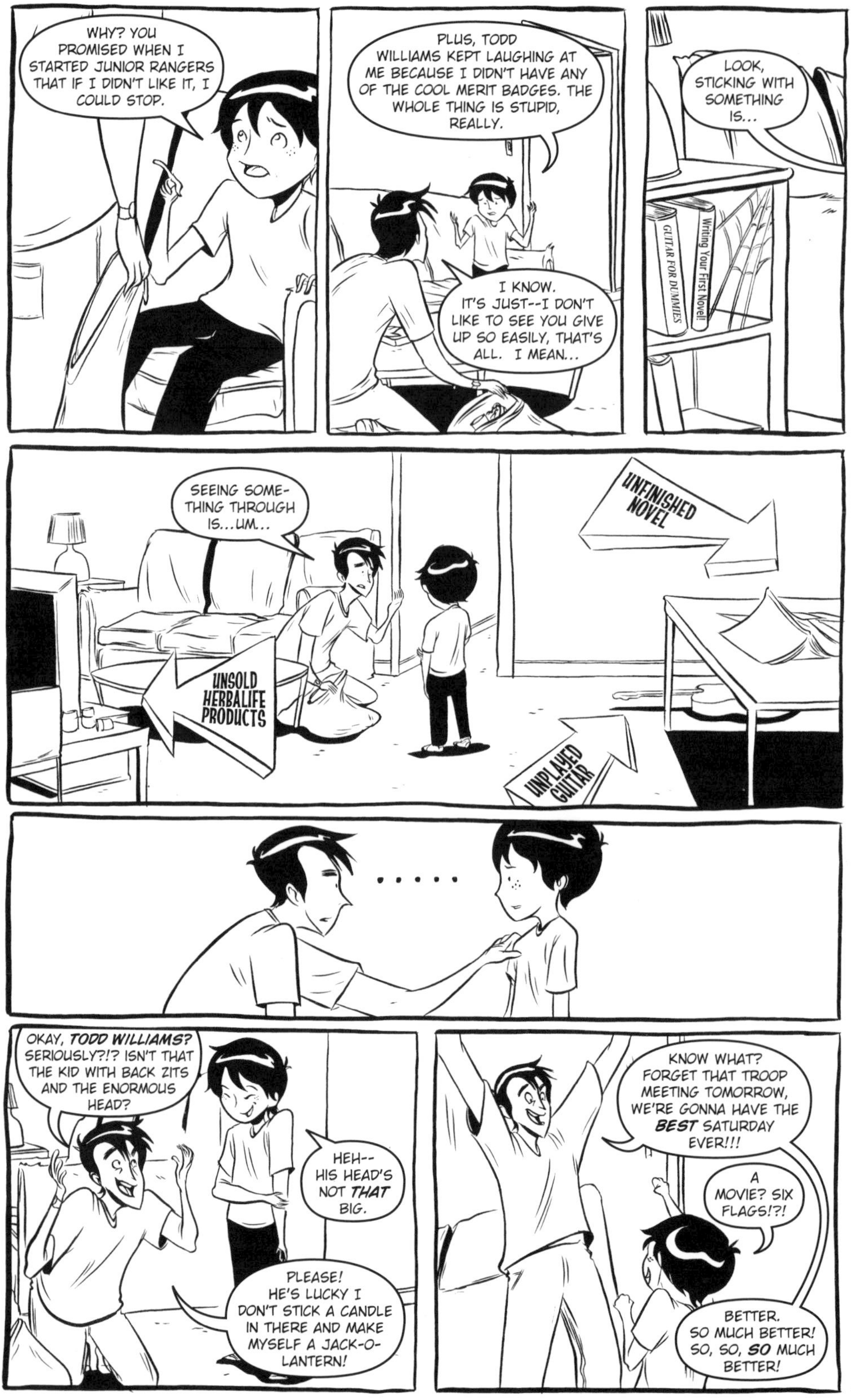
WHY? YOU PROMISED WHEN I STARTED JUNIOR RANGERS THAT IF I DIDN'T LIKE IT, I COULD STOP.
PLUS, TODD WILLIAMS KEPT LAUGHING AT ME BECAUSE I DIDN'T HAVE ANY OF THE COOL MERIT BADGES. THE WHOLE THING IS STUPID, REALLY.
I KNOW. IT'S JUST--I DON'T LIKE TO SEE YOU GIVE UP SO EASILY, THAT'S ALL. I MEAN...
LOOK, STICKING WITH SOMETHING IS...
GUITAR FOR DUMMIES
Writing Your First Novel!
SEEING SOME-THING THROUGH IS...UM...
UNFINISHED NOVEL
UNSOLD HERBALIFE PRODUCTS
UNPLAYED GUITAR
......
OKAY, ***TODD WILLIAMS?*** SERIOUSLY?!? ISN'T THAT THE KID WITH BACK ZITS AND THE ENORMOUS HEAD?
HEH-- HIS HEAD'S NOT ***THAT*** BIG.
PLEASE! HE'S LUCKY I DON'T STICK A CANDLE IN THERE AND MAKE MYSELF A JACK-O-LANTERN!
KNOW WHAT? FORGET THAT TROOP MEETING TOMORROW, WE'RE GONNA HAVE THE ***BEST*** SATURDAY EVER!!!
A MOVIE? SIX FLAGS!?!
BETTER. SO MUCH BETTER! SO, SO, ***SO*** MUCH BETTER!

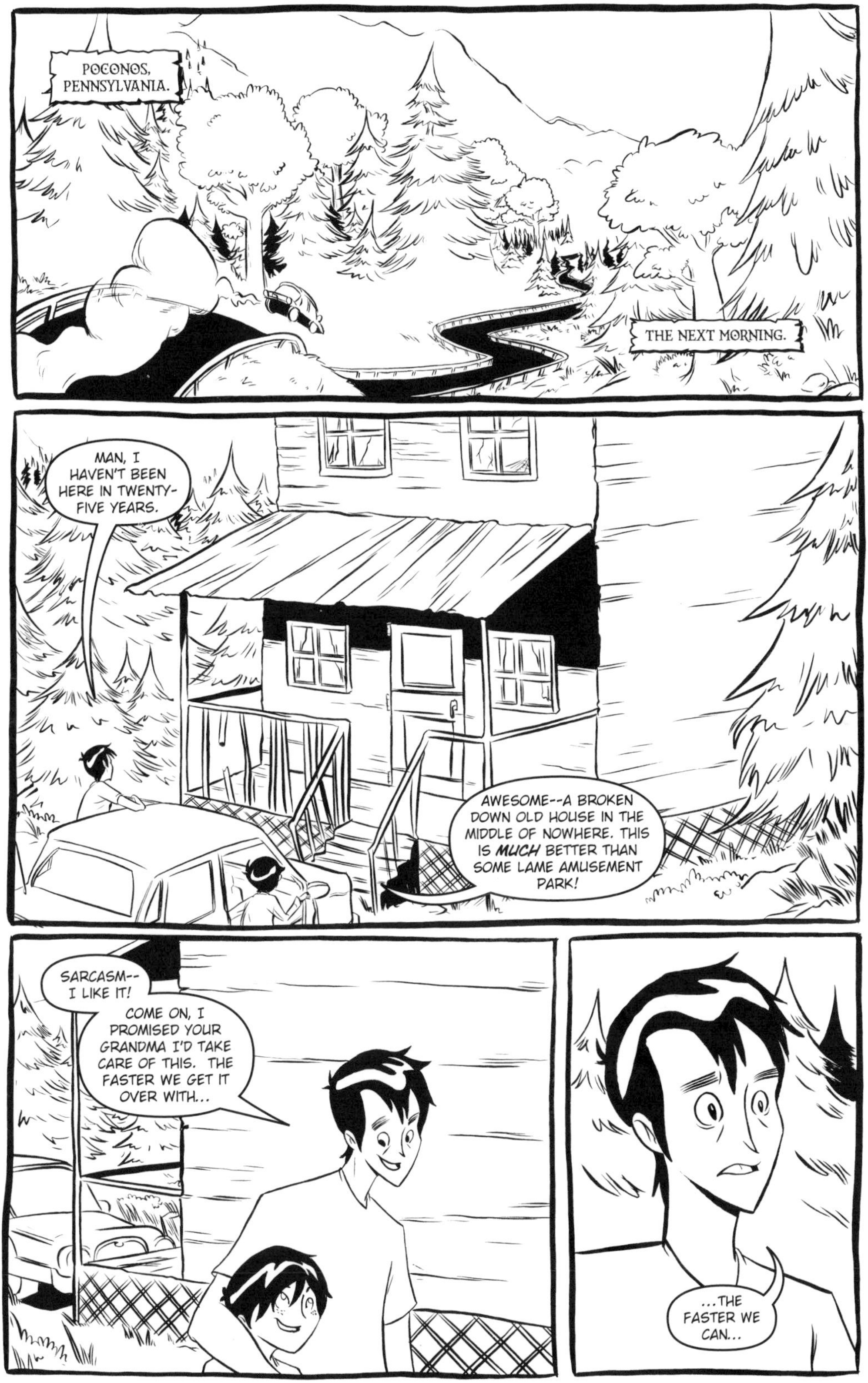

POCONOS, PENNSYLVANIA.
THE NEXT MORNING.
MAN, I HAVEN'T BEEN HERE IN TWENTY-FIVE YEARS.
AWESOME--A BROKEN DOWN OLD HOUSE IN THE MIDDLE OF NOWHERE. THIS IS MUCH BETTER THAN SOME LAME AMUSEMENT PARK!
SARCASM--I LIKE IT!
COME ON, I PROMISED YOUR GRANDMA I'D TAKE CARE OF THIS. THE FASTER WE GET IT OVER WITH...
...THE FASTER WE CAN...

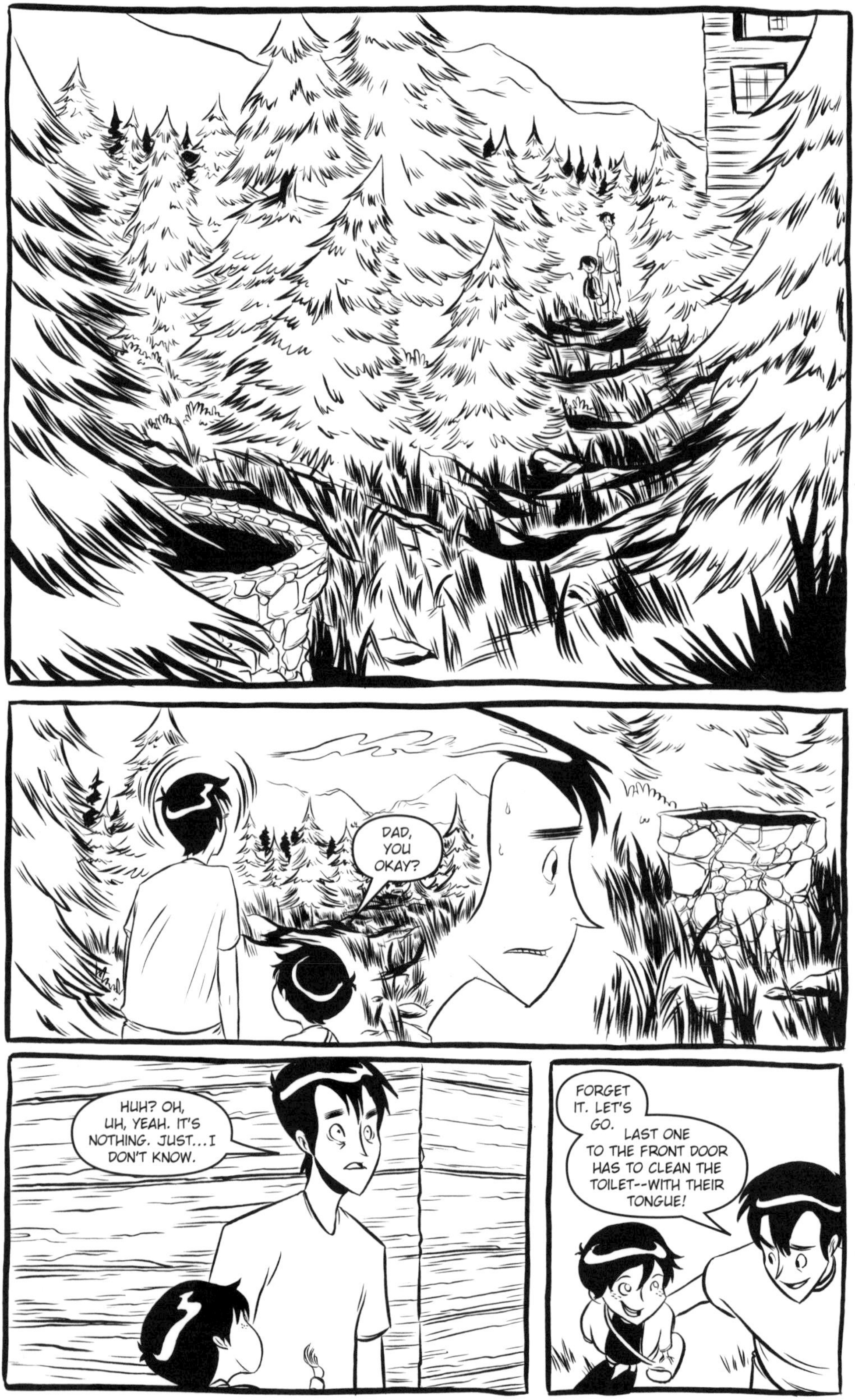
DAD, YOU OKAY?
HUH? OH, UH, YEAH. IT'S NOTHING. JUST...I DON'T KNOW.
FORGET IT. LET'S GO.
LAST ONE TO THE FRONT DOOR HAS TO CLEAN THE TOILET--WITH THEIR TONGUE!

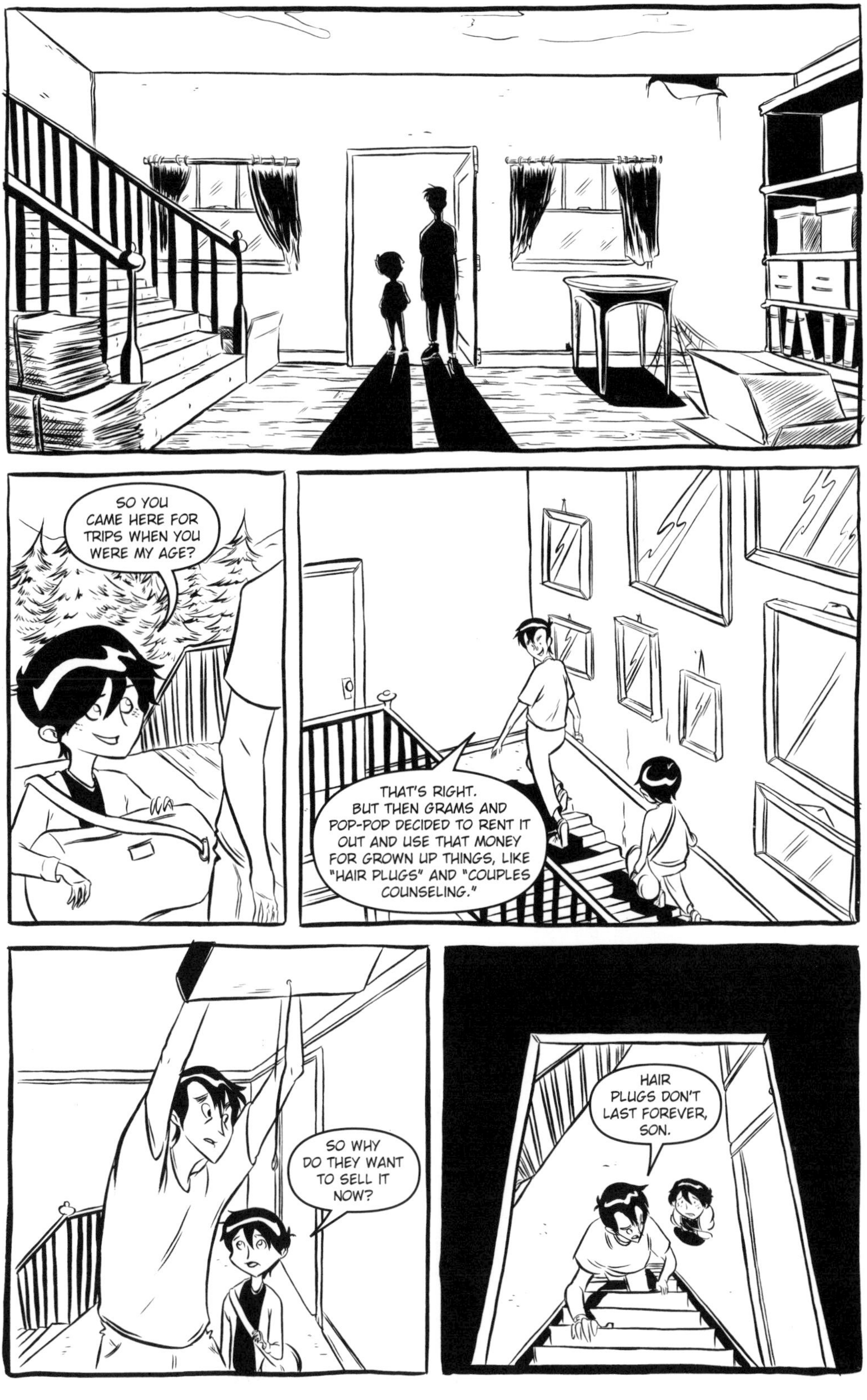
SO YOU CAME HERE FOR TRIPS WHEN YOU WERE MY AGE?
THAT'S RIGHT. BUT THEN GRAMS AND POP-POP DECIDED TO RENT IT OUT AND USE THAT MONEY FOR GROWN UP THINGS, LIKE "HAIR PLUGS" AND "COUPLES COUNSELING."
SO WHY DO THEY WANT TO SELL IT NOW?
HAIR PLUGS DON'T LAST FOREVER, SON.

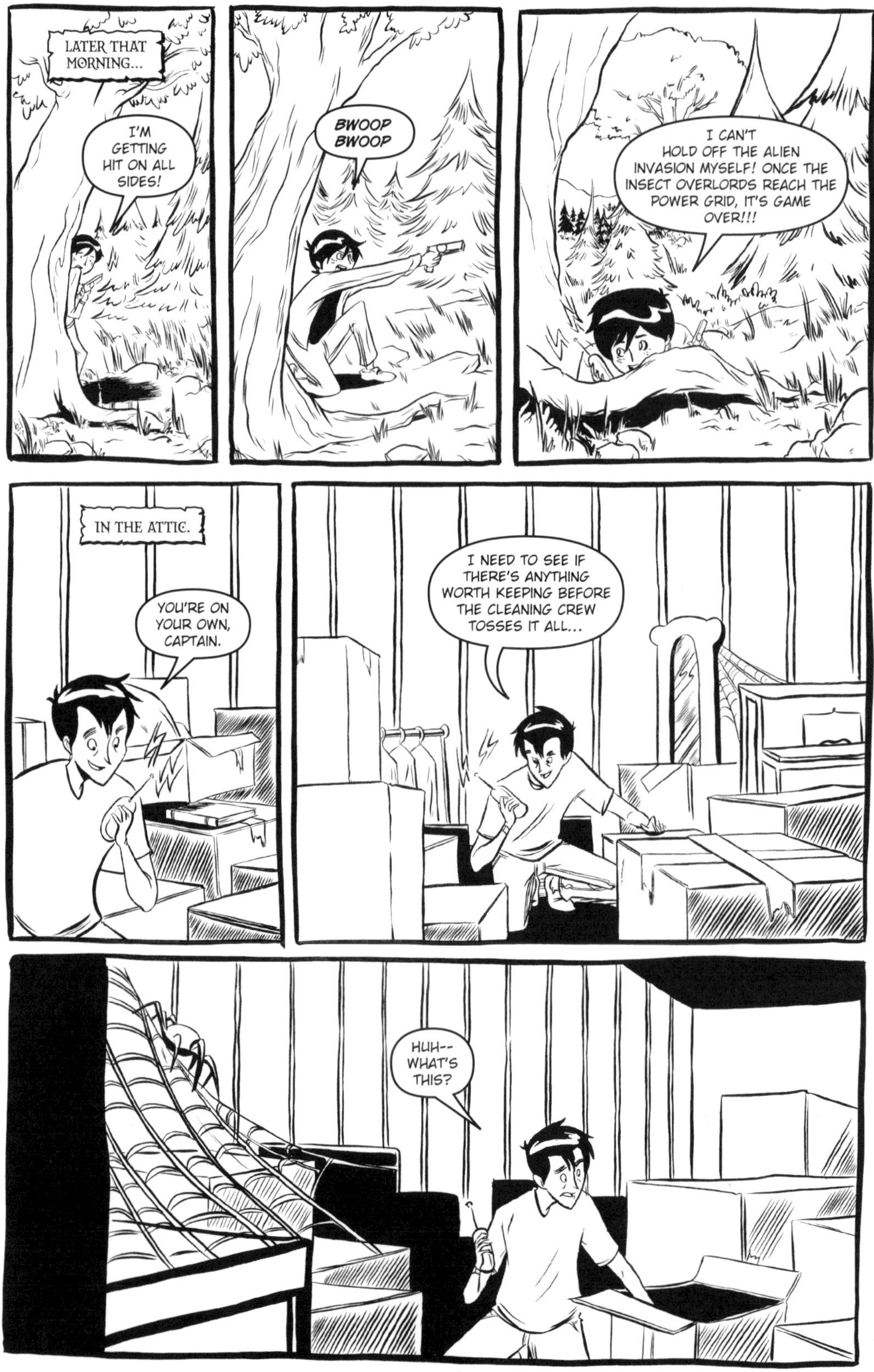
LATER THAT MORNING...
I'M GETTING HIT ON ALL SIDES!
BWOOP BWOOP
I CAN'T HOLD OFF THE ALIEN INVASION MYSELF! ONCE THE INSECT OVERLORDS REACH THE POWER GRID, IT'S GAME OVER!!!
IN THE ATTIC.
YOU'RE ON YOUR OWN, CAPTAIN.
I NEED TO SEE IF THERE'S ANYTHING WORTH KEEPING BEFORE THE CLEANING CREW TOSSES IT ALL...
HUH-- WHAT'S THIS?

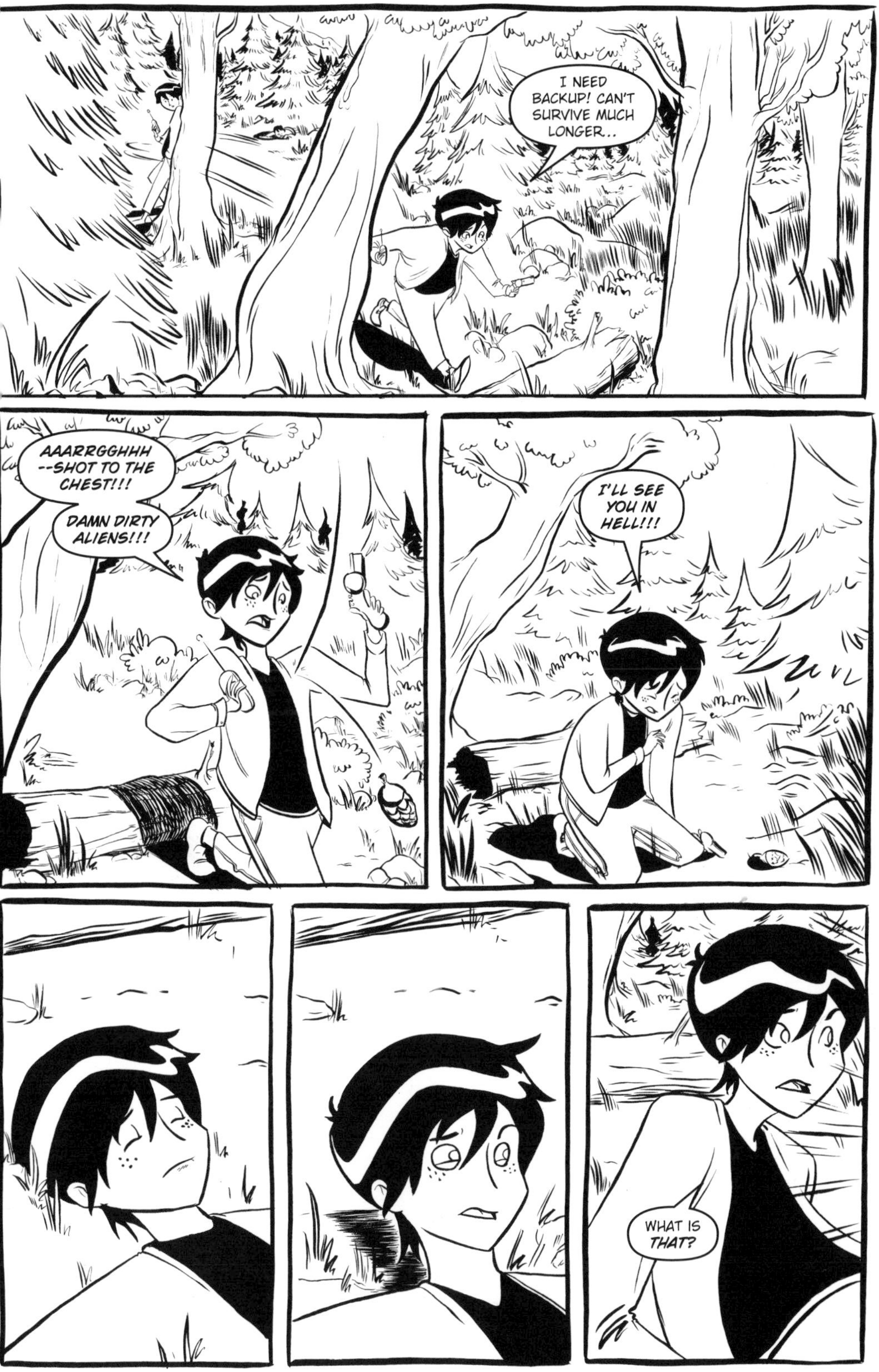
I NEED BACKUP! CAN'T SURVIVE MUCH LONGER..
AAARRGGHHH --SHOT TO THE CHEST!!!
DAMN DIRTY ALIENS!!!
I'LL SEE YOU IN HELL!!!
WHAT IS *THAT?*

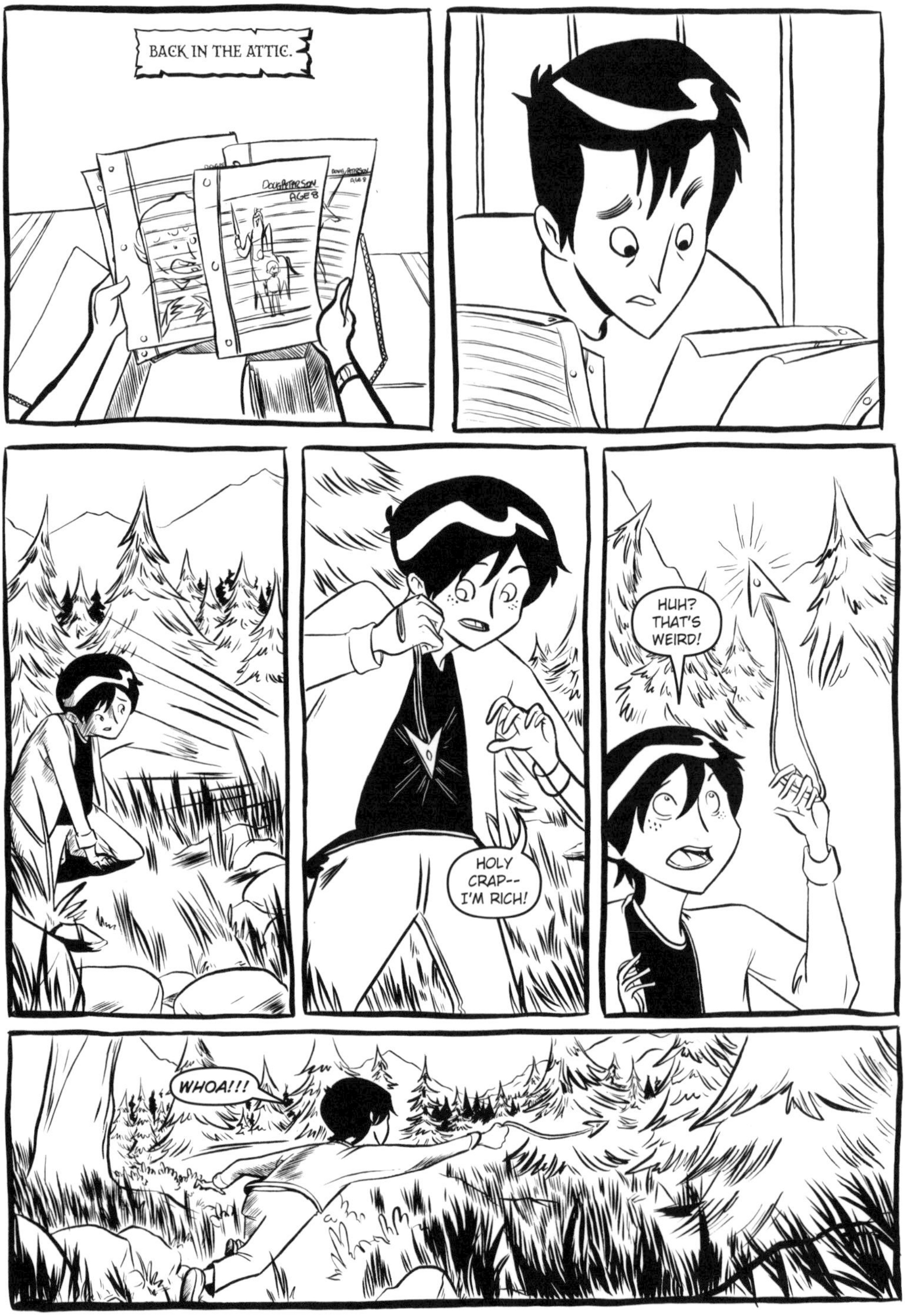
BACK IN THE ATTIC.
DOUG PETERSON
AGE 8
HOLY CRAP-- I'M RICH!
HUH? THAT'S WEIRD!
WHOA!!!

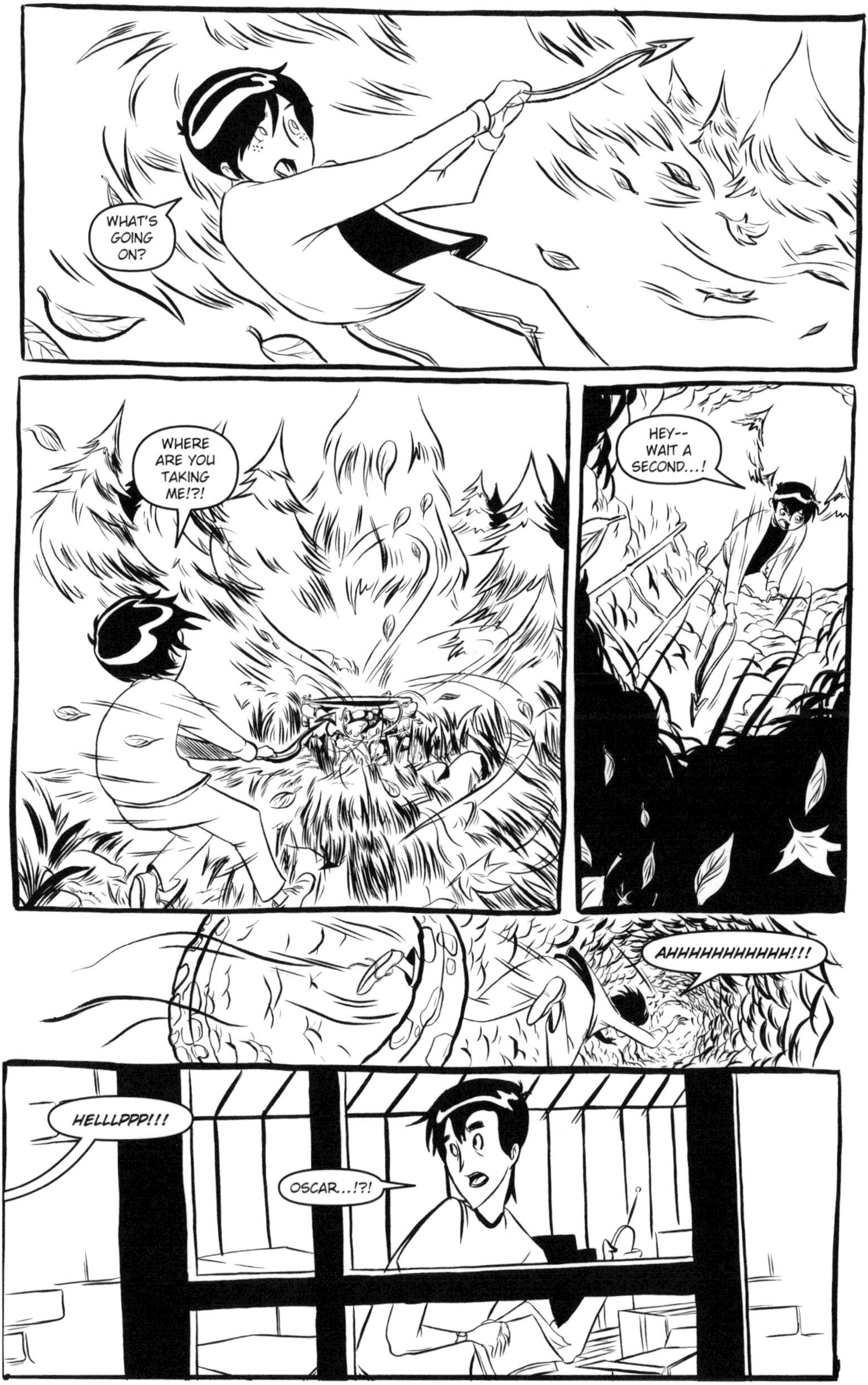
WHAT'S GOING ON?
WHERE ARE YOU TAKING ME!?!
HEY-- WAIT A SECOND...!
AHHHHHHHHHHH!!!
HELLLPPP!!!
OSCAR...!?!

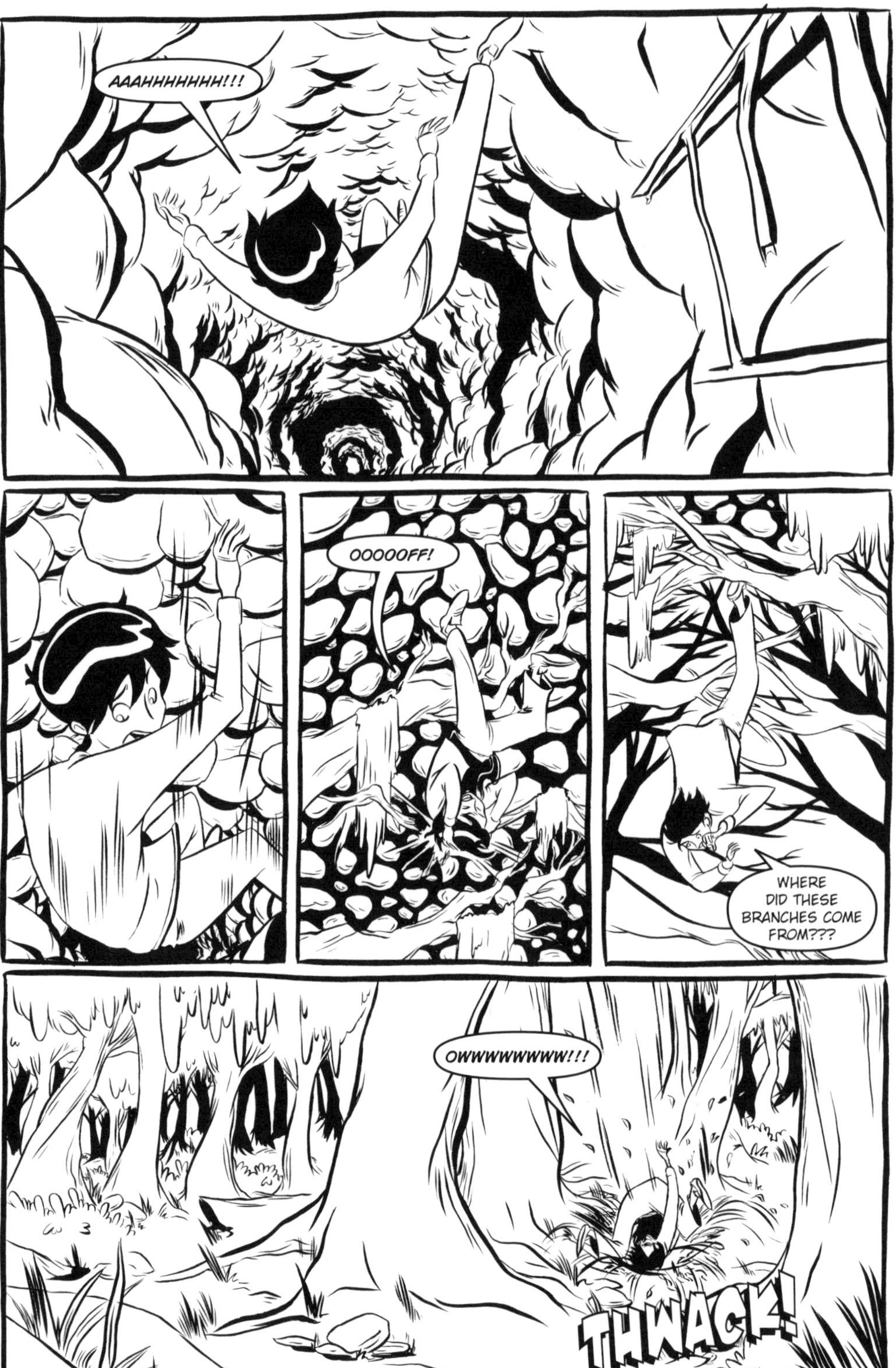
AAAHHHHHHH!!!
OOOOOFF!
WHERE DID THESE BRANCHES COME FROM???
OWWWWWWWW!!!
THWACK!

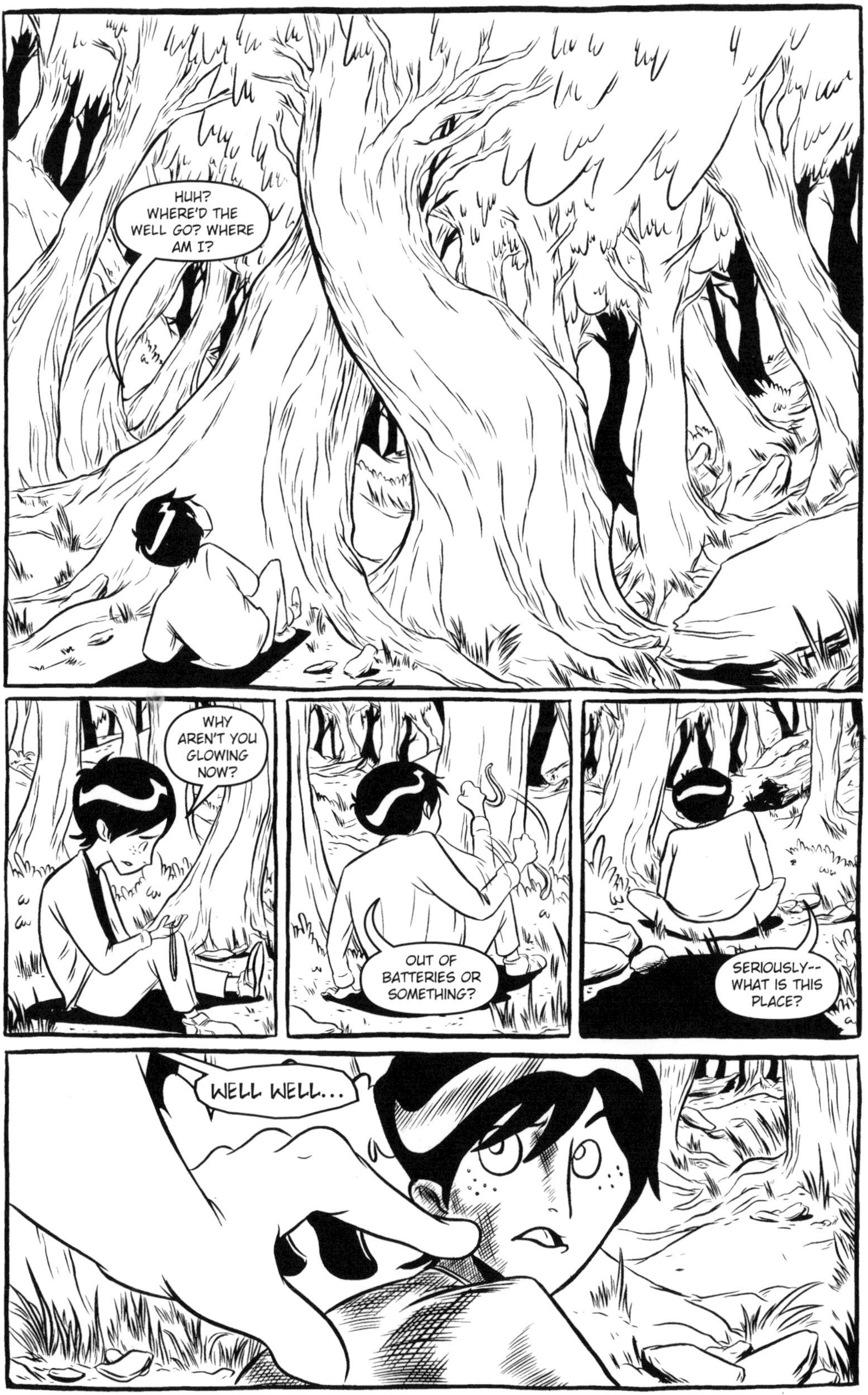
HUH? WHERE'D THE WELL GO? WHERE AM I?
WHY AREN'T YOU GLOWING NOW?
OUT OF BATTERIES OR SOMETHING?
SERIOUSLY-- WHAT IS THIS PLACE?
WELL WELL...

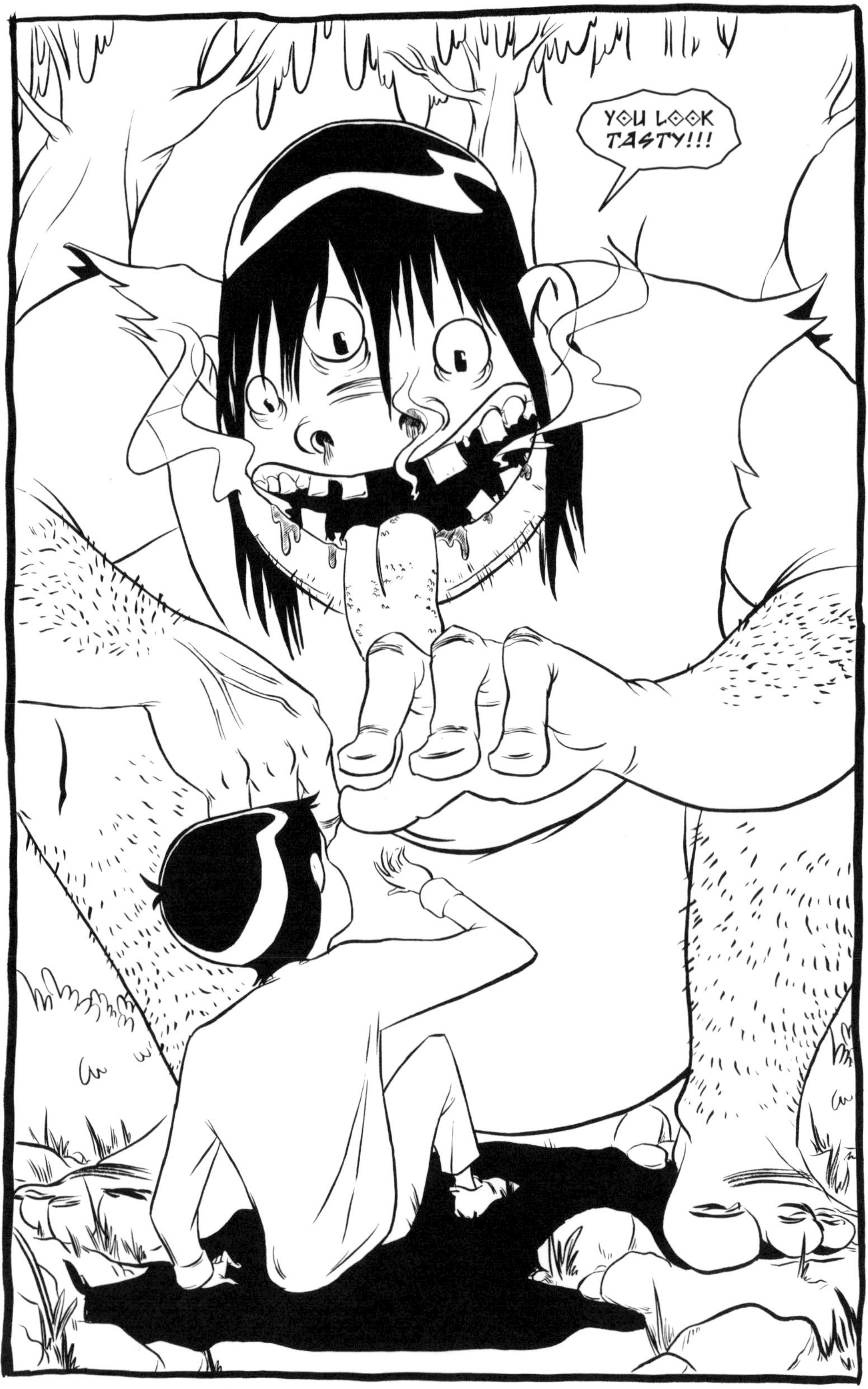
YOU LOOK TASTY!!!

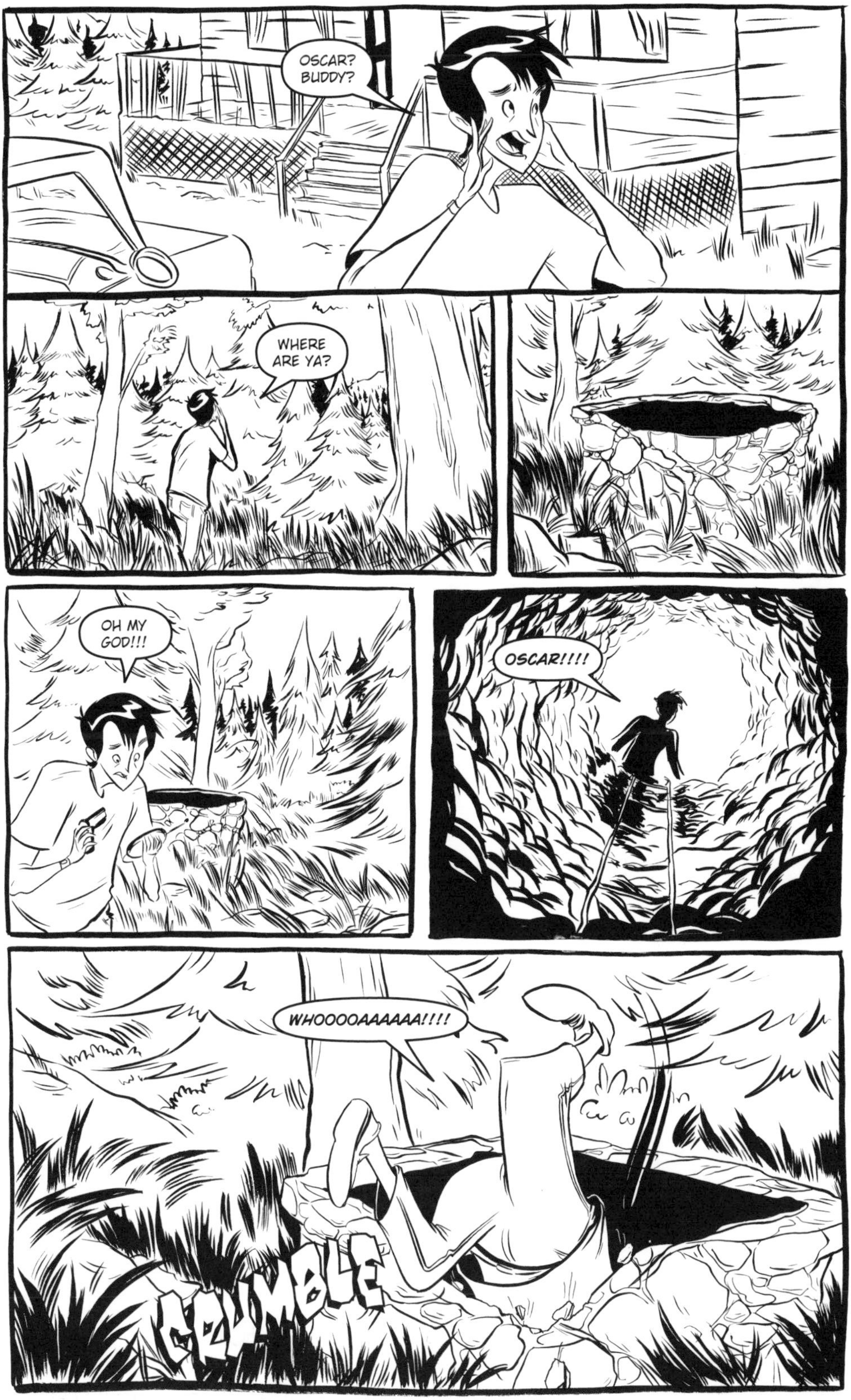
OSCAR? BUDDY?
WHERE ARE YA?
OH MY GOD!!!
OSCAR!!!!
WHOOOOAAAAAA!!!!
CRUMBLE

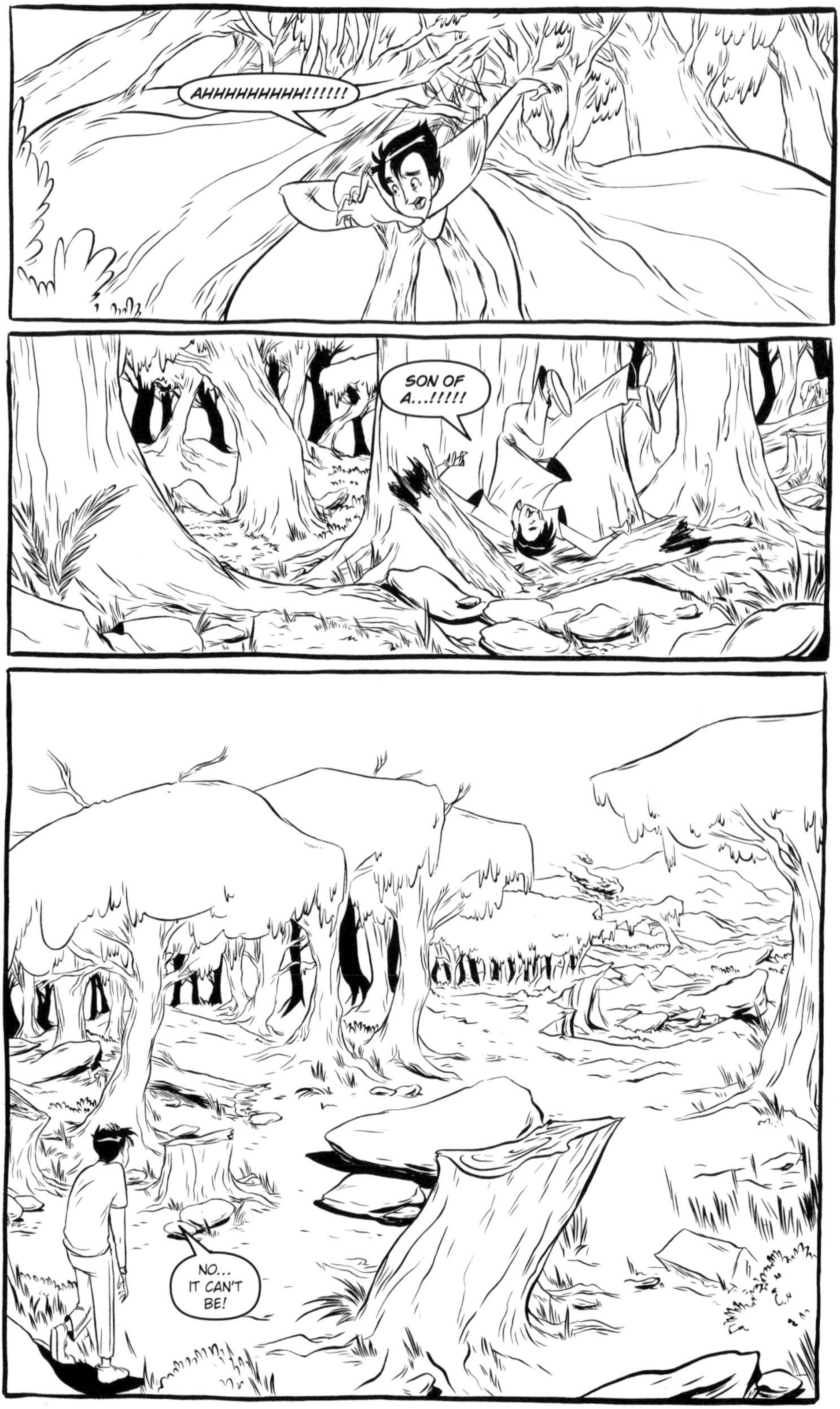
AHHHHHHHHH!!!!!!
SON OF A...!!!!!
NO... IT CAN'T BE!

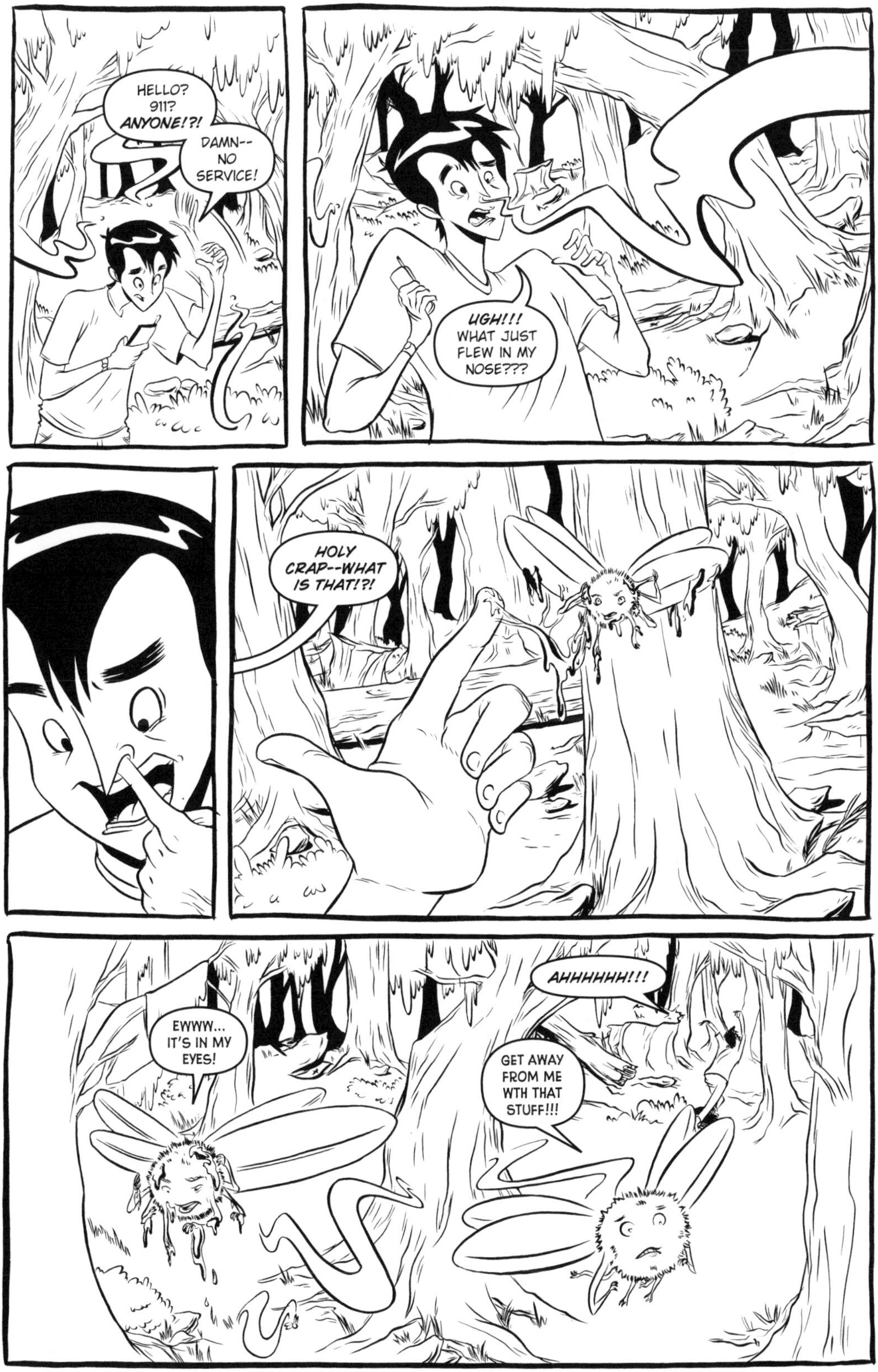
HELLO? 911? ANYONE!?!
DAMN-- NO SERVICE!
UGH!!! WHAT JUST FLEW IN MY NOSE???
HOLY CRAP--WHAT IS THAT!?!
EWWW... IT'S IN MY EYES!
AHHHHHH!!!
GET AWAY FROM ME WTH THAT STUFF!!!

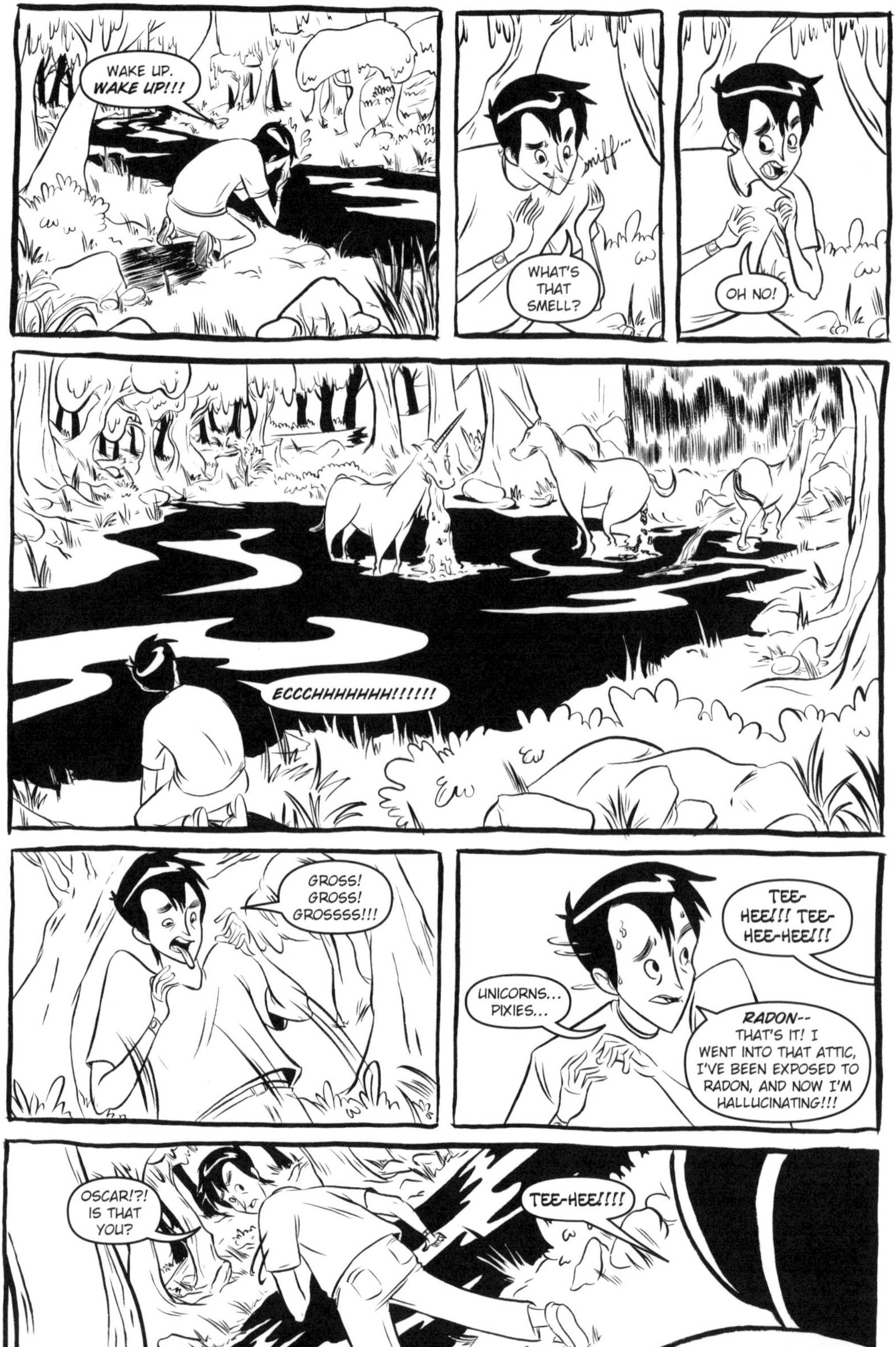
WAKE UP. **WAKE UP!!!**
sniff...
WHAT'S THAT SMELL?
OH NO!
ECCCHHHHHHH!!!!!!
GROSS! GROSS! GROSSSS!!!
TEE-HEE!!! TEE-HEE-HEE!!!
UNICORNS... PIXIES...
RADON-- THAT'S IT! I WENT INTO THAT ATTIC, I'VE BEEN EXPOSED TO RADON, AND NOW I'M HALLUCINATING!!!
OSCAR!?! IS THAT YOU?
TEE-HEE!!!!

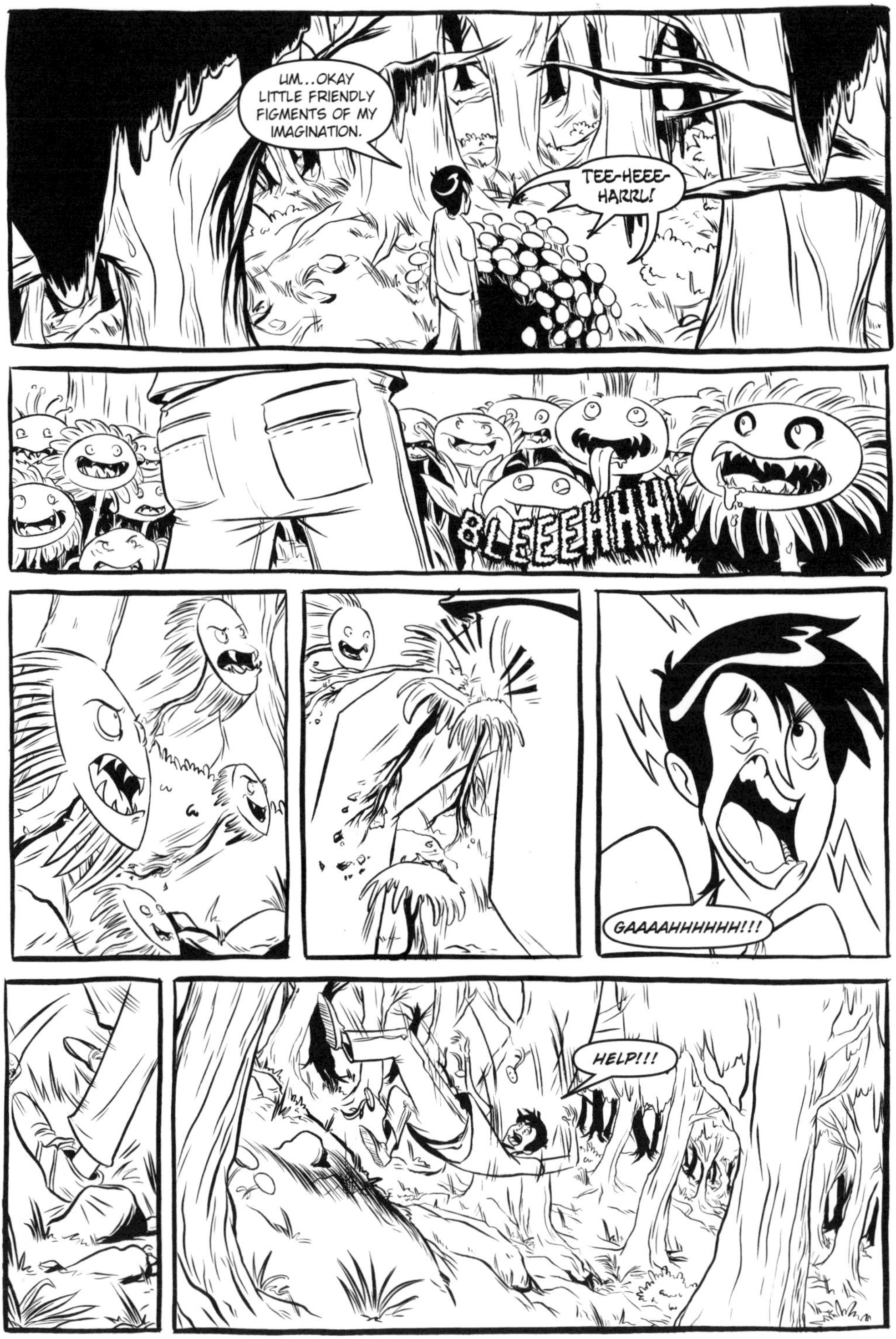
UM...OKAY LITTLE FRIENDLY FIGMENTS OF MY IMAGINATION.
TEE-HEEE-HARRL!
BLEEEHHH!
GAAAAHHHHHH!!!
HELP!!!

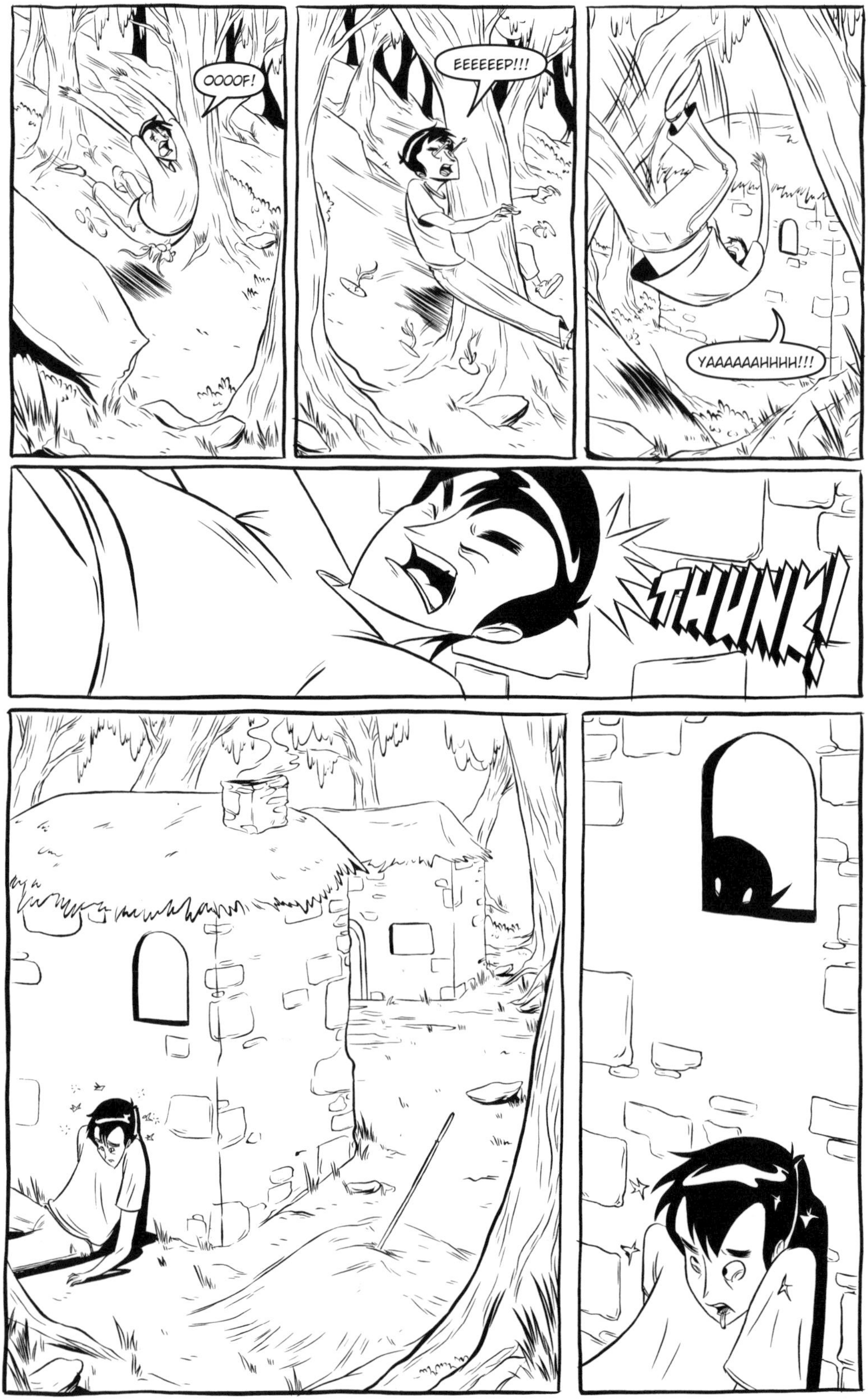
OOOOF!
EEEEEEP!!!
YAAAAAAHHHH!!!
THUNK!

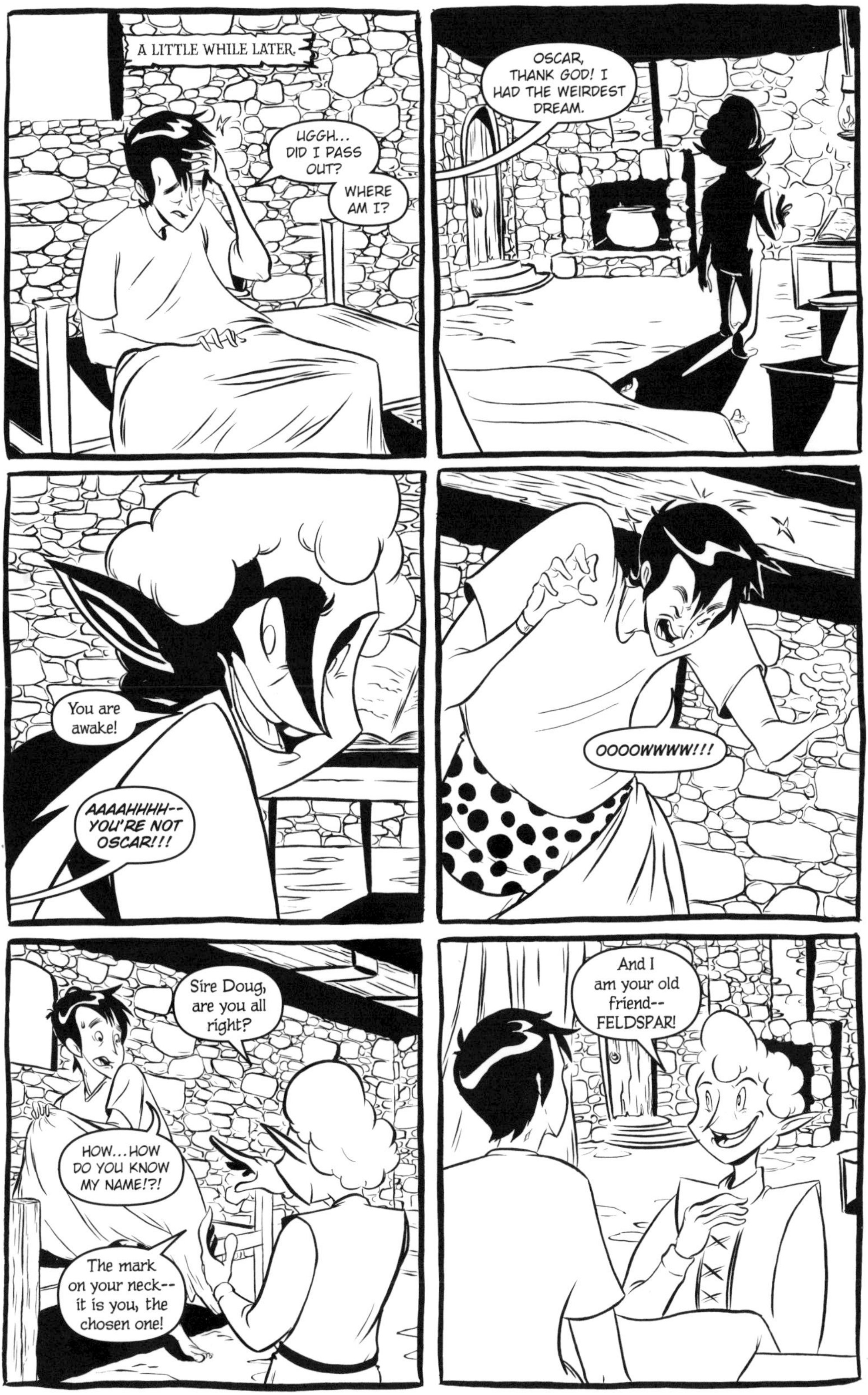
A LITTLE WHILE LATER.
UGGH... DID I PASS OUT?
WHERE AM I?
OSCAR, THANK GOD! I HAD THE WEIRDEST DREAM.
You are awake!
AAAAHHHH-- YOU'RE NOT OSCAR!!!
OOOOWWWW!!!
Sire Doug, are you all right?
HOW...HOW DO YOU KNOW MY NAME!?!
The mark on your neck-- it is you, the chosen one!
And I am your old friend-- FELDSPAR!

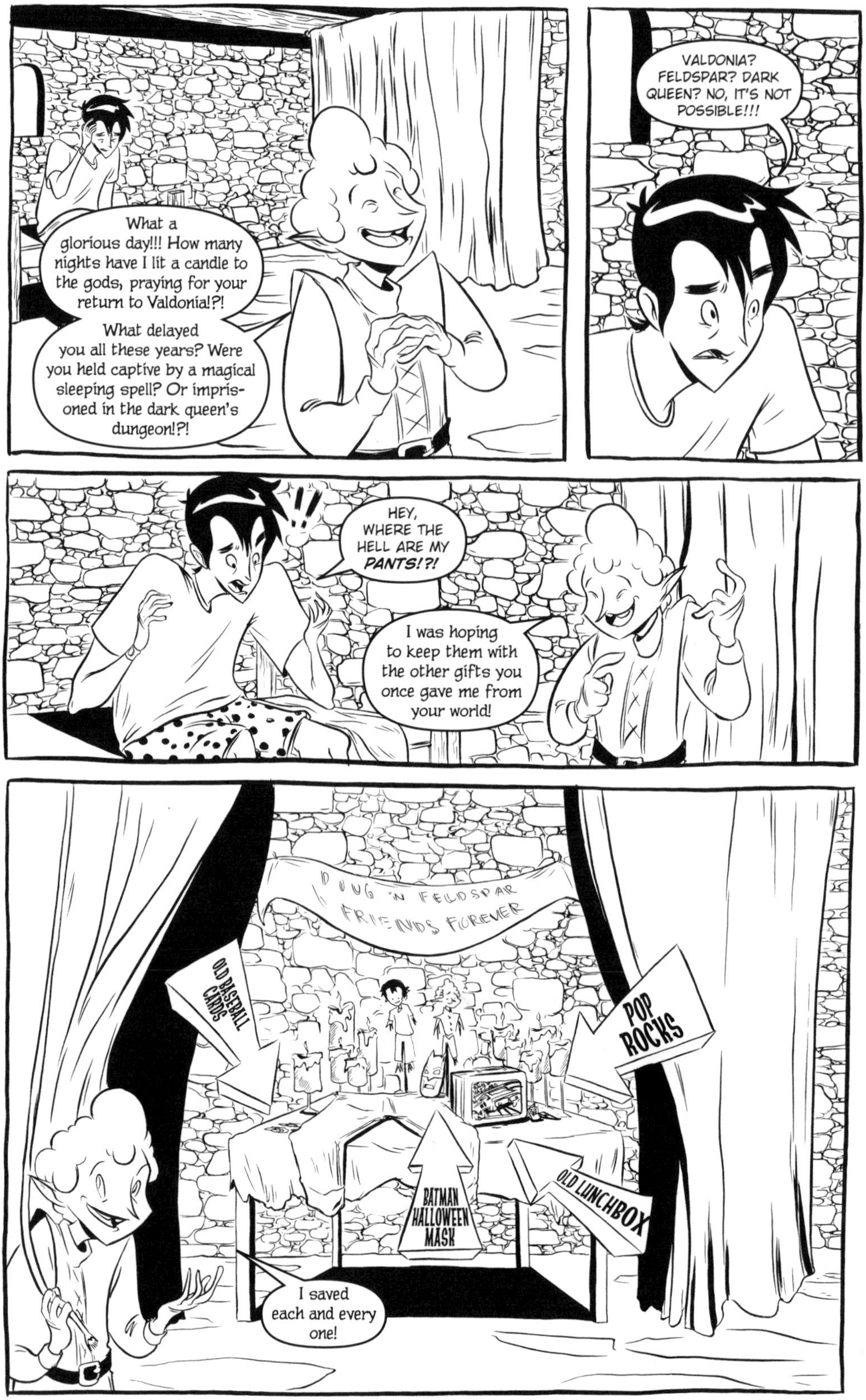
What a glorious day!!! How many nights have I lit a candle to the gods, praying for your return to Valdonia!?!
What delayed you all these years? Were you held captive by a magical sleeping spell? Or imprisoned in the dark queen's dungeon!?!
VALDONIA? FELDSPAR? DARK QUEEN? NO, IT'S NOT POSSIBLE!!!
HEY, WHERE THE HELL ARE MY *PANTS!?!*
I was hoping to keep them with the other gifts you once gave me from your world!
DOUG 'N FELDSPAR FRIENDS FOREVER
OLD BASEBALL CARDS
POP ROCKS
BATMAN HALLOWEEN MASK
OLD LUNCHBOX
I saved each and every one!

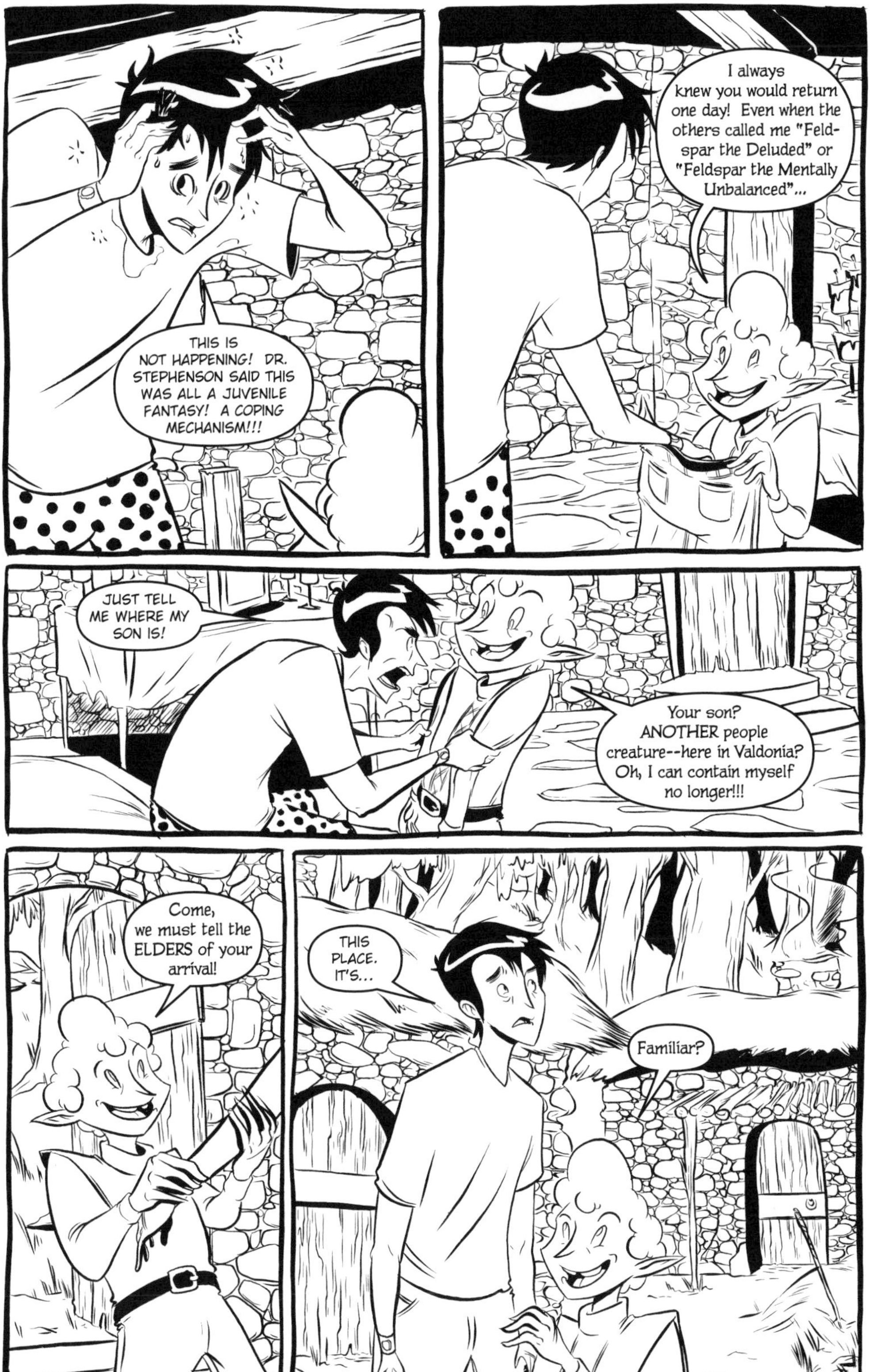
THIS IS NOT HAPPENING! DR. STEPHENSON SAID THIS WAS ALL A JUVENILE FANTASY! A COPING MECHANISM!!!
I always knew you would return one day! Even when the others called me "Feld-spar the Deluded" or "Feldspar the Mentally Unbalanced"...
JUST TELL ME WHERE MY SON IS!
Your son? ANOTHER people creature--here in Valdonia? Oh, I can contain myself no longer!!!
Come, we must tell the ELDERS of your arrival!
THIS PLACE. IT'S...
Familiar?

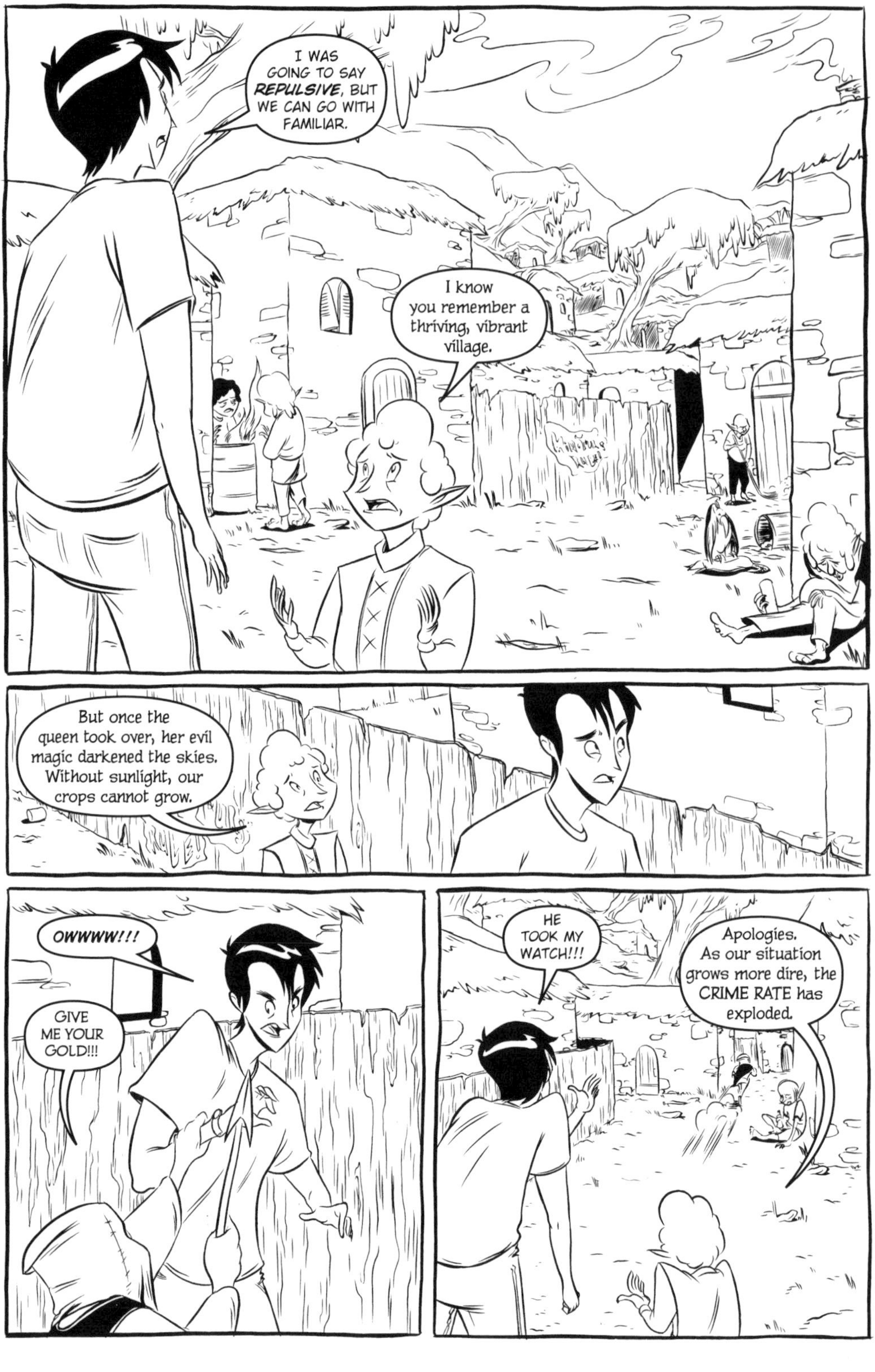
I WAS GOING TO SAY **REPULSIVE**, BUT WE CAN GO WITH FAMILIAR.
I know you remember a thriving, vibrant village.
But once the queen took over, her evil magic darkened the skies. Without sunlight, our crops cannot grow.
OWWWW!!!
GIVE ME YOUR GOLD!!!
HE TOOK MY WATCH!!!
Apologies. As our situation grows more dire, the CRIME RATE has exploded.

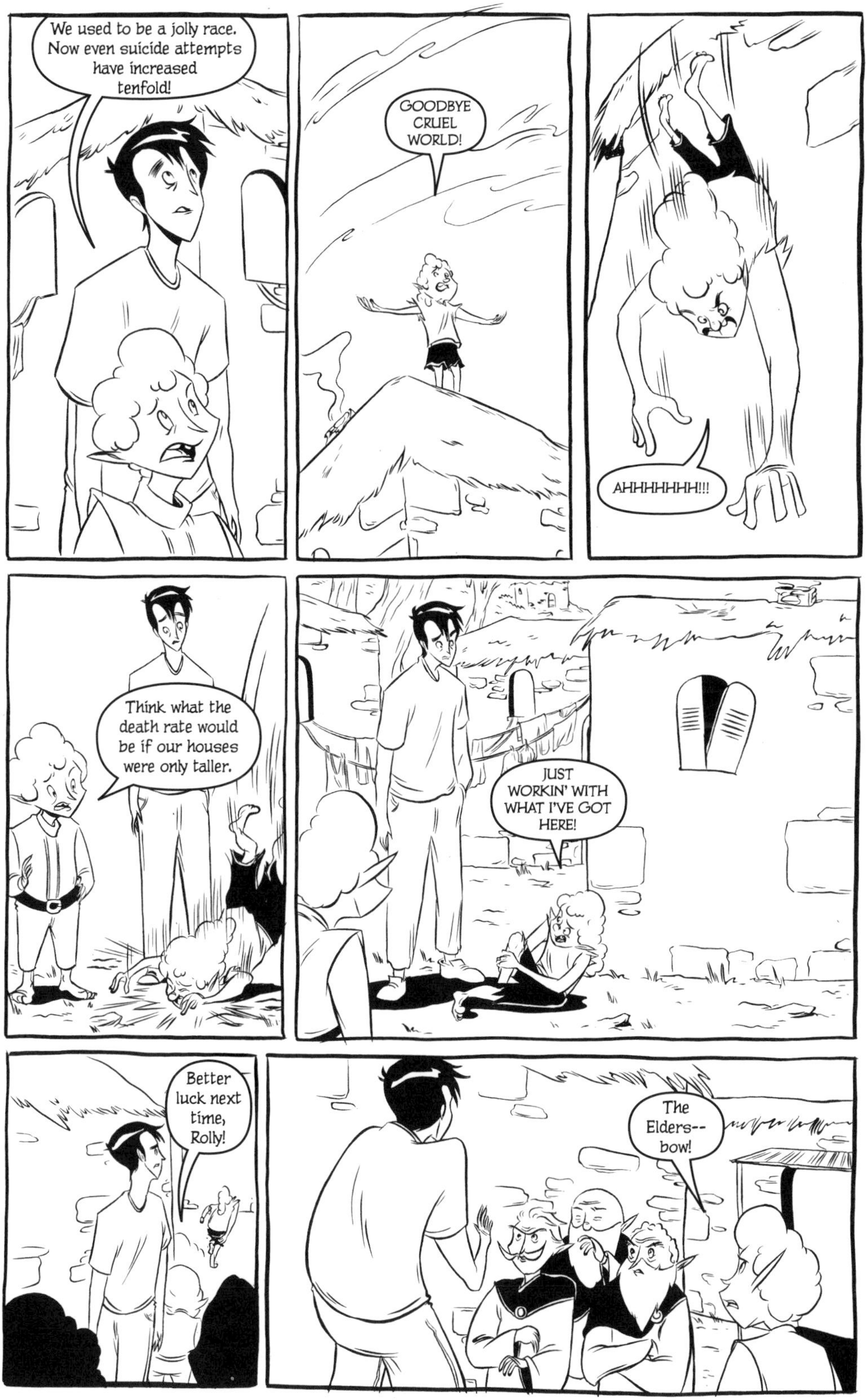
We used to be a jolly race. Now even suicide attempts have increased tenfold!
GOODBYE CRUEL WORLD!
AHHHHHHH!!!
Think what the death rate would be if our houses were only taller.
JUST WORKIN' WITH WHAT I'VE GOT HERE!
Better luck next time, Rolly!
The Elders-- bow!

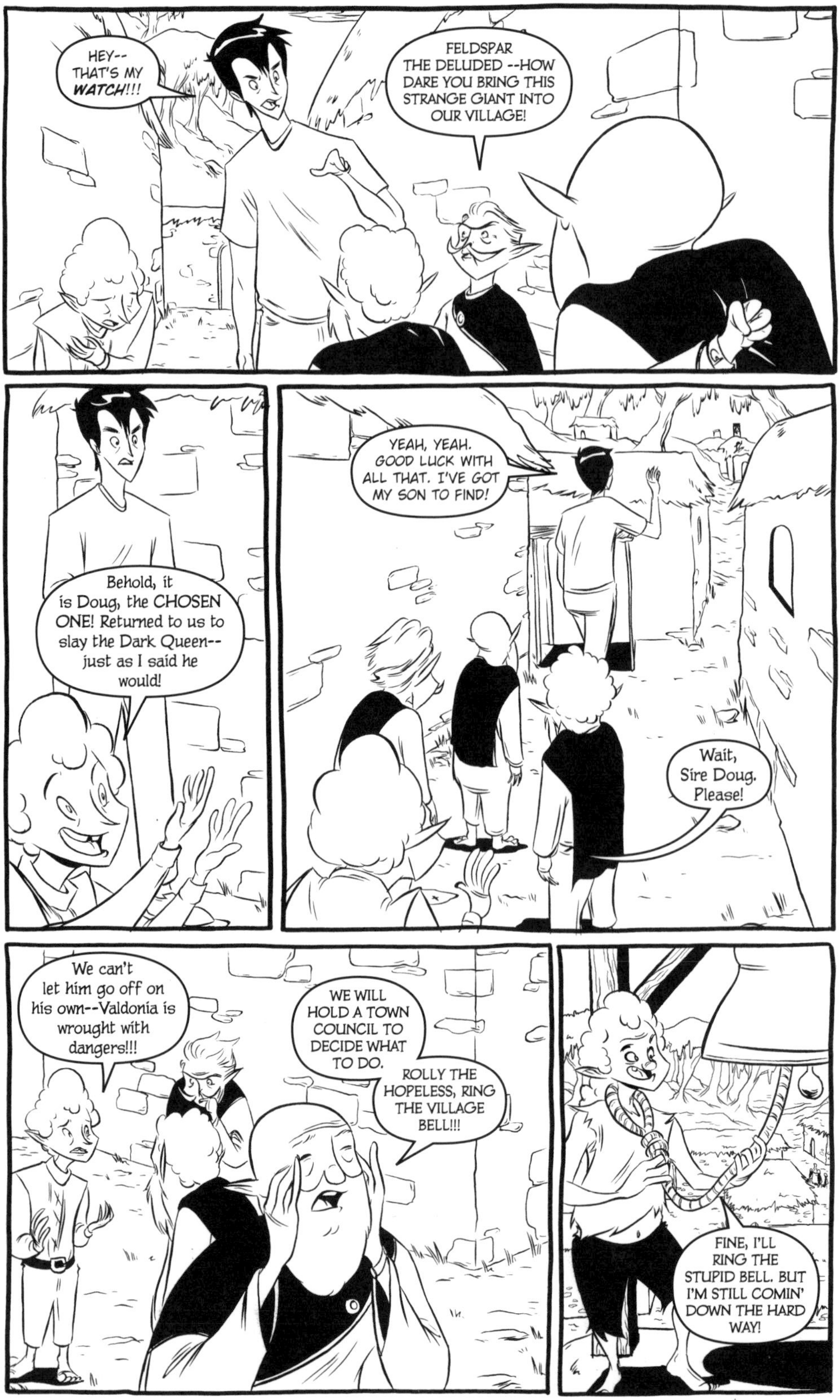
HEY-- THAT'S MY WATCH!!!
FELDSPAR THE DELUDED --HOW DARE YOU BRING THIS STRANGE GIANT INTO OUR VILLAGE!
Behold, it is Doug, the CHOSEN ONE! Returned to us to slay the Dark Queen-- just as I said he would!
YEAH, YEAH. GOOD LUCK WITH ALL THAT. I'VE GOT MY SON TO FIND!
Wait, Sire Doug. Please!
We can't let him go off on his own--Valdonia is wrought with dangers!!!
WE WILL HOLD A TOWN COUNCIL TO DECIDE WHAT TO DO.
ROLLY THE HOPELESS, RING THE VILLAGE BELL!!!
FINE, I'LL RING THE STUPID BELL. BUT I'M STILL COMIN' DOWN THE HARD WAY!

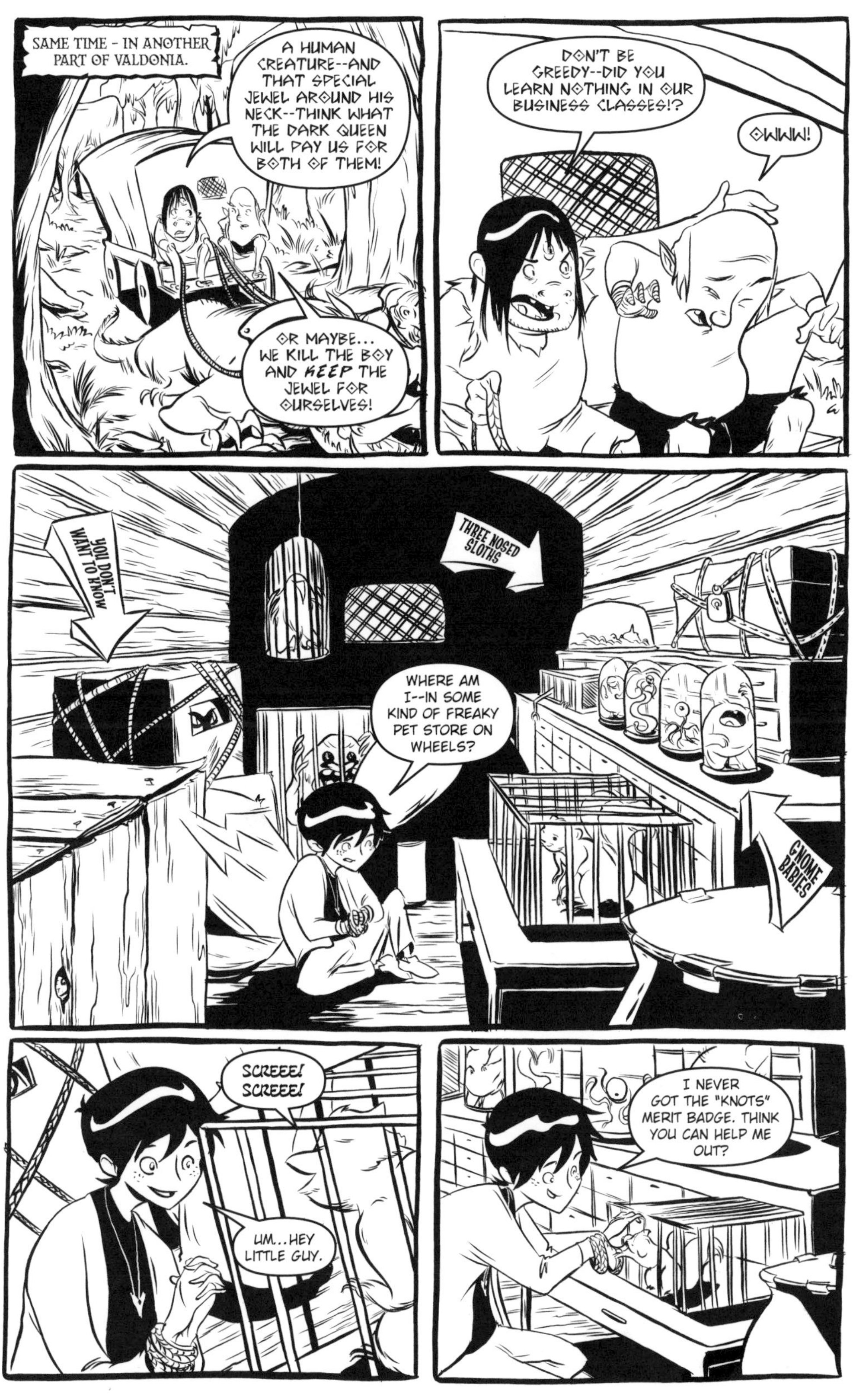
SAME TIME - IN ANOTHER PART OF VALDONIA.
A HUMAN CREATURE--AND THAT SPECIAL JEWEL AROUND HIS NECK--THINK WHAT THE DARK QUEEN WILL PAY US FOR BOTH OF THEM!
OR MAYBE... WE KILL THE BOY AND KEEP THE JEWEL FOR OURSELVES!
DON'T BE GREEDY--DID YOU LEARN NOTHING IN OUR BUSINESS CLASSES!?
OWWW!
YOU DON'T WANT TO KNOW
THREE NOSED SLOTHS
WHERE AM I--IN SOME KIND OF FREAKY PET STORE ON WHEELS?
GNOME BABIES
SCREEE! SCREEE!
UM...HEY LITTLE GUY.
I NEVER GOT THE "KNOTS" MERIT BADGE. THINK YOU CAN HELP ME OUT?

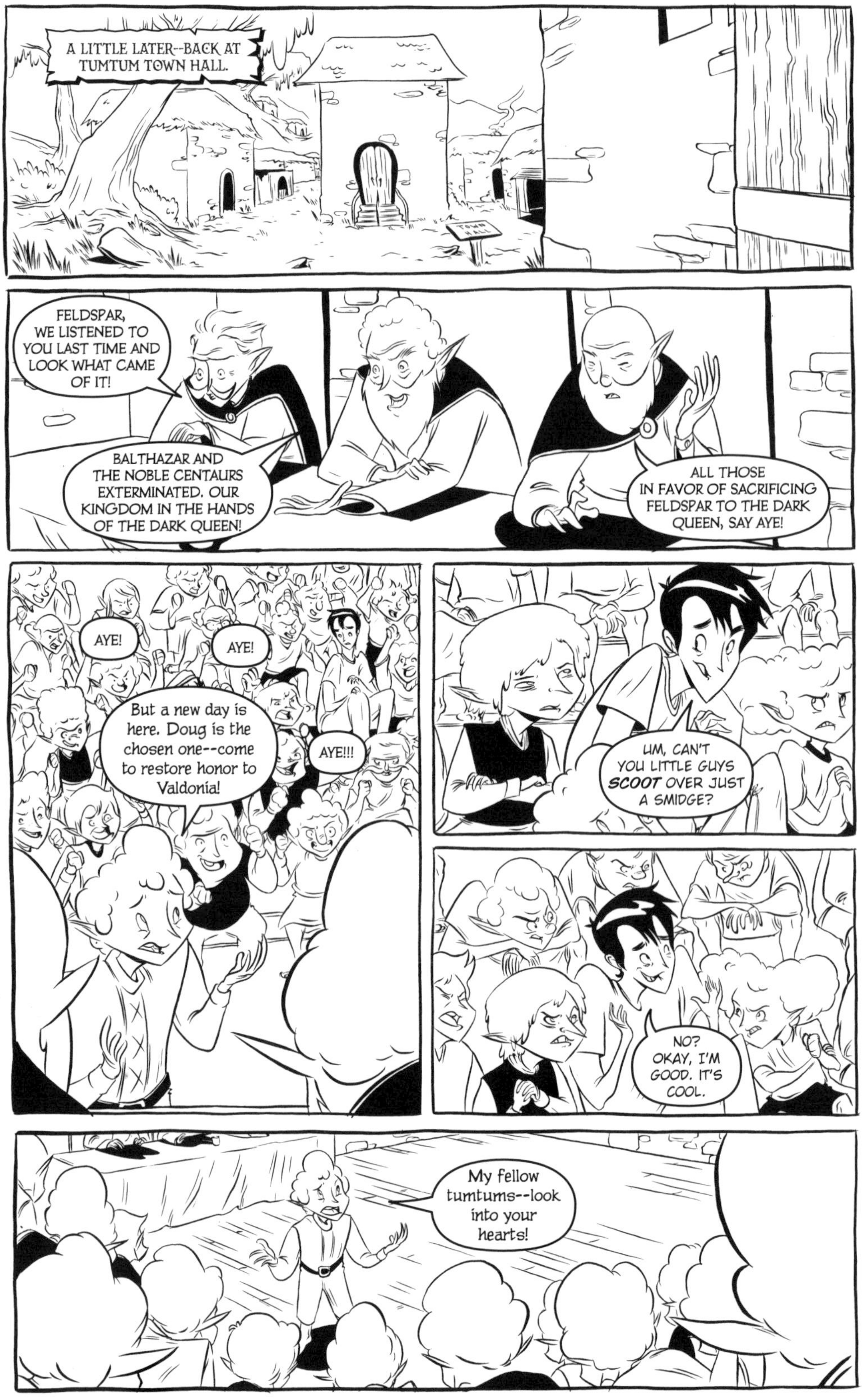
A LITTLE LATER--BACK AT TUMTUM TOWN HALL.
FELDSPAR, WE LISTENED TO YOU LAST TIME AND LOOK WHAT CAME OF IT!
BALTHAZAR AND THE NOBLE CENTAURS EXTERMINATED. OUR KINGDOM IN THE HANDS OF THE DARK QUEEN!
ALL THOSE IN FAVOR OF SACRIFICING FELDSPAR TO THE DARK QUEEN, SAY AYE!
AYE!
AYE!
AYE!!!
But a new day is here. Doug is the chosen one--come to restore honor to Valdonia!
UM, CAN'T YOU LITTLE GUYS SCOOT OVER JUST A SMIDGE?
NO? OKAY, I'M GOOD. IT'S COOL.
My fellow tumtums--look into your hearts!

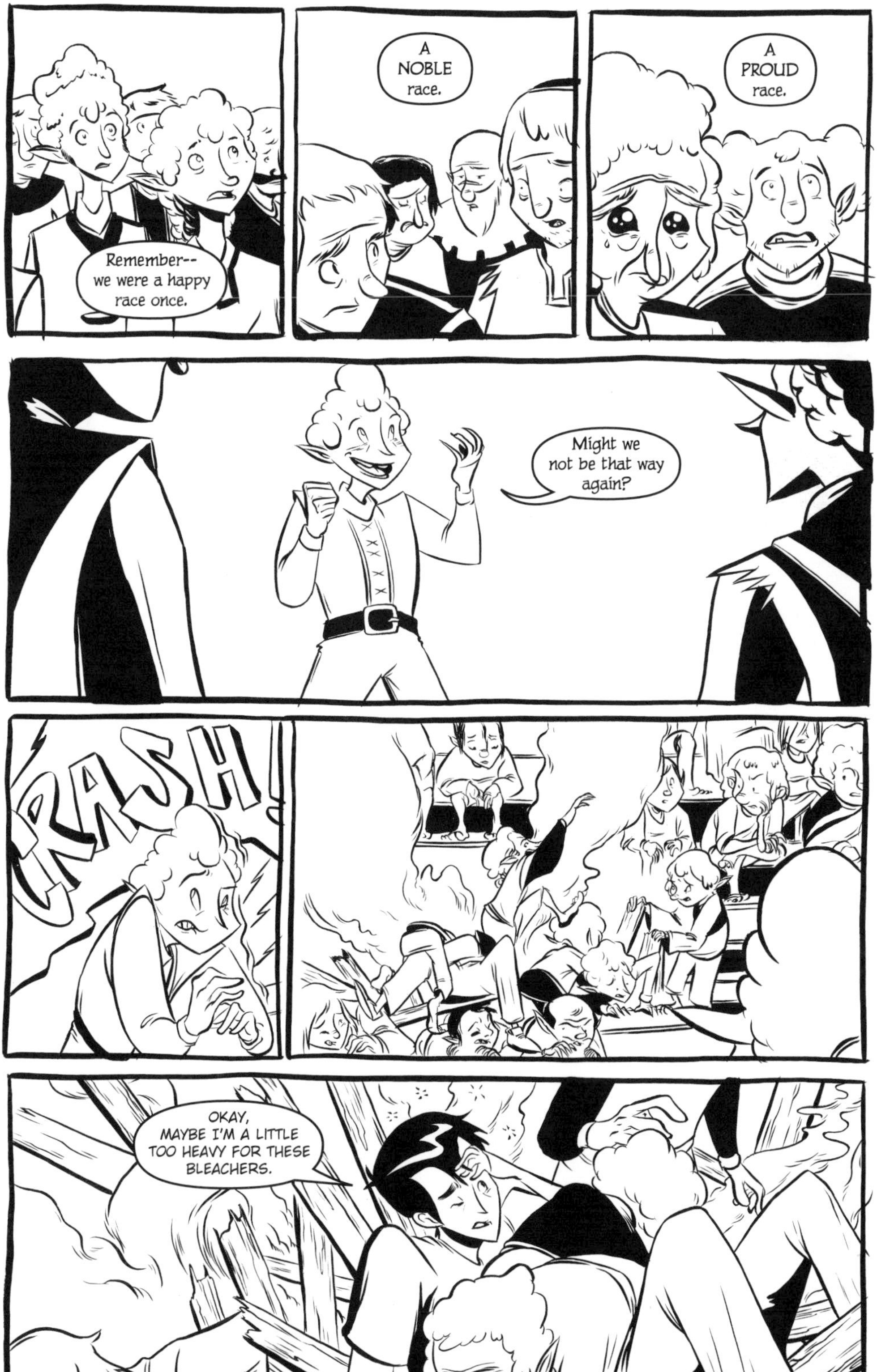
Remember-- we were a happy race once.
A NOBLE race.
A PROUD race.
Might we not be that way again?
CRASH!
OKAY, MAYBE I'M A LITTLE TOO HEAVY FOR THESE BLEACHERS.

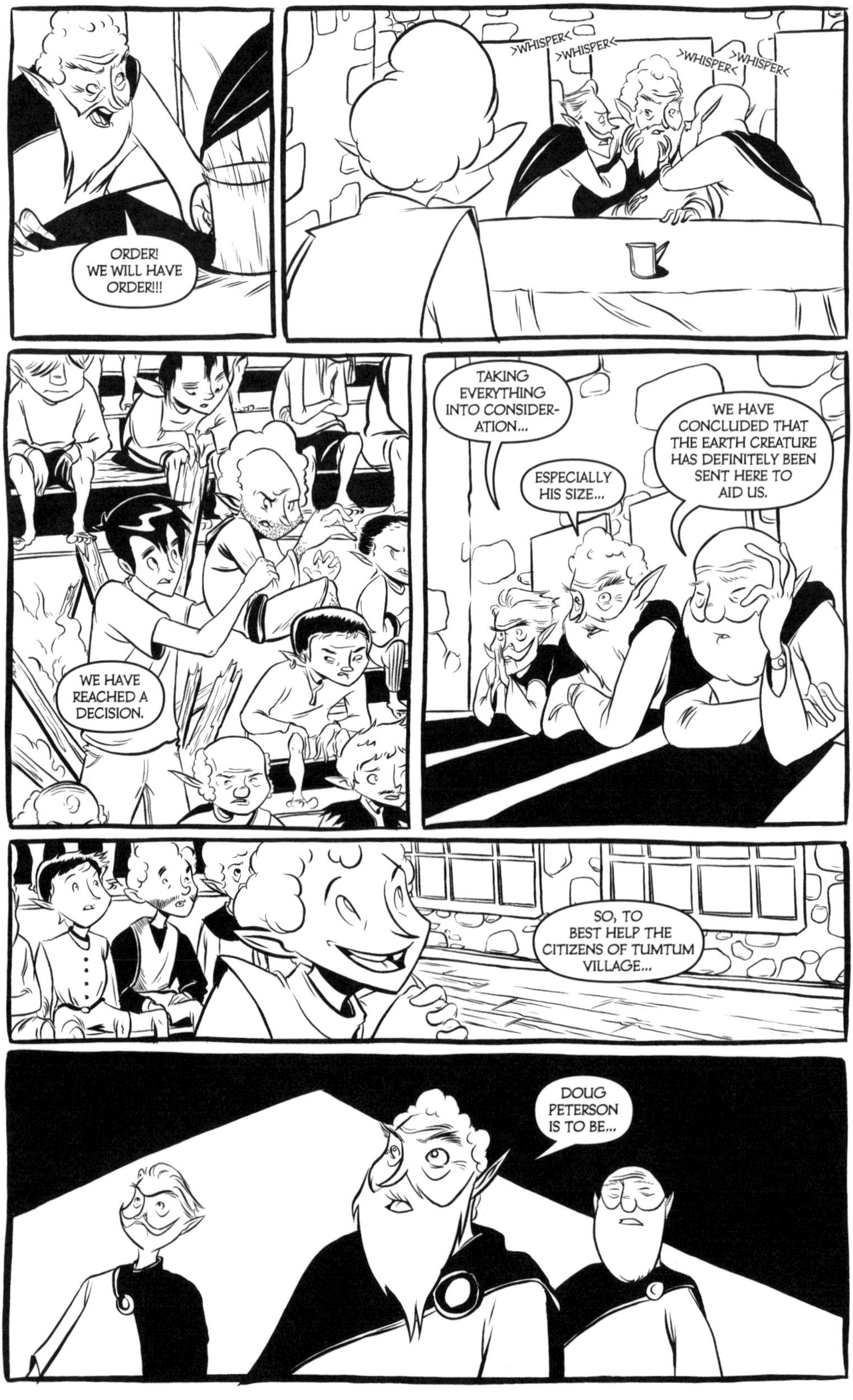
ORDER! WE WILL HAVE ORDER!!!
>WHISPER< >WHISPER< >WHISPER< >WHISPER<
WE HAVE REACHED A DECISION.
TAKING EVERYTHING INTO CONSIDER-ATION...
ESPECIALLY HIS SIZE...
WE HAVE CONCLUDED THAT THE EARTH CREATURE HAS DEFINITELY BEEN SENT HERE TO AID US.
SO, TO BEST HELP THE CITIZENS OF TUMTUM VILLAGE...
DOUG PETERSON IS TO BE...

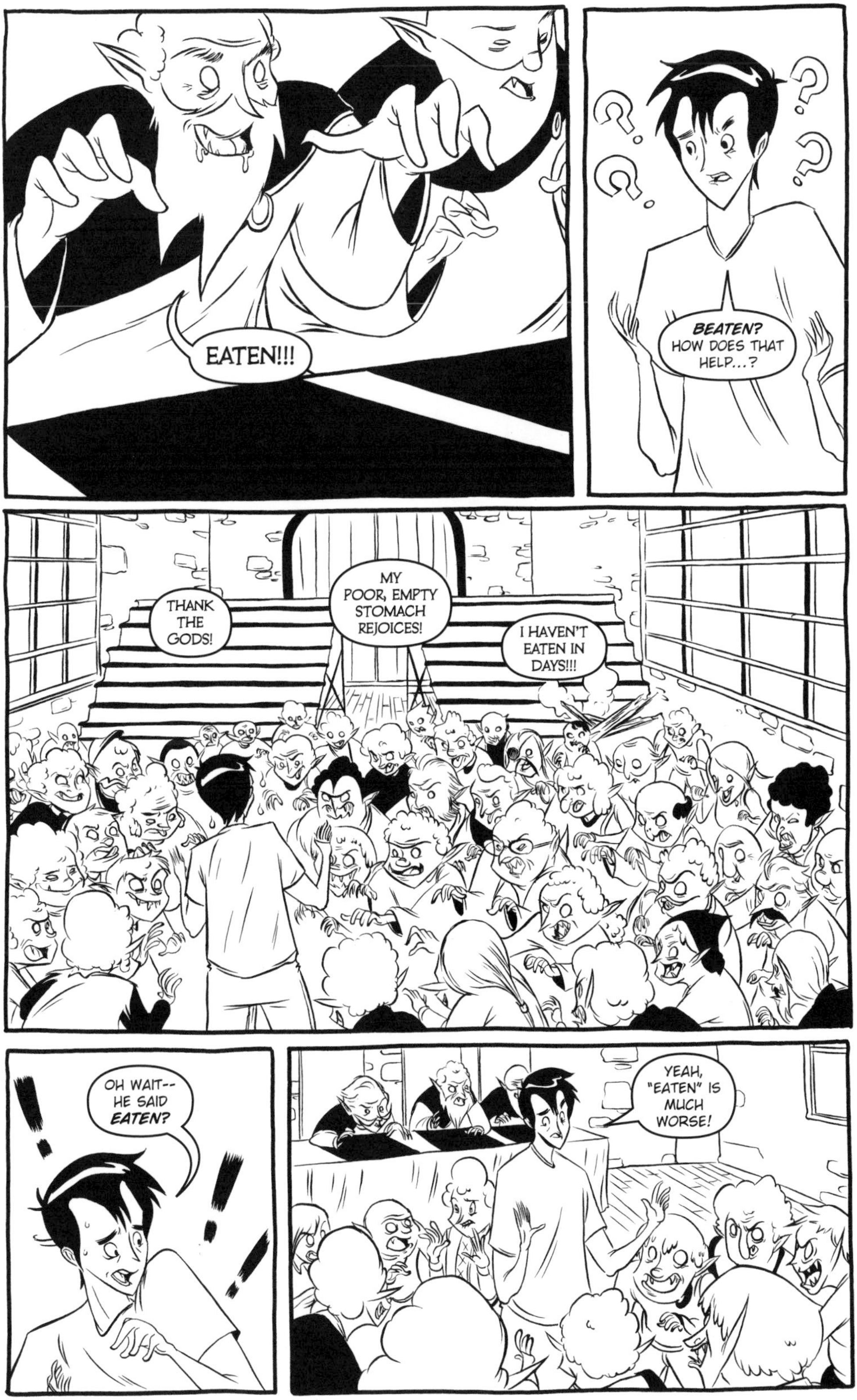
EATEN!!!
BEATEN? HOW DOES THAT HELP...?
THANK THE GODS!
MY POOR, EMPTY STOMACH REJOICES!
I HAVEN'T EATEN IN DAYS!!!
OH WAIT-- HE SAID *EATEN?*
YEAH, "EATEN" IS MUCH WORSE!

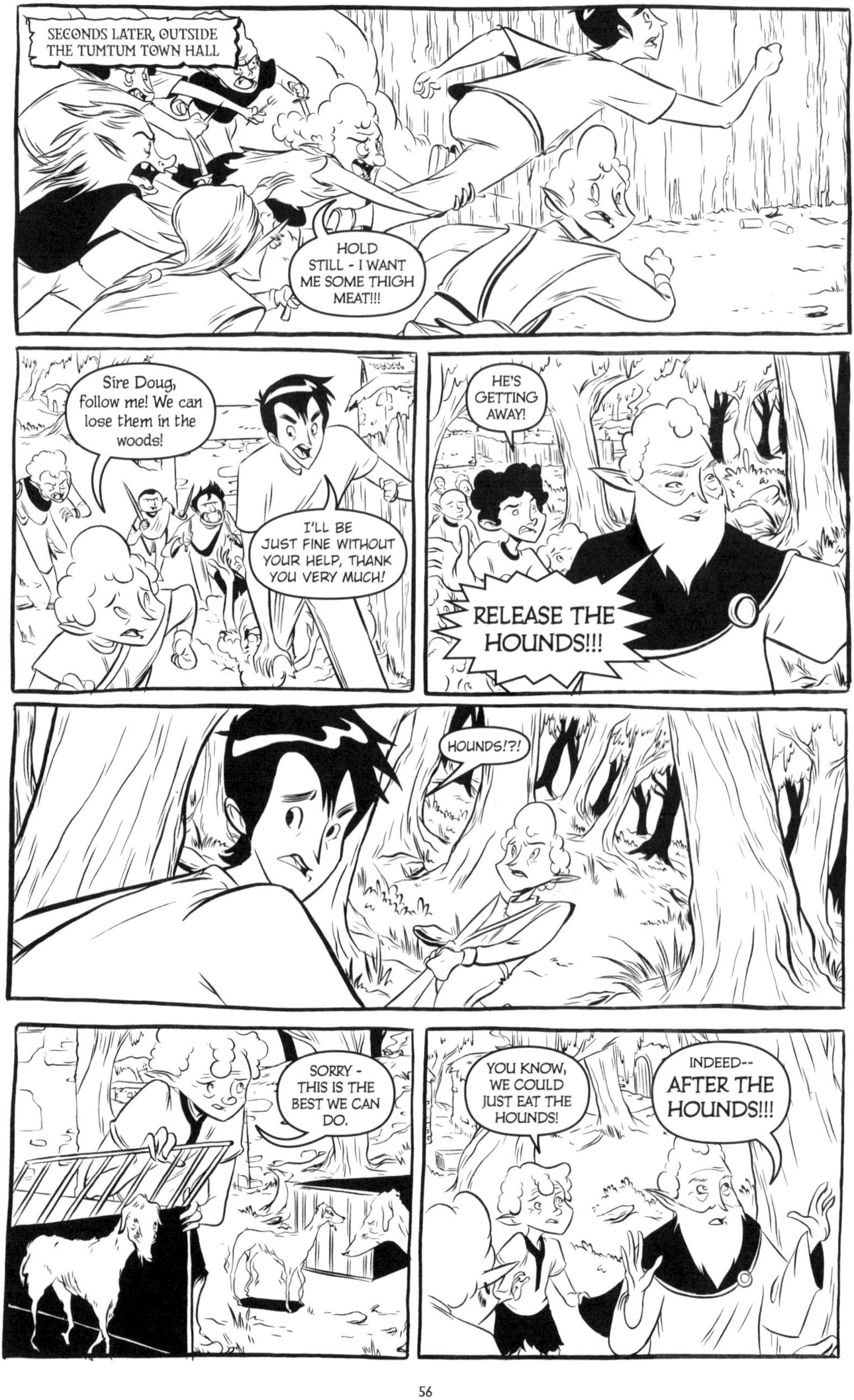
SECONDS LATER, OUTSIDE THE TUMTUM TOWN HALL
HOLD STILL - I WANT ME SOME THIGH MEAT!!!
Sire Doug, follow me! We can lose them in the woods!
I'LL BE JUST FINE WITHOUT YOUR HELP, THANK YOU VERY MUCH!
HE'S GETTING AWAY!
RELEASE THE HOUNDS!!!
HOUNDS!?!
SORRY - THIS IS THE BEST WE CAN DO.
YOU KNOW, WE COULD JUST EAT THE HOUNDS!
INDEED-- AFTER THE HOUNDS!!!

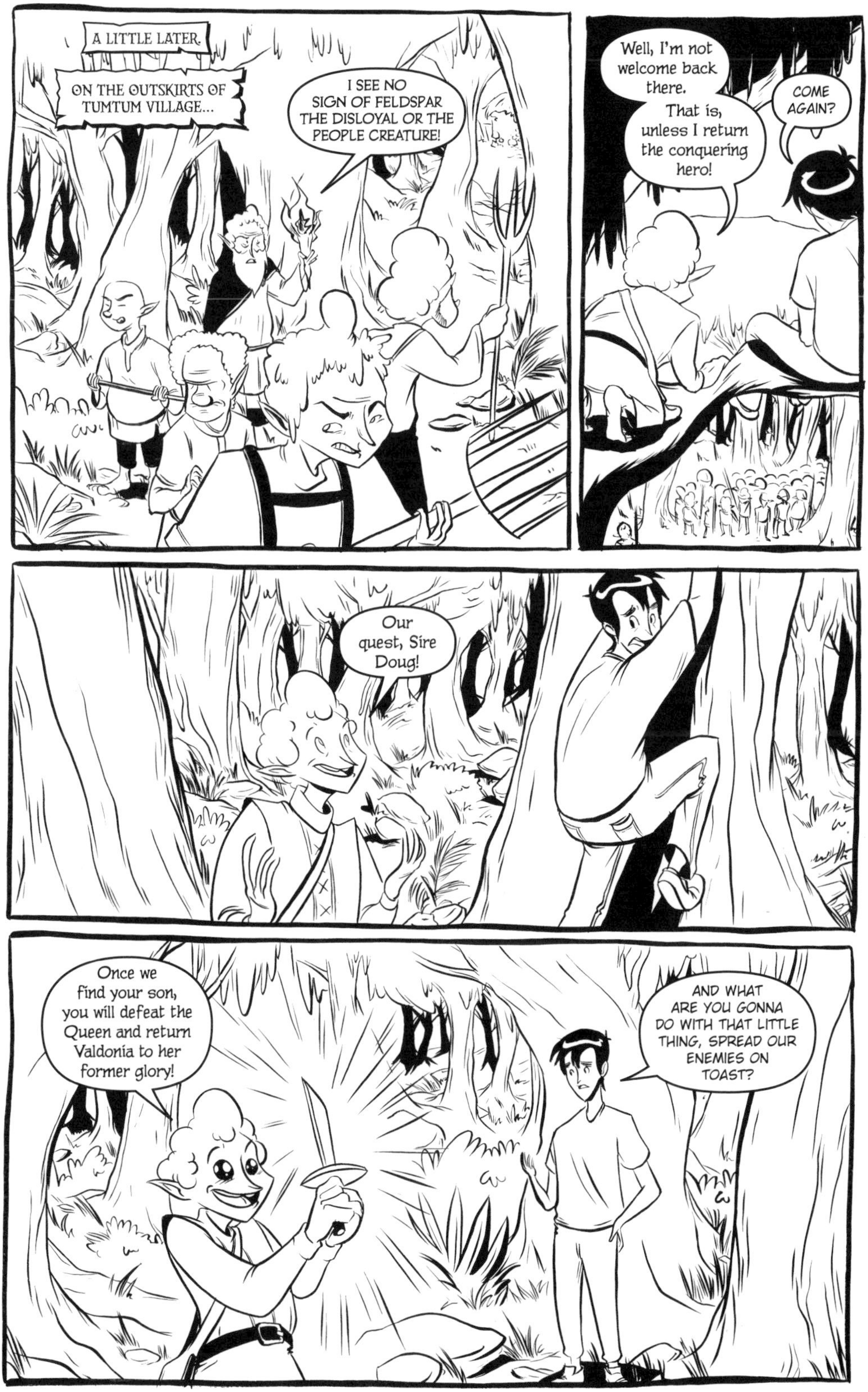

A LITTLE LATER.
ON THE OUTSKIRTS OF TUMTUM VILLAGE...
I SEE NO SIGN OF FELDSPAR THE DISLOYAL OR THE PEOPLE CREATURE!
Well, I'm not welcome back there.
That is, unless I return the conquering hero!
COME AGAIN?
Our quest, Sire Doug!
Once we find your son, you will defeat the Queen and return Valdonia to her former glory!
AND WHAT ARE YOU GONNA DO WITH THAT LITTLE THING, SPREAD OUR ENEMIES ON TOAST?

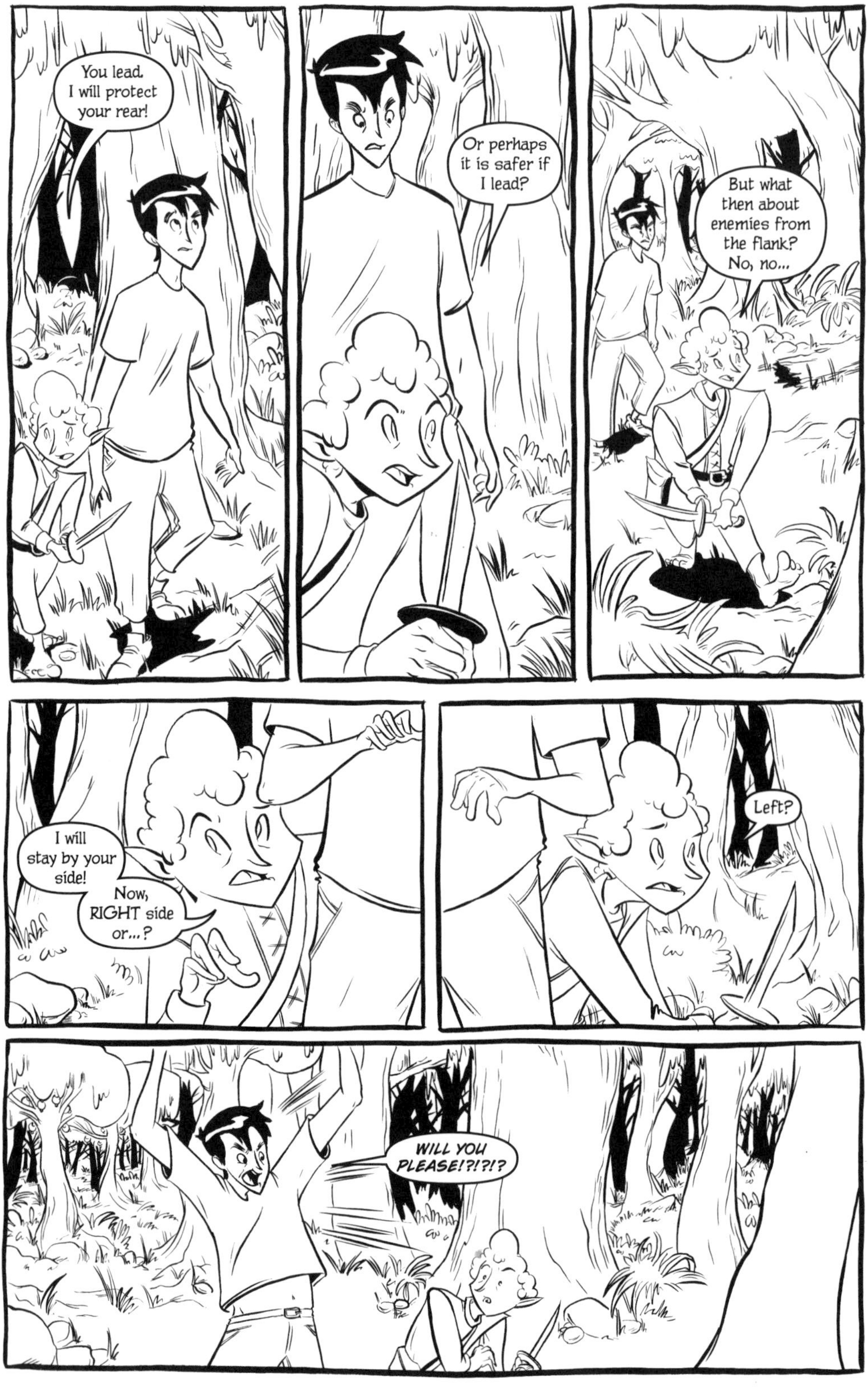
You lead. I will protect your rear!
Or perhaps it is safer if I lead?
But what then about enemies from the flank? No, no...
I will stay by your side!
Now, RIGHT side or...?
Left?
WILL YOU PLEASE!?!?!?

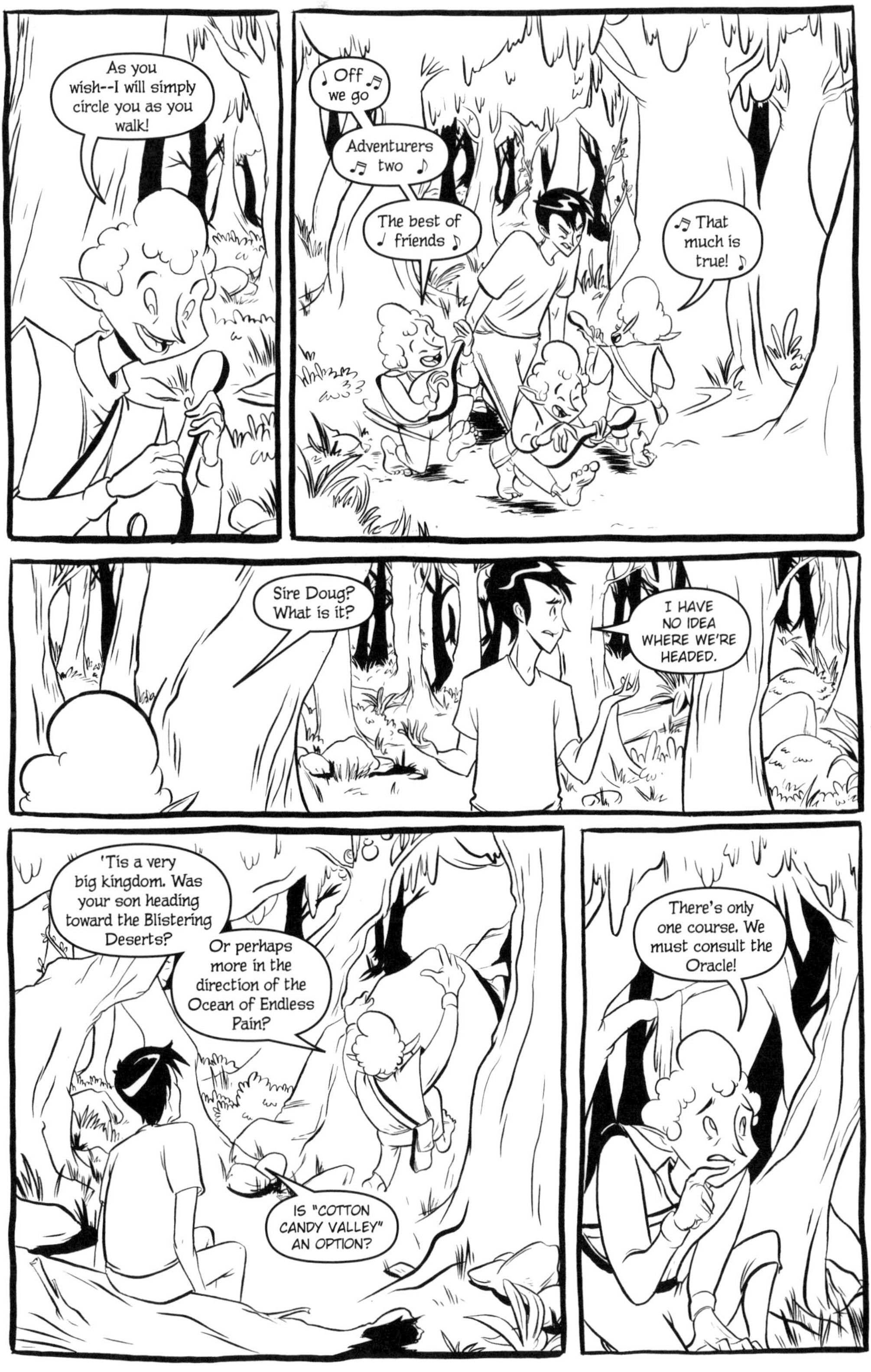
As you wish--I will simply circle you as you walk!
♩ Off ♫ we go
Adventurers ♫ two ♪
The best of ♩ friends ♪
♫ That much is true! ♪
Sire Doug? What is it?
I HAVE NO IDEA WHERE WE'RE HEADED.
'Tis a very big kingdom. Was your son heading toward the Blistering Deserts?
Or perhaps more in the direction of the Ocean of Endless Pain?
IS "COTTON CANDY VALLEY" AN OPTION?
There's only one course. We must consult the Oracle!

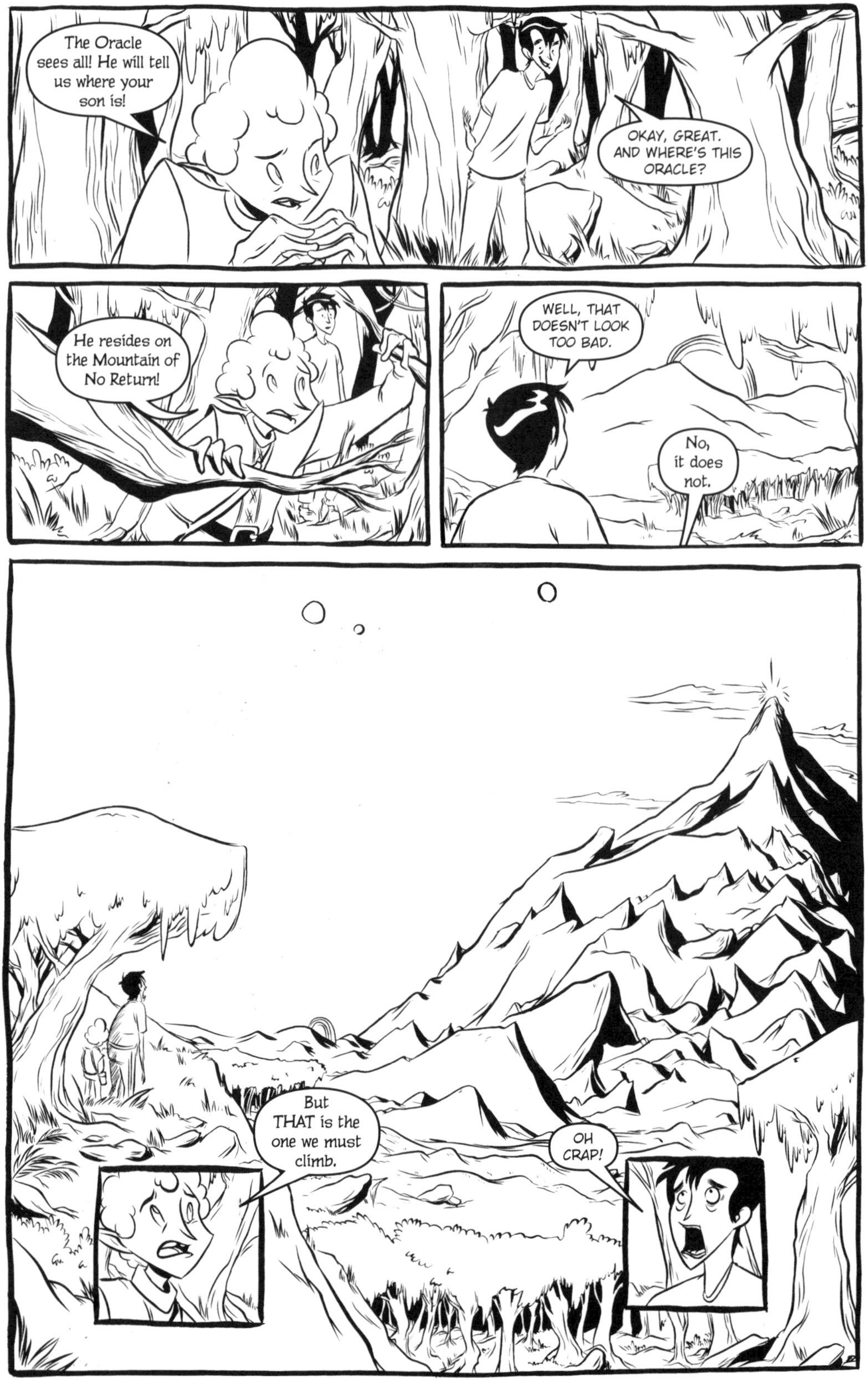
The Oracle sees all! He will tell us where your son is!
OKAY, GREAT. AND WHERE'S THIS ORACLE?
He resides on the Mountain of No Return!
WELL, THAT DOESN'T LOOK TOO BAD.
No, it does not.
But THAT is the one we must climb.
OH CRAP!

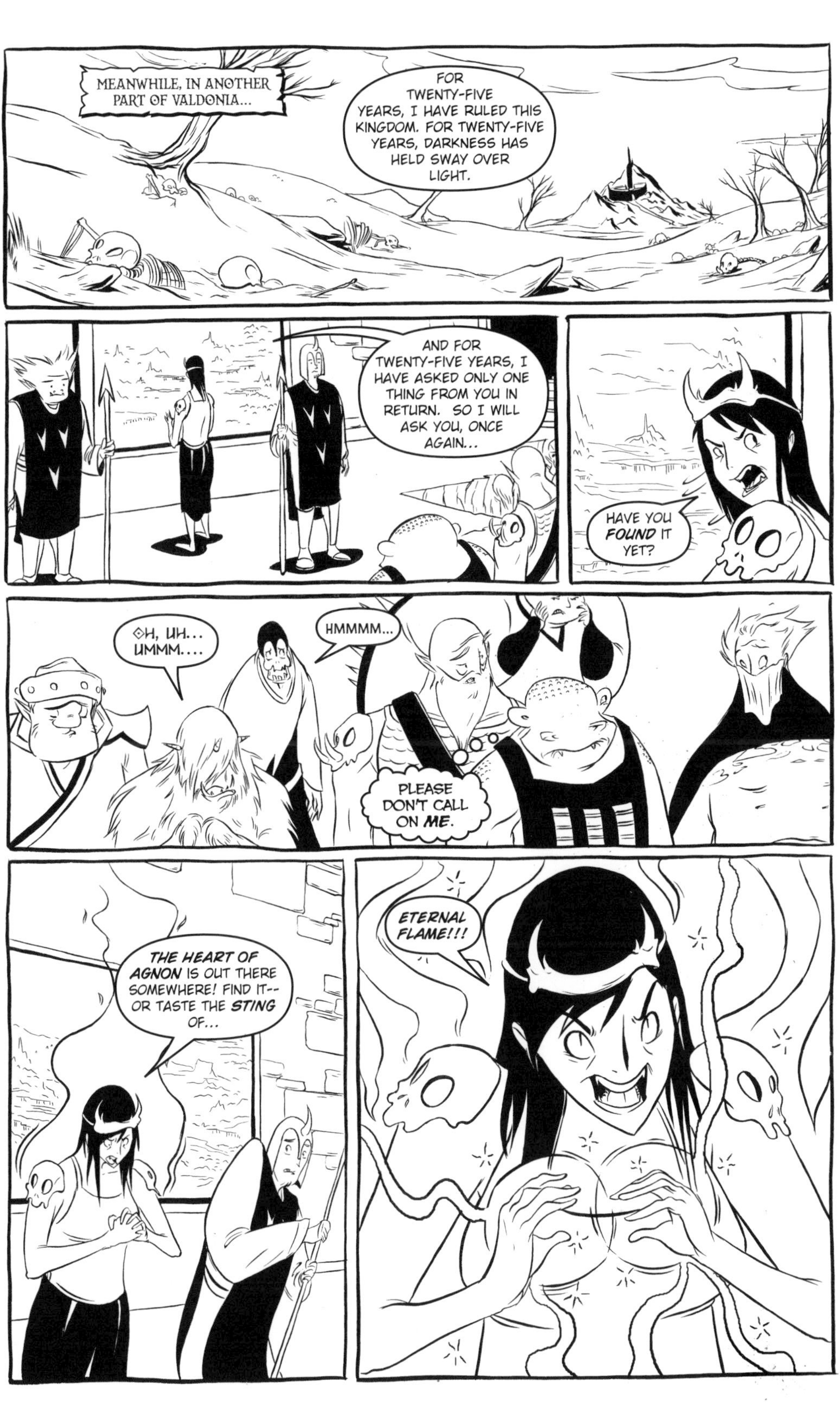
MEANWHILE, IN ANOTHER PART OF VALDONIA...
FOR TWENTY-FIVE YEARS, I HAVE RULED THIS KINGDOM. FOR TWENTY-FIVE YEARS, DARKNESS HAS HELD SWAY OVER LIGHT.
AND FOR TWENTY-FIVE YEARS, I HAVE ASKED ONLY ONE THING FROM YOU IN RETURN. SO I WILL ASK YOU, ONCE AGAIN...
HAVE YOU *FOUND* IT YET?
OH, UH... UMMM....
HMMMM...
PLEASE DON'T CALL ON *ME*.
THE HEART OF AGNON IS OUT THERE SOMEWHERE! FIND IT-- OR TASTE THE *STING* OF...
ETERNAL FLAME!!!

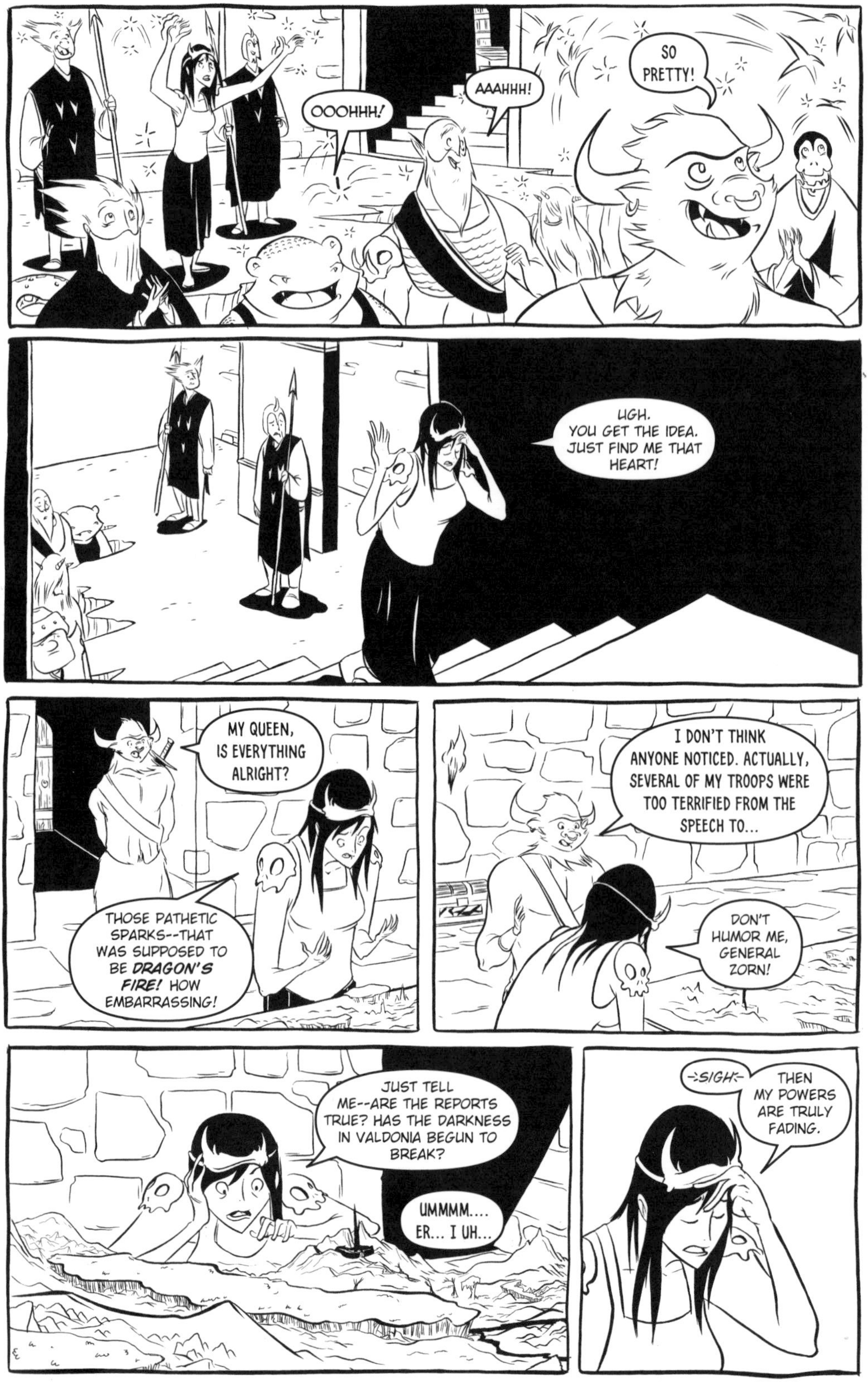
OOOHHH!
AAAHHH!
SO PRETTY!
UGH. YOU GET THE IDEA. JUST FIND ME THAT HEART!
MY QUEEN, IS EVERYTHING ALRIGHT?
THOSE PATHETIC SPARKS--THAT WAS SUPPOSED TO BE ***DRAGON'S FIRE!*** HOW EMBARRASSING!
I DON'T THINK ANYONE NOTICED. ACTUALLY, SEVERAL OF MY TROOPS WERE TOO TERRIFIED FROM THE SPEECH TO...
DON'T HUMOR ME, GENERAL ZORN!
JUST TELL ME--ARE THE REPORTS TRUE? HAS THE DARKNESS IN VALDONIA BEGUN TO BREAK?
UMMMM.... ER... I UH...
-SIGH-
THEN MY POWERS ARE TRULY FADING.

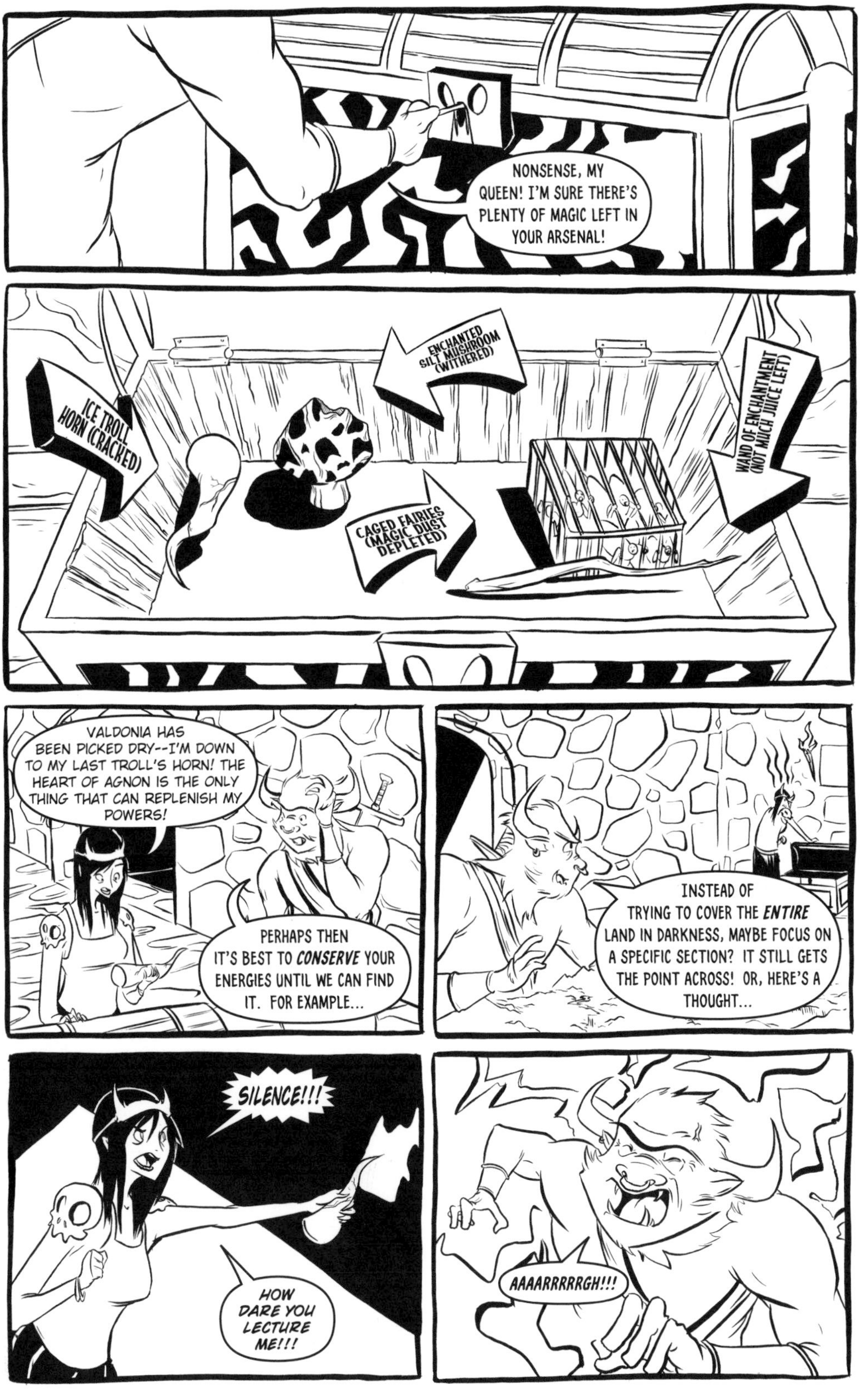
NONSENSE, MY QUEEN! I'M SURE THERE'S PLENTY OF MAGIC LEFT IN YOUR ARSENAL!
ICE TROLL HORN (CRACKED)
ENCHANTED SILT MUSHROOM (WITHERED)
CAGED FAIRIES (MAGIC DUST DEPLETED)
WAND OF ENCHANTMENT (NOT MUCH JUICE LEFT)
VALDONIA HAS BEEN PICKED DRY--I'M DOWN TO MY LAST TROLL'S HORN! THE HEART OF AGNON IS THE ONLY THING THAT CAN REPLENISH MY POWERS!
PERHAPS THEN IT'S BEST TO *CONSERVE* YOUR ENERGIES UNTIL WE CAN FIND IT. FOR EXAMPLE...
INSTEAD OF TRYING TO COVER THE *ENTIRE* LAND IN DARKNESS, MAYBE FOCUS ON A SPECIFIC SECTION? IT STILL GETS THE POINT ACROSS! OR, HERE'S A THOUGHT...
SILENCE!!!
HOW DARE YOU LECTURE ME!!!
AAAARRRRRGH!!!

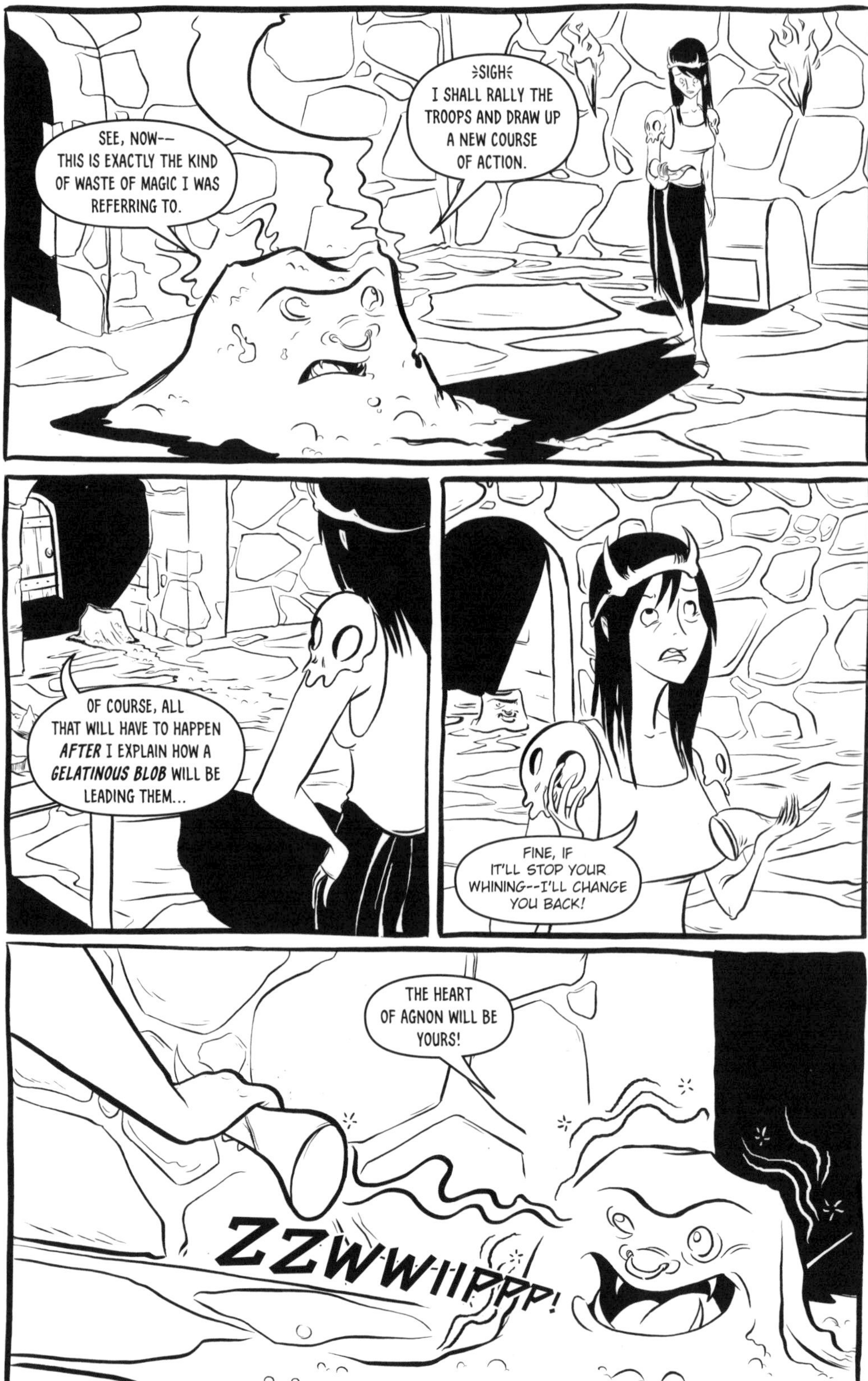
SEE, NOW-- THIS IS EXACTLY THE KIND OF WASTE OF MAGIC I WAS REFERRING TO.
SIGH I SHALL RALLY THE TROOPS AND DRAW UP A NEW COURSE OF ACTION.
OF COURSE, ALL THAT WILL HAVE TO HAPPEN ***AFTER*** I EXPLAIN HOW A ***GELATINOUS BLOB*** WILL BE LEADING THEM...
FINE, IF IT'LL STOP YOUR WHINING--I'LL CHANGE YOU BACK!
THE HEART OF AGNON WILL BE YOURS!
ZZWWIIPPPP!

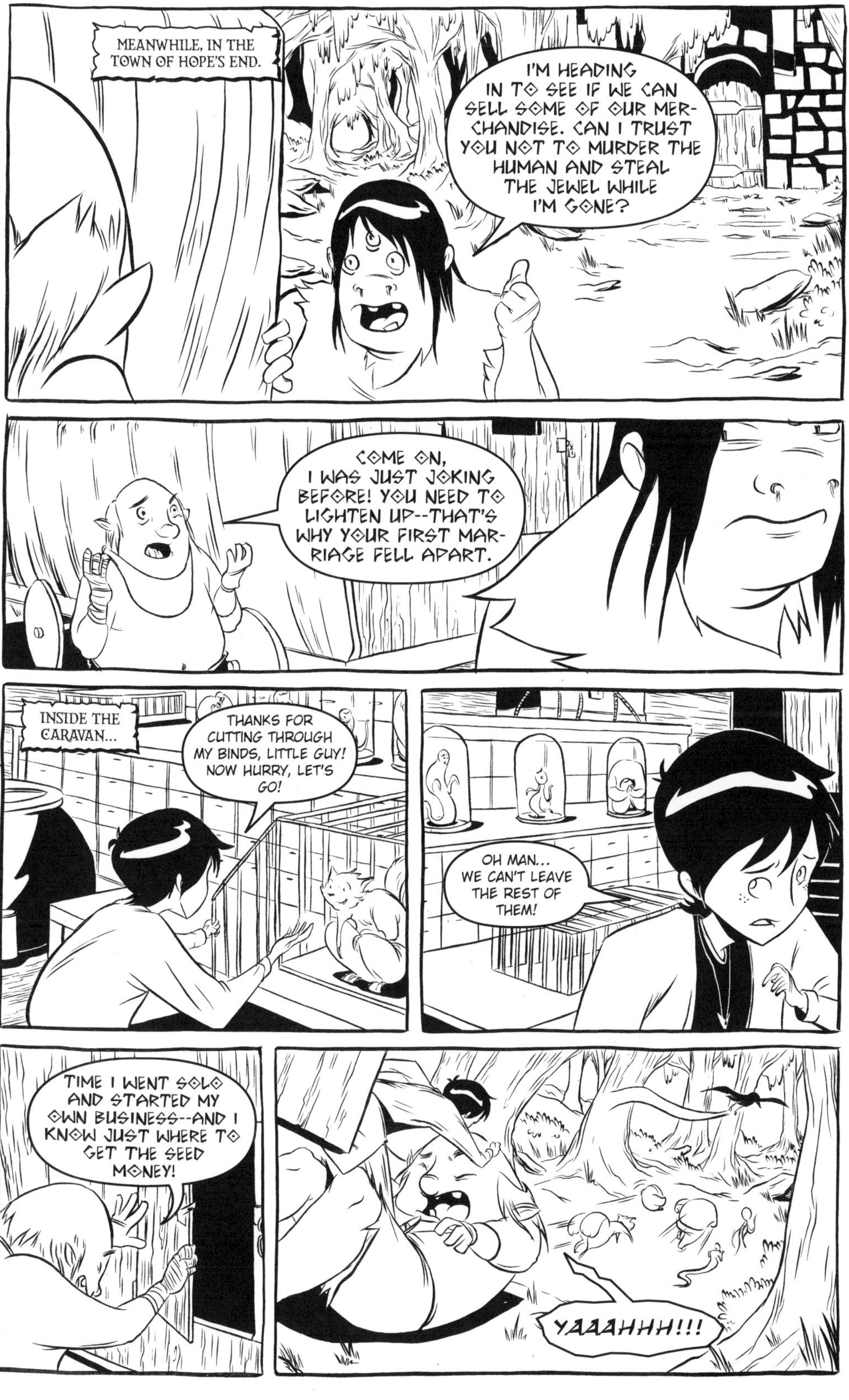

MEANWHILE, IN THE TOWN OF HOPE'S END.
I'M HEADING IN TO SEE IF WE CAN SELL SOME OF OUR MER-CHANDISE. CAN I TRUST YOU NOT TO MURDER THE HUMAN AND STEAL THE JEWEL WHILE I'M GONE?
COME ON, I WAS JUST JOKING BEFORE! YOU NEED TO LIGHTEN UP--THAT'S WHY YOUR FIRST MAR-RIAGE FELL APART.
INSIDE THE CARAVAN...
THANKS FOR CUTTING THROUGH MY BINDS, LITTLE GUY! NOW HURRY, LET'S GO!
OH MAN... WE CAN'T LEAVE THE REST OF THEM!
TIME I WENT SOLO AND STARTED MY OWN BUSINESS--AND I KNOW JUST WHERE TO GET THE SEED MONEY!
YAAAHHH!!!

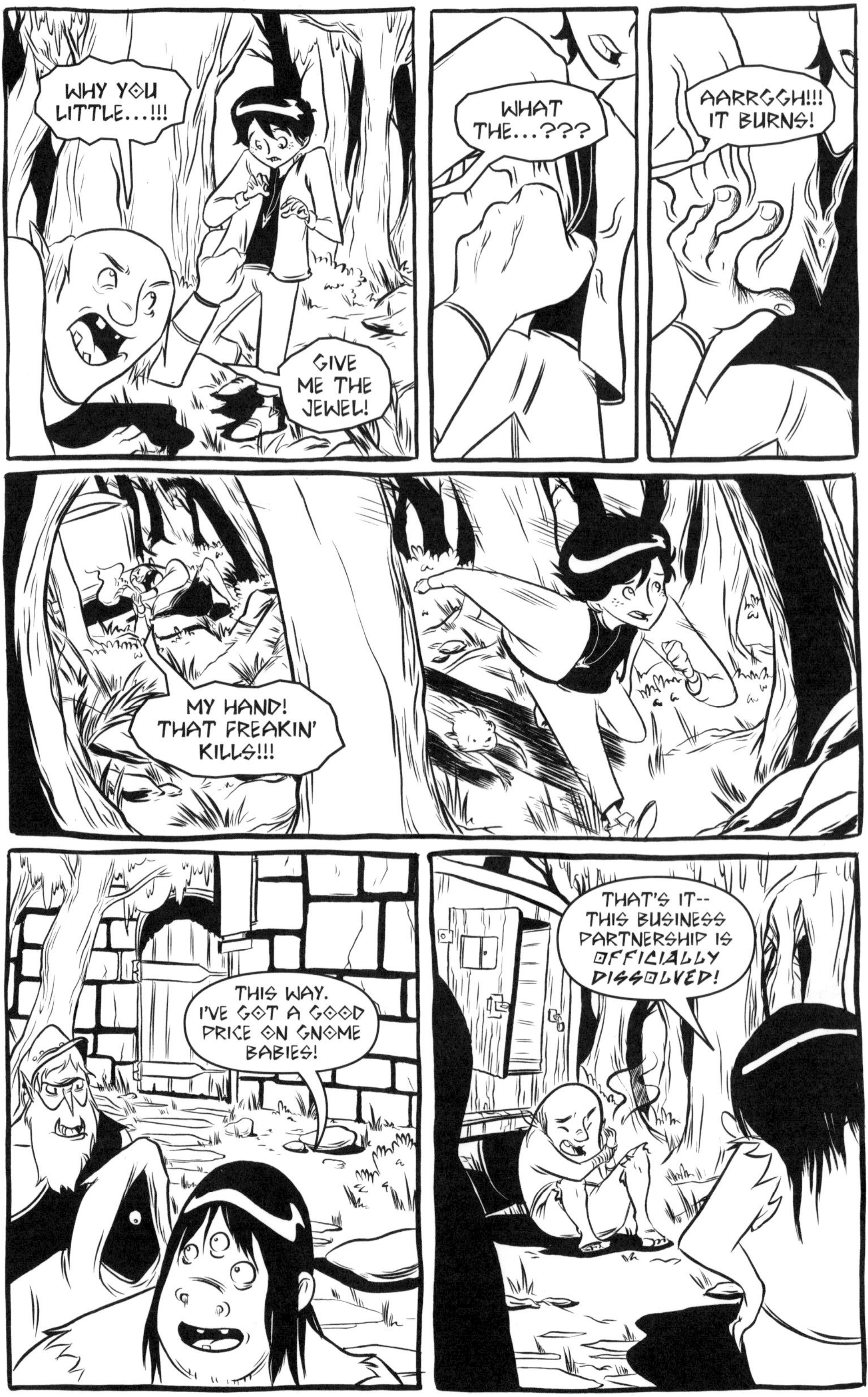
WHY YOU LITTLE...!!!
GIVE ME THE JEWEL!
WHAT THE...???
AARRGGH!!! IT BURNS!
MY HAND! THAT FREAKIN' KILLS!!!
THIS WAY. I'VE GOT A GOOD PRICE ON GNOME BABIES!
THAT'S IT-- THIS BUSINESS PARTNERSHIP IS *OFFICIALLY DISSOLVED!*

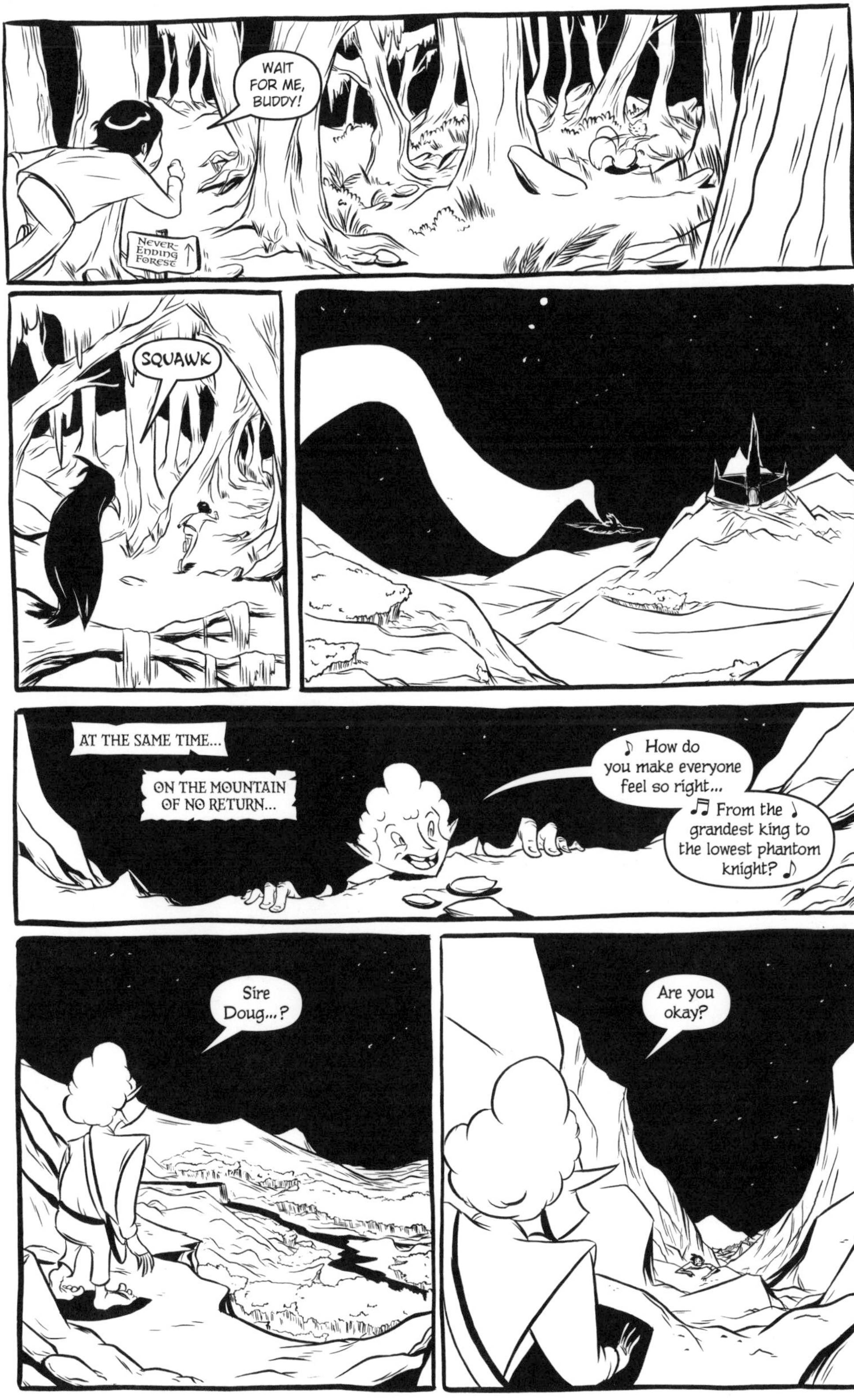

WAIT FOR ME, BUDDY!
NEVER-ENDING FOREST
SQUAWK
AT THE SAME TIME...
ON THE MOUNTAIN OF NO RETURN...
♪ How do you make everyone feel so right...
♫ From the ♪ grandest king to the lowest phantom knight? ♪
Sire Doug...?
Are you okay?

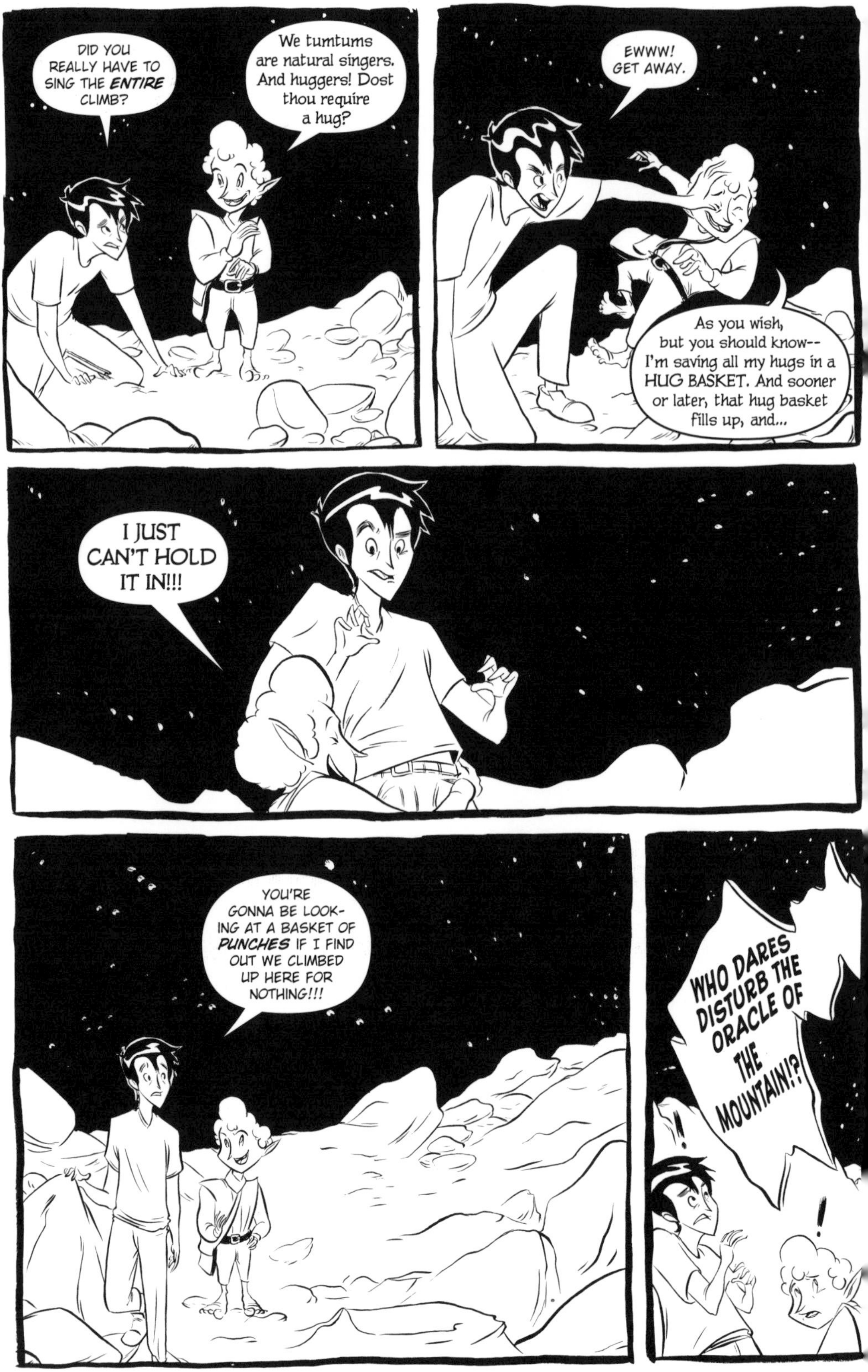
DID YOU REALLY HAVE TO SING THE ENTIRE CLIMB?
We tumtums are natural singers. And huggers! Dost thou require a hug?
EWWW! GET AWAY.
As you wish, but you should know-- I'm saving all my hugs in a HUG BASKET. And sooner or later, that hug basket fills up, and...
I JUST CAN'T HOLD IT IN!!!
YOU'RE GONNA BE LOOKING AT A BASKET OF PUNCHES IF I FIND OUT WE CLIMBED UP HERE FOR NOTHING!!!
WHO DARES DISTURB THE ORACLE OF THE MOUNTAIN!?
!!
!

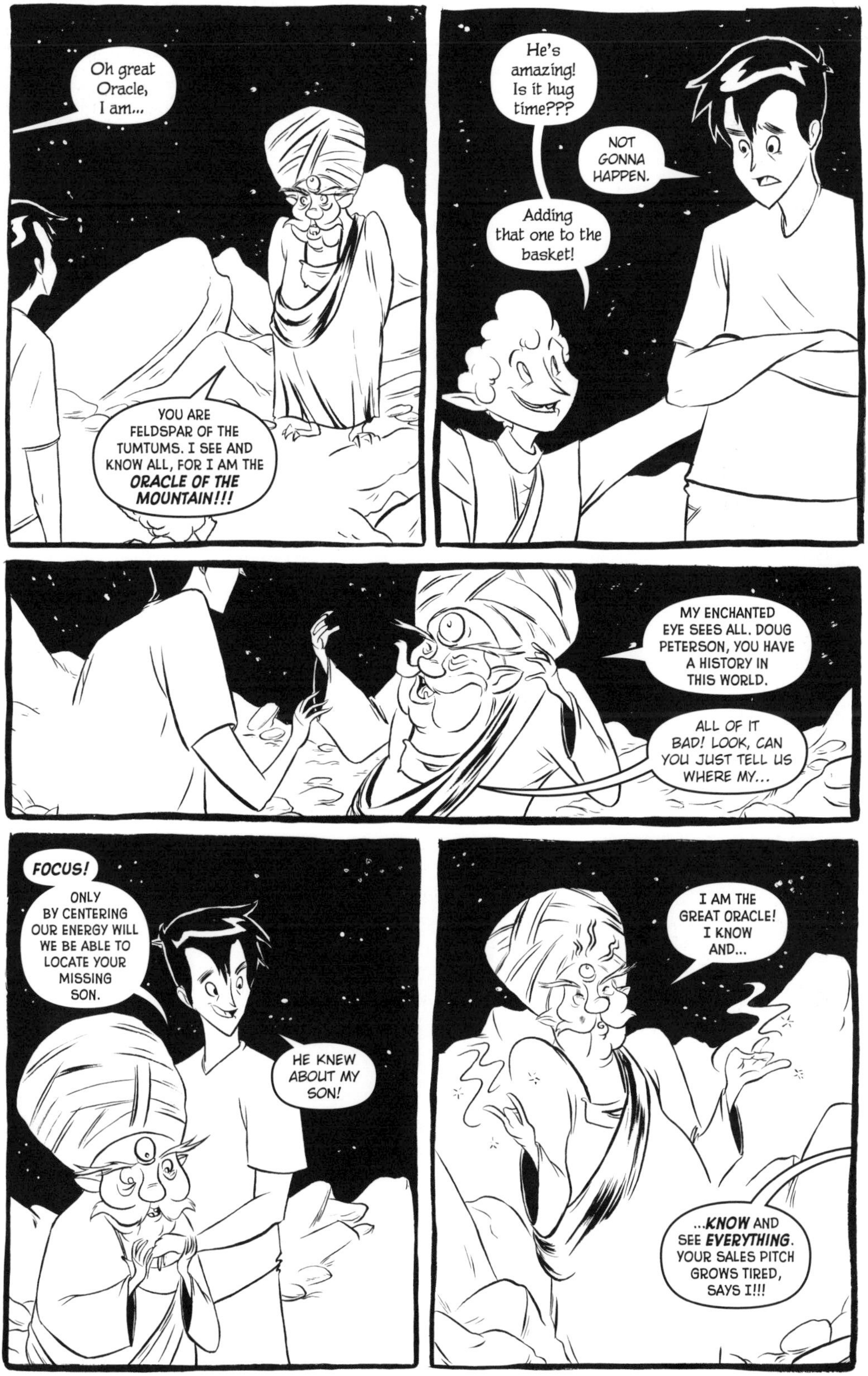

Oh great Oracle, I am...
YOU ARE FELDSPAR OF THE TUMTUMS. I SEE AND KNOW ALL, FOR I AM THE ***ORACLE OF THE MOUNTAIN!!!***
He's amazing! Is it hug time???
NOT GONNA HAPPEN.
Adding that one to the basket!
MY ENCHANTED EYE SEES ALL. DOUG PETERSON, YOU HAVE A HISTORY IN THIS WORLD.
ALL OF IT BAD! LOOK, CAN YOU JUST TELL US WHERE MY...
FOCUS!
ONLY BY CENTERING OUR ENERGY WILL WE BE ABLE TO LOCATE YOUR MISSING SON.
HE KNEW ABOUT MY SON!
I AM THE GREAT ORACLE! I KNOW AND...
...***KNOW*** AND SEE ***EVERYTHING***. YOUR SALES PITCH GROWS TIRED, SAYS I!!!

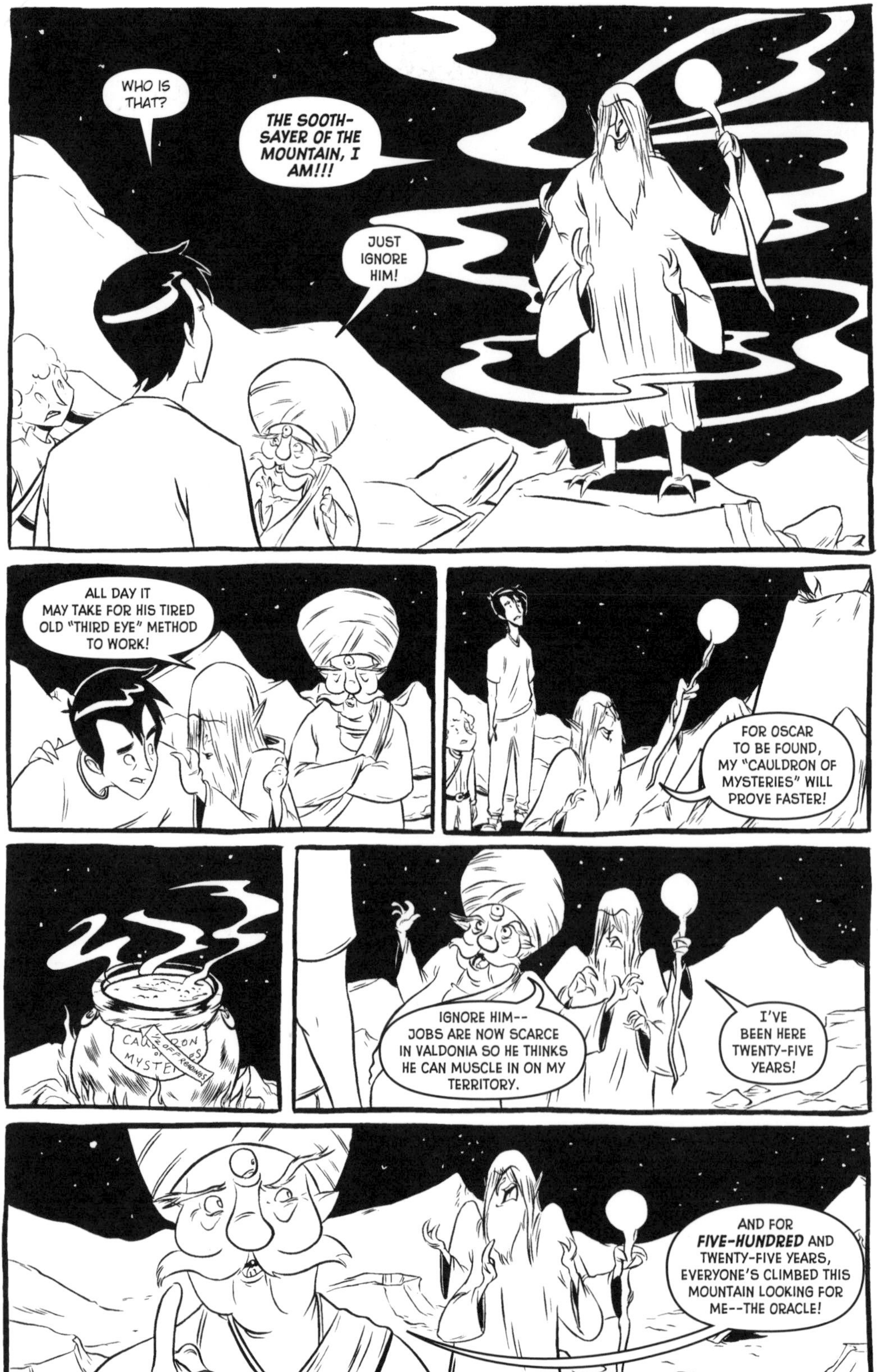

WHO IS THAT?
THE SOOTH-SAYER OF THE MOUNTAIN, I AM!!!
JUST IGNORE HIM!
ALL DAY IT MAY TAKE FOR HIS TIRED OLD "THIRD EYE" METHOD TO WORK!
FOR OSCAR TO BE FOUND, MY "CAULDRON OF MYSTERIES" WILL PROVE FASTER!
½ OFF READINGS
IGNORE HIM-- JOBS ARE NOW SCARCE IN VALDONIA SO HE THINKS HE CAN MUSCLE IN ON MY TERRITORY.
I'VE BEEN HERE TWENTY-FIVE YEARS!
AND FOR FIVE-HUNDRED AND TWENTY-FIVE YEARS, EVERYONE'S CLIMBED THIS MOUNTAIN LOOKING FOR ME--THE ORACLE!

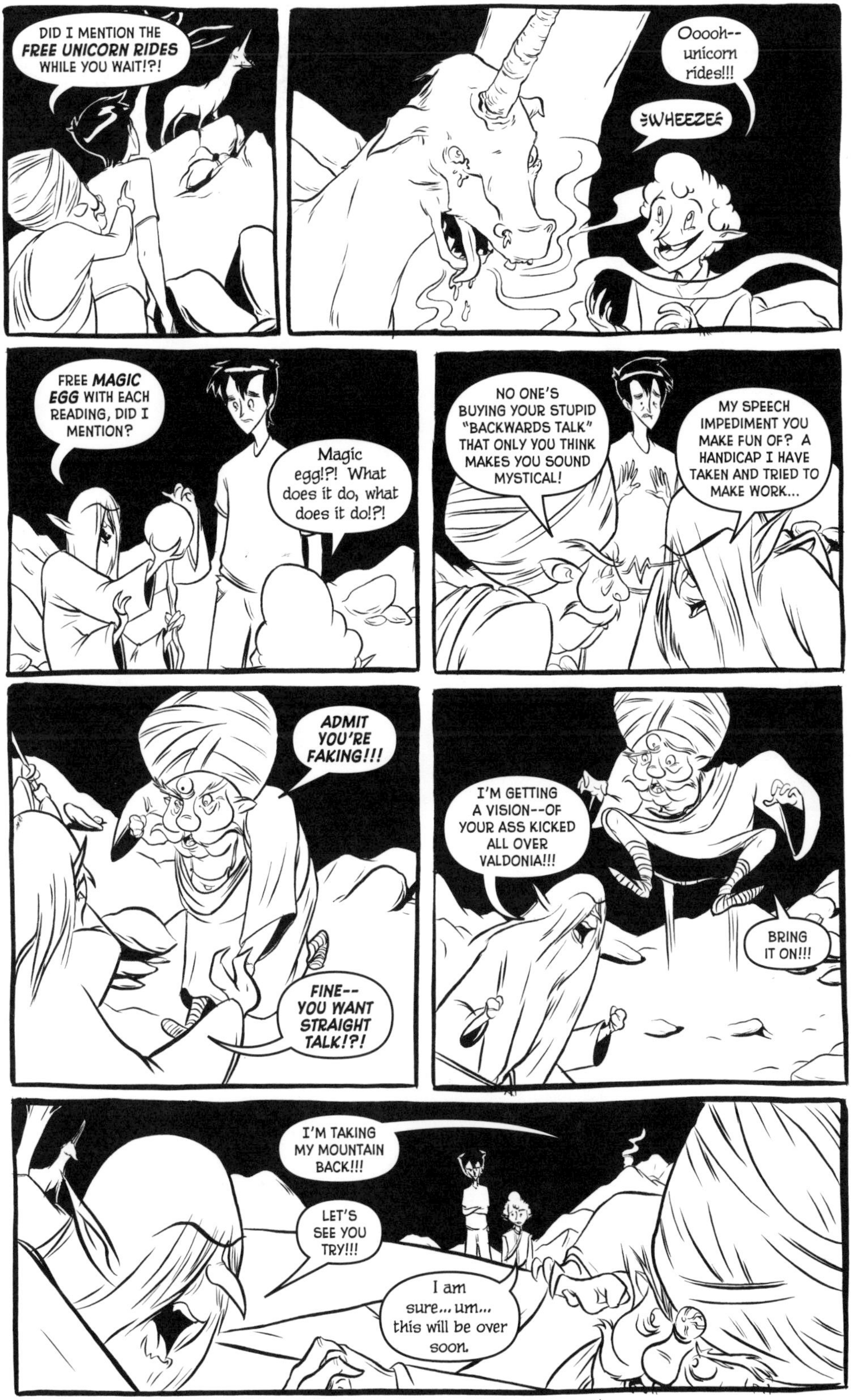
DID I MENTION THE FREE UNICORN RIDES WHILE YOU WAIT!?!
Ooooh-- unicorn rides!!!
WHEEZE
FREE MAGIC EGG WITH EACH READING, DID I MENTION?
Magic egg!?! What does it do, what does it do!?!
NO ONE'S BUYING YOUR STUPID "BACKWARDS TALK" THAT ONLY YOU THINK MAKES YOU SOUND MYSTICAL!
MY SPEECH IMPEDIMENT YOU MAKE FUN OF? A HANDICAP I HAVE TAKEN AND TRIED TO MAKE WORK...
ADMIT YOU'RE FAKING!!!
FINE-- YOU WANT STRAIGHT TALK!?!
I'M GETTING A VISION--OF YOUR ASS KICKED ALL OVER VALDONIA!!!
BRING IT ON!!!
I'M TAKING MY MOUNTAIN BACK!!!
LET'S SEE YOU TRY!!!
I am sure... um... this will be over soon.

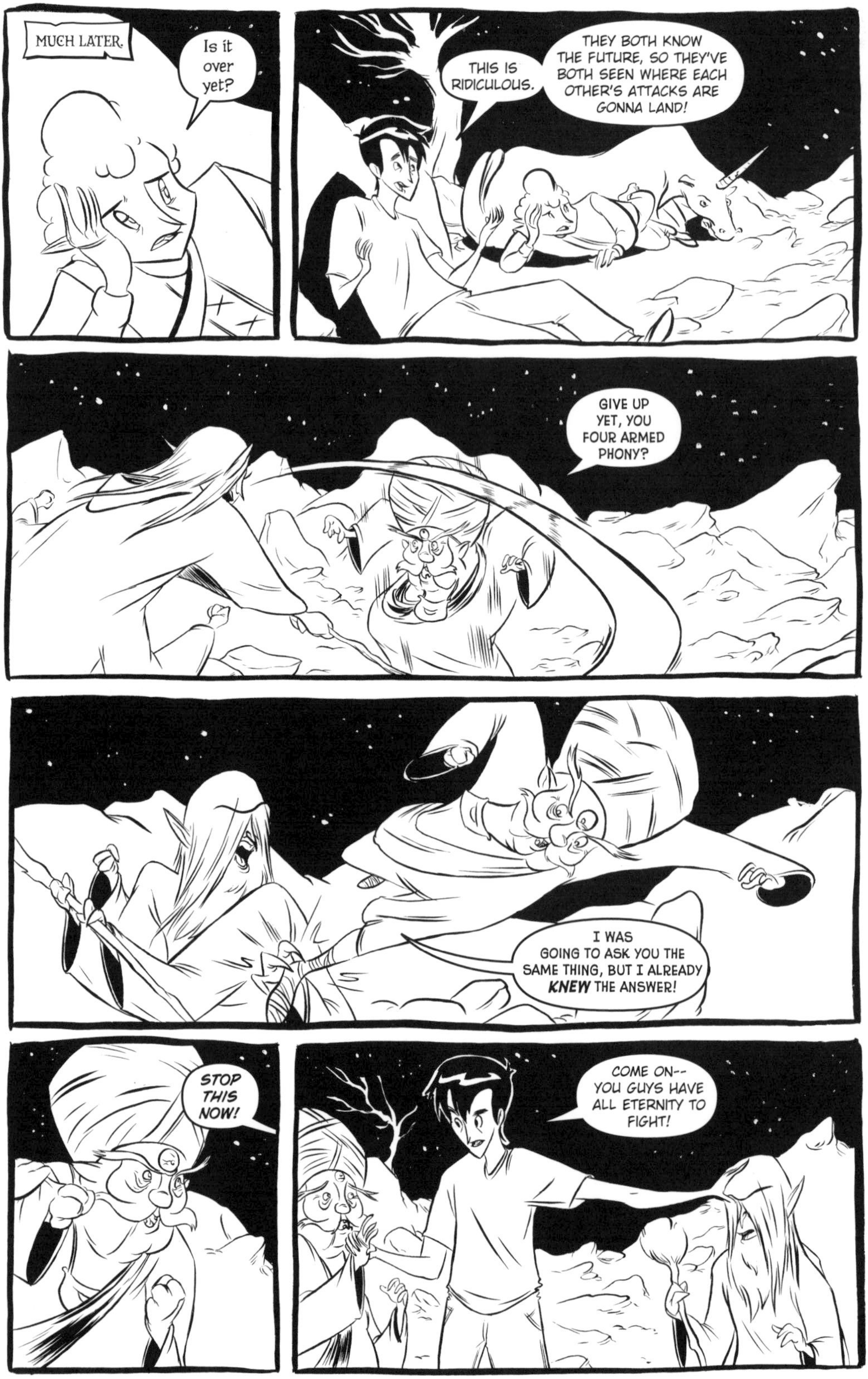
MUCH LATER.
Is it over yet?
THIS IS RIDICULOUS.
THEY BOTH KNOW THE FUTURE, SO THEY'VE BOTH SEEN WHERE EACH OTHER'S ATTACKS ARE GONNA LAND!
GIVE UP YET, YOU FOUR ARMED PHONY?
I WAS GOING TO ASK YOU THE SAME THING, BUT I ALREADY ***KNEW*** THE ANSWER!
STOP THIS NOW!
COME ON-- YOU GUYS HAVE ALL ETERNITY TO FIGHT!

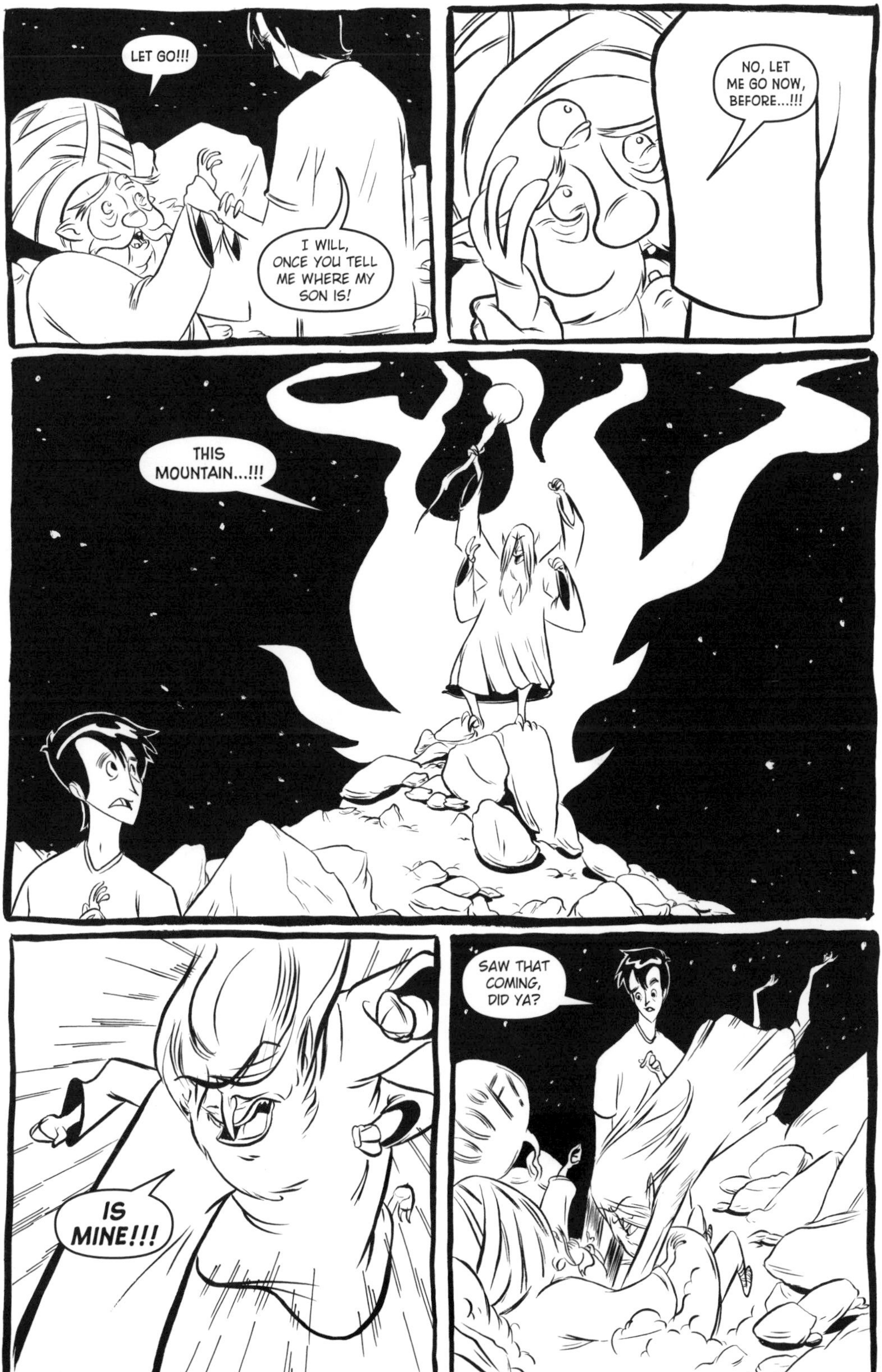
LET GO!!!
I WILL, ONCE YOU TELL ME WHERE MY SON IS!
NO, LET ME GO NOW, BEFORE...!!!
THIS MOUNTAIN...!!!
IS MINE!!!
SAW THAT COMING, DID YA?

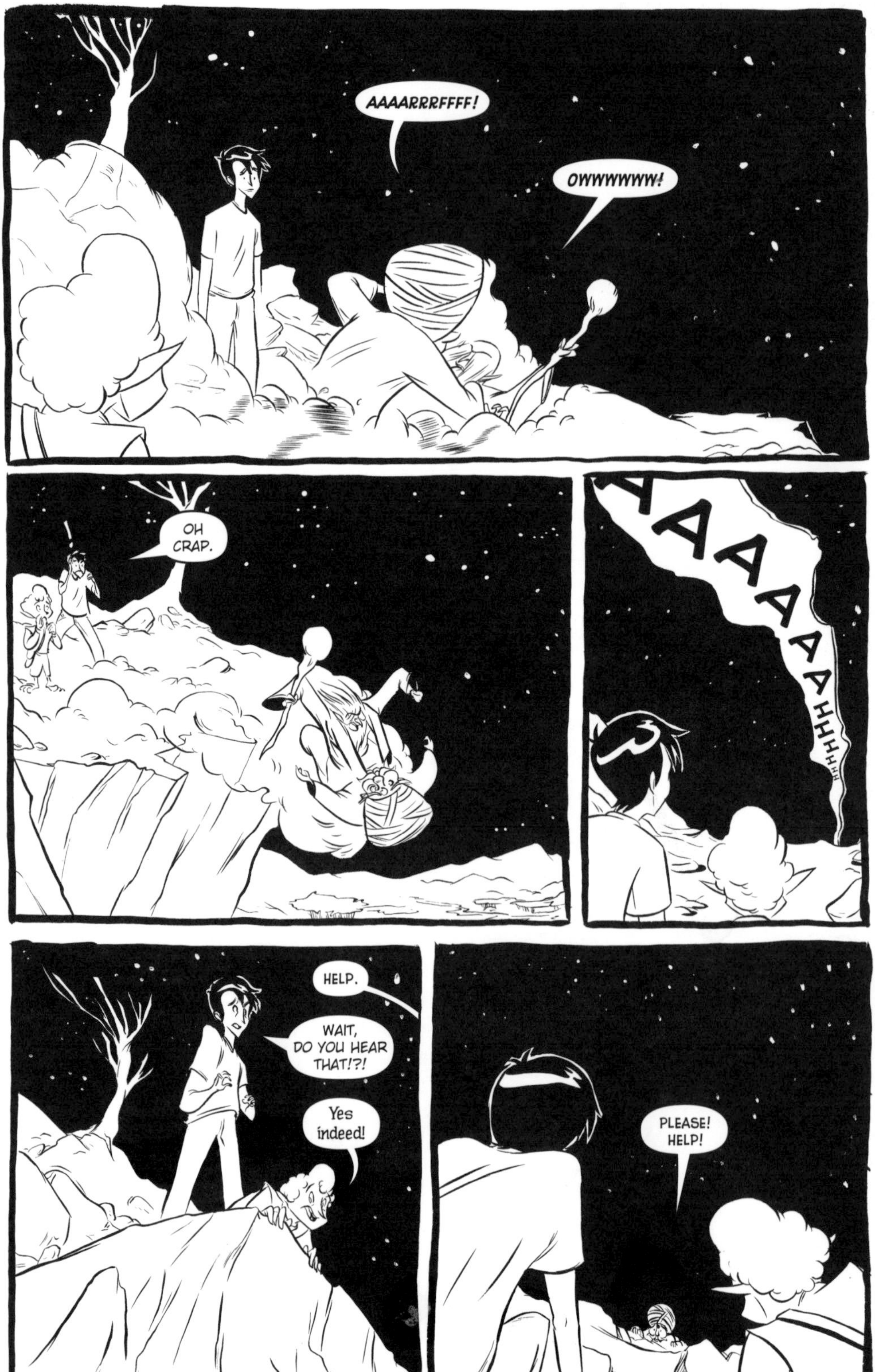
AAAARRRFFFF!
OWWWWWW!
OH CRAP.
AAAAAAAHHHHHH
HELP.
WAIT, DO YOU HEAR THAT!?!
Yes indeed!
PLEASE! HELP!

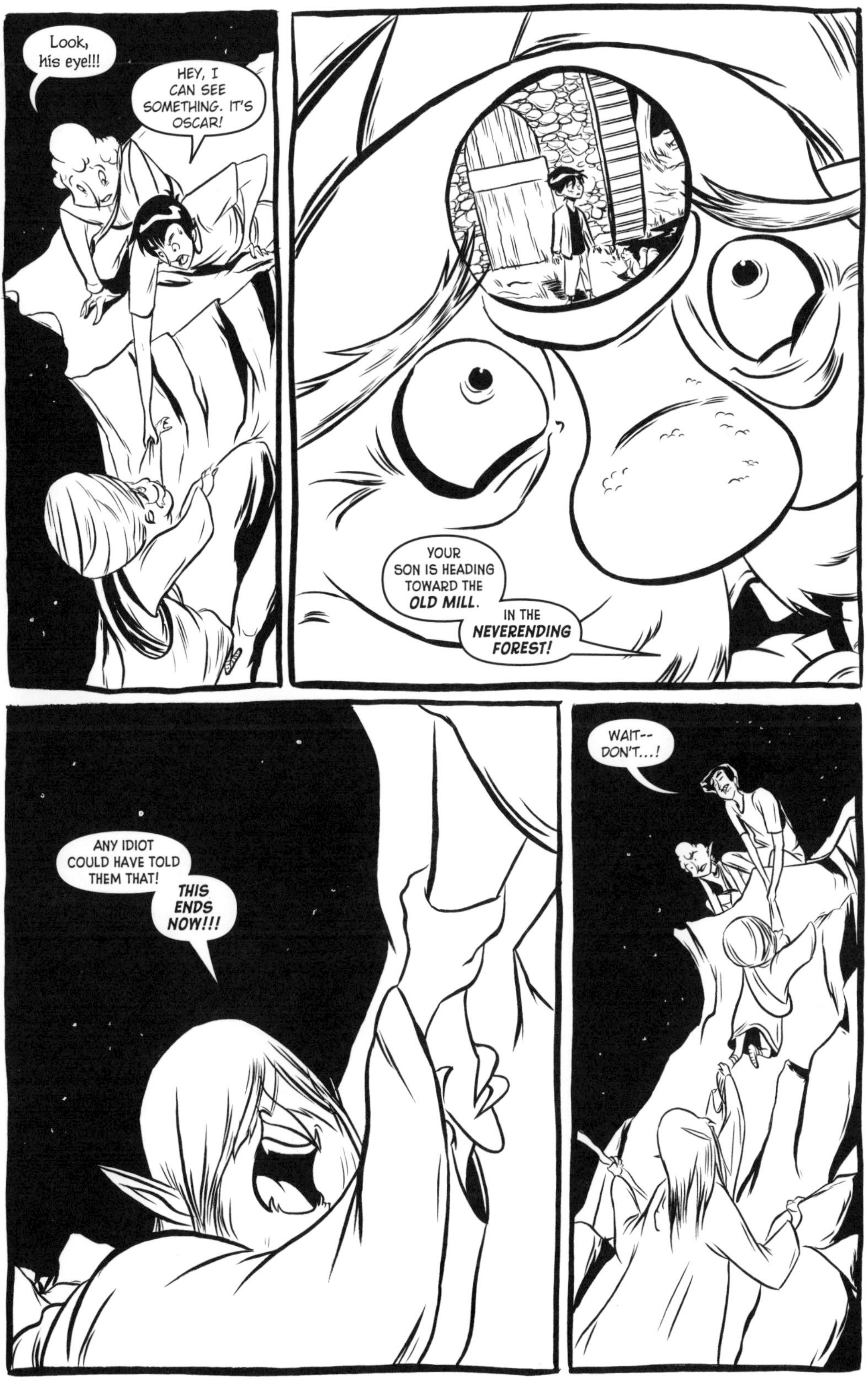
Look, his eye!!!
HEY, I CAN SEE SOMETHING. IT'S OSCAR!
YOUR SON IS HEADING TOWARD THE OLD MILL.
IN THE NEVERENDING FOREST!
ANY IDIOT COULD HAVE TOLD THEM THAT!
THIS ENDS NOW!!!
WAIT-- DON'T...!

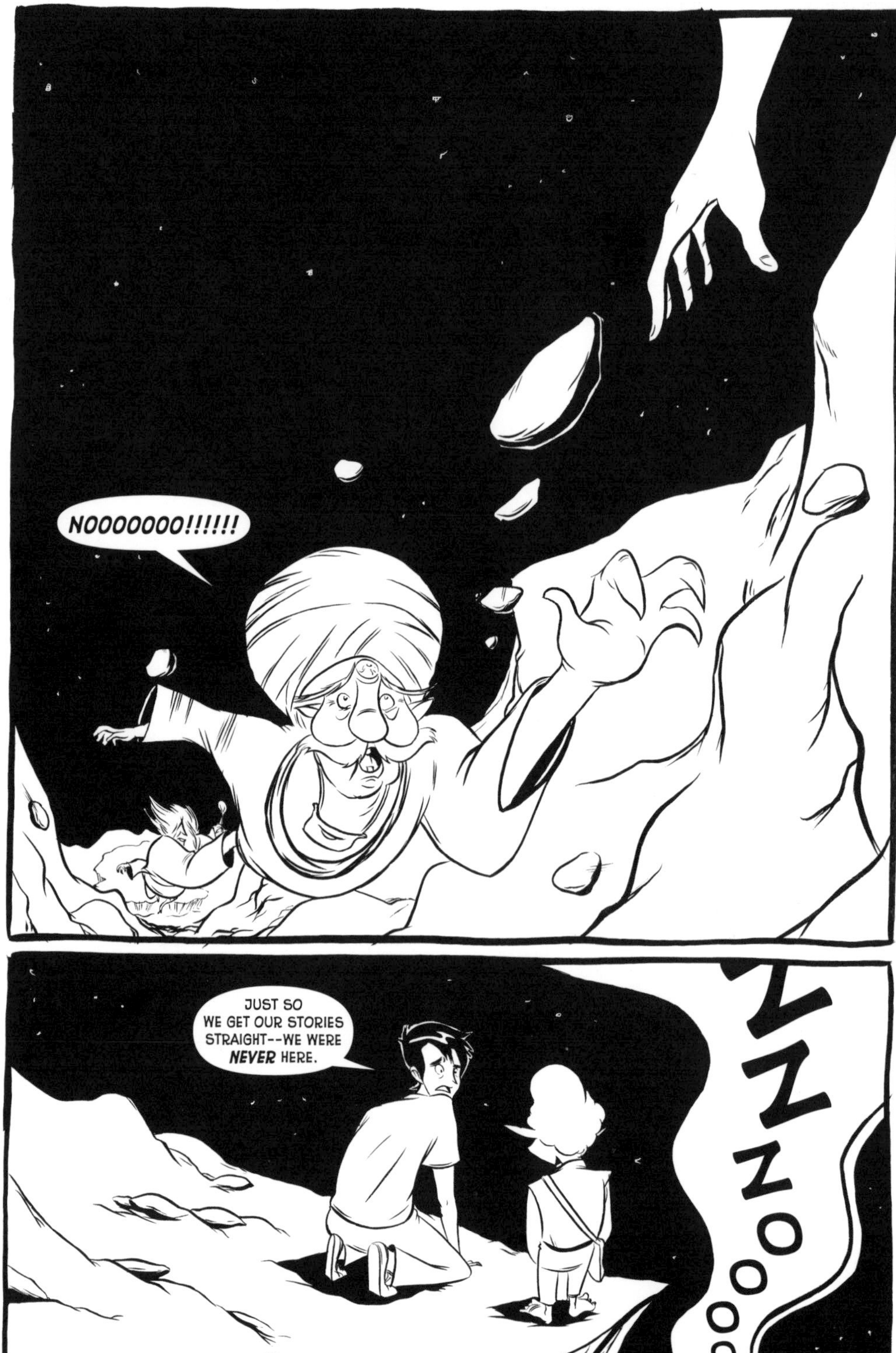
NOOOOOOO!!!!!!
JUST SO WE GET OUR STORIES STRAIGHT--WE WERE **NEVER** HERE.
ZZZOOOOOOO

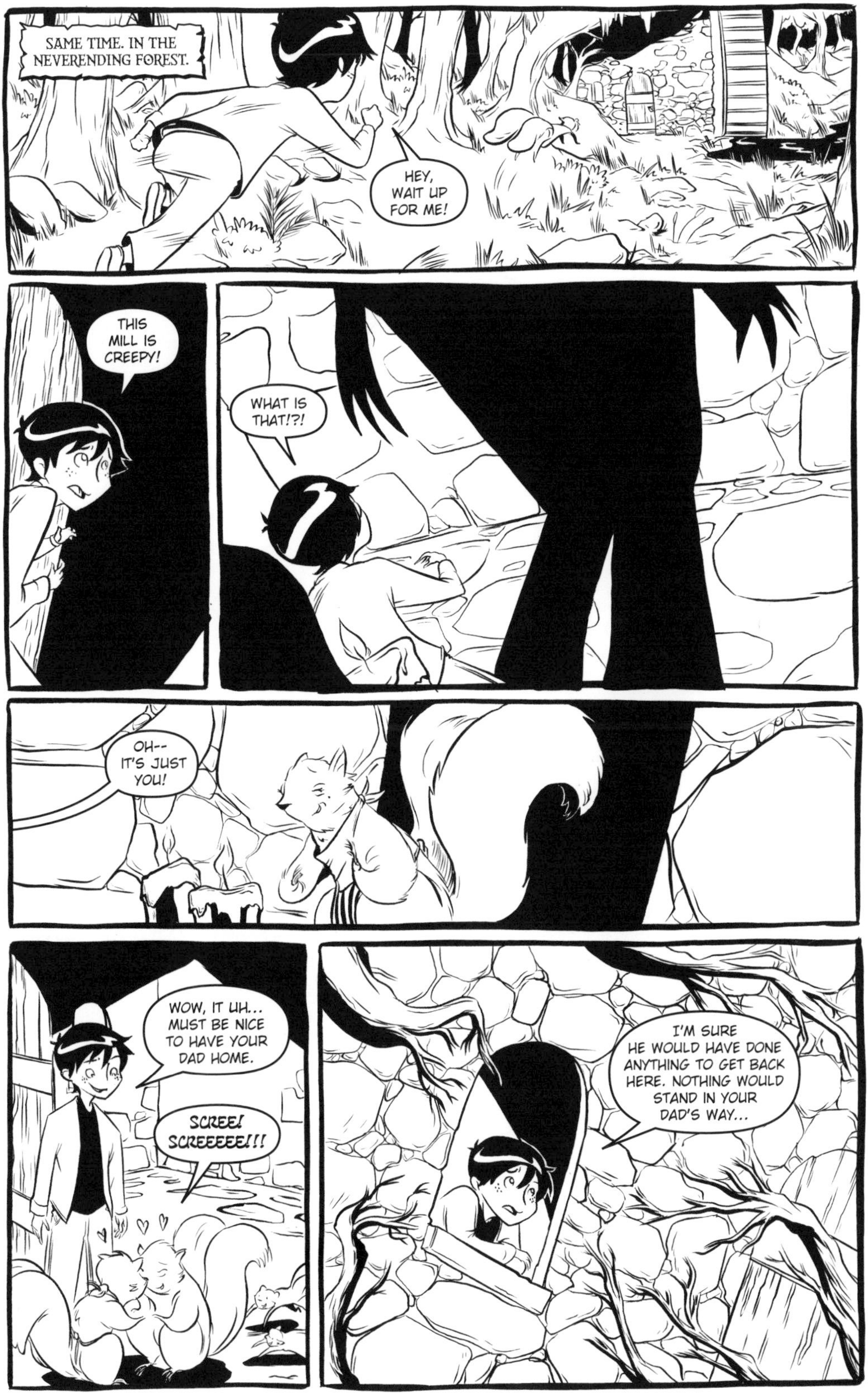
SAME TIME. IN THE NEVERENDING FOREST.
HEY, WAIT UP FOR ME!
THIS MILL IS CREEPY!
WHAT IS THAT!?!
OH-- IT'S JUST YOU!
WOW, IT UH... MUST BE NICE TO HAVE YOUR DAD HOME.
SCREE! SCREEEEEE!!!
I'M SURE HE WOULD HAVE DONE ANYTHING TO GET BACK HERE. NOTHING WOULD STAND IN YOUR DAD'S WAY...

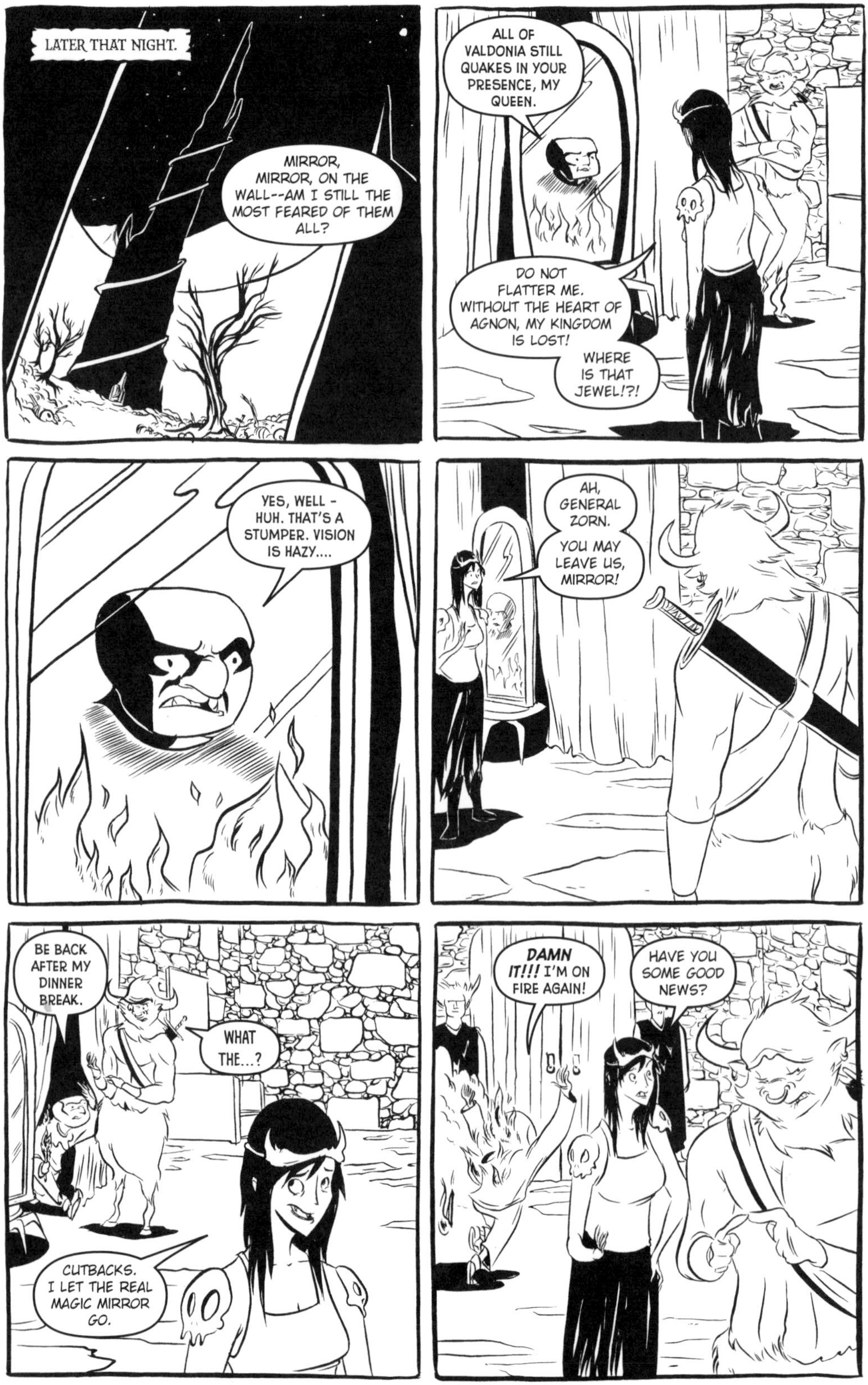
LATER THAT NIGHT.
MIRROR, MIRROR, ON THE WALL--AM I STILL THE MOST FEARED OF THEM ALL?
ALL OF VALDONIA STILL QUAKES IN YOUR PRESENCE, MY QUEEN.
DO NOT FLATTER ME. WITHOUT THE HEART OF AGNON, MY KINGDOM IS LOST!
WHERE IS THAT JEWEL!?!
YES, WELL - HUH. THAT'S A STUMPER. VISION IS HAZY....
AH, GENERAL ZORN.
YOU MAY LEAVE US, MIRROR!
BE BACK AFTER MY DINNER BREAK.
WHAT THE...?
CUTBACKS. I LET THE REAL MAGIC MIRROR GO.
DAMN IT!!! I'M ON FIRE AGAIN!
HAVE YOU SOME GOOD NEWS?

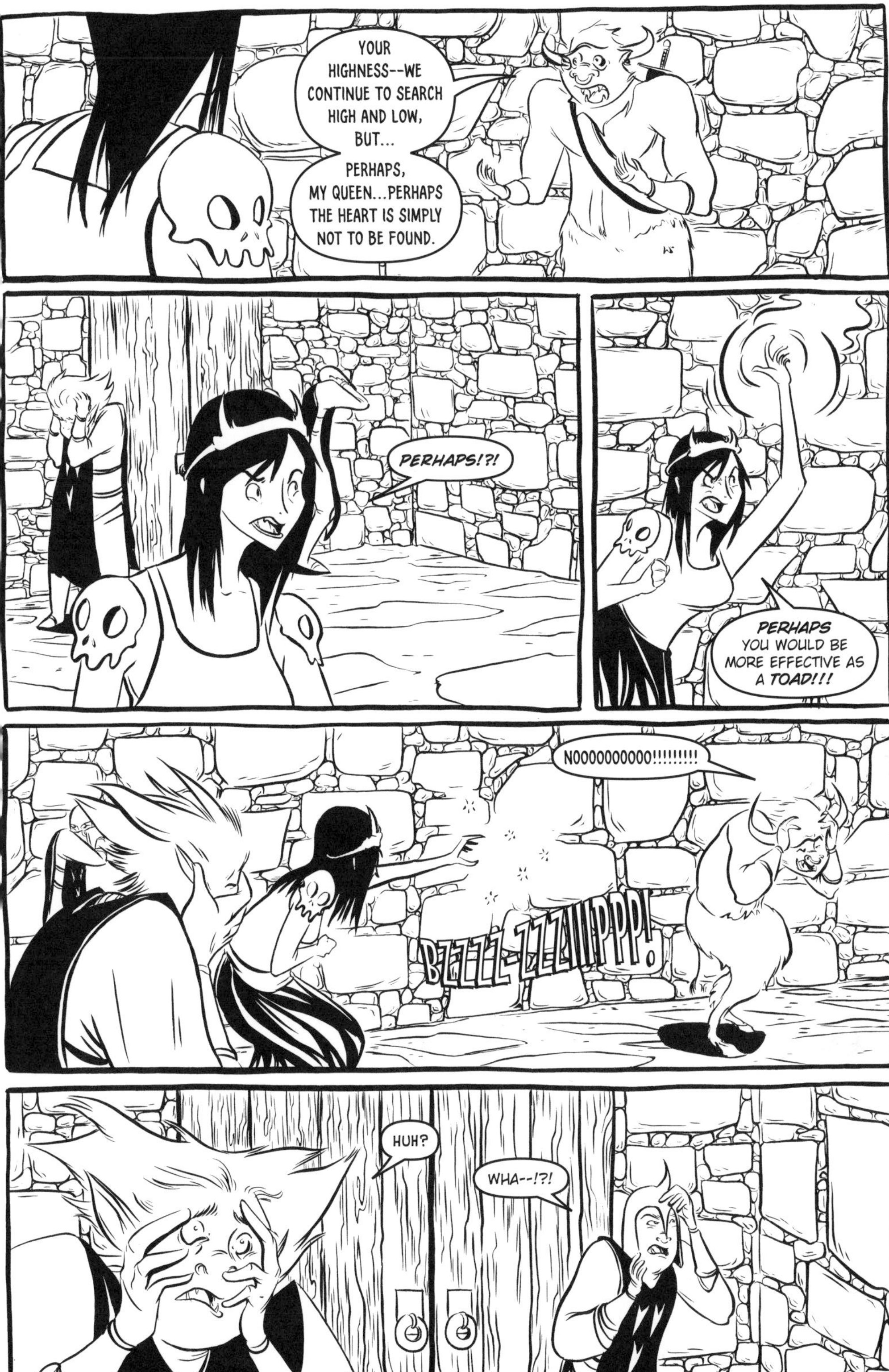
YOUR HIGHNESS--WE CONTINUE TO SEARCH HIGH AND LOW, BUT...
PERHAPS, MY QUEEN...PERHAPS THE HEART IS SIMPLY NOT TO BE FOUND.
PERHAPS!?!
PERHAPS YOU WOULD BE MORE EFFECTIVE AS A TOAD!!!
NOOOOOOOOOO!!!!!!!!!
BZZZZ-ZZZIIIPPP!
HUH?
WHA--!?!

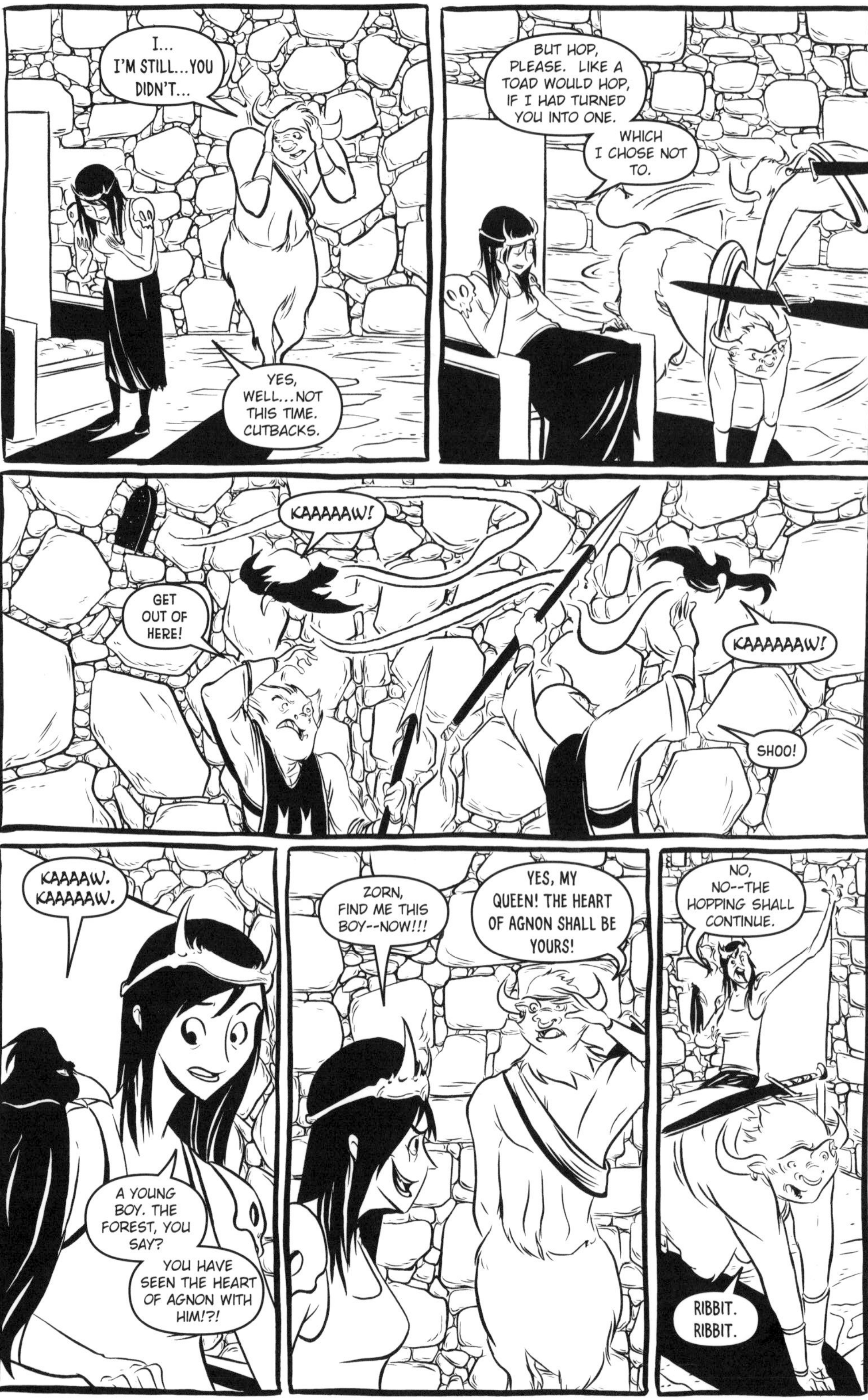
I... I'M STILL...YOU DIDN'T...
YES, WELL...NOT THIS TIME. CUTBACKS.
BUT HOP, PLEASE. LIKE A TOAD WOULD HOP, IF I HAD TURNED YOU INTO ONE.
WHICH I CHOSE NOT TO.
KAAAAAW!
GET OUT OF HERE!
KAAAAAAW!
SHOO!
KAAAAW. KAAAAAW.
A YOUNG BOY. THE FOREST, YOU SAY?
YOU HAVE SEEN THE HEART OF AGNON WITH HIM!?!
ZORN, FIND ME THIS BOY--NOW!!!
YES, MY QUEEN! THE HEART OF AGNON SHALL BE YOURS!
NO, NO--THE HOPPING SHALL CONTINUE.
RIBBIT. RIBBIT.

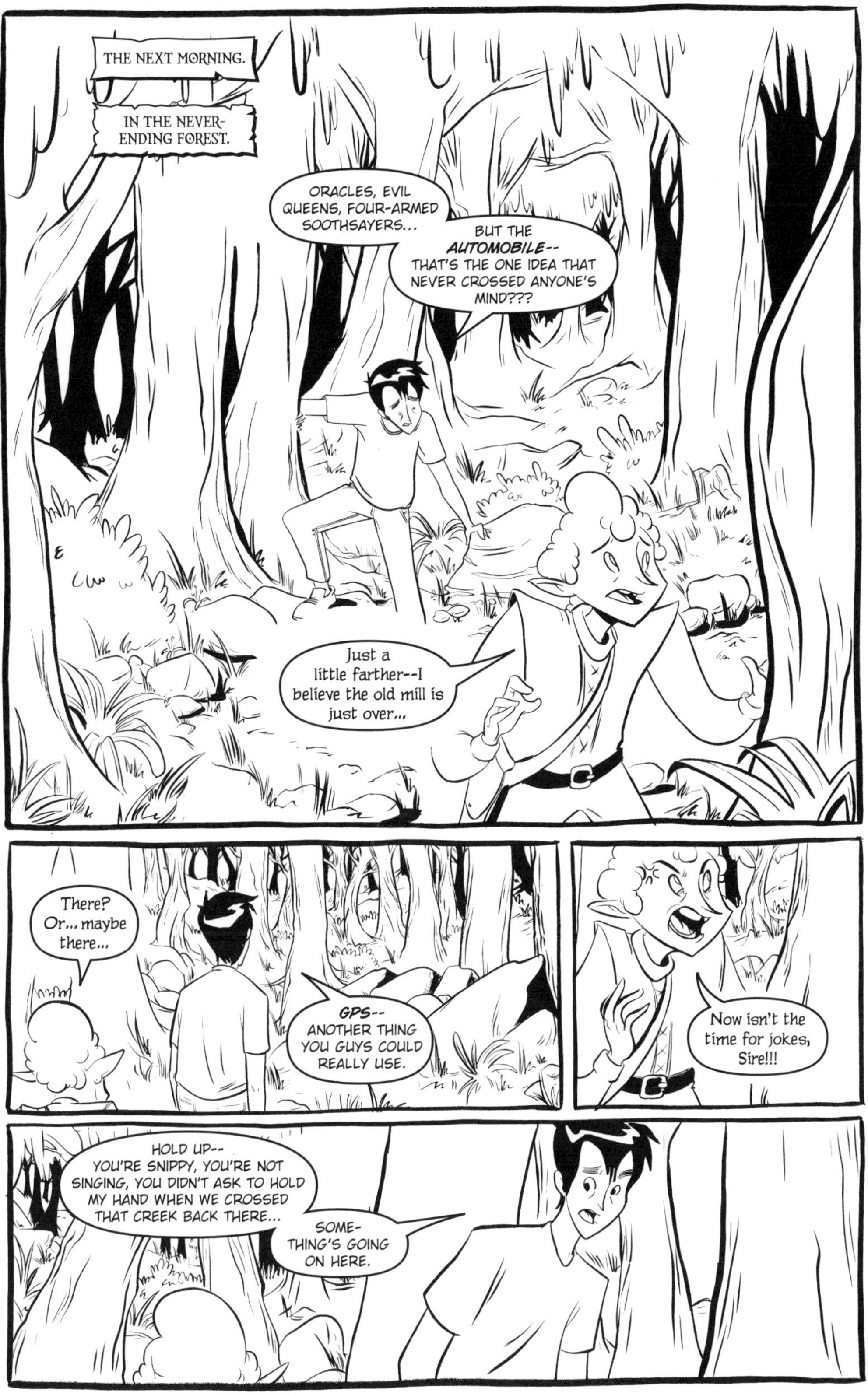
THE NEXT MORNING.
IN THE NEVER-ENDING FOREST.
ORACLES, EVIL QUEENS, FOUR-ARMED SOOTHSAYERS...
BUT THE *AUTOMOBILE*-- THAT'S THE ONE IDEA THAT NEVER CROSSED ANYONE'S MIND???
Just a little farther--I believe the old mill is just over...
There? Or... maybe there...
GPS-- ANOTHER THING YOU GUYS COULD REALLY USE.
Now isn't the time for jokes, Sire!!!
HOLD UP-- YOU'RE SNIPPY, YOU'RE NOT SINGING, YOU DIDN'T ASK TO HOLD MY HAND WHEN WE CROSSED THAT CREEK BACK THERE...
SOME-THING'S GOING ON HERE.

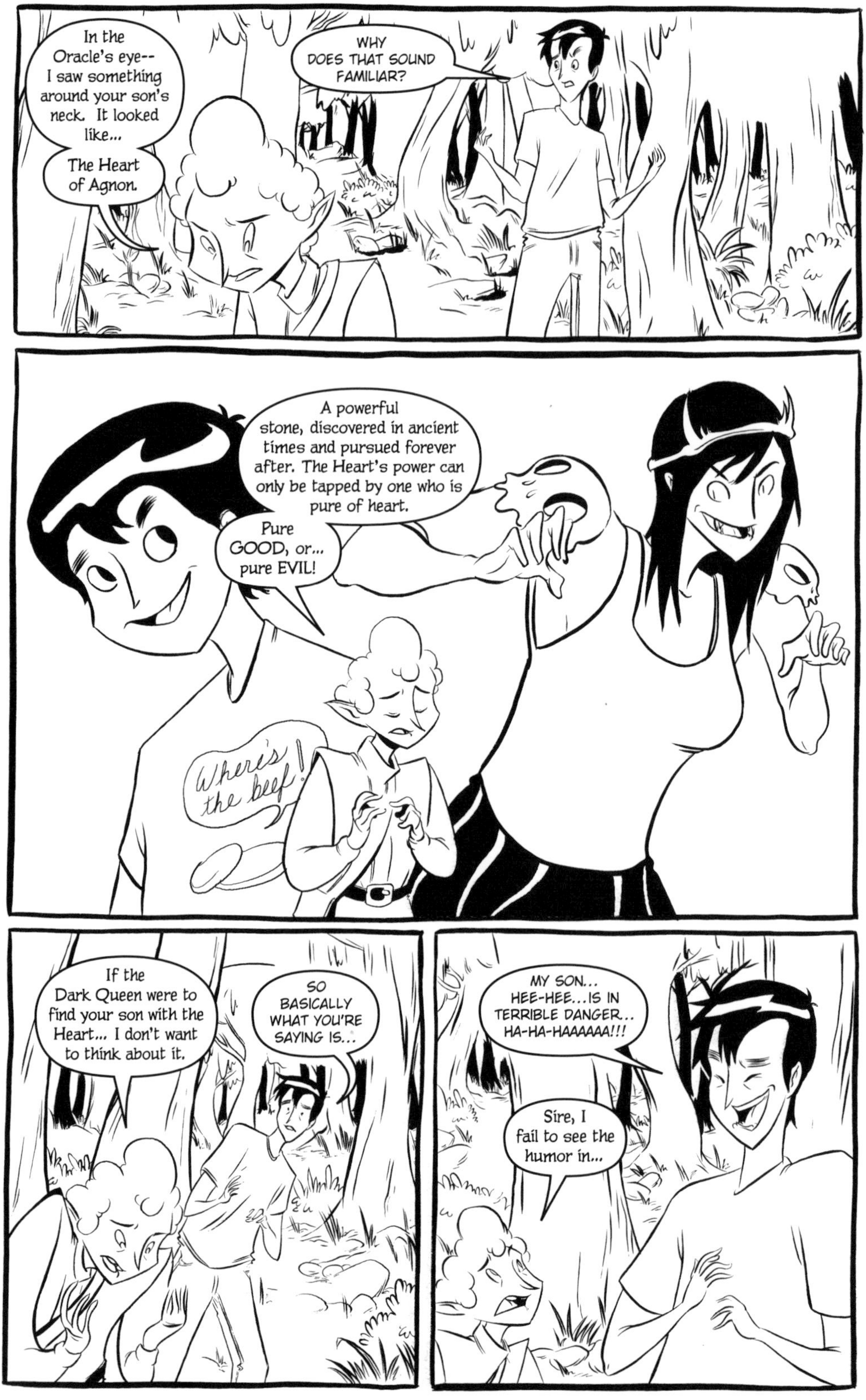
In the Oracle's eye-- I saw something around your son's neck. It looked like...
The Heart of Agnon.
WHY DOES THAT SOUND FAMILIAR?
A powerful stone, discovered in ancient times and pursued forever after. The Heart's power can only be tapped by one who is pure of heart.
Pure GOOD, or... pure EVIL!
Where's the beef!
If the Dark Queen were to find your son with the Heart... I don't want to think about it.
SO BASICALLY WHAT YOU'RE SAYING IS...
MY SON... HEE-HEE... IS IN TERRIBLE DANGER... HA-HA-HAAAAAA!!!
Sire, I fail to see the humor in...

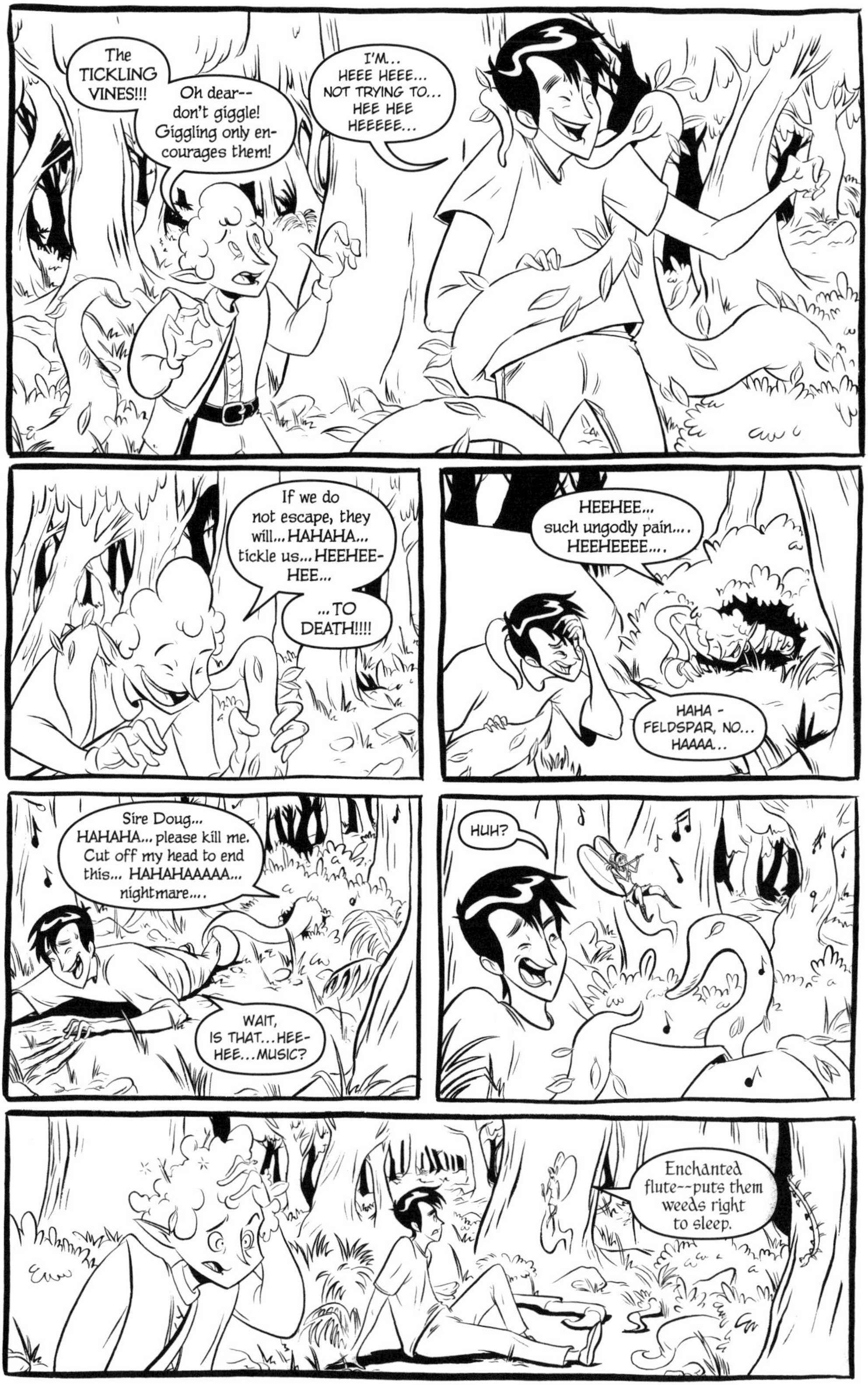

The TICKLING VINES!!!
Oh dear--don't giggle! Giggling only encourages them!
I'M... HEEE HEEE... NOT TRYING TO... HEE HEE HEEEEE...
If we do not escape, they will... HAHAHA... tickle us... HEEHEE-HEE...
...TO DEATH!!!!
HEEHEE... such ungodly pain.... HEEHEEEE....
HAHA - FELDSPAR, NO... HAAAA...
Sire Doug... HAHAHA... please kill me. Cut off my head to end this... HAHAHAAAAA... nightmare....
WAIT, IS THAT... HEE-HEE... MUSIC?
HUH?
Enchanted flute--puts them weeds right to sleep.

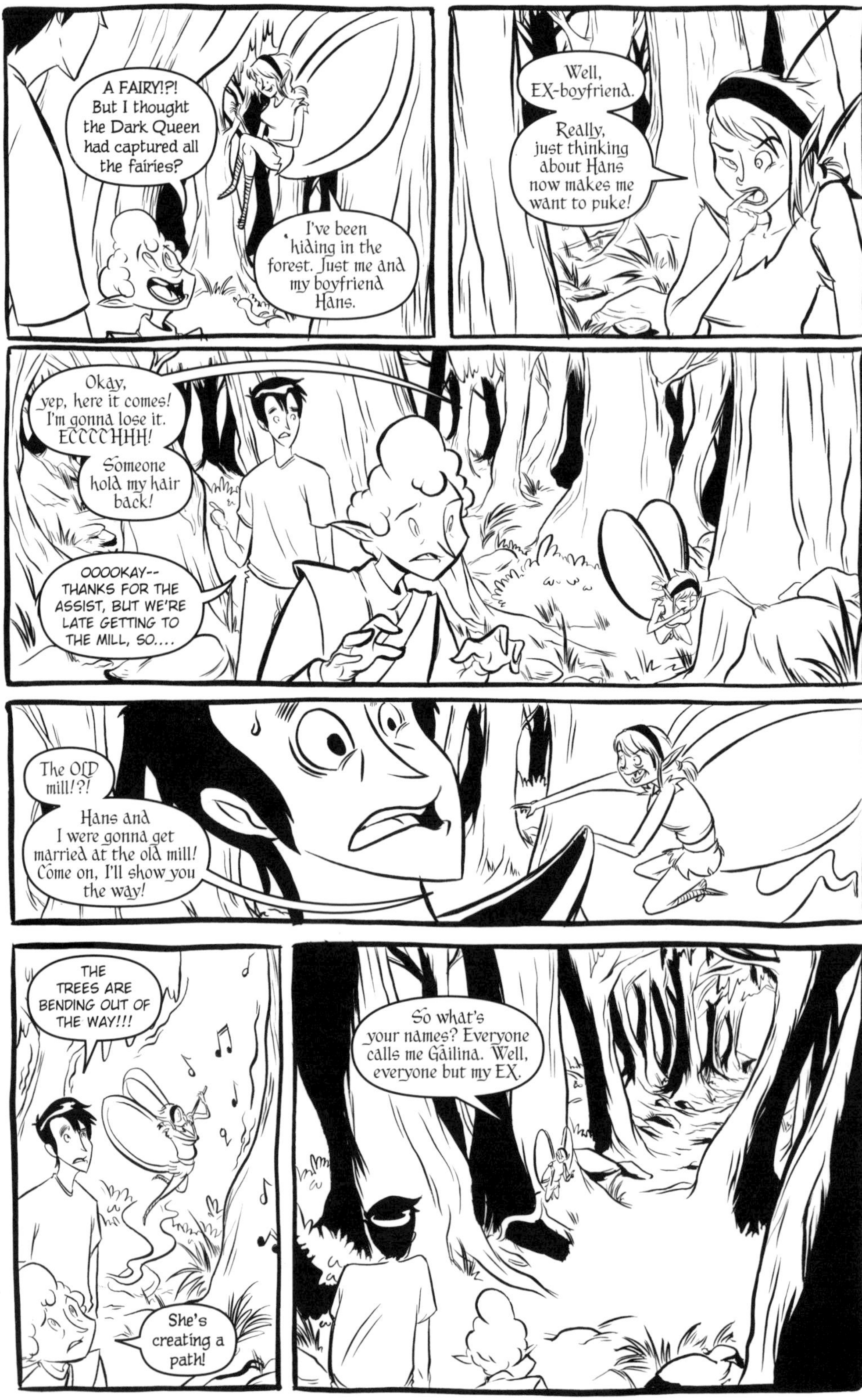
A FAIRY!?! But I thought the Dark Queen had captured all the fairies?
I've been hiding in the forest. Just me and my boyfriend Hans.
Well, EX-boyfriend.
Really, just thinking about Hans now makes me want to puke!
Okay, yep, here it comes! I'm gonna lose it. ECCCCHHH!
Someone hold my hair back!
OOOOKAY-- THANKS FOR THE ASSIST, BUT WE'RE LATE GETTING TO THE MILL, SO....
The OLD mill!?!
Hans and I were gonna get married at the old mill! Come on, I'll show you the way!
THE TREES ARE BENDING OUT OF THE WAY!!!
She's creating a path!
So what's your names? Everyone calls me Gailina. Well, everyone but my EX.

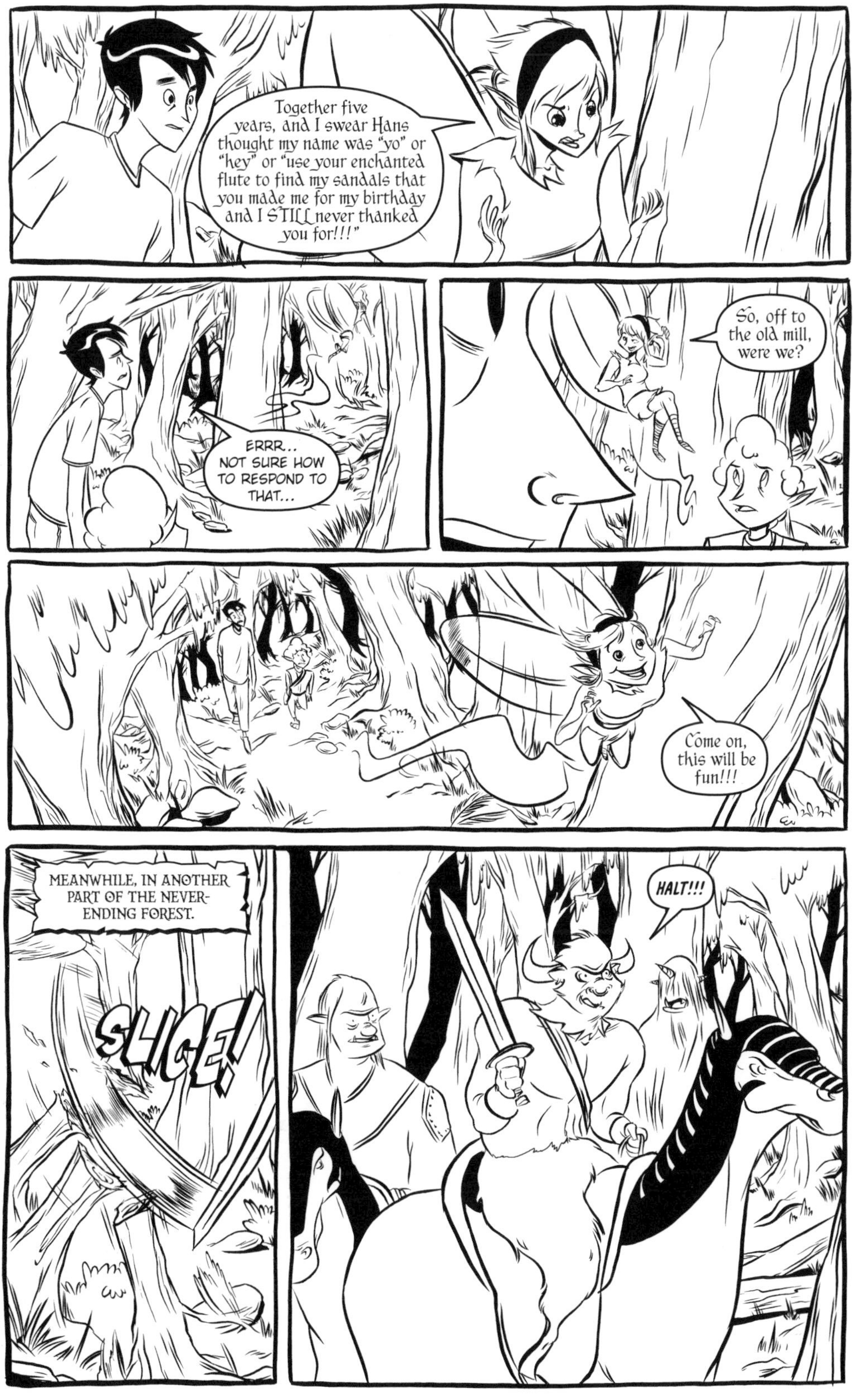
Together five years, and I swear Hans thought my name was "yo" or "hey" or "use your enchanted flute to find my sandals that you made me for my birthday and I STILL never thanked you for!!!"
ERRR... NOT SURE HOW TO RESPOND TO THAT...
So, off to the old mill, were we?
Come on, this will be fun!!!
MEANWHILE, IN ANOTHER PART OF THE NEVER-ENDING FOREST.
SLICE!
HALT!!!

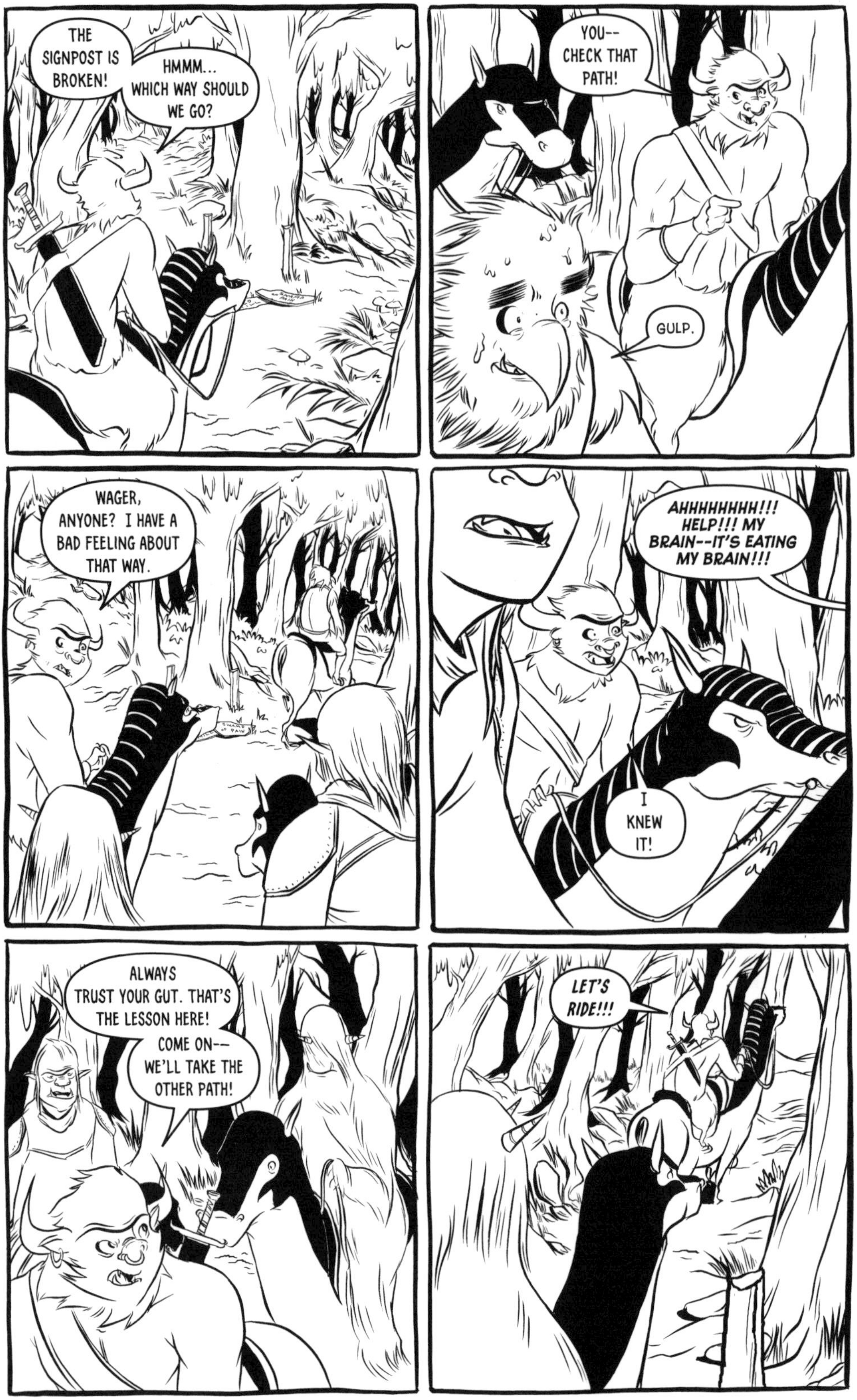
THE SIGNPOST IS BROKEN!
HMMM... WHICH WAY SHOULD WE GO?
YOU-- CHECK THAT PATH!
GULP.
WAGER, ANYONE? I HAVE A BAD FEELING ABOUT THAT WAY.
AHHHHHHHH!!! HELP!!! MY BRAIN--IT'S EATING MY BRAIN!!!
I KNEW IT!
ALWAYS TRUST YOUR GUT. THAT'S THE LESSON HERE!
COME ON-- WE'LL TAKE THE OTHER PATH!
LET'S RIDE!!!

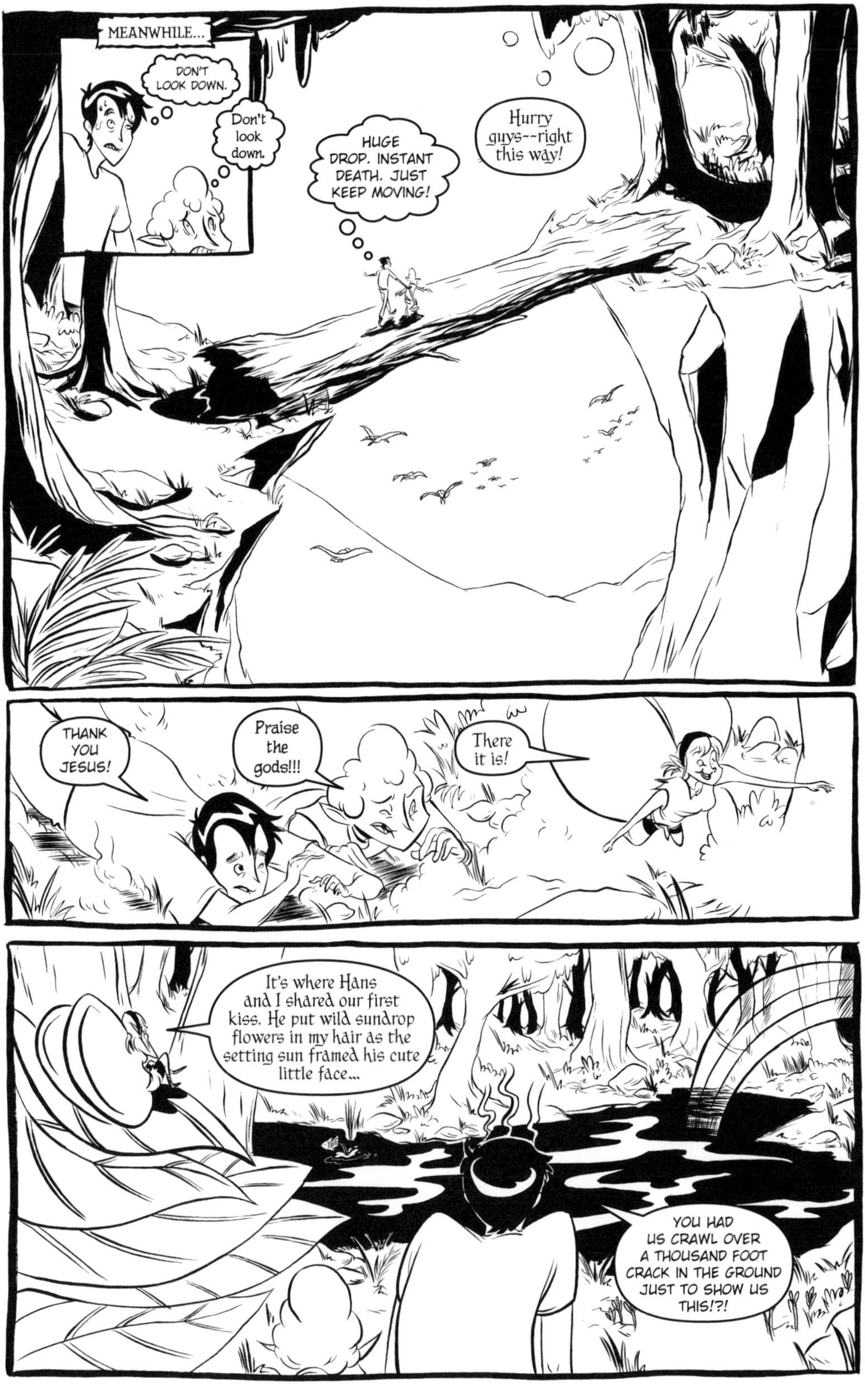
MEANWHILE...
DON'T LOOK DOWN.
Don't look down.
HUGE DROP. INSTANT DEATH. JUST KEEP MOVING!
Hurry guys--right this way!
THANK YOU JESUS!
Praise the gods!!!
There it is!
It's where Hans and I shared our first kiss. He put wild sundrop flowers in my hair as the setting sun framed his cute little face...
YOU HAD US CRAWL OVER A THOUSAND FOOT CRACK IN THE GROUND JUST TO SHOW US THIS!?!

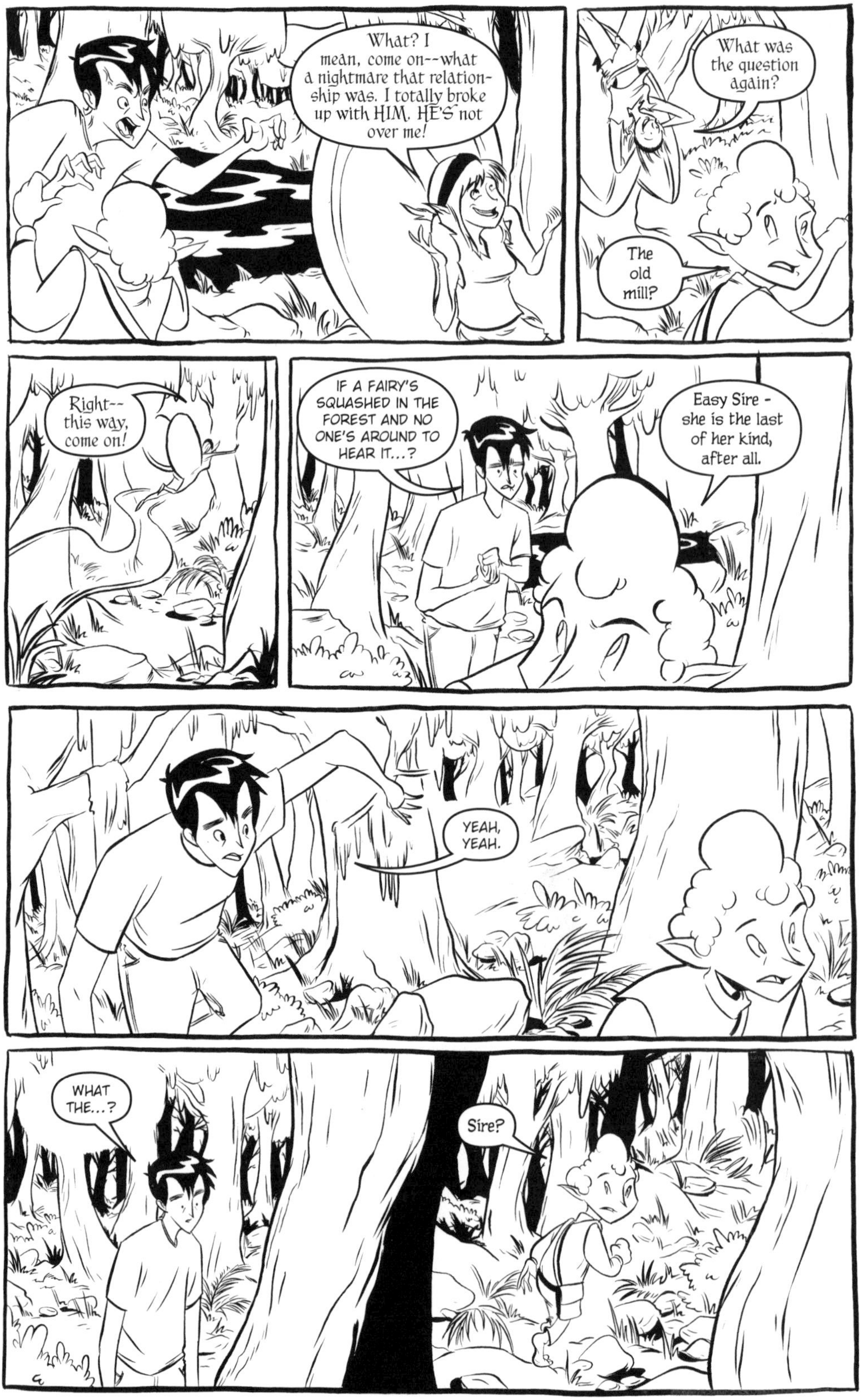
What? I mean, come on--what a nightmare that relationship was. I totally broke up with HIM. HE'S not over me!
What was the question again?
The old mill?
Right-- this way, come on!
IF A FAIRY'S SQUASHED IN THE FOREST AND NO ONE'S AROUND TO HEAR IT...?
Easy Sire - she is the last of her kind, after all.
YEAH, YEAH.
WHAT THE...?
Sire?

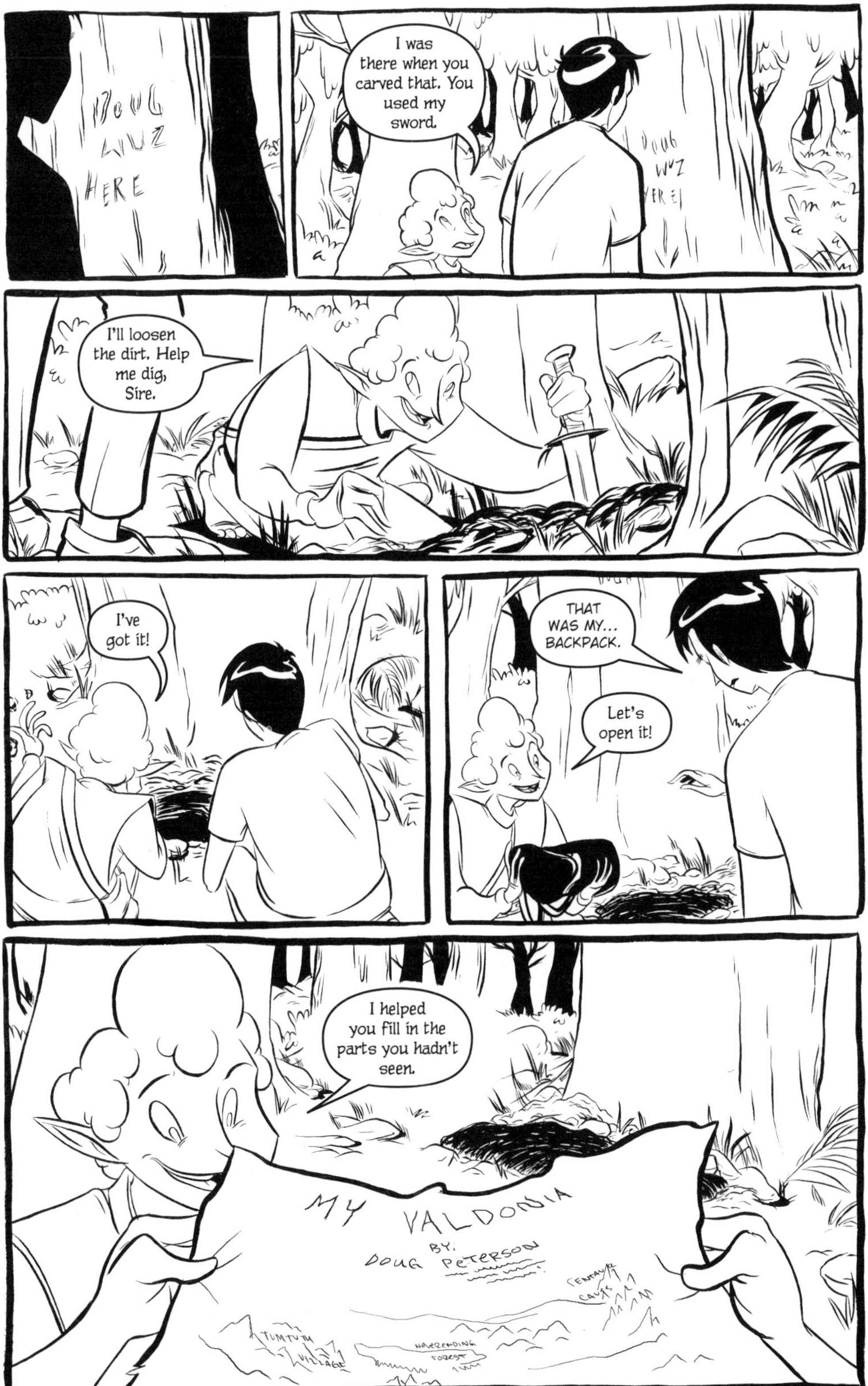
DOUG
WUZ
HERE
I was there when you carved that. You used my sword.
DOUG
WUZ
HERE
I'll loosen the dirt. Help me dig, Sire.
I've got it!
THAT WAS MY... BACKPACK.
Let's open it!
I helped you fill in the parts you hadn't seen.
MY VALDONIA
BY:
DOUG PETERSON
CENTAUR CAVES
TUMTUM VILLAGE
NEVERENDING FOREST

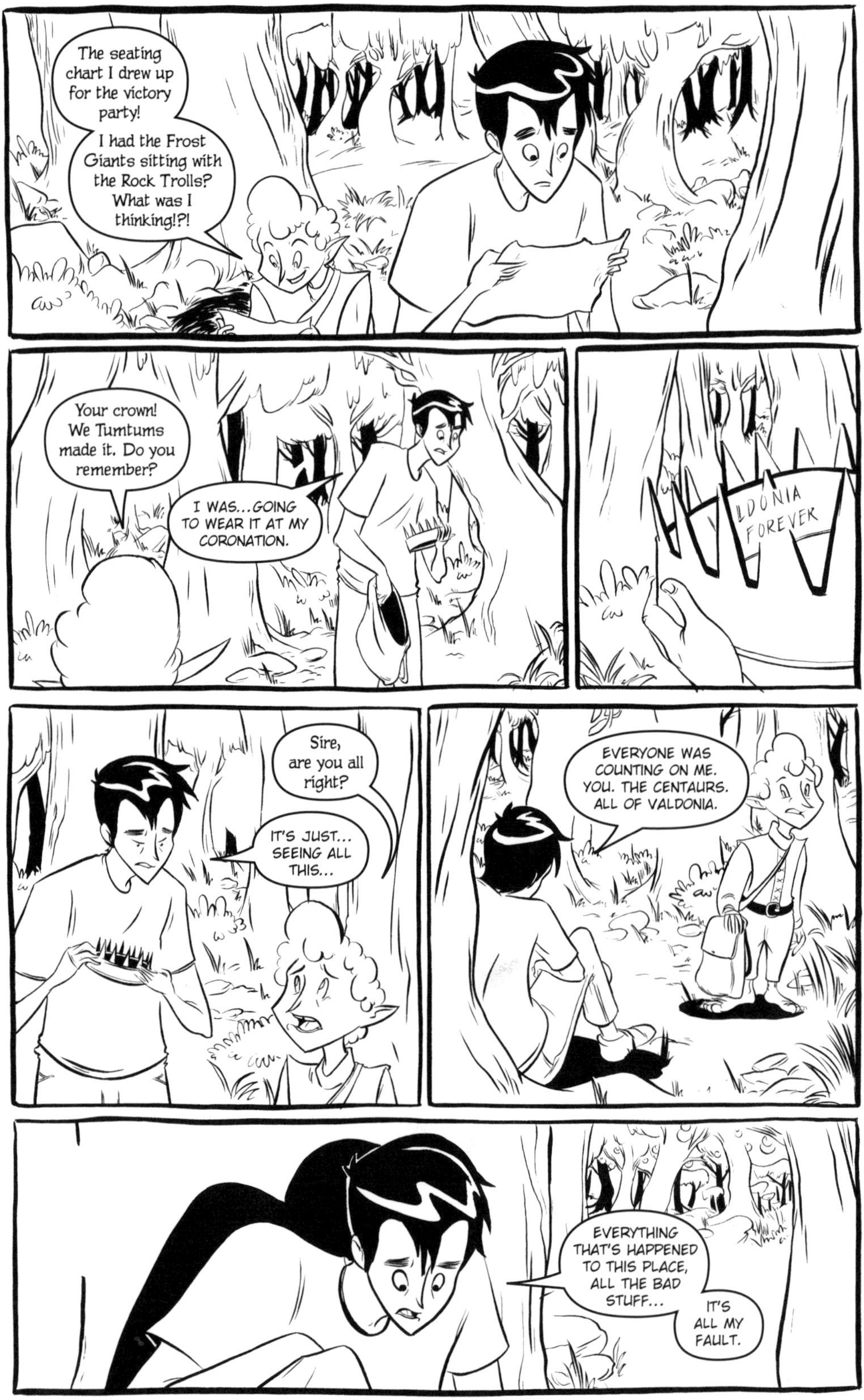
The seating chart I drew up for the victory party!
I had the Frost Giants sitting with the Rock Trolls? What was I thinking!?!
Your crown! We Tumtums made it. Do you remember?
I WAS...GOING TO WEAR IT AT MY CORONATION.
LDONIA FOREVER
Sire, are you all right?
IT'S JUST... SEEING ALL THIS...
EVERYONE WAS COUNTING ON ME. YOU. THE CENTAURS. ALL OF VALDONIA.
EVERYTHING THAT'S HAPPENED TO THIS PLACE, ALL THE BAD STUFF...
IT'S ALL MY FAULT.

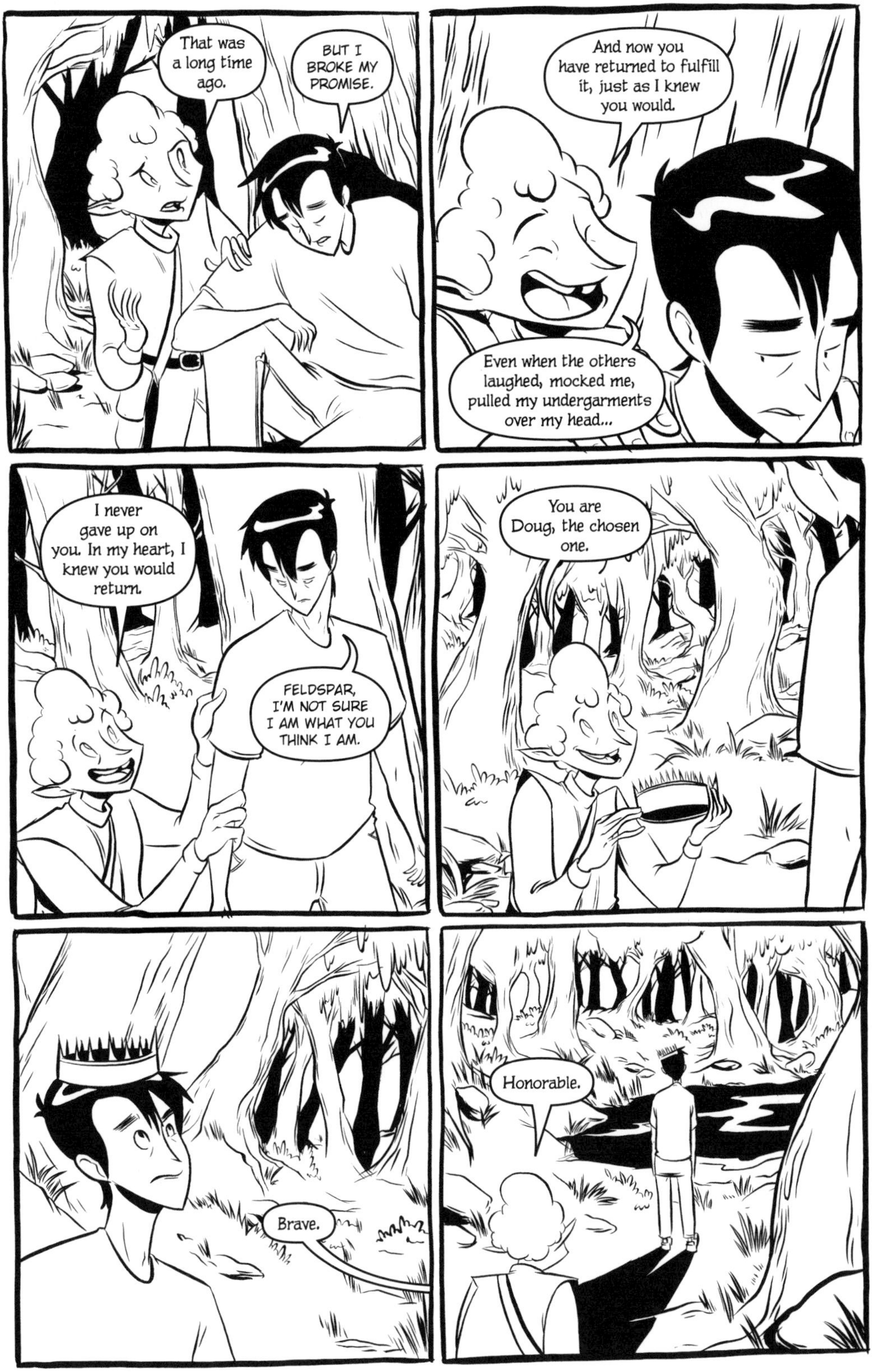
That was a long time ago.
BUT I BROKE MY PROMISE.
And now you have returned to fulfill it, just as I knew you would.
Even when the others laughed, mocked me, pulled my undergarments over my head...
I never gave up on you. In my heart, I knew you would return.
FELDSPAR, I'M NOT SURE I AM WHAT YOU THINK I AM.
You are Doug, the chosen one.
Brave.
Honorable.

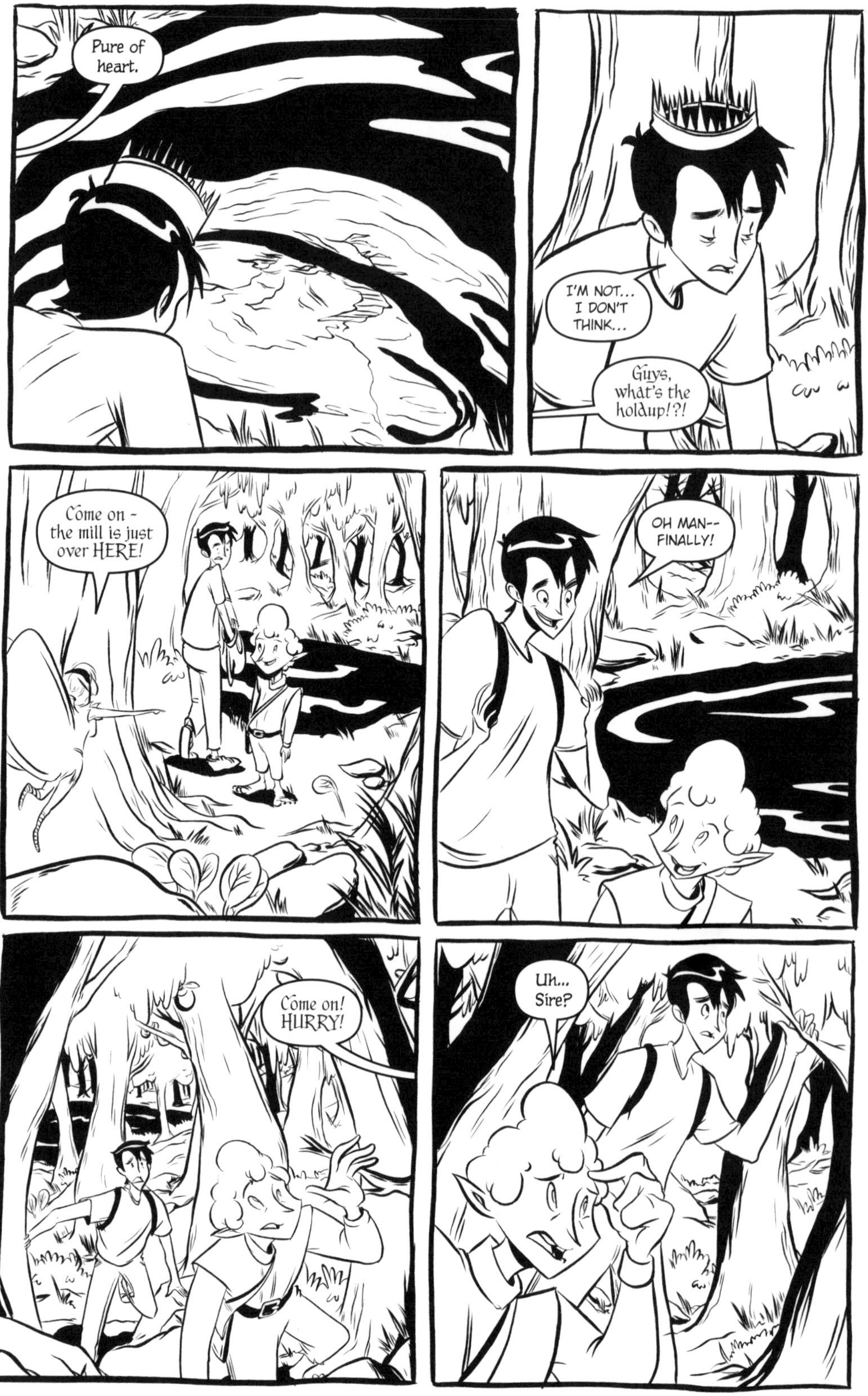
Pure of heart.
I'M NOT... I DON'T THINK...
Guys, what's the holdup!?!
Come on - the mill is just over HERE!
OH MAN-- FINALLY!
Come on! HURRY!
Uh... Sire?

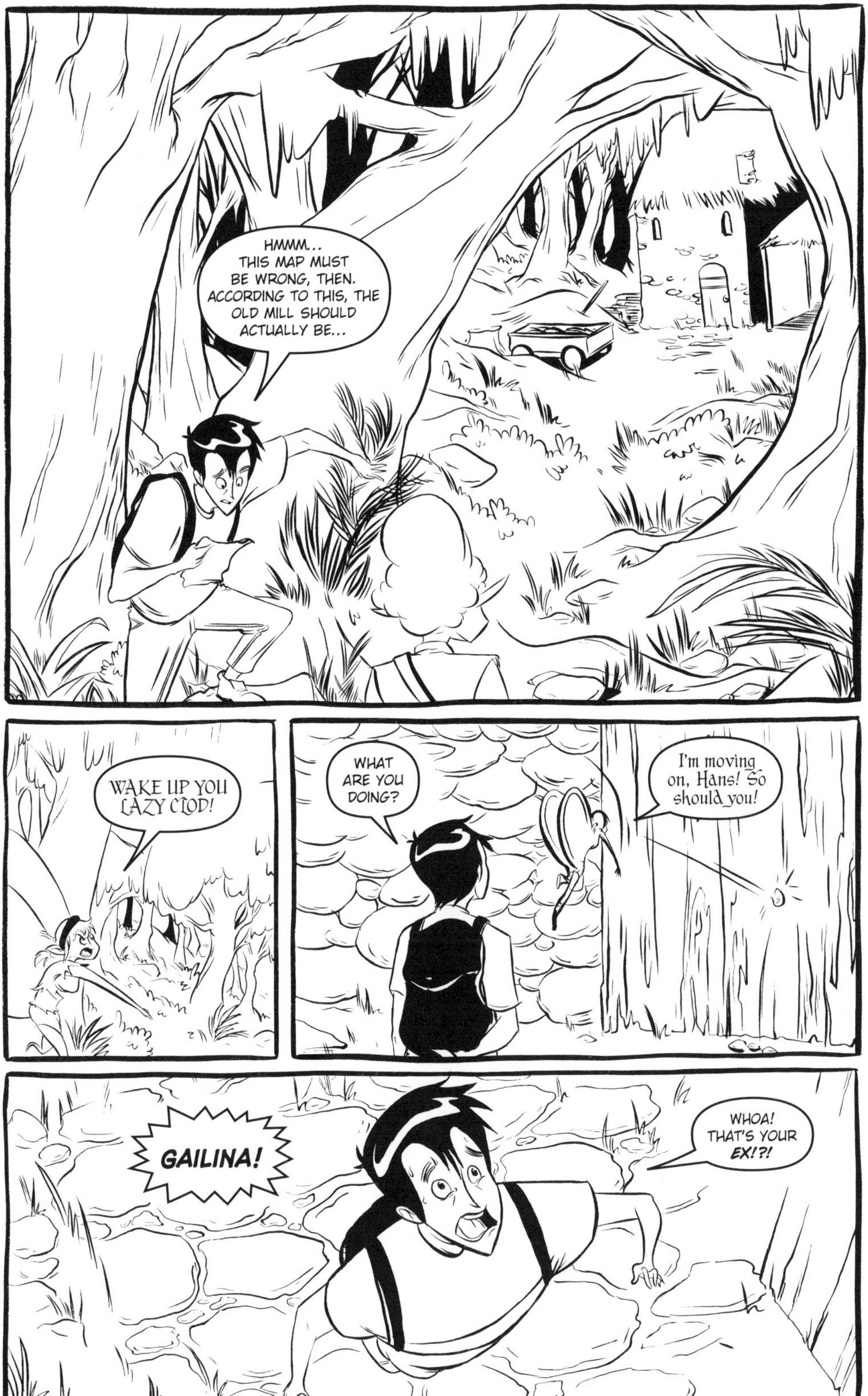
HMMM...
THIS MAP MUST BE WRONG, THEN. ACCORDING TO THIS, THE OLD MILL SHOULD ACTUALLY BE...
WAKE UP YOU LAZY CLOD!
WHAT ARE YOU DOING?
I'm moving on, Hans! So should you!
GAILINA!
WHOA! THAT'S YOUR EX!?!

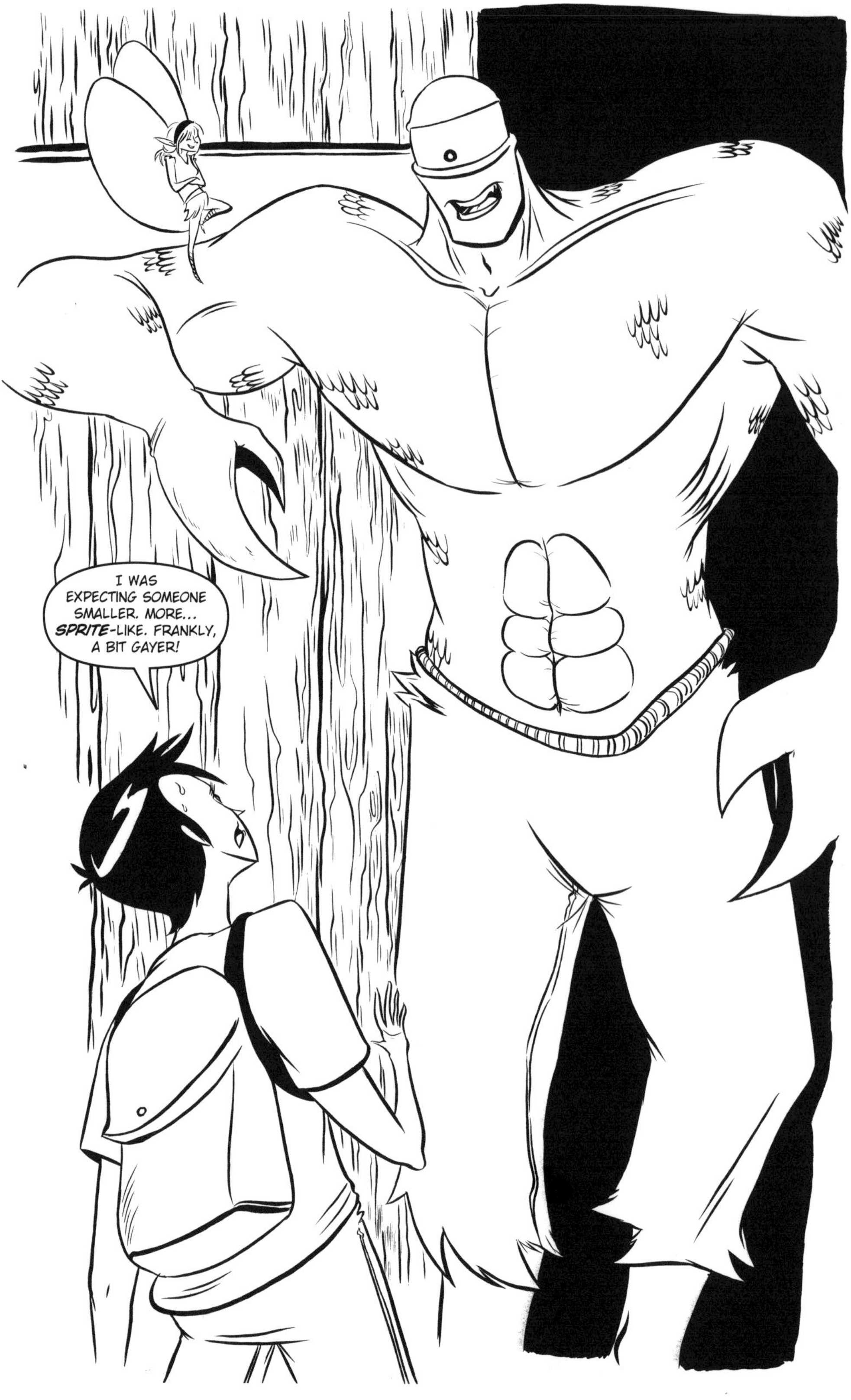
I WAS EXPECTING SOMEONE SMALLER. MORE... **SPRITE**-LIKE. FRANKLY, A BIT GAYER!

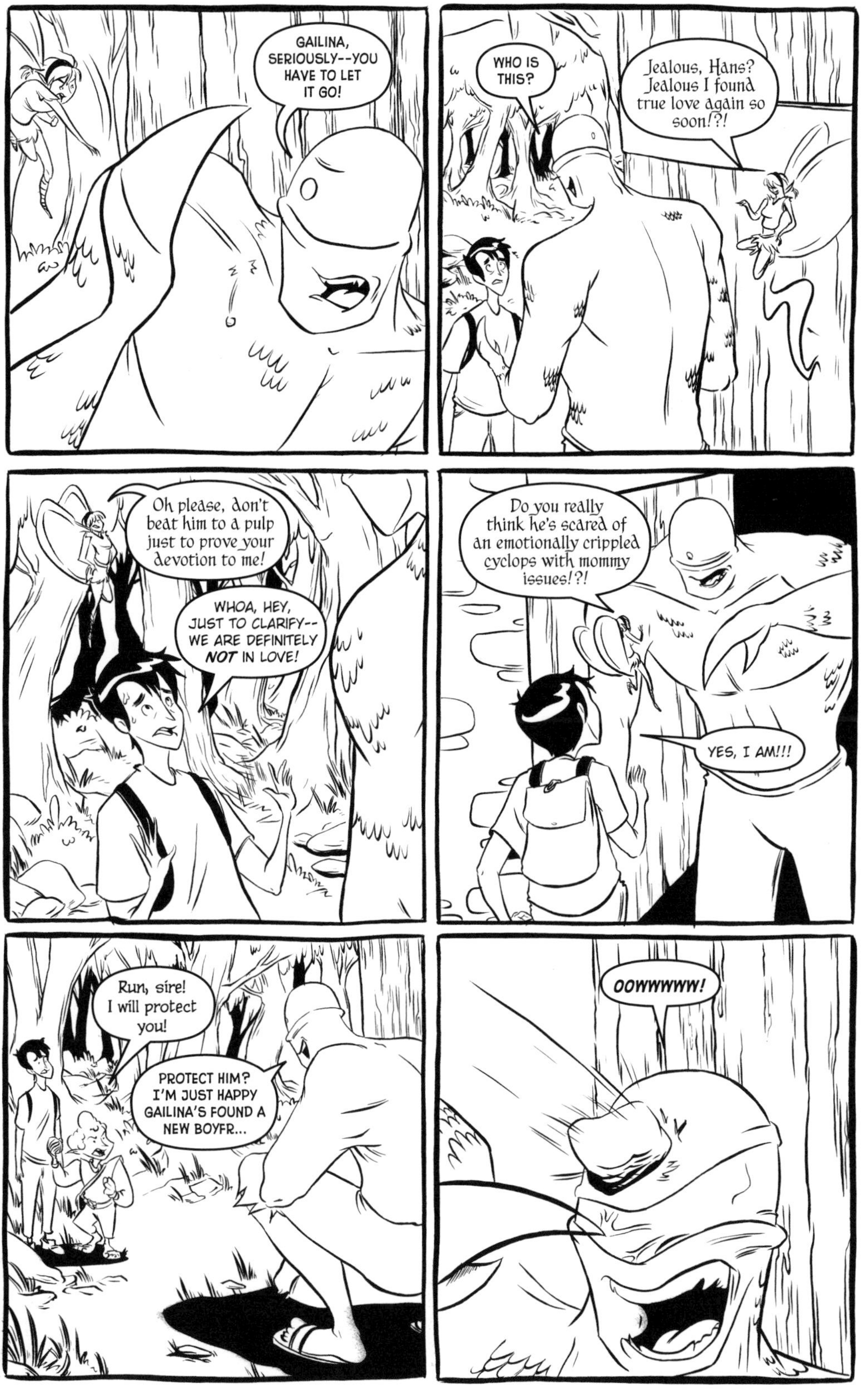
GAILINA, SERIOUSLY--YOU HAVE TO LET IT GO!
WHO IS THIS?
Jealous, Hans? Jealous I found true love again so soon!?!
Oh please, don't beat him to a pulp just to prove your devotion to me!
WHOA, HEY, JUST TO CLARIFY-- WE ARE DEFINITELY ***NOT*** IN LOVE!
Do you really think he's scared of an emotionally crippled cyclops with mommy issues!?!
YES, I AM!!!
Run, sire! I will protect you!
PROTECT HIM? I'M JUST HAPPY GAILINA'S FOUND A NEW BOYFR...
OOWWWWW!

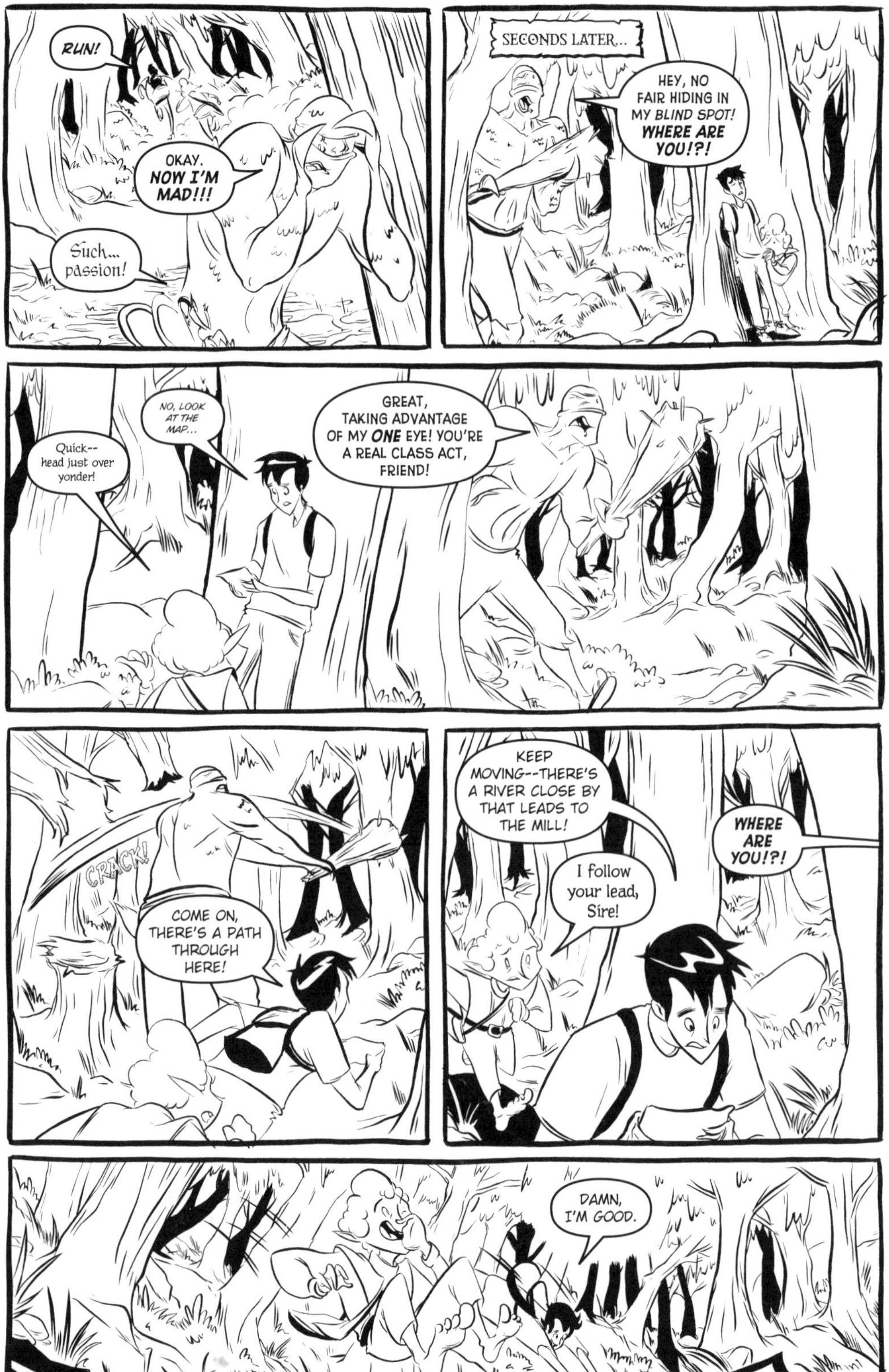
RUN!
OKAY. NOW I'M MAD!!!
Such... passion!
SECONDS LATER...
HEY, NO FAIR HIDING IN MY BLIND SPOT! WHERE ARE YOU!?!
Quick-- head just over yonder!
NO, LOOK AT THE MAP...
GREAT, TAKING ADVANTAGE OF MY ONE EYE! YOU'RE A REAL CLASS ACT, FRIEND!
CRACK!
COME ON, THERE'S A PATH THROUGH HERE!
KEEP MOVING--THERE'S A RIVER CLOSE BY THAT LEADS TO THE MILL!
I follow your lead, Sire!
WHERE ARE YOU!?!
DAMN, I'M GOOD.

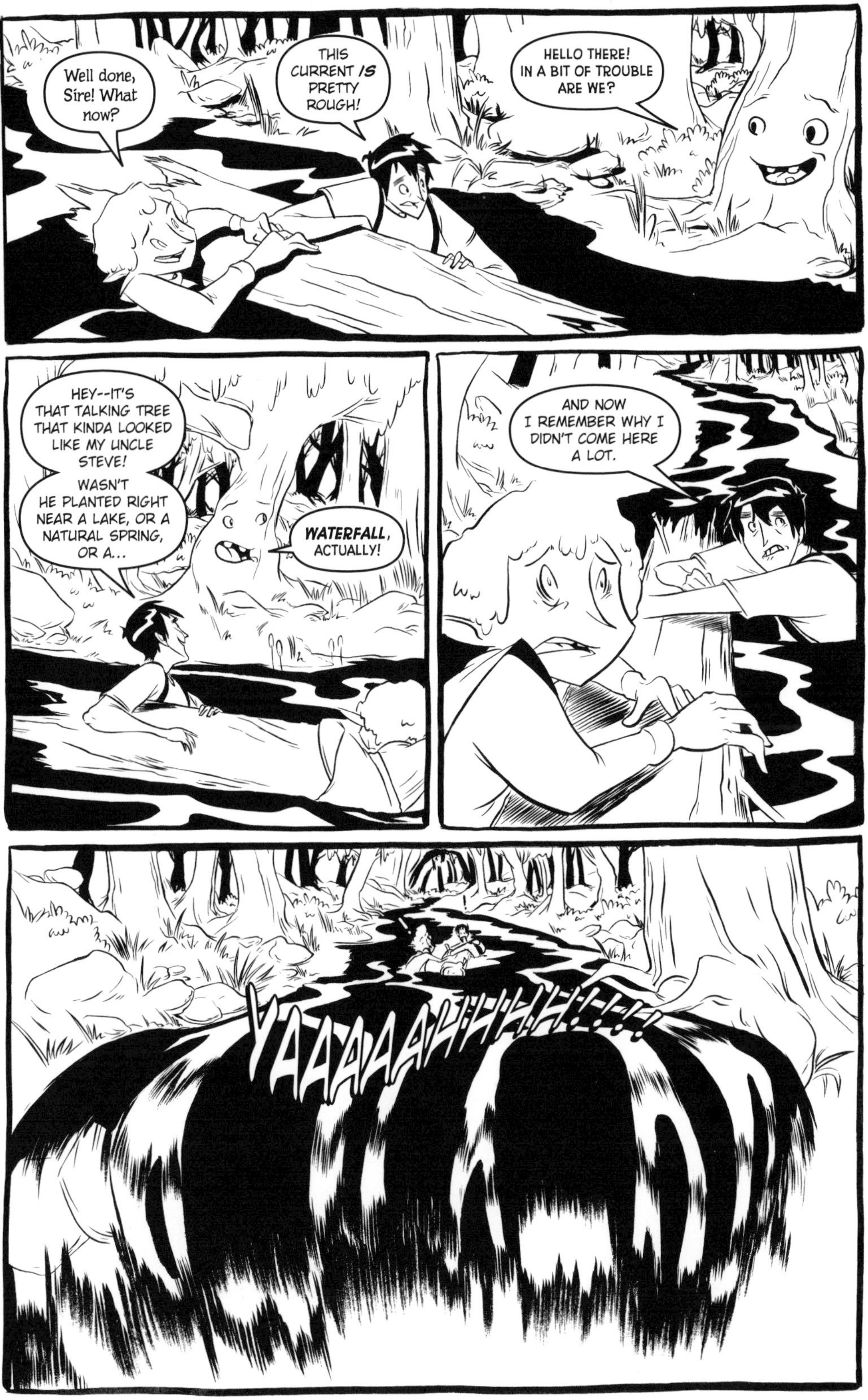
Well done, Sire! What now?
THIS CURRENT IS PRETTY ROUGH!
HELLO THERE! IN A BIT OF TROUBLE ARE WE?
HEY--IT'S THAT TALKING TREE THAT KINDA LOOKED LIKE MY UNCLE STEVE!
WASN'T HE PLANTED RIGHT NEAR A LAKE, OR A NATURAL SPRING, OR A...
WATERFALL, ACTUALLY!
AND NOW I REMEMBER WHY I DIDN'T COME HERE A LOT.
YAAAAAHHHHH!!!!!

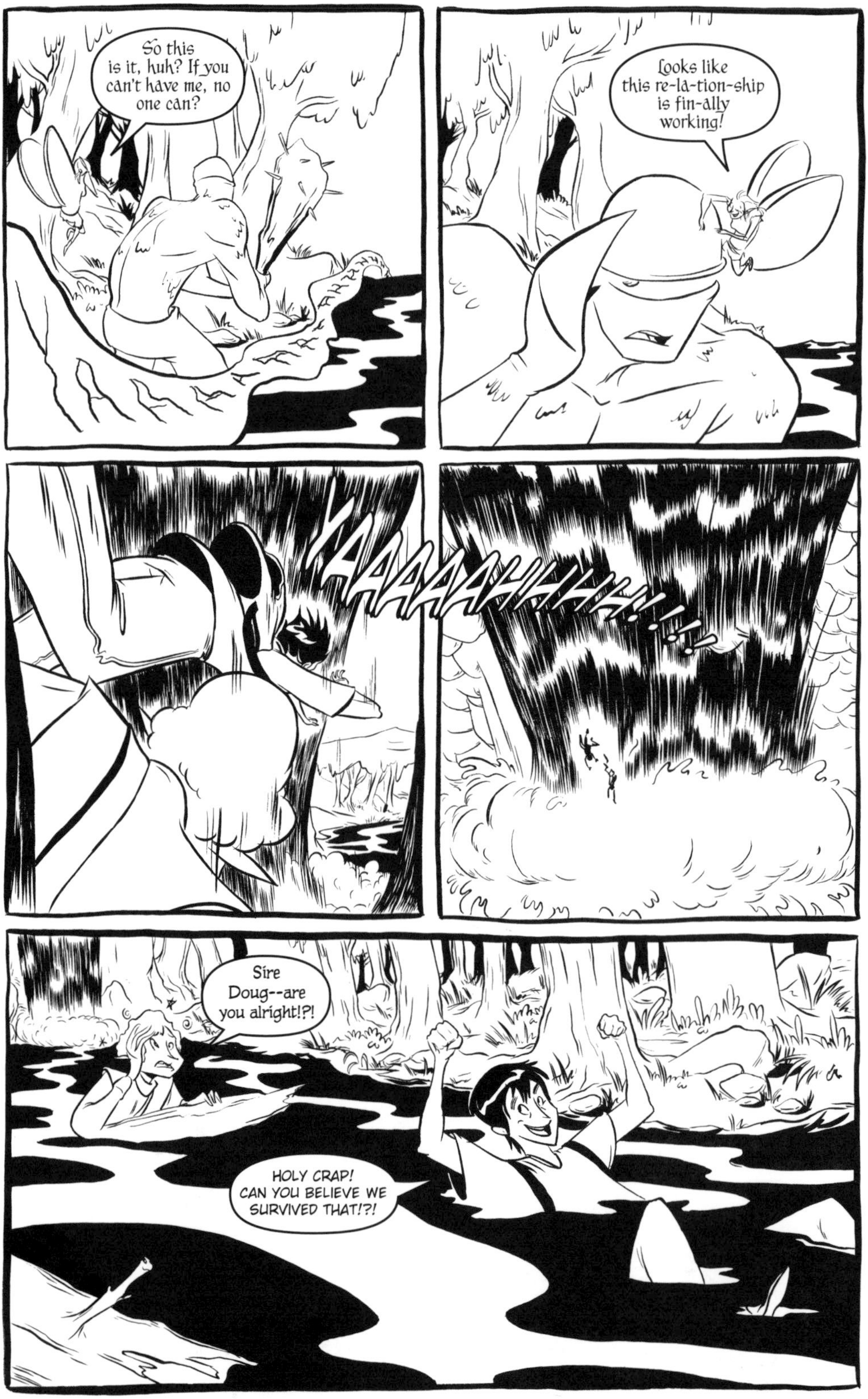
So this is it, huh? If you can't have me, no one can?
Looks like this re-la-tion-ship is fin-ally working!
YAAAAAHHHHH!!!!!
Sire Doug--are you alright!?!
HOLY CRAP! CAN YOU BELIEVE WE SURVIVED THAT!?!

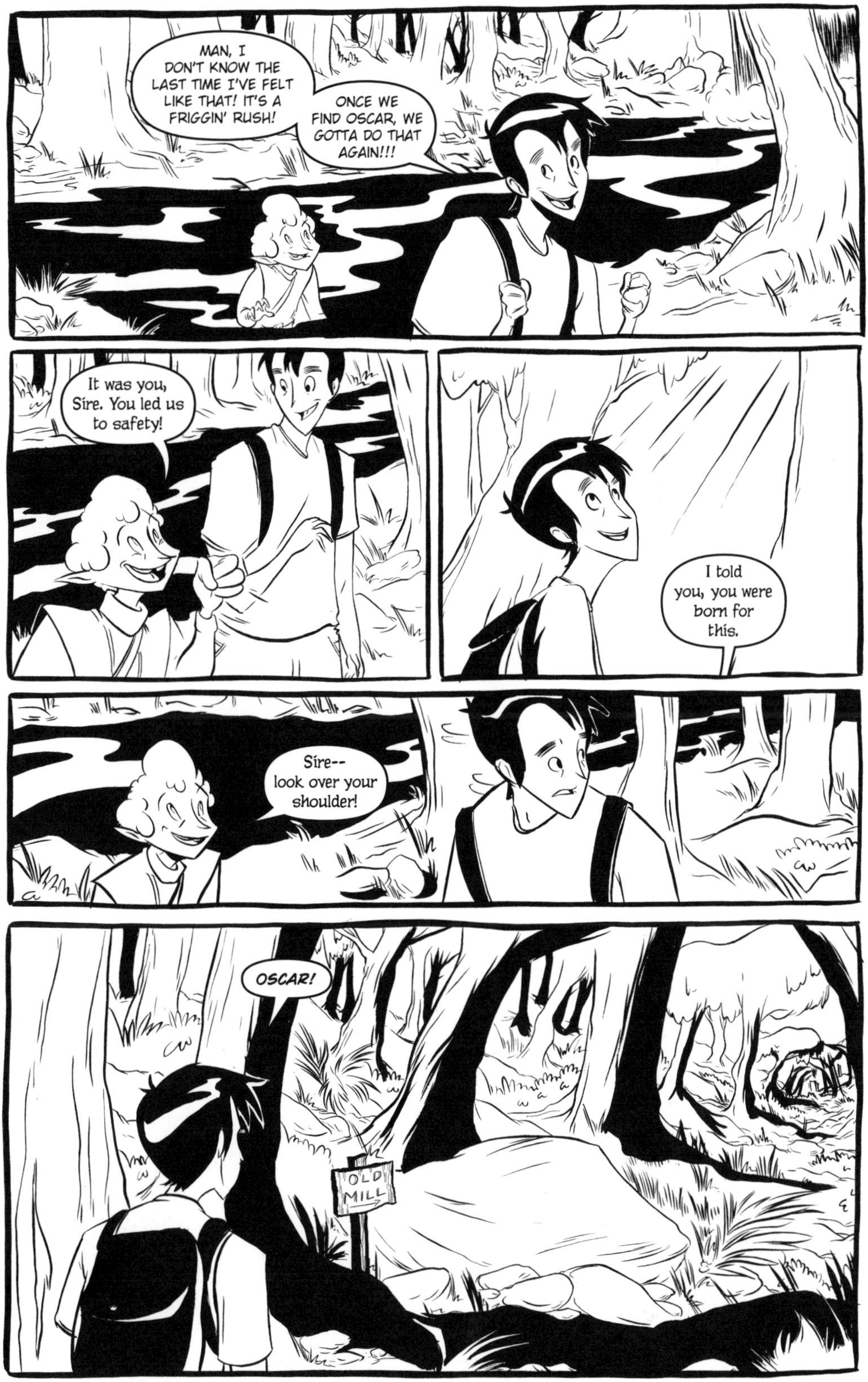
MAN, I DON'T KNOW THE LAST TIME I'VE FELT LIKE THAT! IT'S A FRIGGIN' RUSH!
ONCE WE FIND OSCAR, WE GOTTA DO THAT AGAIN!!!
It was you, Sire. You led us to safety!
I told you, you were born for this.
Sire-- look over your shoulder!
OSCAR!
OLD MILL

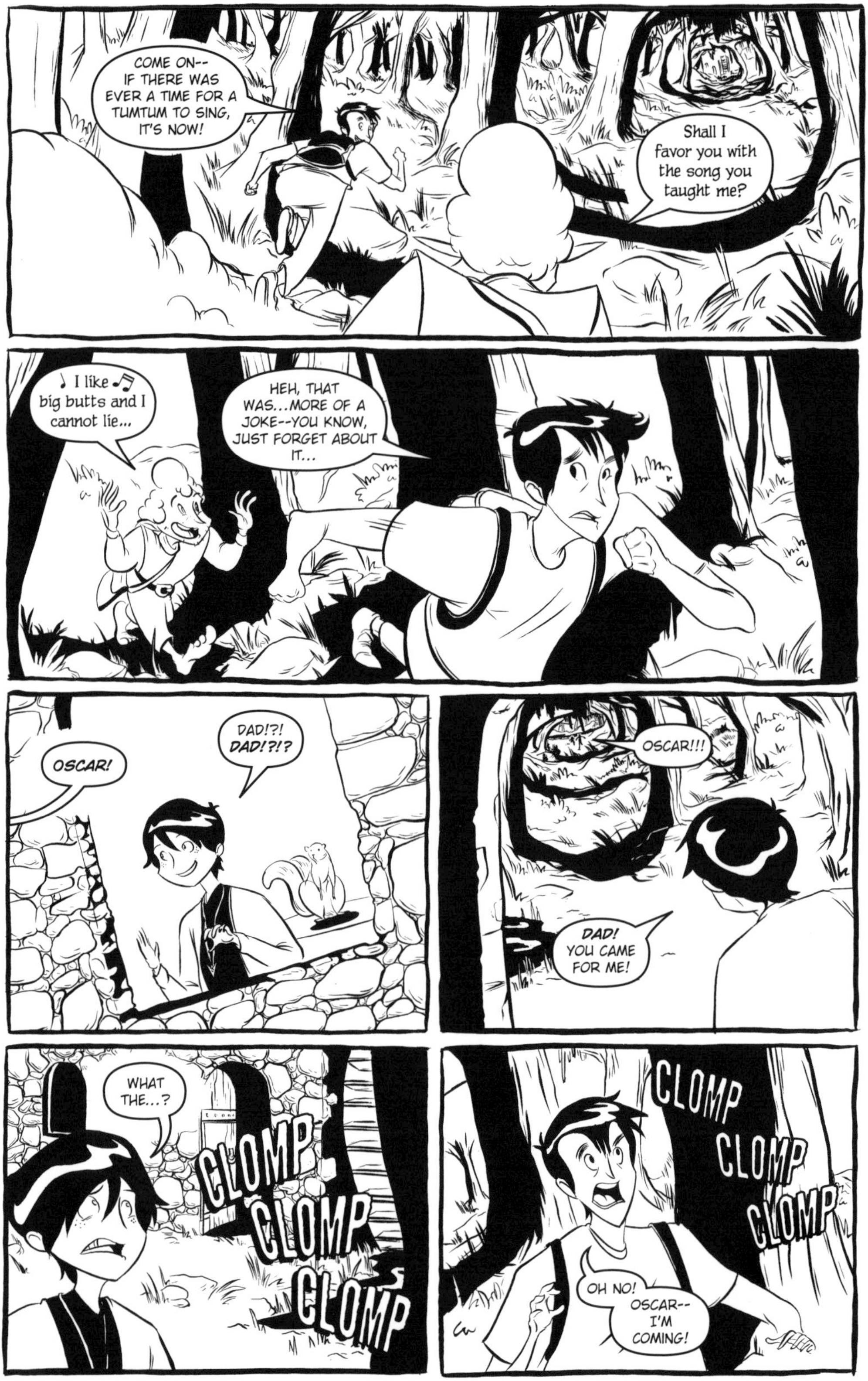
COME ON--
IF THERE WAS EVER A TIME FOR A TUMTUM TO SING, IT'S NOW!
Shall I favor you with the song you taught me?
♪ I like ♫ big butts and I cannot lie...
HEH, THAT WAS...MORE OF A JOKE--YOU KNOW, JUST FORGET ABOUT IT...
OSCAR!
DAD!?! DAD!?!?
OSCAR!!!
DAD! YOU CAME FOR ME!
WHAT THE...?
CLOMP CLOMP CLOMP
CLOMP CLOMP CLOMP
OH NO! OSCAR-- I'M COMING!

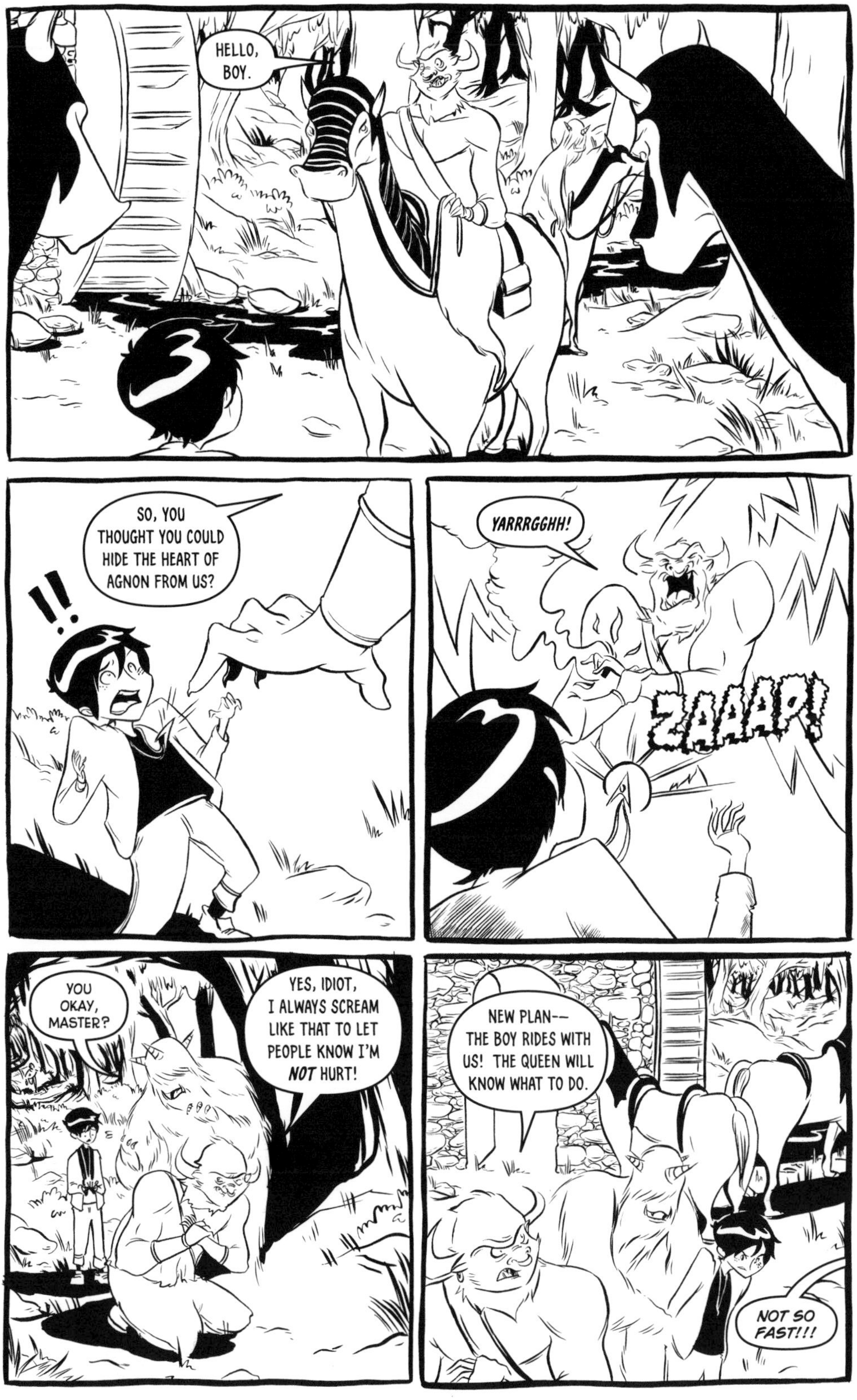
HELLO, BOY.
SO, YOU THOUGHT YOU COULD HIDE THE HEART OF AGNON FROM US?
!!
YARRRGGHH!
ZAAAP!
YOU OKAY, MASTER?
YES, IDIOT, I ALWAYS SCREAM LIKE THAT TO LET PEOPLE KNOW I'M *NOT* HURT!
NEW PLAN-- THE BOY RIDES WITH US! THE QUEEN WILL KNOW WHAT TO DO.
NOT SO FAST!!!

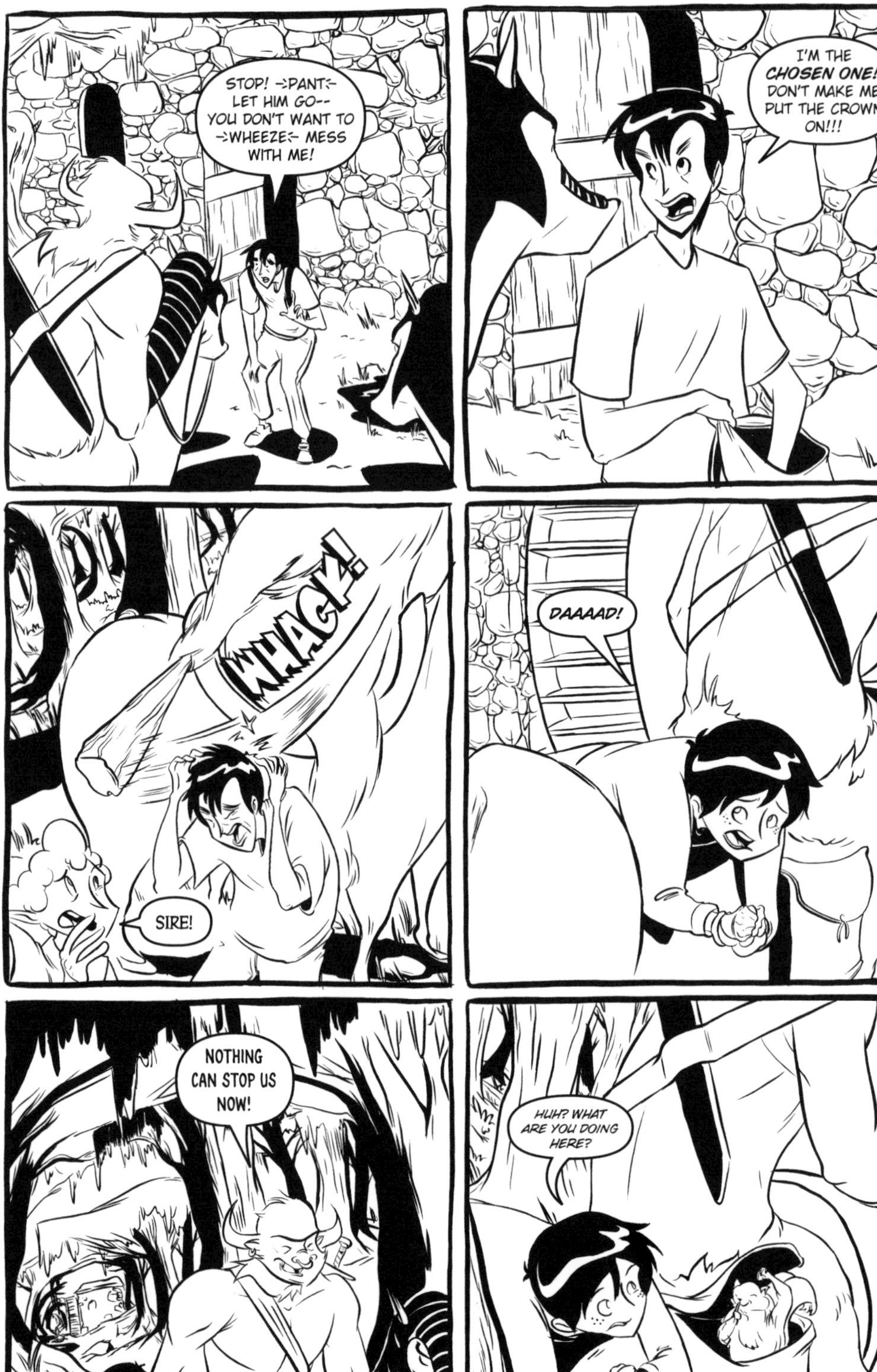
STOP! -PANT- LET HIM GO-- YOU DON'T WANT TO -WHEEZE- MESS WITH ME!
I'M THE **CHOSEN ONE!** DON'T MAKE ME PUT THE CROWN ON!!!
WHACK!
SIRE!
DAAAAD!
NOTHING CAN STOP US NOW!
HUH? WHAT ARE YOU DOING HERE?

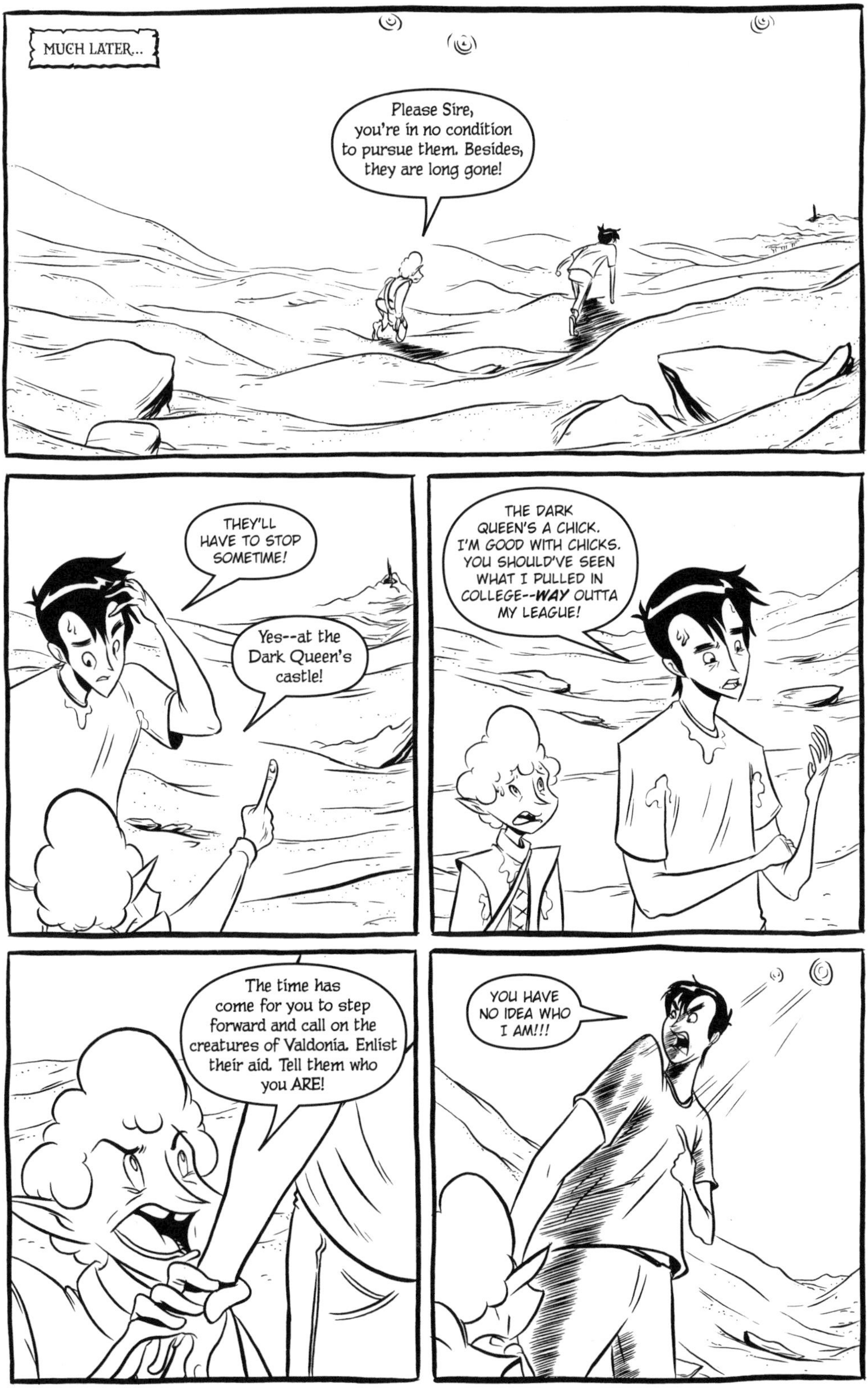
MUCH LATER...
Please Sire, you're in no condition to pursue them. Besides, they are long gone!
THEY'LL HAVE TO STOP SOMETIME!
Yes--at the Dark Queen's castle!
THE DARK QUEEN'S A CHICK. I'M GOOD WITH CHICKS. YOU SHOULD'VE SEEN WHAT I PULLED IN COLLEGE--*WAY* OUTTA MY LEAGUE!
The time has come for you to step forward and call on the creatures of Valdonia. Enlist their aid. Tell them who you ARE!
YOU HAVE NO IDEA WHO I AM!!!

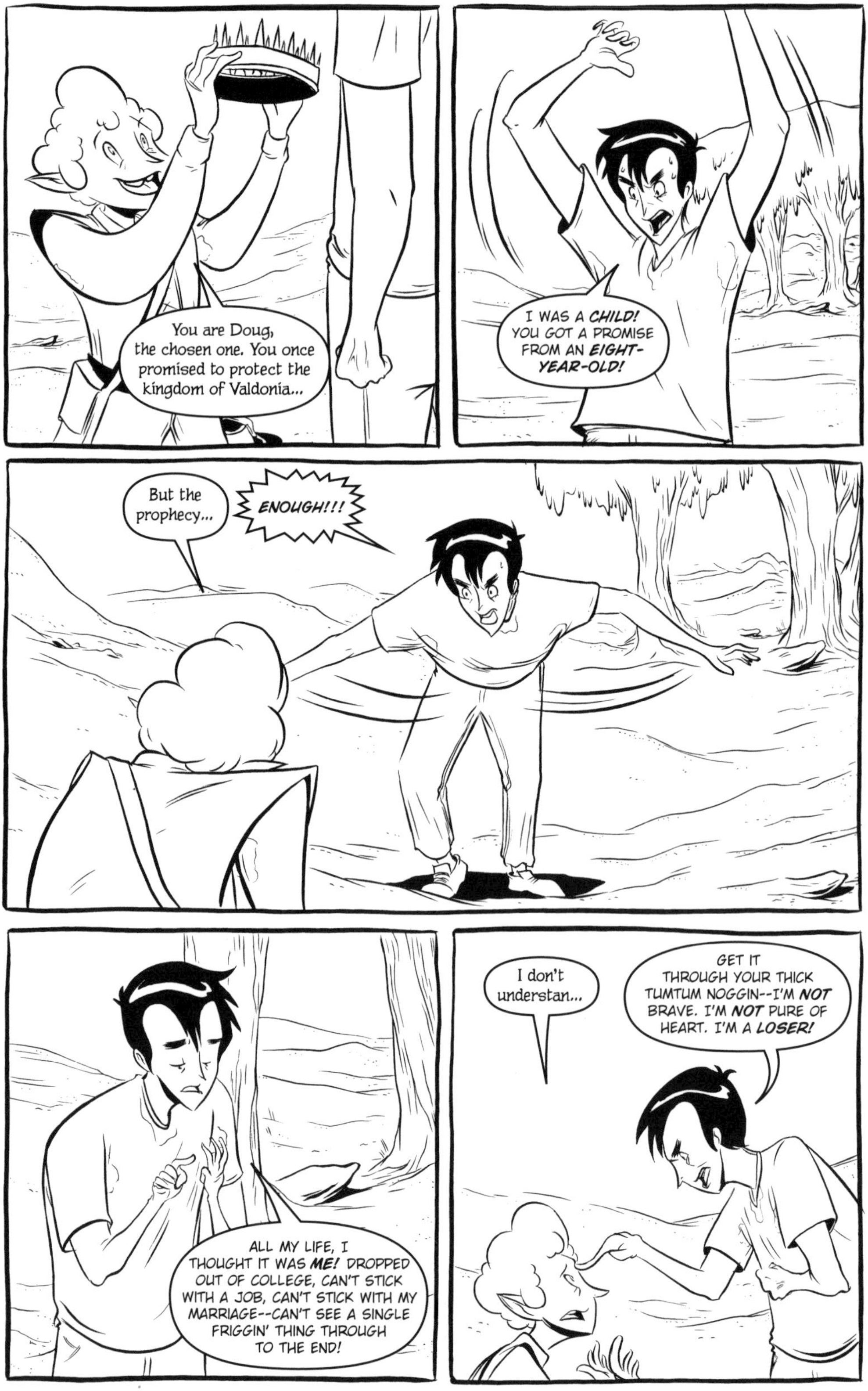
You are Doug, the chosen one. You once promised to protect the kingdom of Valdonia...
I WAS A CHILD! YOU GOT A PROMISE FROM AN EIGHT-YEAR-OLD!
But the prophecy...
ENOUGH!!!
ALL MY LIFE, I THOUGHT IT WAS ME! DROPPED OUT OF COLLEGE, CAN'T STICK WITH A JOB, CAN'T STICK WITH MY MARRIAGE--CAN'T SEE A SINGLE FRIGGIN' THING THROUGH TO THE END!
I don't understan...
GET IT THROUGH YOUR THICK TUMTUM NOGGIN--I'M NOT BRAVE. I'M NOT PURE OF HEART. I'M A LOSER!

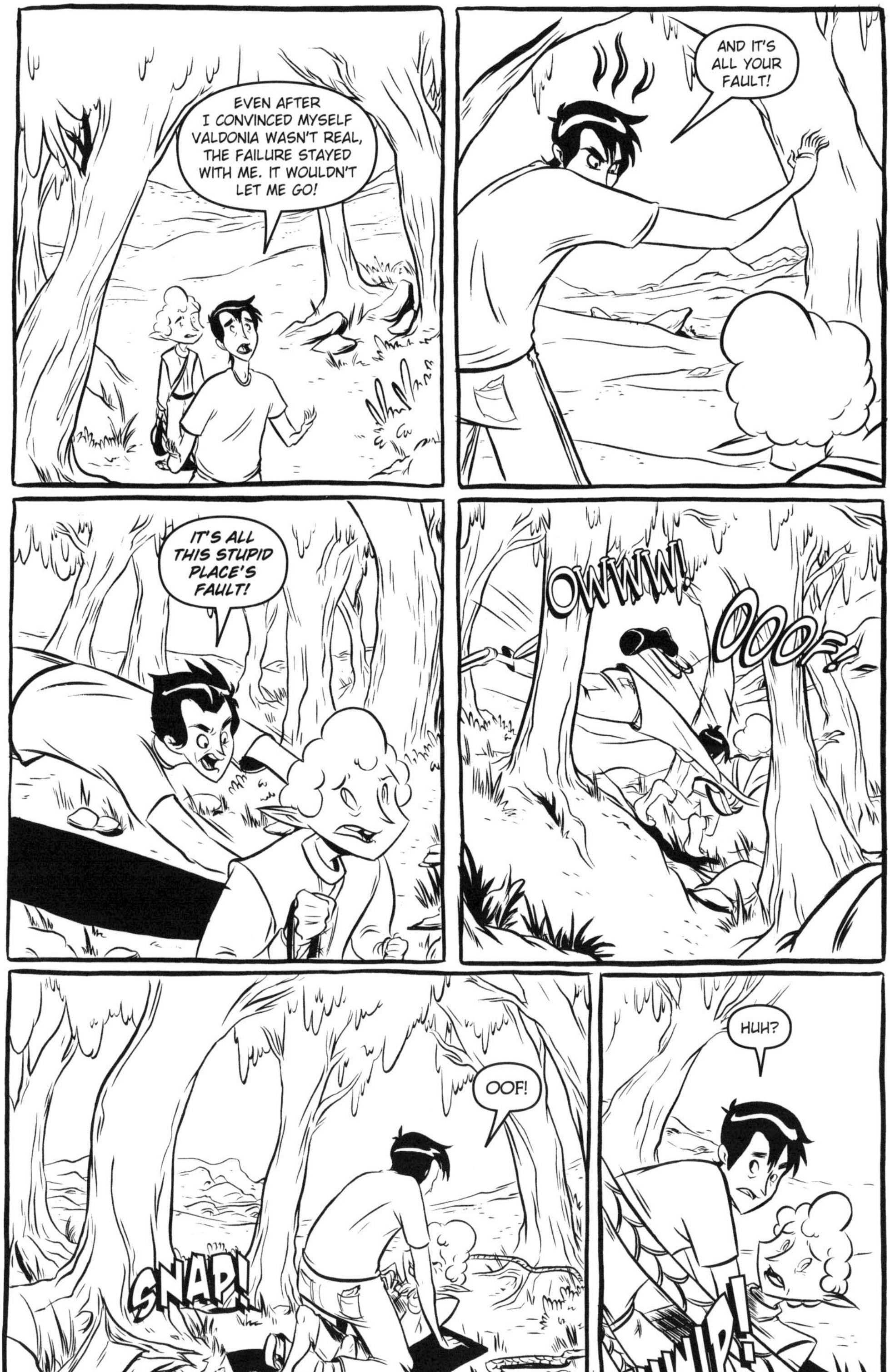
EVEN AFTER I CONVINCED MYSELF VALDONIA WASN'T REAL, THE FAILURE STAYED WITH ME. IT WOULDN'T LET ME GO!
AND IT'S ALL YOUR FAULT!
IT'S ALL THIS STUPID PLACE'S FAULT!
OWWW!
OOOF!
SNAP!
OOF!
HUH?
THWIP!

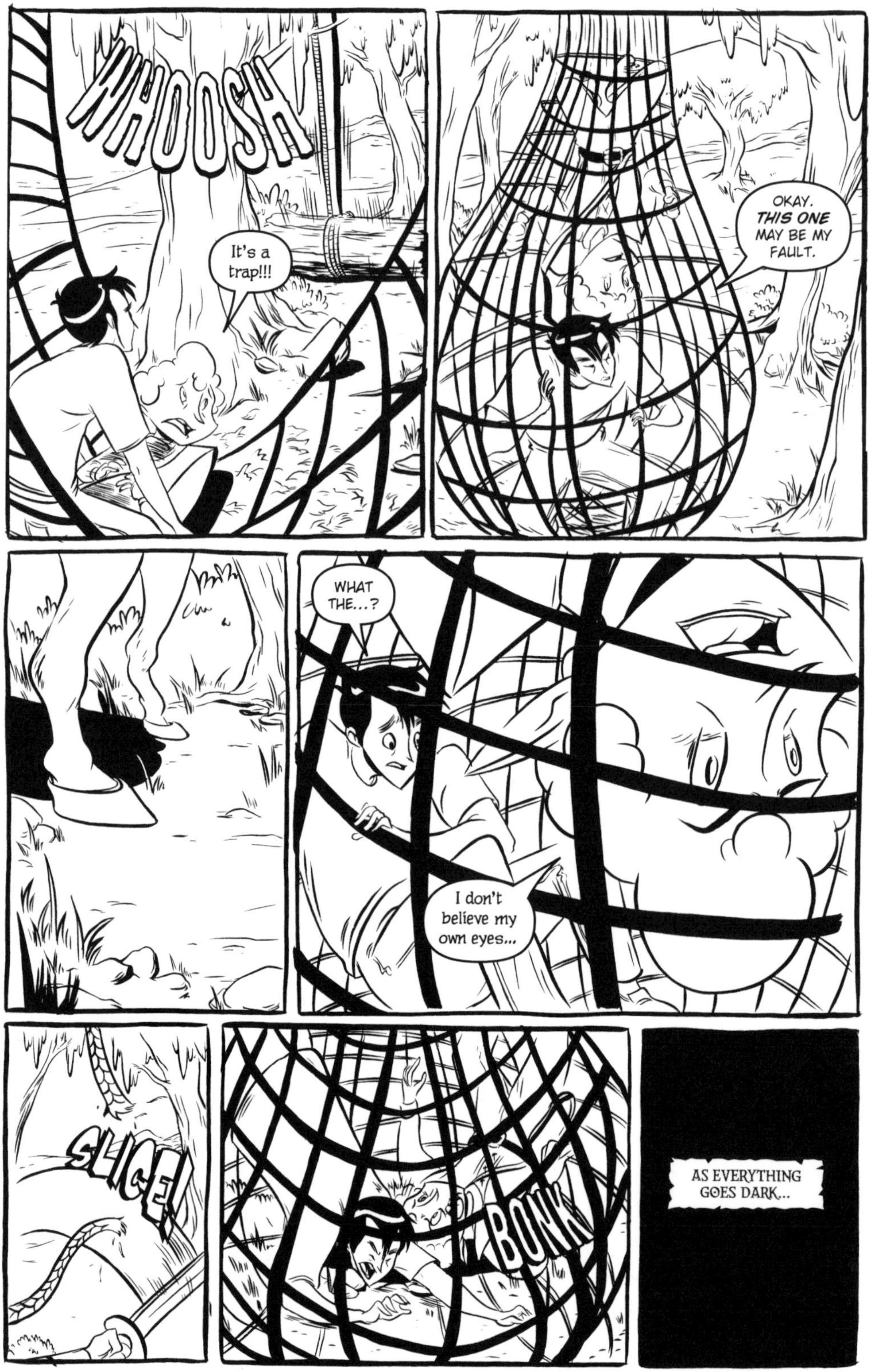
WHOOSH
It's a trap!!!
OKAY. THIS ONE MAY BE MY FAULT.
WHAT THE...?
I don't believe my own eyes...
SLICE!
BONK
AS EVERYTHING GOES DARK...

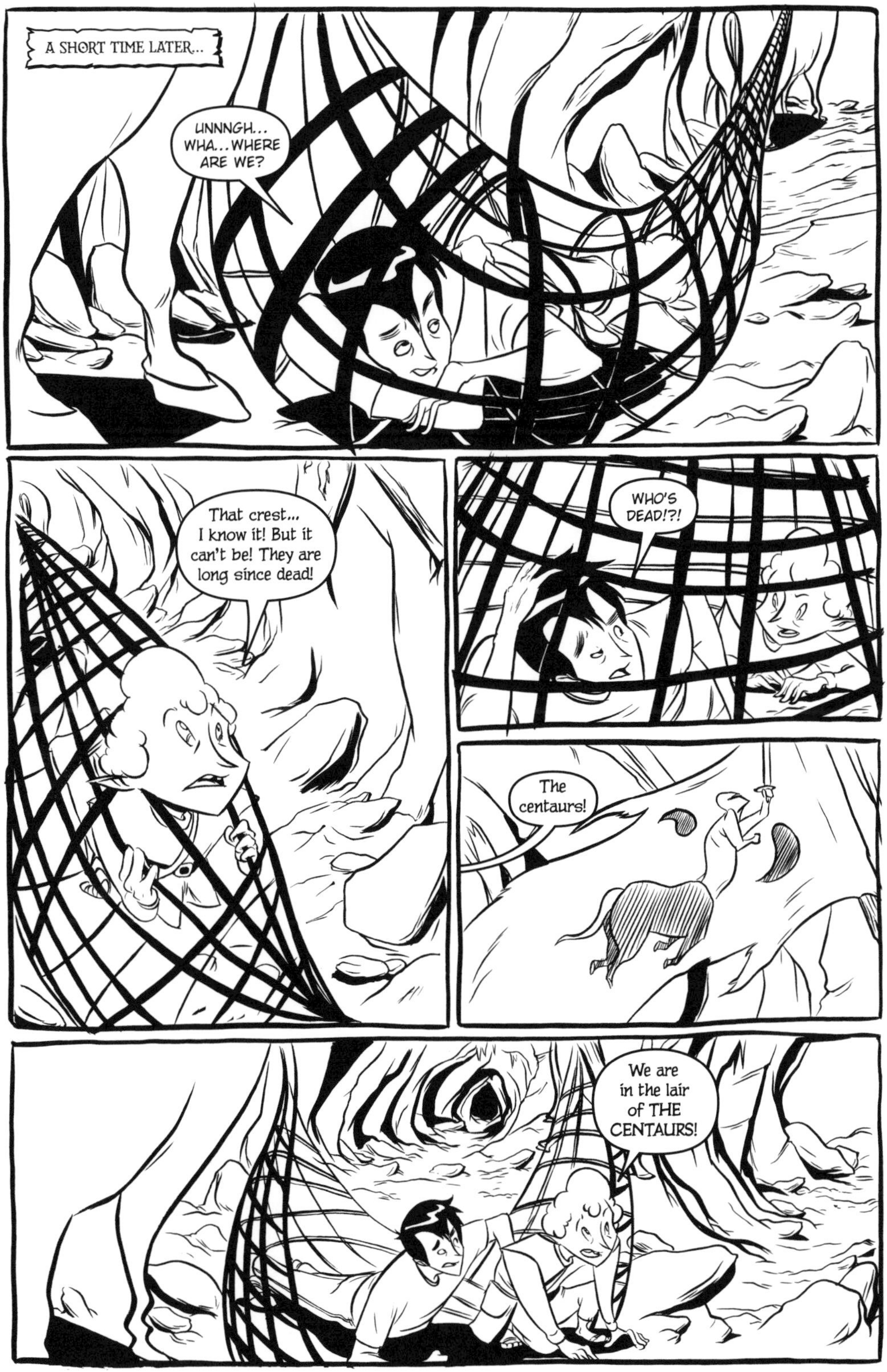
A SHORT TIME LATER...
UNNNGH... WHA...WHERE ARE WE?
That crest... I know it! But it can't be! They are long since dead!
WHO'S DEAD!?!
The centaurs!
We are in the lair of THE CENTAURS!

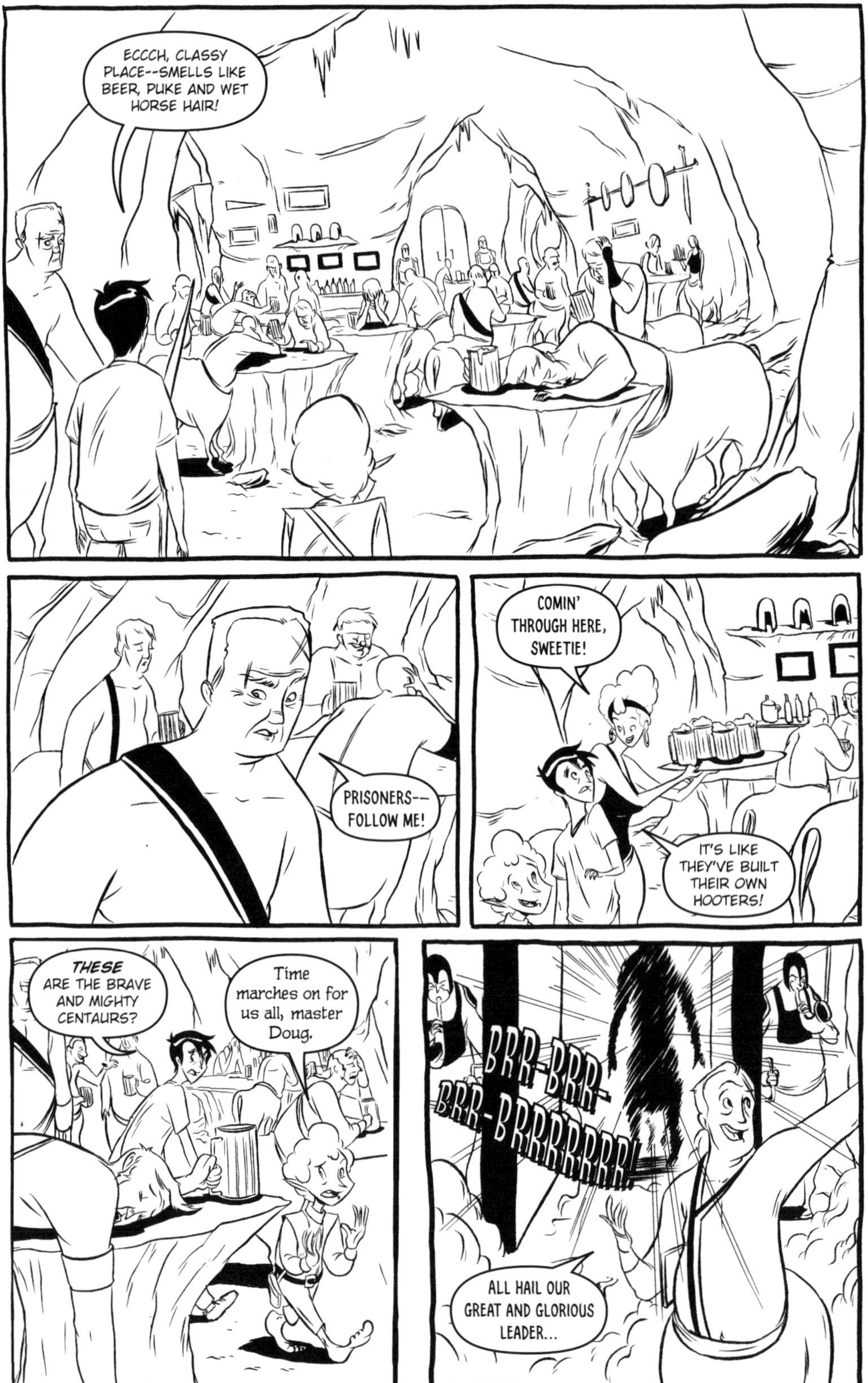
ECCCH, CLASSY PLACE--SMELLS LIKE BEER, PUKE AND WET HORSE HAIR!
PRISONERS-- FOLLOW ME!
COMIN' THROUGH HERE, SWEETIE!
IT'S LIKE THEY'VE BUILT THEIR OWN HOOTERS!
THESE ARE THE BRAVE AND MIGHTY CENTAURS?
Time marches on for us all, master Doug.
BRR-BRR BRR-BRRRRRRRR!
ALL HAIL OUR GREAT AND GLORIOUS LEADER...

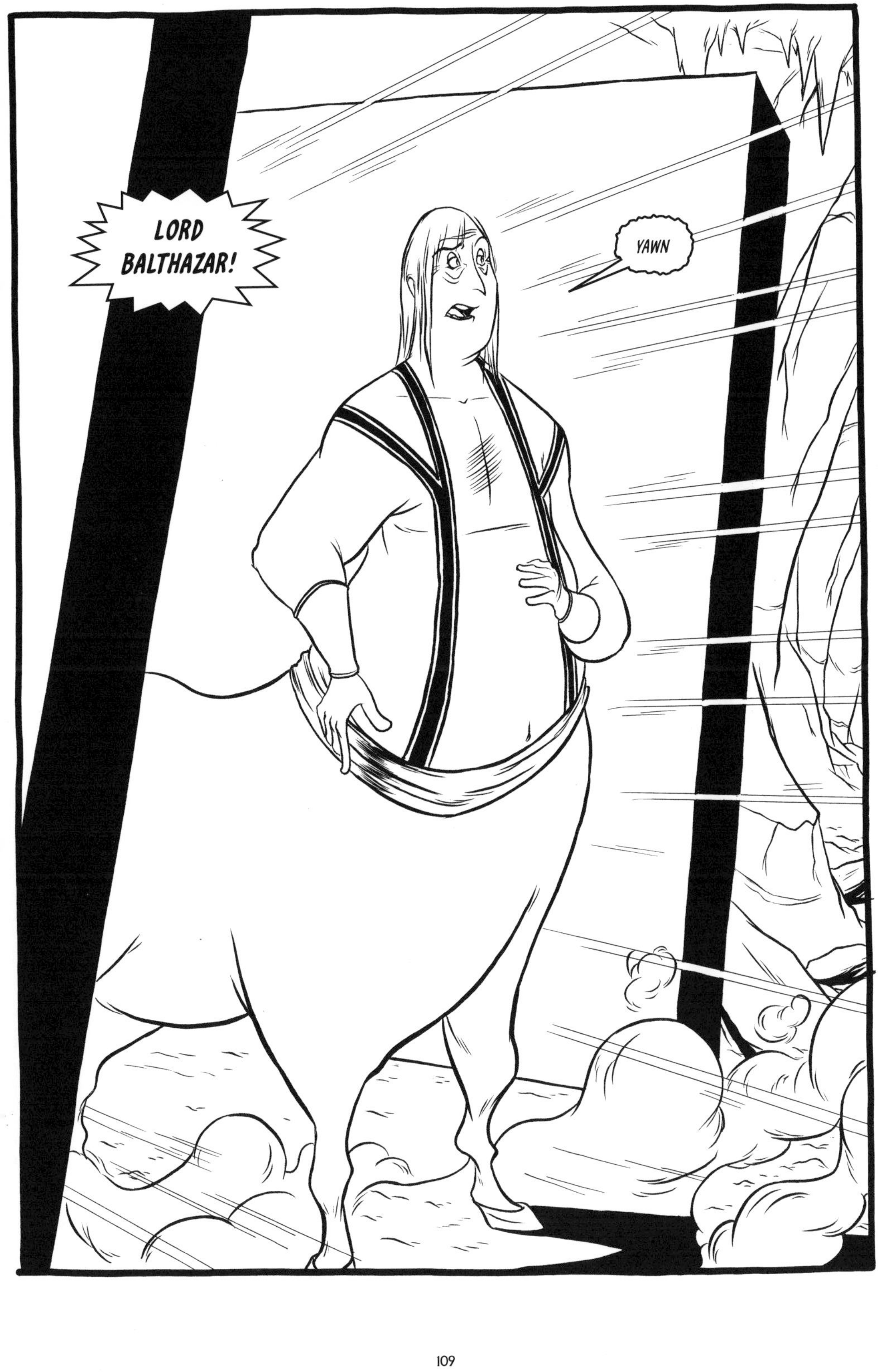
LORD BALTHAZAR!
YAWN

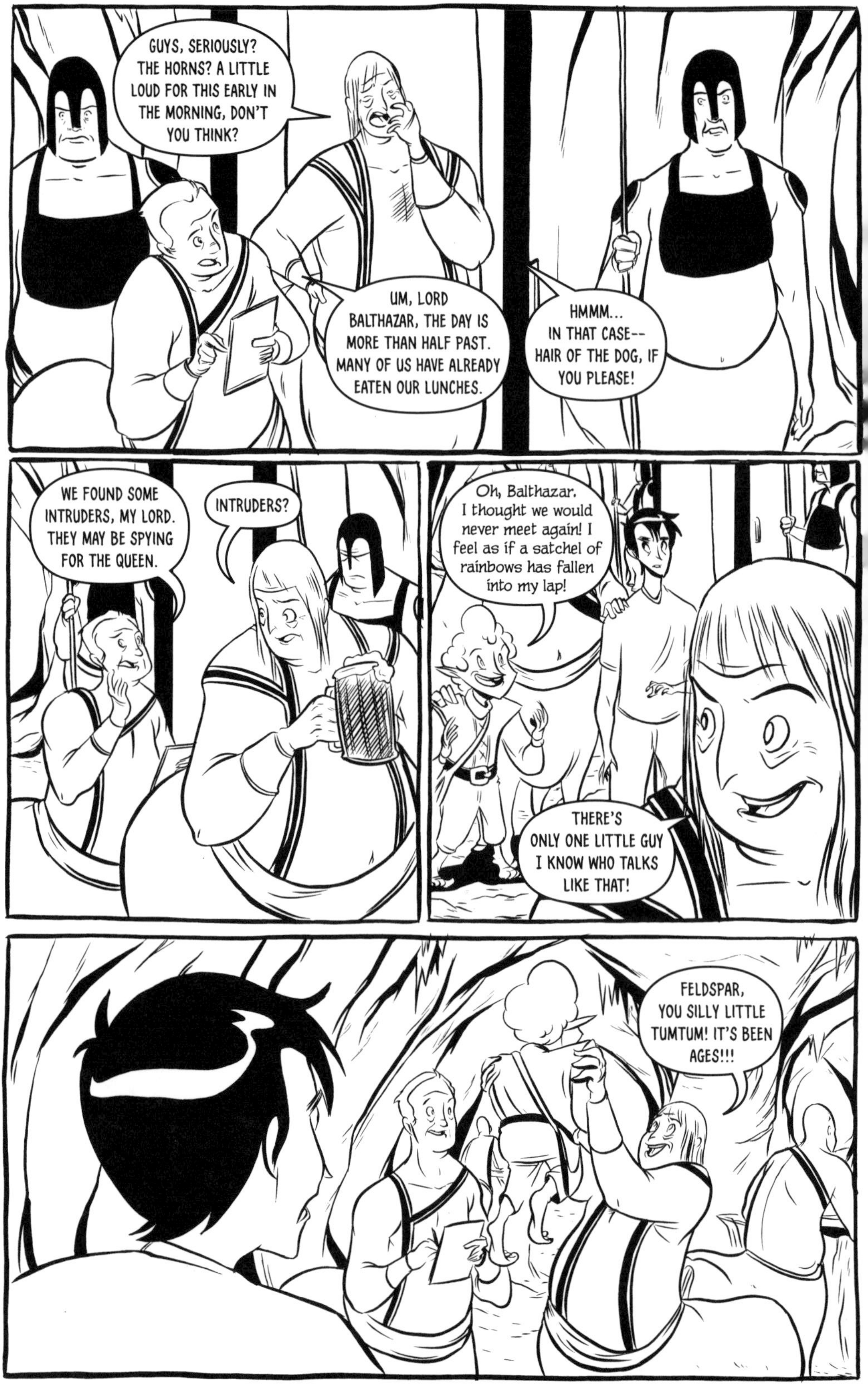
GUYS, SERIOUSLY? THE HORNS? A LITTLE LOUD FOR THIS EARLY IN THE MORNING, DON'T YOU THINK?
UM, LORD BALTHAZAR, THE DAY IS MORE THAN HALF PAST. MANY OF US HAVE ALREADY EATEN OUR LUNCHES.
HMMM... IN THAT CASE-- HAIR OF THE DOG, IF YOU PLEASE!
WE FOUND SOME INTRUDERS, MY LORD. THEY MAY BE SPYING FOR THE QUEEN.
INTRUDERS?
Oh, Balthazar. I thought we would never meet again! I feel as if a satchel of rainbows has fallen into my lap!
THERE'S ONLY ONE LITTLE GUY I KNOW WHO TALKS LIKE THAT!
FELDSPAR, YOU SILLY LITTLE TUMTUM! IT'S BEEN AGES!!!

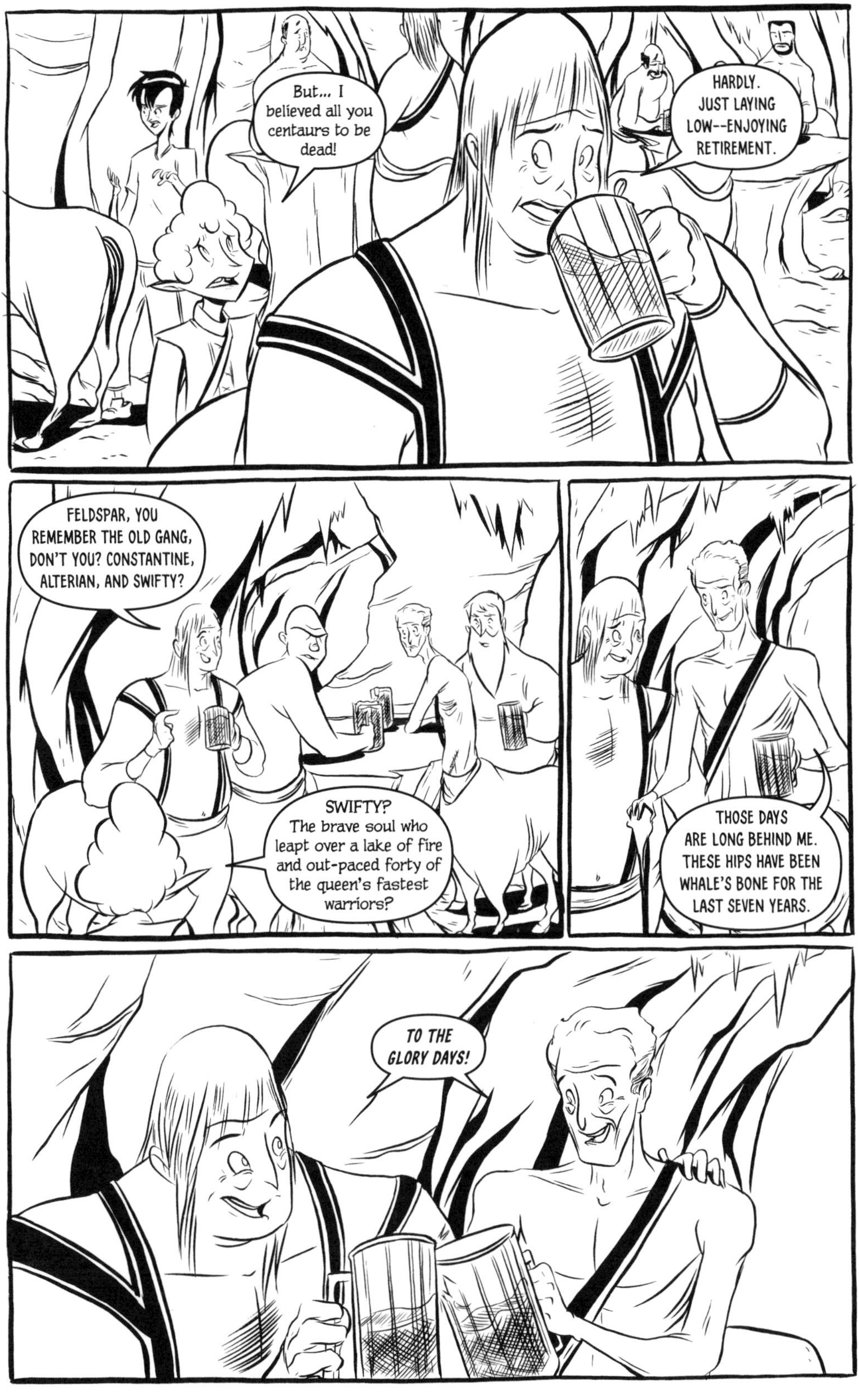
But... I believed all you centaurs to be dead!
HARDLY. JUST LAYING LOW--ENJOYING RETIREMENT.
FELDSPAR, YOU REMEMBER THE OLD GANG, DON'T YOU? CONSTANTINE, ALTERIAN, AND SWIFTY?
SWIFTY? The brave soul who leapt over a lake of fire and out-paced forty of the queen's fastest warriors?
THOSE DAYS ARE LONG BEHIND ME. THESE HIPS HAVE BEEN WHALE'S BONE FOR THE LAST SEVEN YEARS.
TO THE GLORY DAYS!

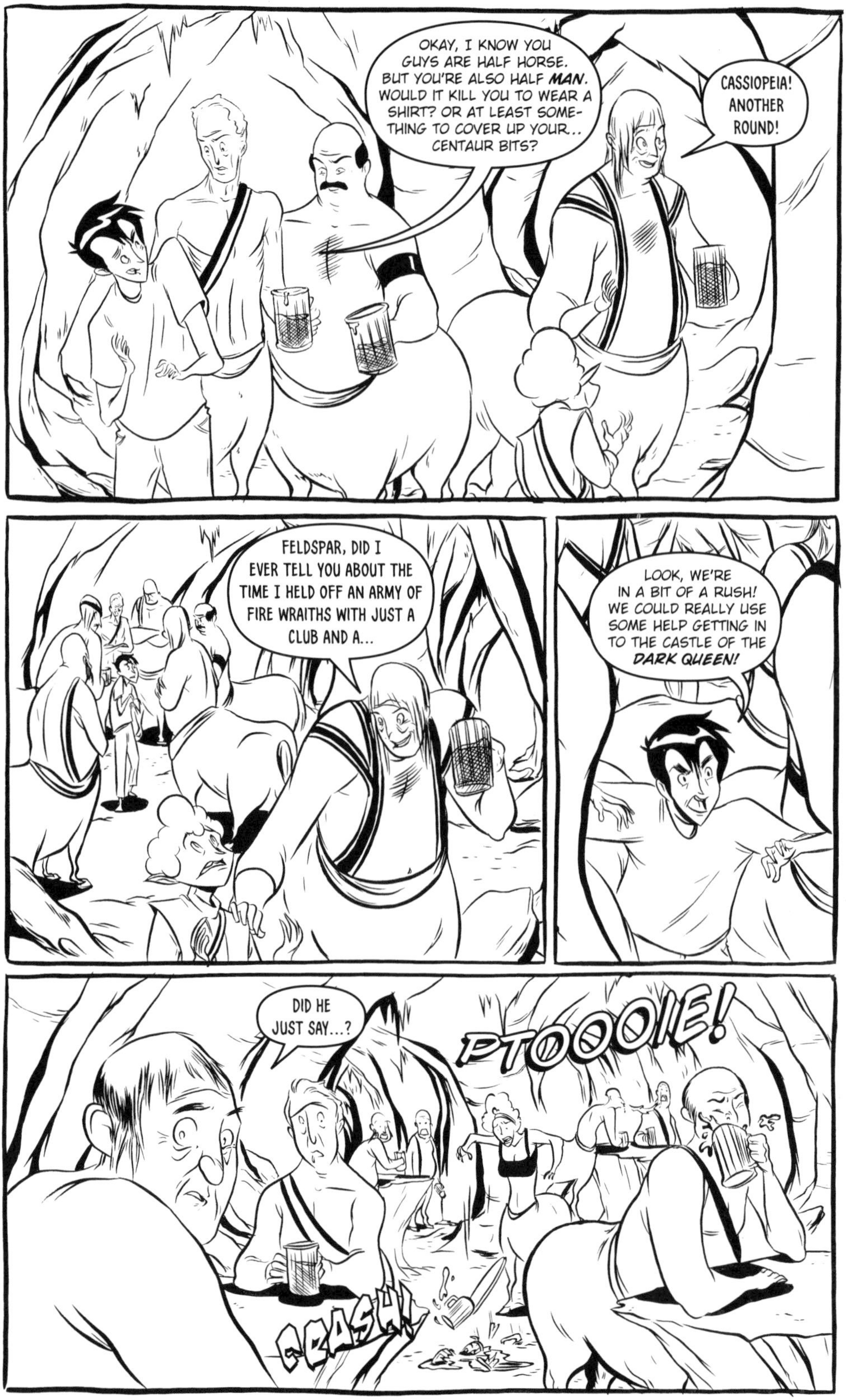
OKAY, I KNOW YOU GUYS ARE HALF HORSE. BUT YOU'RE ALSO HALF **MAN**. WOULD IT KILL YOU TO WEAR A SHIRT? OR AT LEAST SOME-THING TO COVER UP YOUR.. CENTAUR BITS?
CASSIOPEIA! ANOTHER ROUND!
FELDSPAR, DID I EVER TELL YOU ABOUT THE TIME I HELD OFF AN ARMY OF FIRE WRAITHS WITH JUST A CLUB AND A...
LOOK, WE'RE IN A BIT OF A RUSH! WE COULD REALLY USE SOME HELP GETTING IN TO THE CASTLE OF THE **DARK QUEEN!**
DID HE JUST SAY...?
PTOOOOIE!
CRASH!

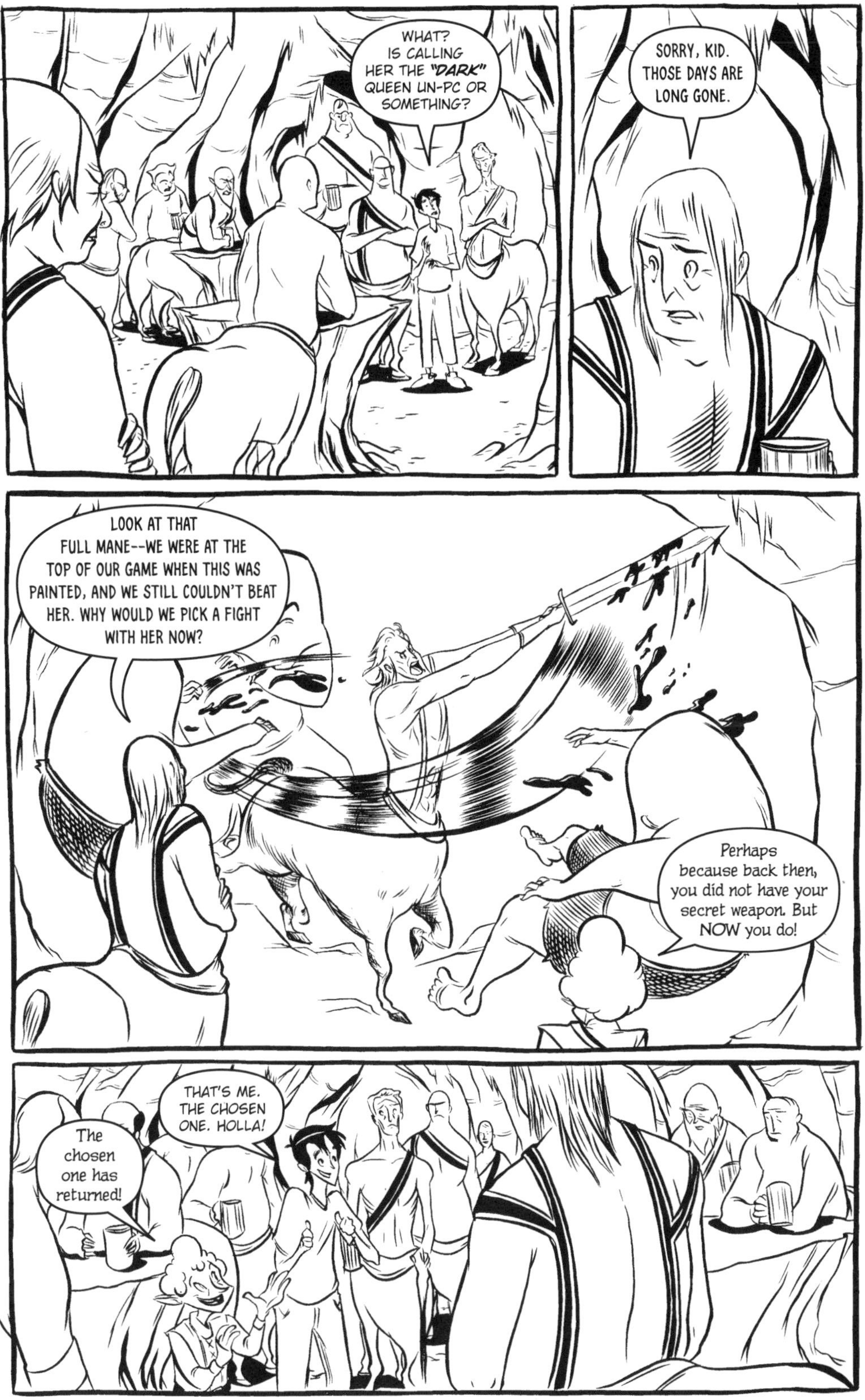
WHAT? IS CALLING HER THE "DARK" QUEEN UN-PC OR SOMETHING?
SORRY, KID. THOSE DAYS ARE LONG GONE.
LOOK AT THAT FULL MANE--WE WERE AT THE TOP OF OUR GAME WHEN THIS WAS PAINTED, AND WE STILL COULDN'T BEAT HER. WHY WOULD WE PICK A FIGHT WITH HER NOW?
Perhaps because back then, you did not have your secret weapon. But NOW you do!
The chosen one has returned!
THAT'S ME. THE CHOSEN ONE. HOLLA!

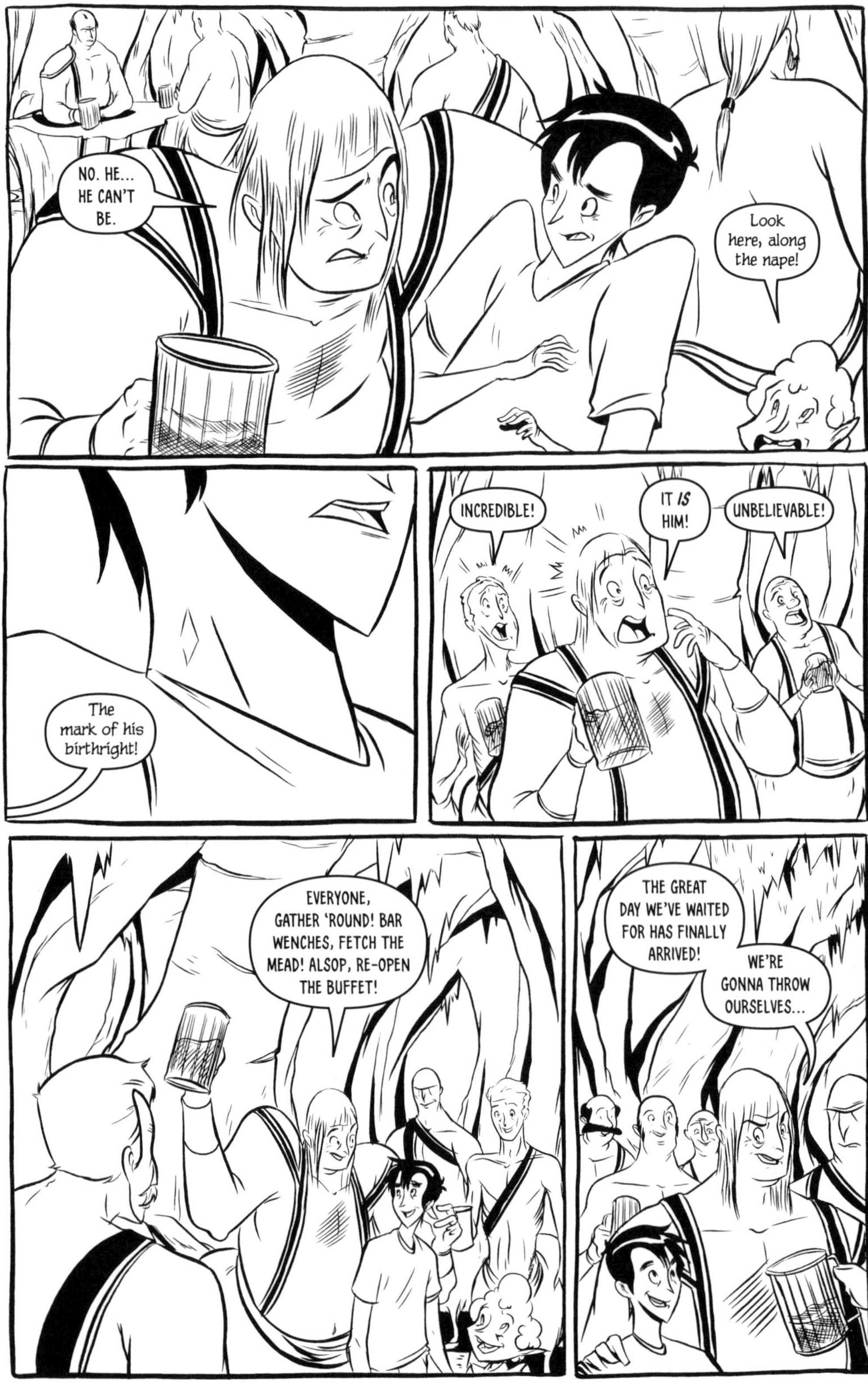
NO. HE... HE CAN'T BE.
Look here, along the nape!
The mark of his birthright!
INCREDIBLE!
IT IS HIM!
UNBELIEVABLE!
EVERYONE, GATHER 'ROUND! BAR WENCHES, FETCH THE MEAD! ALSOP, RE-OPEN THE BUFFET!
THE GREAT DAY WE'VE WAITED FOR HAS FINALLY ARRIVED!
WE'RE GONNA THROW OURSELVES...

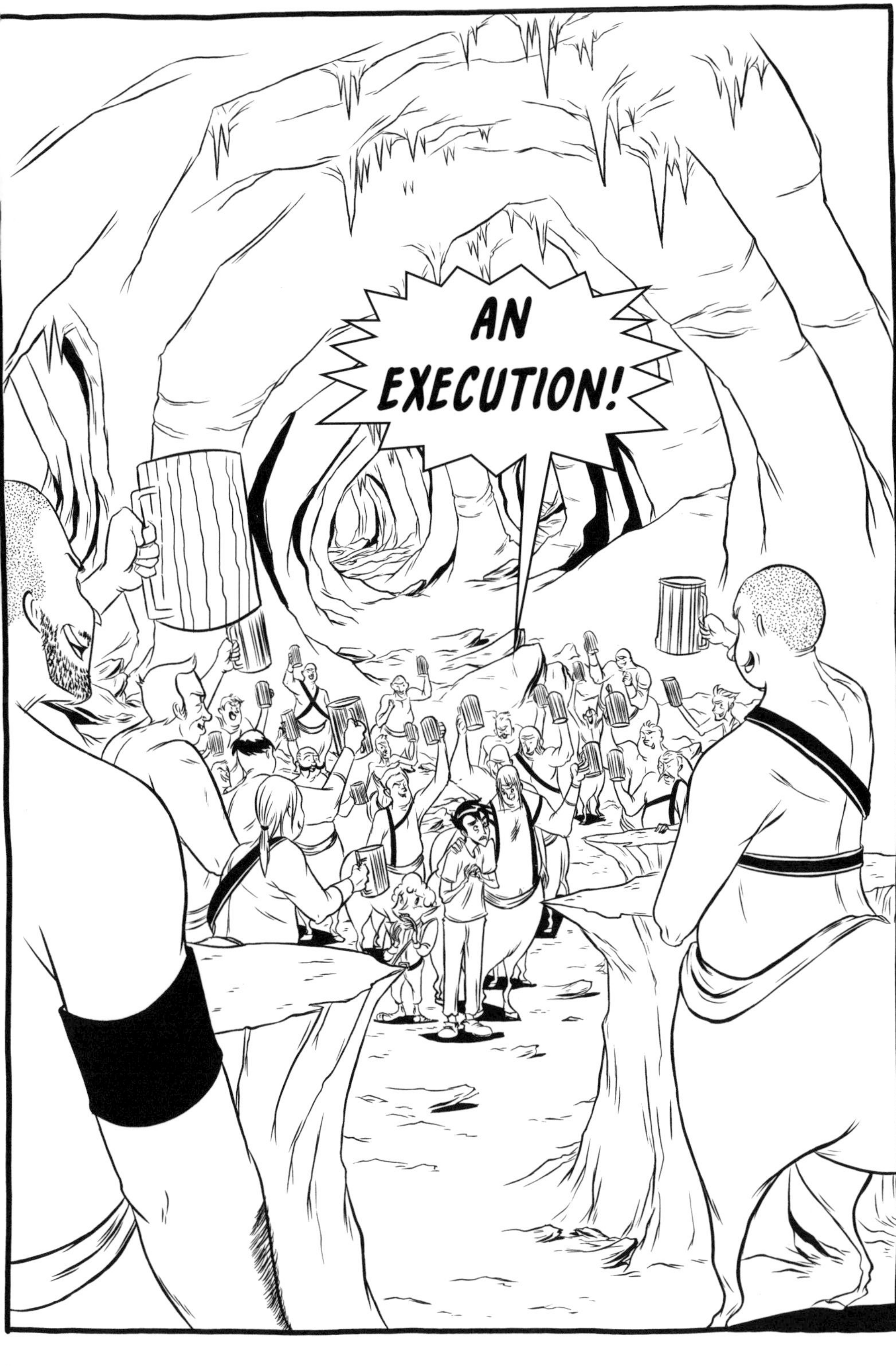
AN EXECUTION!

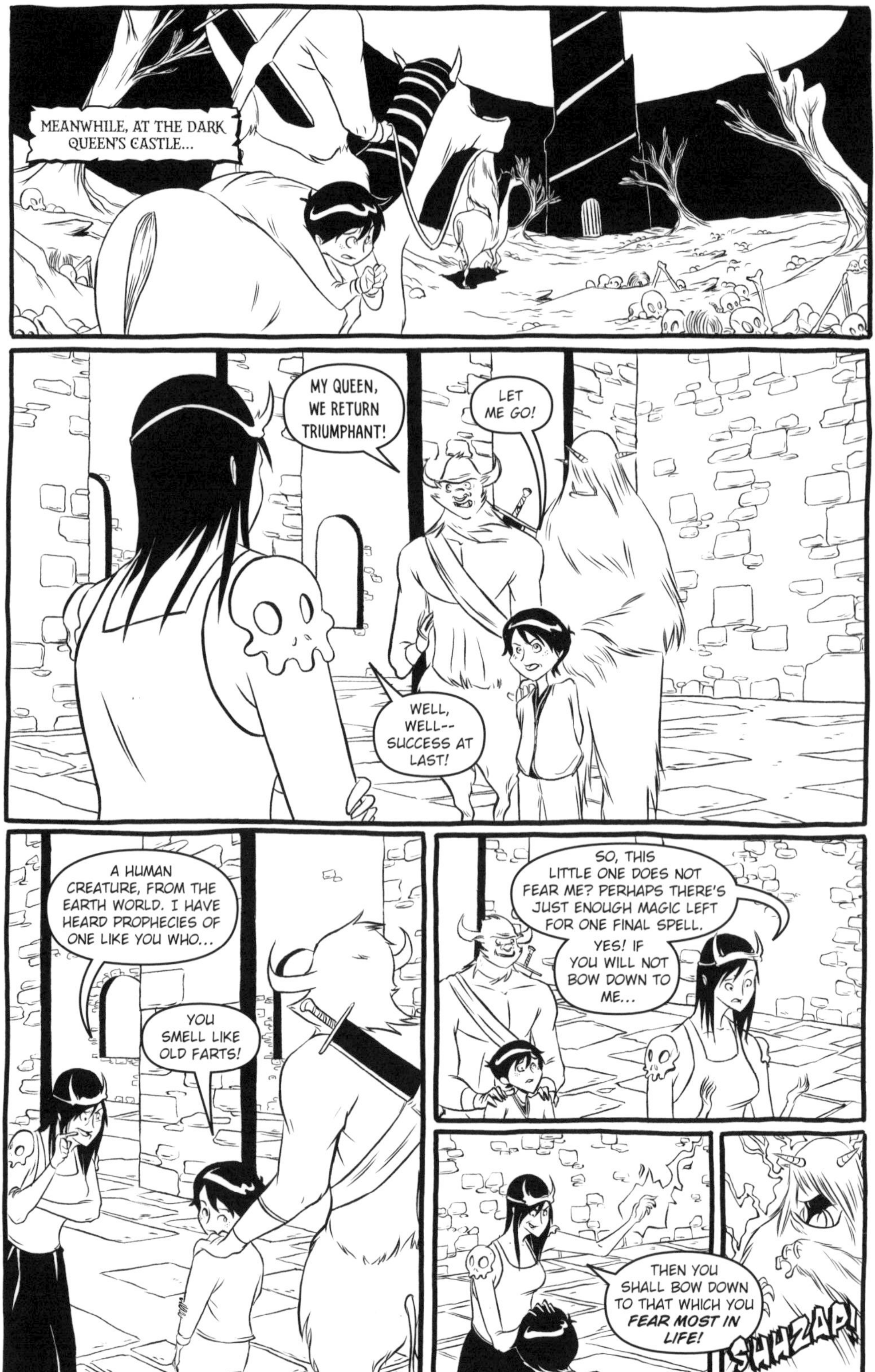
MEANWHILE, AT THE DARK QUEEN'S CASTLE...
MY QUEEN, WE RETURN TRIUMPHANT!
LET ME GO!
WELL, WELL-- SUCCESS AT LAST!
A HUMAN CREATURE, FROM THE EARTH WORLD. I HAVE HEARD PROPHECIES OF ONE LIKE YOU WHO...
YOU SMELL LIKE OLD FARTS!
SO, THIS LITTLE ONE DOES NOT FEAR ME? PERHAPS THERE'S JUST ENOUGH MAGIC LEFT FOR ONE FINAL SPELL.
YES! IF YOU WILL NOT BOW DOWN TO ME...
THEN YOU SHALL BOW DOWN TO THAT WHICH YOU ***FEAR MOST IN LIFE!***
SHHZAP!

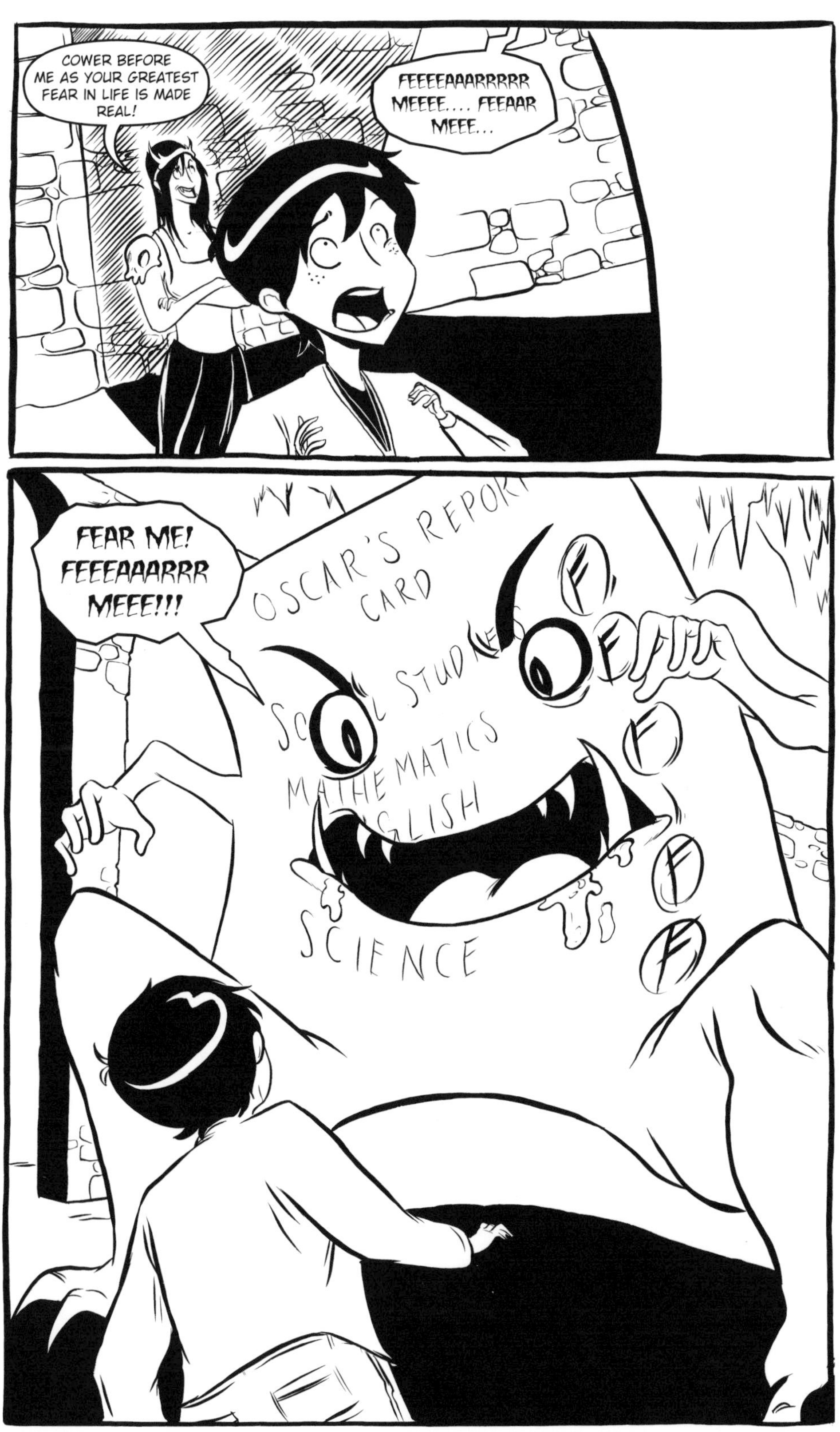
COWER BEFORE ME AS YOUR GREATEST FEAR IN LIFE IS MADE REAL!
FEEEEAAARRRRR MEEEE.... FEEAAR MEEE...
FEAR ME! FEEEAAARRR MEEE!!!
CARD
MATHEMATICS
SCIENCE

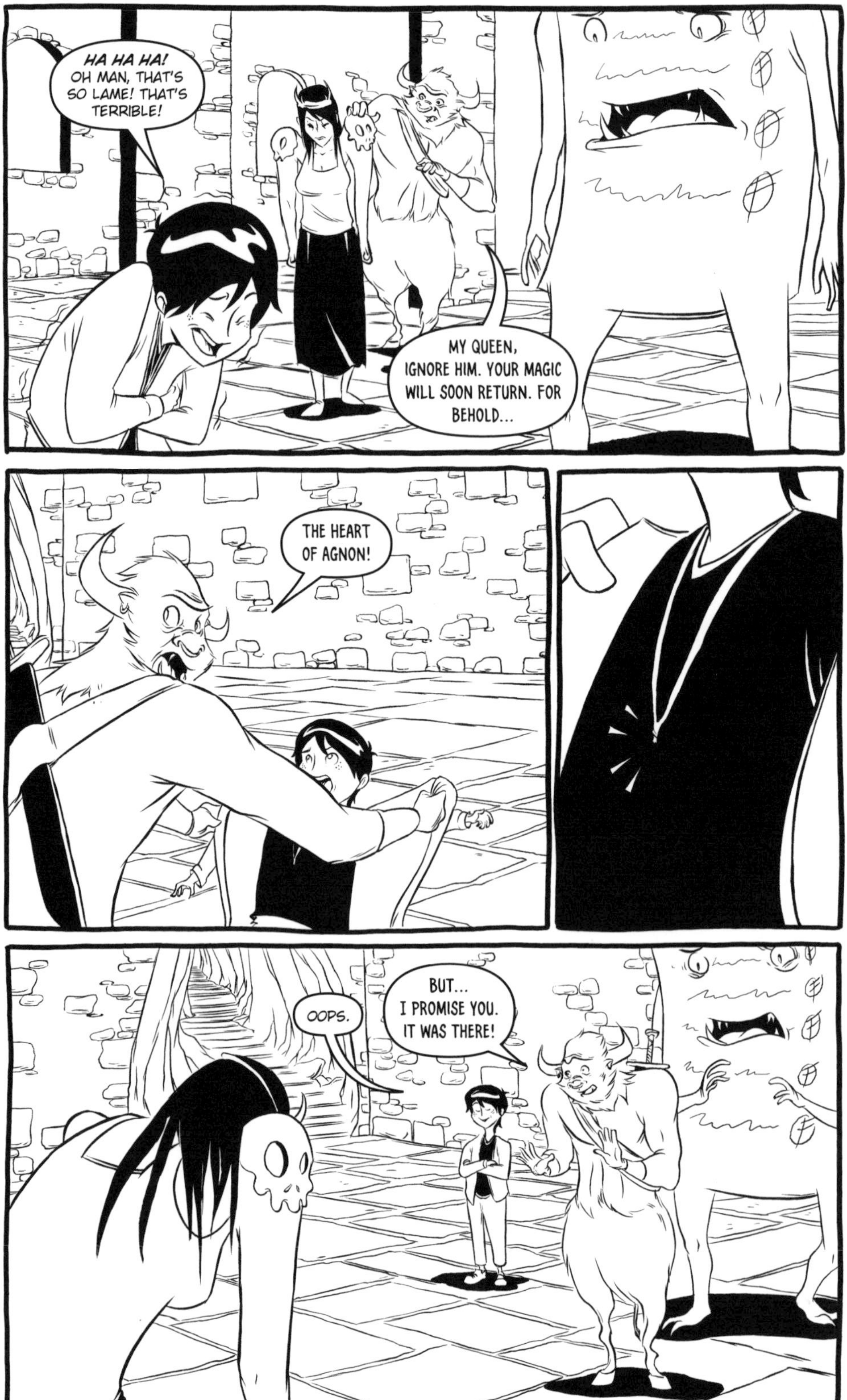
HA HA HA!
OH MAN, THAT'S SO LAME! THAT'S TERRIBLE!
MY QUEEN, IGNORE HIM. YOUR MAGIC WILL SOON RETURN. FOR BEHOLD...
THE HEART OF AGNON!
OOPS.
BUT... I PROMISE YOU. IT WAS THERE!

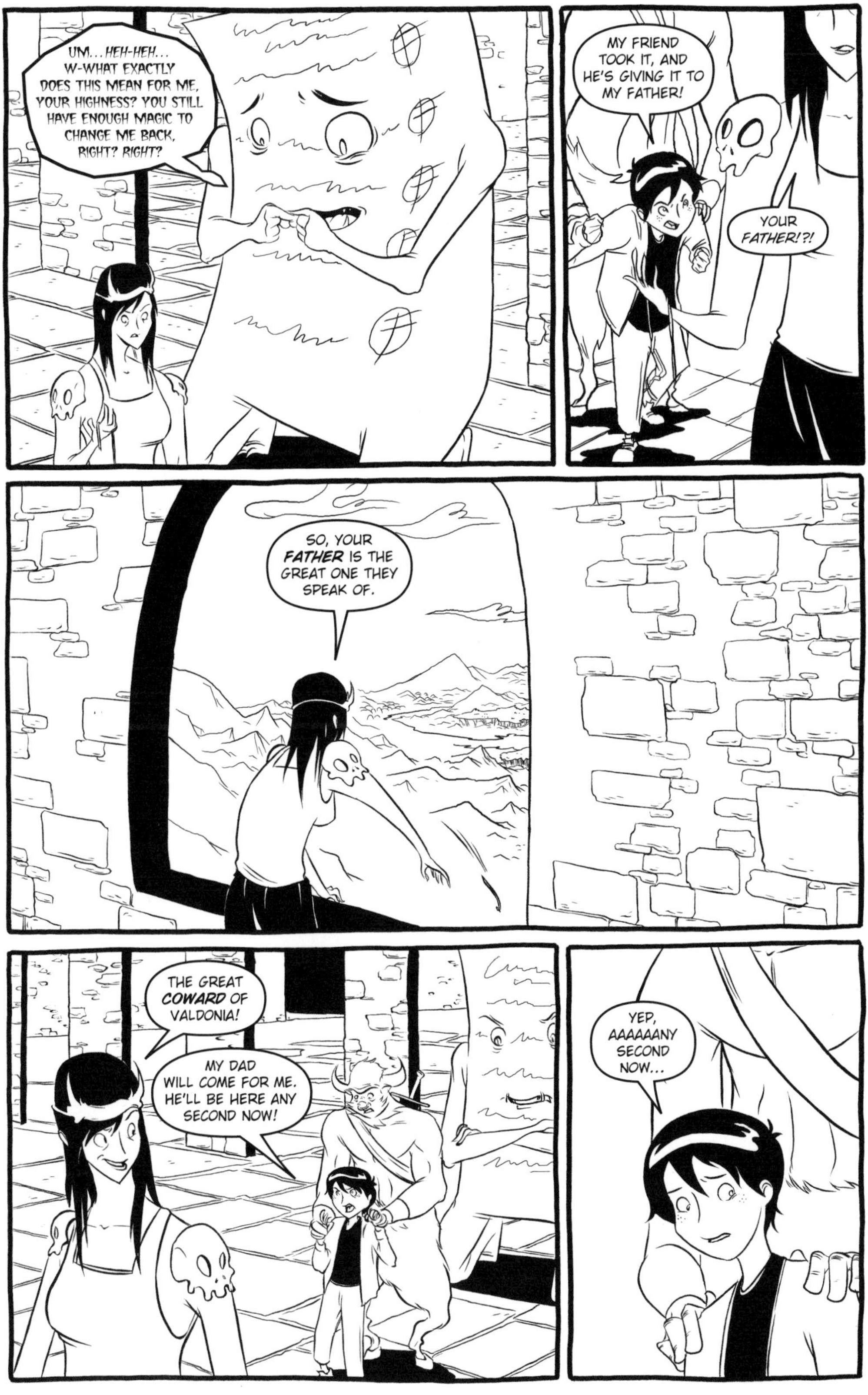
UM... HEH-HEH... W-WHAT EXACTLY DOES THIS MEAN FOR ME, YOUR HIGHNESS? YOU STILL HAVE ENOUGH MAGIC TO CHANGE ME BACK, RIGHT? RIGHT?
MY FRIEND TOOK IT, AND HE'S GIVING IT TO MY FATHER!
YOUR FATHER!?!
SO, YOUR FATHER IS THE GREAT ONE THEY SPEAK OF.
THE GREAT COWARD OF VALDONIA!
MY DAD WILL COME FOR ME. HE'LL BE HERE ANY SECOND NOW!
YEP, AAAAAANY SECOND NOW...

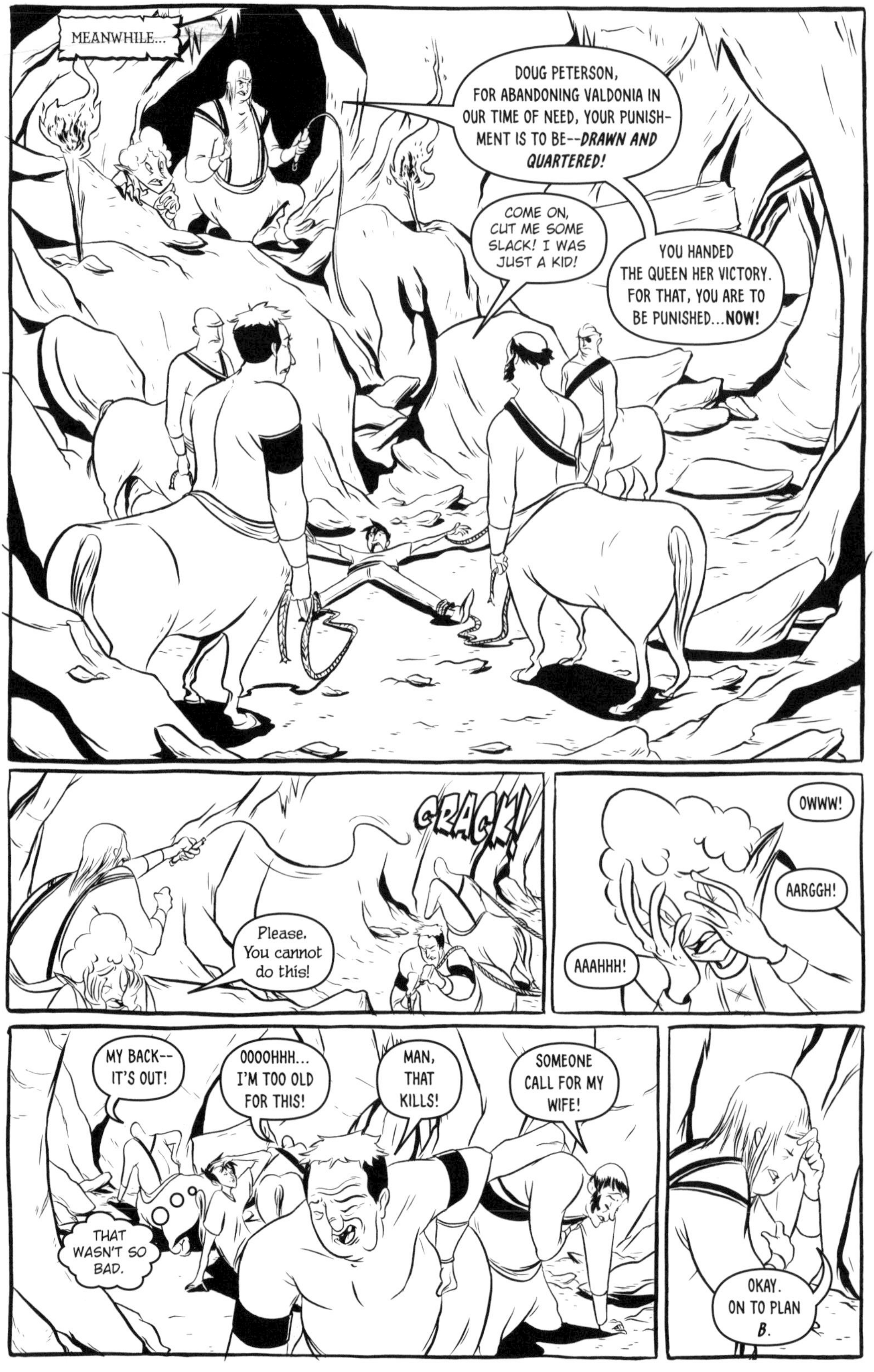
MEANWHILE...
DOUG PETERSON, FOR ABANDONING VALDONIA IN OUR TIME OF NEED, YOUR PUNISHMENT IS TO BE--*DRAWN AND QUARTERED!*
COME ON, CUT ME SOME SLACK! I WAS JUST A KID!
YOU HANDED THE QUEEN HER VICTORY. FOR THAT, YOU ARE TO BE PUNISHED...**NOW!**
CRACK!
Please. You cannot do this!
OWWW!
AARGGH!
AAAHHH!
MY BACK-- IT'S OUT!
THAT WASN'T SO BAD.
OOOOHHH... I'M TOO OLD FOR THIS!
MAN, THAT KILLS!
SOMEONE CALL FOR MY WIFE!
OKAY. ON TO PLAN *B*.

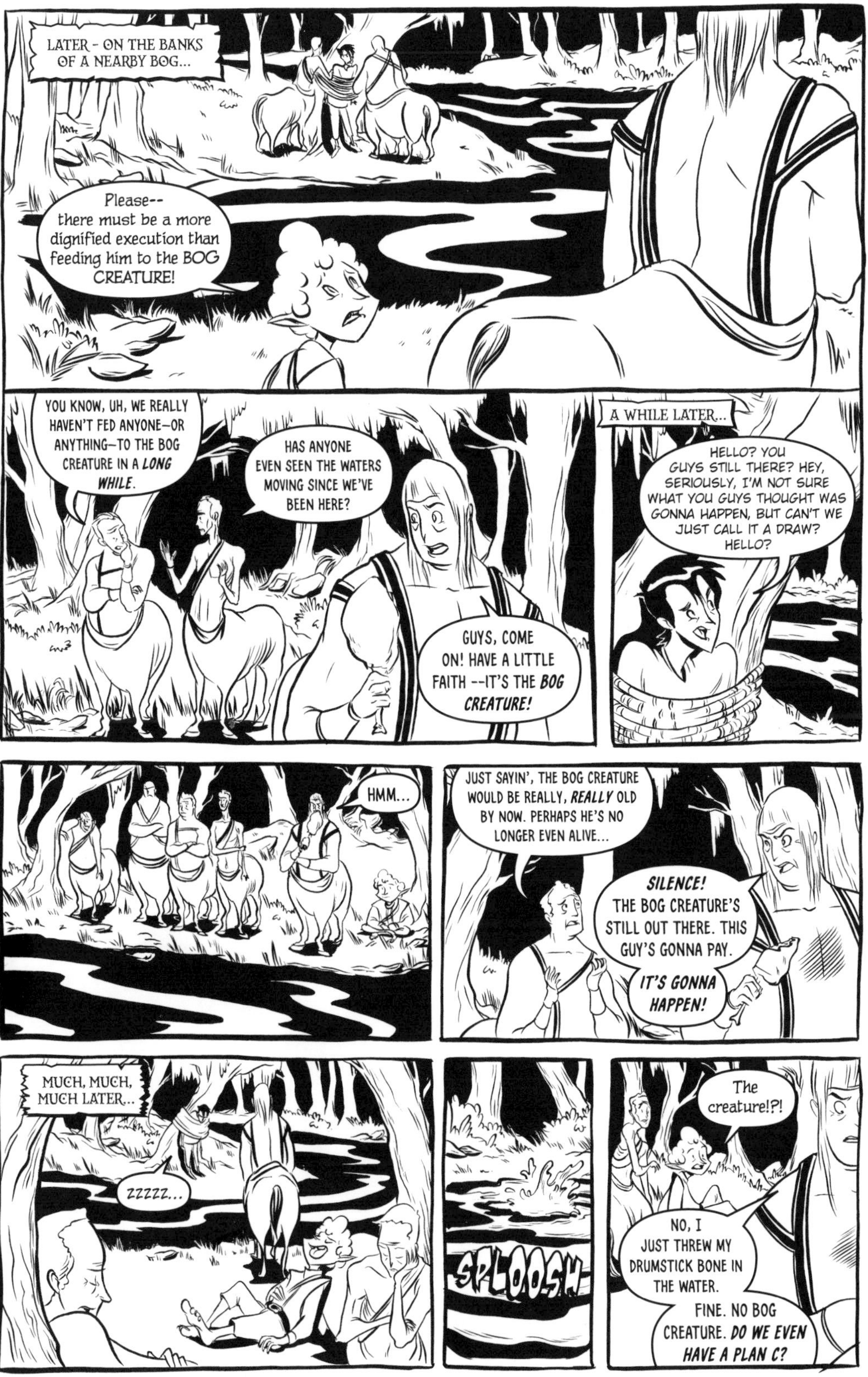
LATER - ON THE BANKS OF A NEARBY BOG...
Please-- there must be a more dignified execution than feeding him to the BOG CREATURE!
YOU KNOW, UH, WE REALLY HAVEN'T FED ANYONE—OR ANYTHING—TO THE BOG CREATURE IN A LONG WHILE.
HAS ANYONE EVEN SEEN THE WATERS MOVING SINCE WE'VE BEEN HERE?
GUYS, COME ON! HAVE A LITTLE FAITH --IT'S THE BOG CREATURE!
A WHILE LATER...
HELLO? YOU GUYS STILL THERE? HEY, SERIOUSLY, I'M NOT SURE WHAT YOU GUYS THOUGHT WAS GONNA HAPPEN, BUT CAN'T WE JUST CALL IT A DRAW? HELLO?
HMM...
JUST SAYIN', THE BOG CREATURE WOULD BE REALLY, REALLY OLD BY NOW. PERHAPS HE'S NO LONGER EVEN ALIVE...
SILENCE! THE BOG CREATURE'S STILL OUT THERE. THIS GUY'S GONNA PAY.
IT'S GONNA HAPPEN!
MUCH, MUCH, MUCH LATER...
ZZZZZ...
SPLOOSH
The creature!?!
NO, I JUST THREW MY DRUMSTICK BONE IN THE WATER.
FINE. NO BOG CREATURE. DO WE EVEN HAVE A PLAN C?

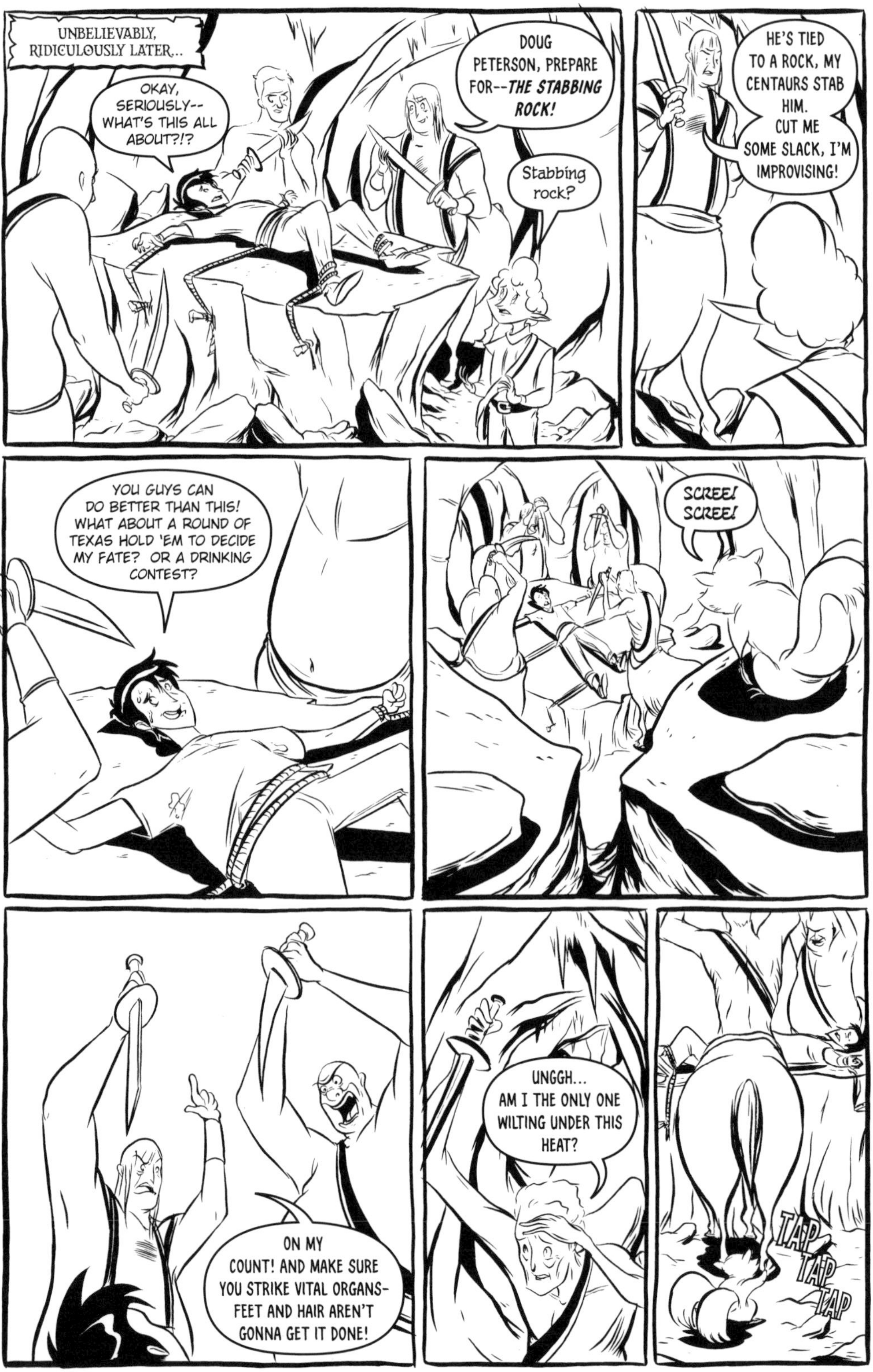
UNBELIEVABLY, RIDICULOUSLY LATER...
OKAY, SERIOUSLY-- WHAT'S THIS ALL ABOUT?!?
DOUG PETERSON, PREPARE FOR--THE STABBING ROCK!
Stabbing rock?
HE'S TIED TO A ROCK, MY CENTAURS STAB HIM.
CUT ME SOME SLACK, I'M IMPROVISING!
YOU GUYS CAN DO BETTER THAN THIS! WHAT ABOUT A ROUND OF TEXAS HOLD 'EM TO DECIDE MY FATE? OR A DRINKING CONTEST?
SCREE! SCREE!
ON MY COUNT! AND MAKE SURE YOU STRIKE VITAL ORGANS- FEET AND HAIR AREN'T GONNA GET IT DONE!
UNGGH... AM I THE ONLY ONE WILTING UNDER THIS HEAT?
TAP TAP TAP

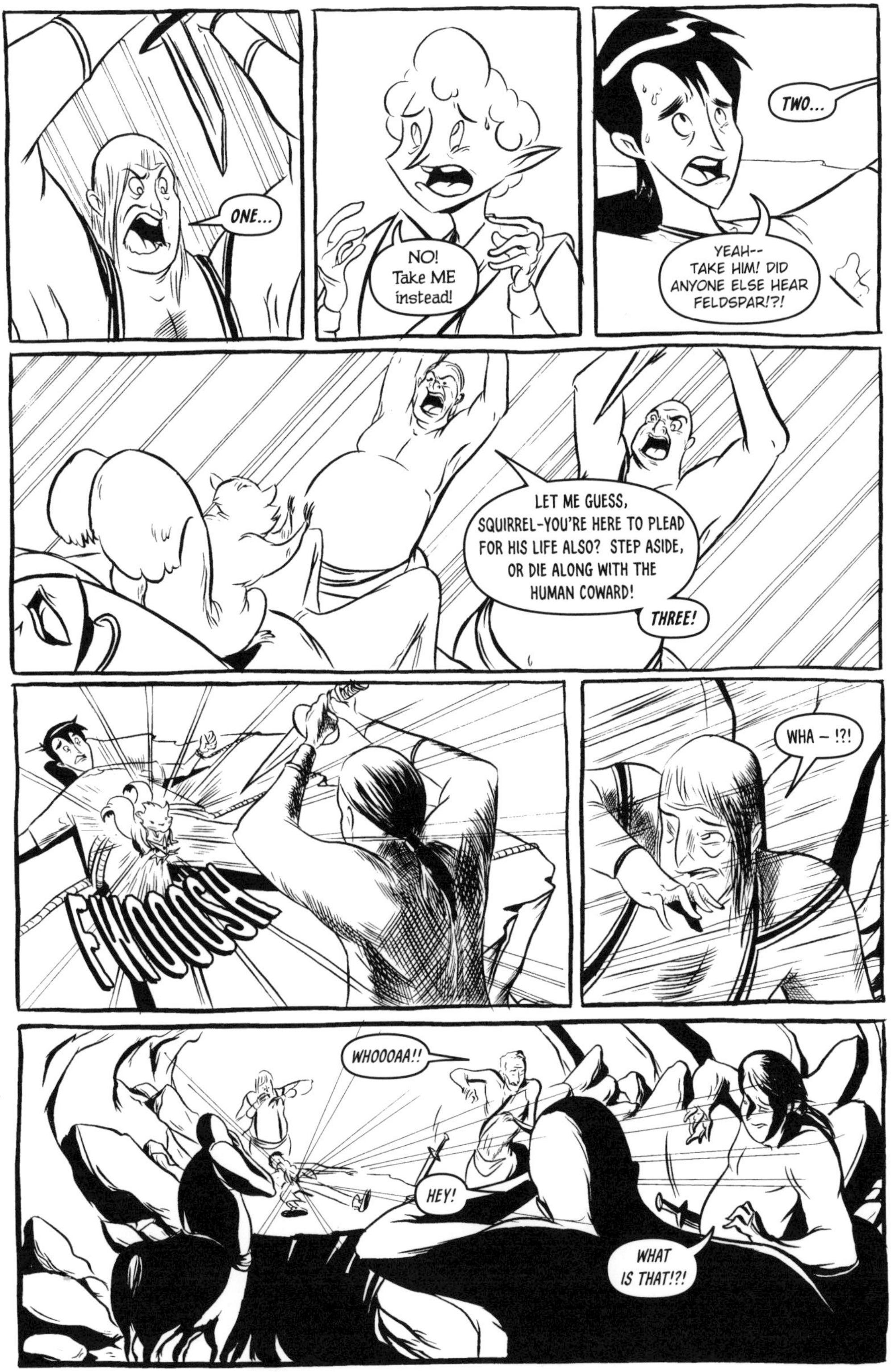
ONE...
NO! Take ME instead!
TWO...
YEAH-- TAKE HIM! DID ANYONE ELSE HEAR FELDSPAR!?!
LET ME GUESS, SQUIRREL-YOU'RE HERE TO PLEAD FOR HIS LIFE ALSO? STEP ASIDE, OR DIE ALONG WITH THE HUMAN COWARD!
THREE!
FWOOSH
WHA – !?!
WHOOOAA!!
HEY!
WHAT IS THAT!?!

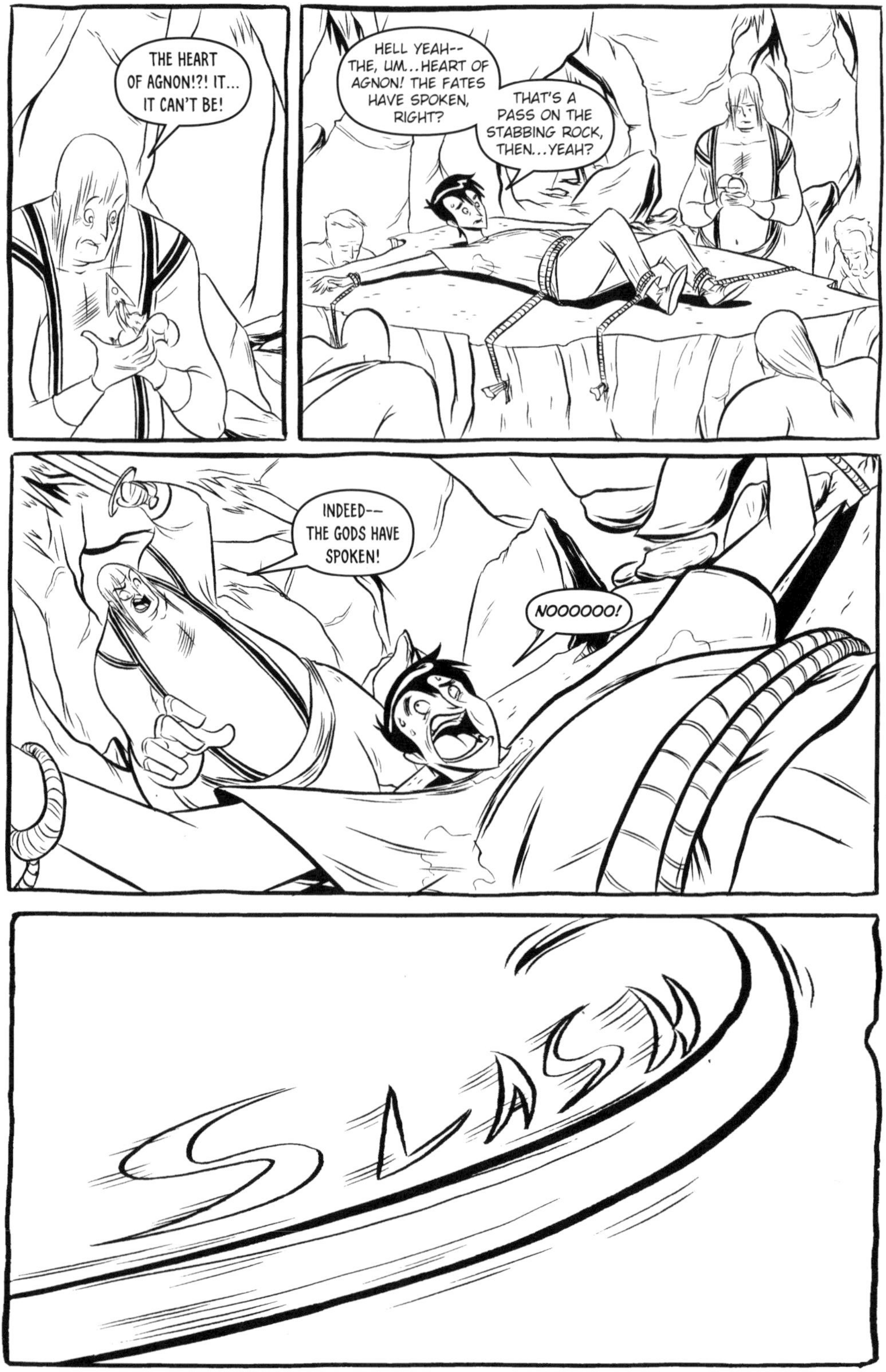
THE HEART OF AGNON!?! IT... IT CAN'T BE!
HELL YEAH-- THE, UM...HEART OF AGNON! THE FATES HAVE SPOKEN, RIGHT?
THAT'S A PASS ON THE STABBING ROCK, THEN...YEAH?
INDEED-- THE GODS HAVE SPOKEN!
NOOOOOO!
SLASH

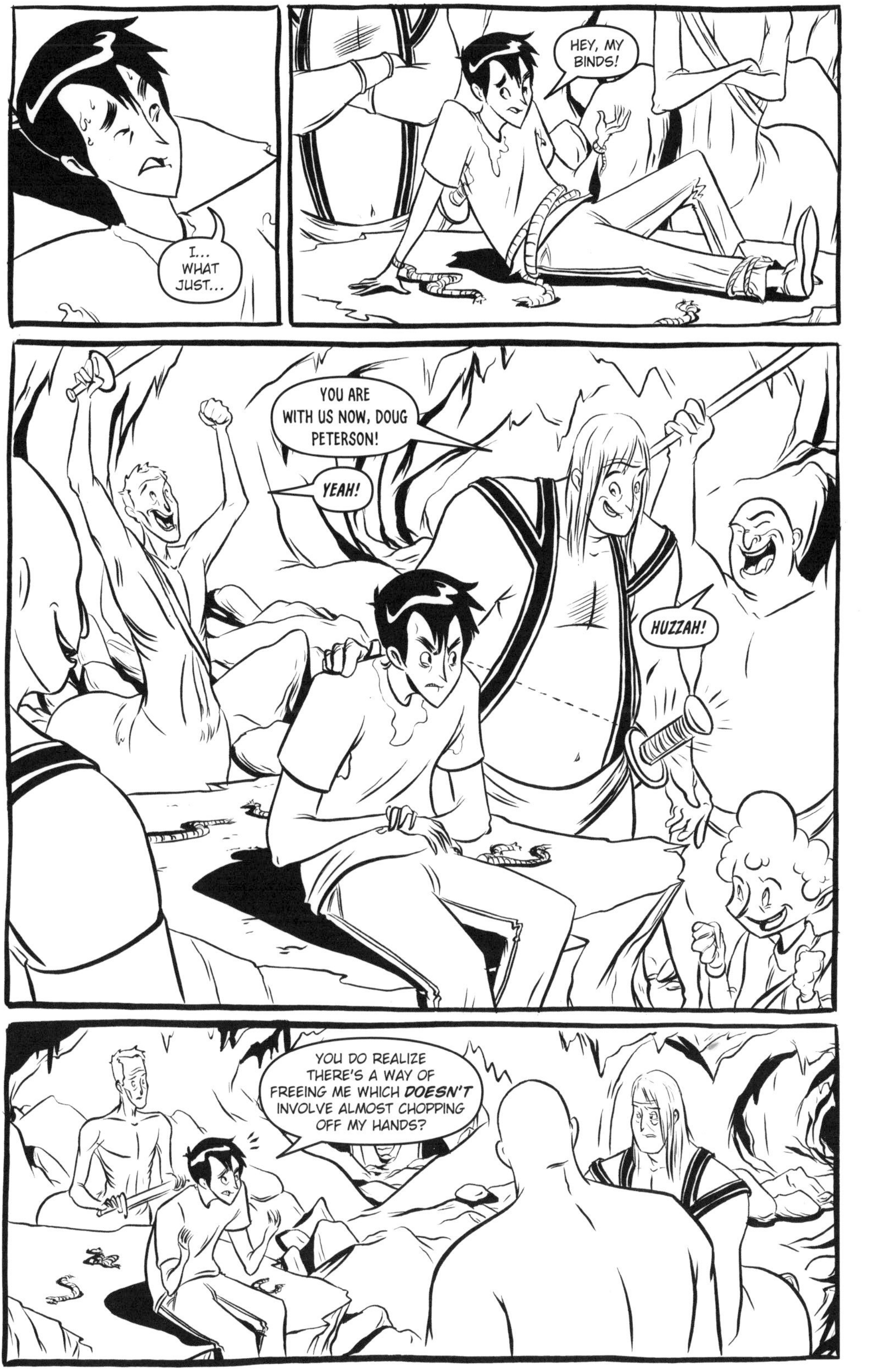
I... WHAT JUST...
HEY, MY BINDS!
YOU ARE WITH US NOW, DOUG PETERSON!
YEAH!
HUZZAH!
YOU DO REALIZE THERE'S A WAY OF FREEING ME WHICH DOESN'T INVOLVE ALMOST CHOPPING OFF MY HANDS?

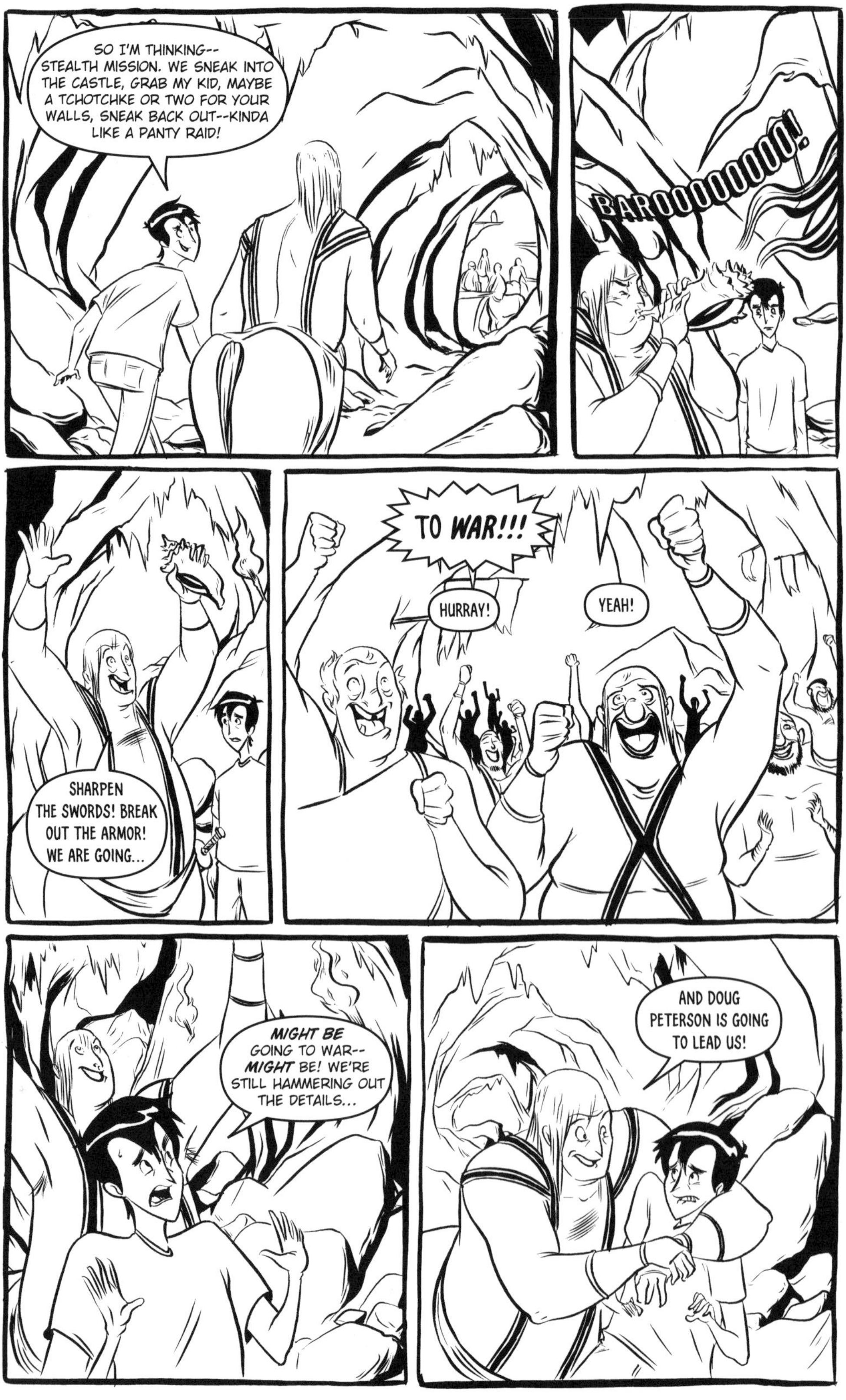
SO I'M THINKING-- STEALTH MISSION. WE SNEAK INTO THE CASTLE, GRAB MY KID, MAYBE A TCHOTCHKE OR TWO FOR YOUR WALLS, SNEAK BACK OUT--KINDA LIKE A PANTY RAID!
BAROOOOOOOOO!
SHARPEN THE SWORDS! BREAK OUT THE ARMOR! WE ARE GOING...
TO WAR!!!
HURRAY!
YEAH!
MIGHT BE GOING TO WAR-- MIGHT BE! WE'RE STILL HAMMERING OUT THE DETAILS...
AND DOUG PETERSON IS GOING TO LEAD US!

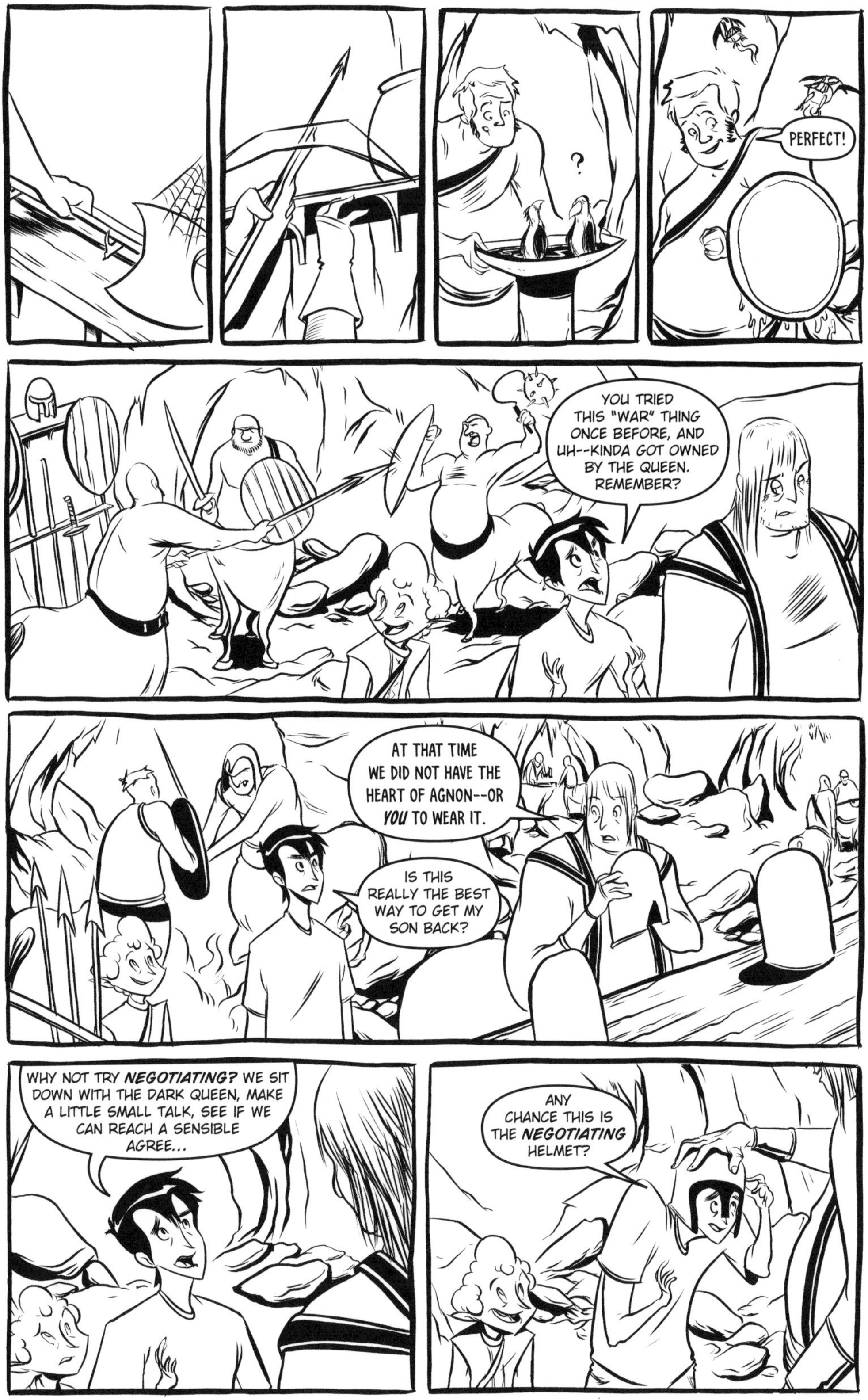
?
PERFECT!
YOU TRIED THIS "WAR" THING ONCE BEFORE, AND UH--KINDA GOT OWNED BY THE QUEEN. REMEMBER?
AT THAT TIME WE DID NOT HAVE THE HEART OF AGNON--OR *YOU* TO WEAR IT.
IS THIS REALLY THE BEST WAY TO GET MY SON BACK?
WHY NOT TRY ***NEGOTIATING?*** WE SIT DOWN WITH THE DARK QUEEN, MAKE A LITTLE SMALL TALK, SEE IF WE CAN REACH A SENSIBLE AGREE...
ANY CHANCE THIS IS THE ***NEGOTIATING*** HELMET?

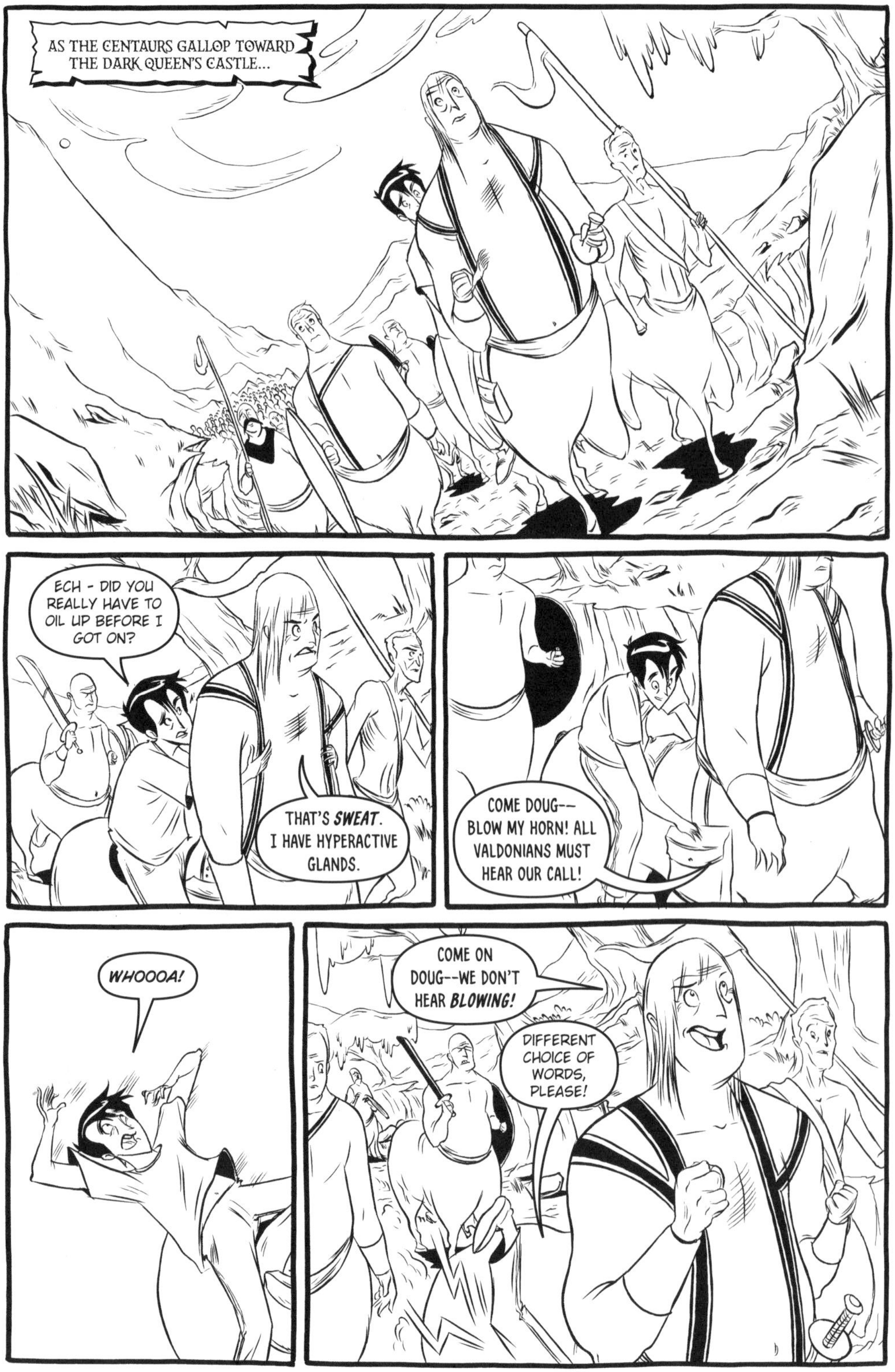
AS THE CENTAURS GALLOP TOWARD THE DARK QUEEN'S CASTLE...
ECH - DID YOU REALLY HAVE TO OIL UP BEFORE I GOT ON?
THAT'S **SWEAT**. I HAVE HYPERACTIVE GLANDS.
COME DOUG-- BLOW MY HORN! ALL VALDONIANS MUST HEAR OUR CALL!
WHOOOA!
COME ON DOUG--WE DON'T HEAR **BLOWING!**
DIFFERENT CHOICE OF WORDS, PLEASE!

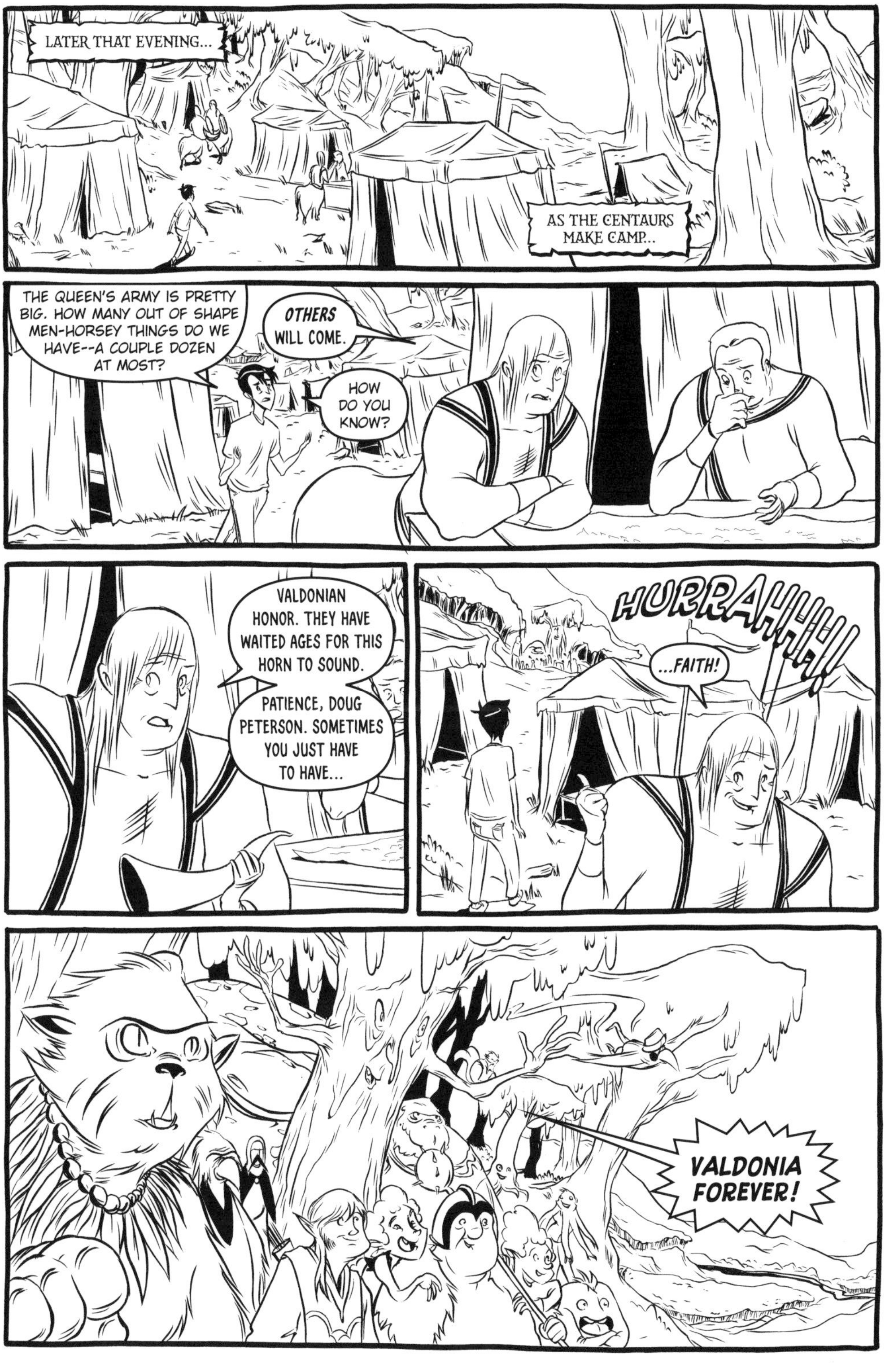
LATER THAT EVENING...
AS THE CENTAURS MAKE CAMP...
THE QUEEN'S ARMY IS PRETTY BIG. HOW MANY OUT OF SHAPE MEN-HORSEY THINGS DO WE HAVE--A COUPLE DOZEN AT MOST?
OTHERS WILL COME.
HOW DO YOU KNOW?
VALDONIAN HONOR. THEY HAVE WAITED AGES FOR THIS HORN TO SOUND.
PATIENCE, DOUG PETERSON. SOMETIMES YOU JUST HAVE TO HAVE...
HURRAHHH!!
...FAITH!
VALDONIA FOREVER!

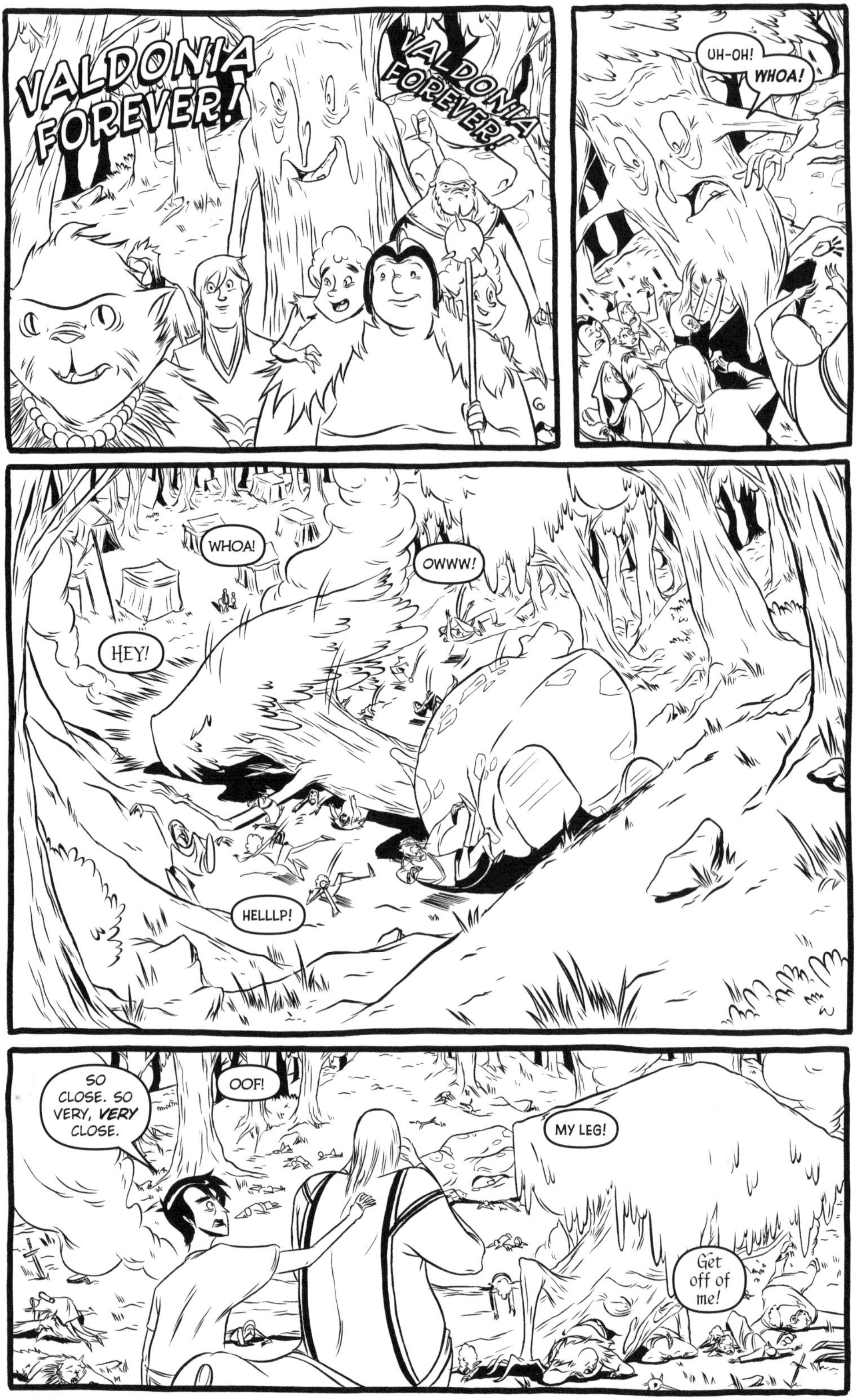
VALDONIA FOREVER!
VALDONIA FOREVER!
UH-OH!
WHOA!
WHOA!
OWWW!
HEY!
HELLLP!
SO CLOSE. SO VERY, VERY CLOSE.
OOF!
MY LEG!
Get off of me!

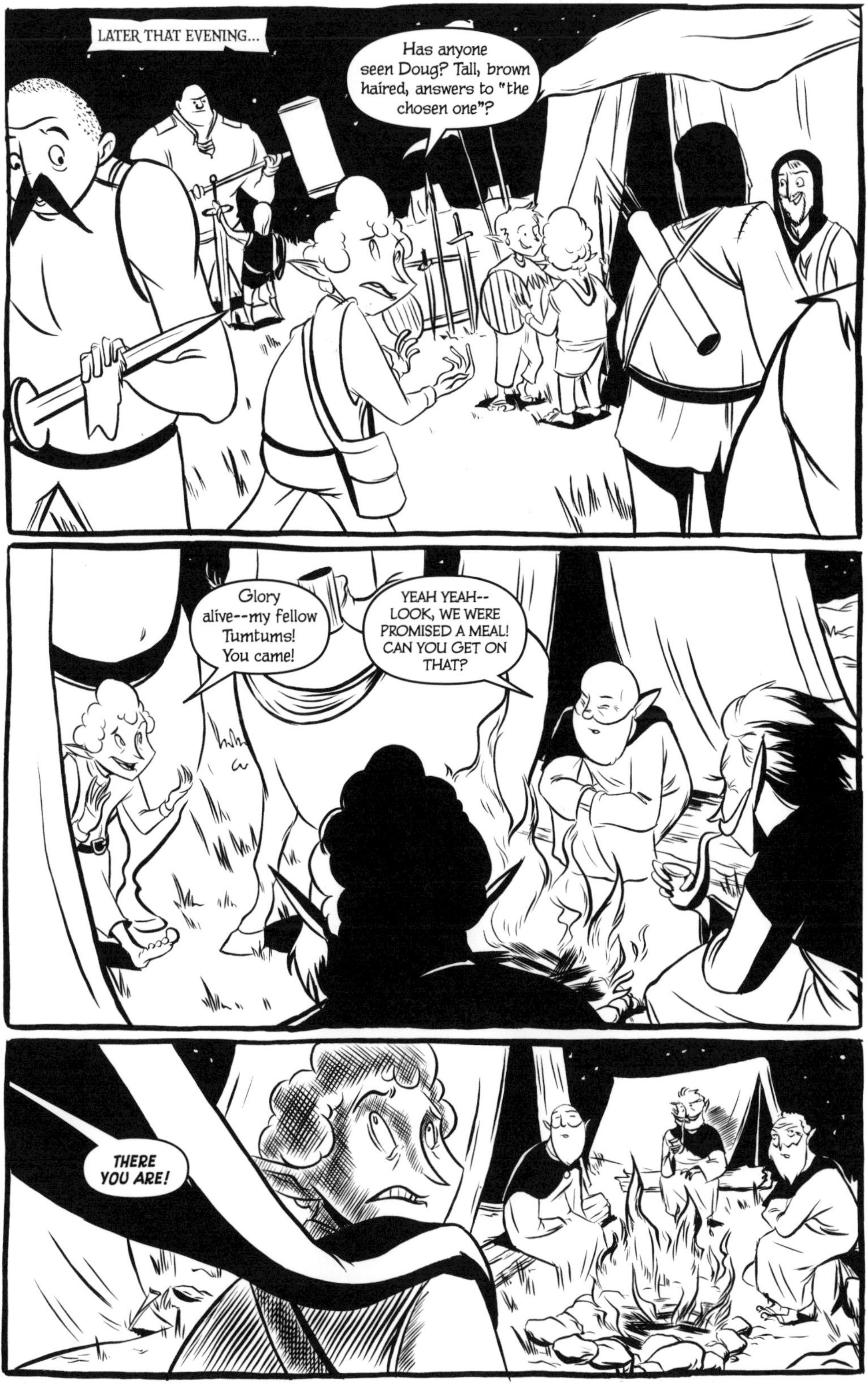
LATER THAT EVENING...
Has anyone seen Doug? Tall, brown haired, answers to "the chosen one"?
Glory alive--my fellow Tumtums! You came!
YEAH YEAH--LOOK, WE WERE PROMISED A MEAL! CAN YOU GET ON THAT?
THERE YOU ARE!

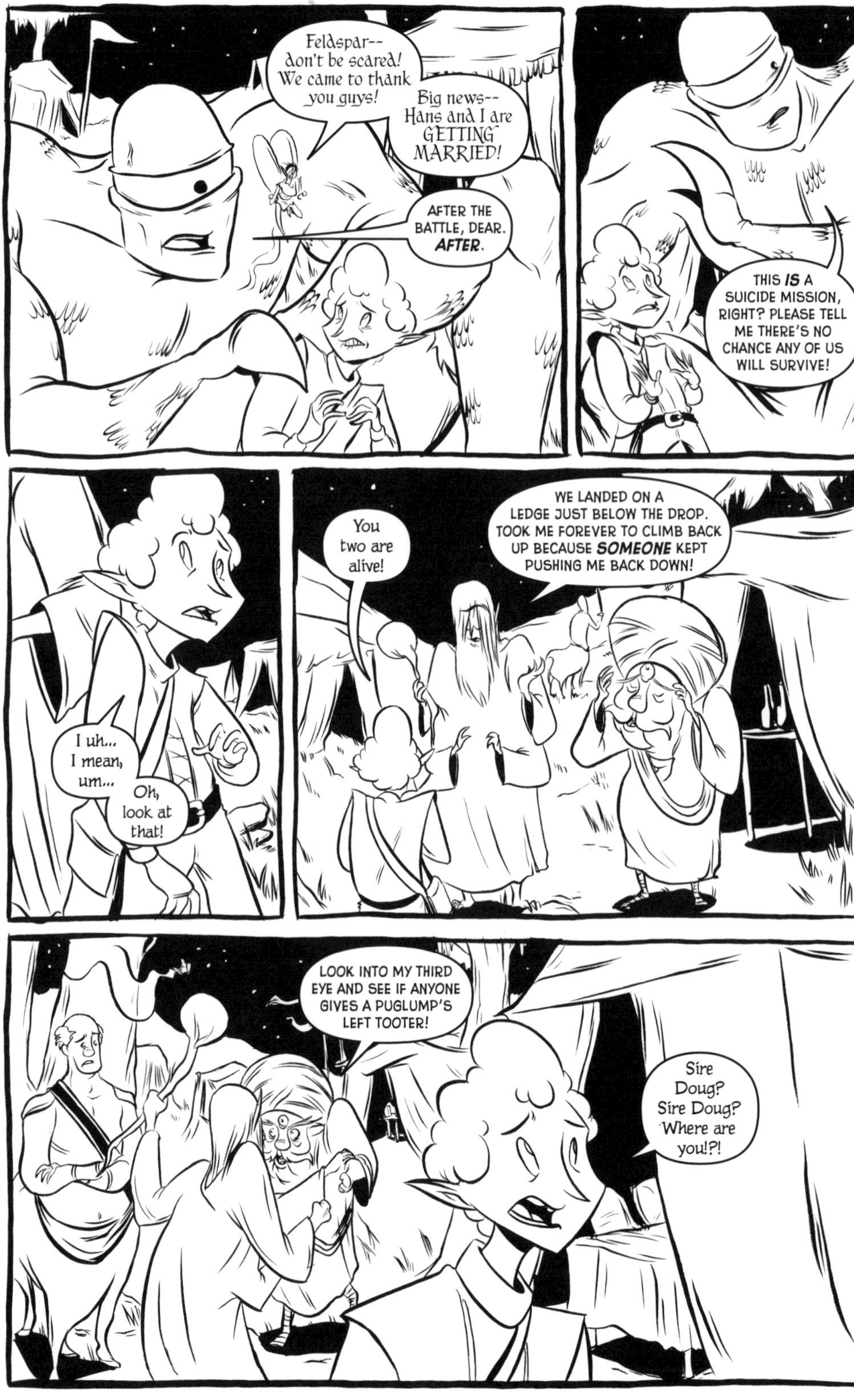
Feldspar-- don't be scared! We came to thank you guys!
Big news-- Hans and I are GETTING MARRIED!
AFTER THE BATTLE, DEAR. **AFTER**.
THIS **IS** A SUICIDE MISSION, RIGHT? PLEASE TELL ME THERE'S NO CHANCE ANY OF US WILL SURVIVE!
I uh... I mean, um...
Oh, look at that!
You two are alive!
WE LANDED ON A LEDGE JUST BELOW THE DROP. TOOK ME FOREVER TO CLIMB BACK UP BECAUSE **SOMEONE** KEPT PUSHING ME BACK DOWN!
LOOK INTO MY THIRD EYE AND SEE IF ANYONE GIVES A PUGLUMP'S LEFT TOOTER!
Sire Doug? Sire Doug? Where are you!?!

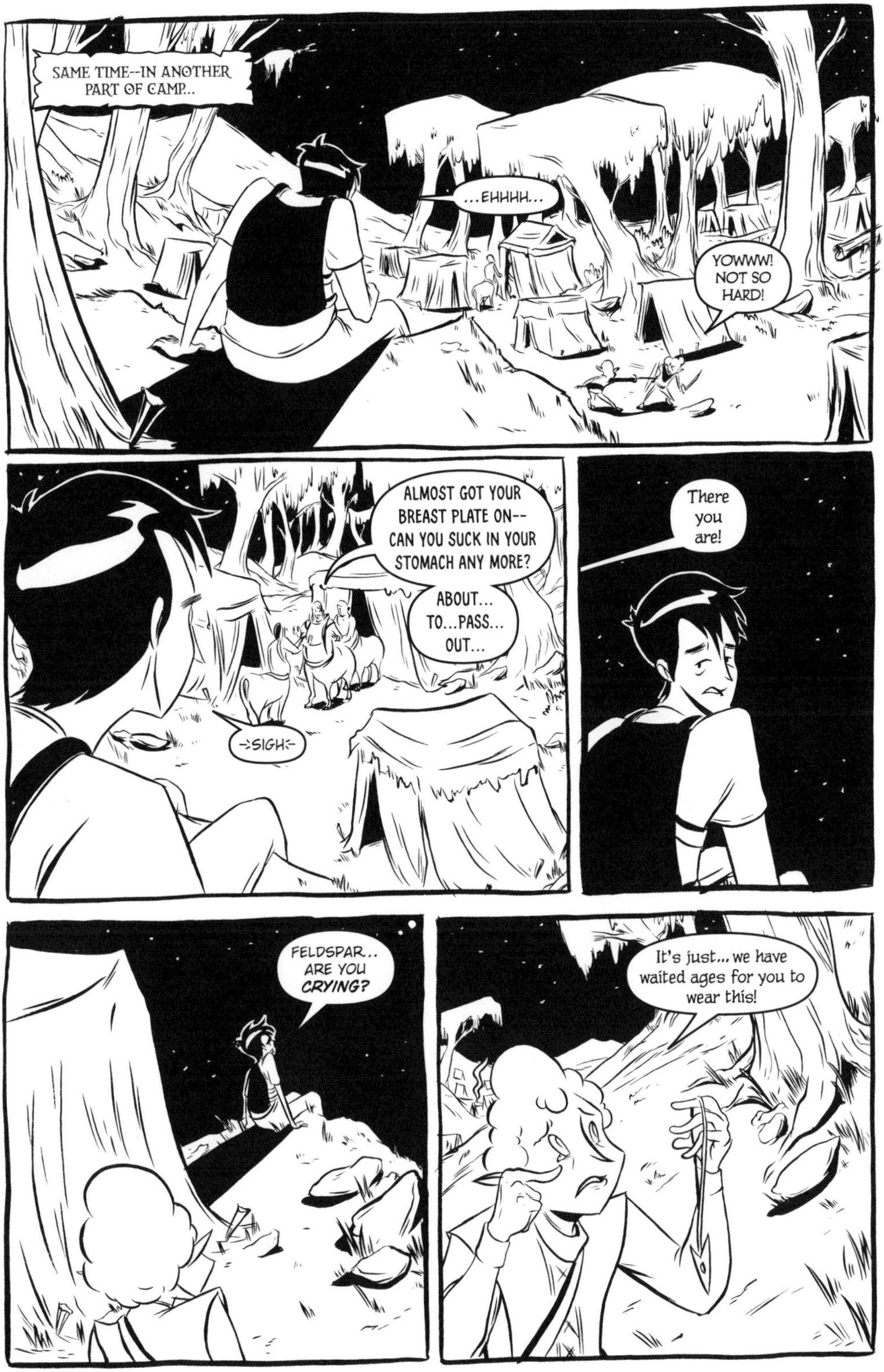
SAME TIME--IN ANOTHER PART OF CAMP...
...EHHHH...
YOWWW! NOT SO HARD!
ALMOST GOT YOUR BREAST PLATE ON-- CAN YOU SUCK IN YOUR STOMACH ANY MORE?
ABOUT... TO...PASS... OUT...
-SIGH-
There you are!
FELDSPAR... ARE YOU *CRYING?*
It's just... we have waited ages for you to wear this!

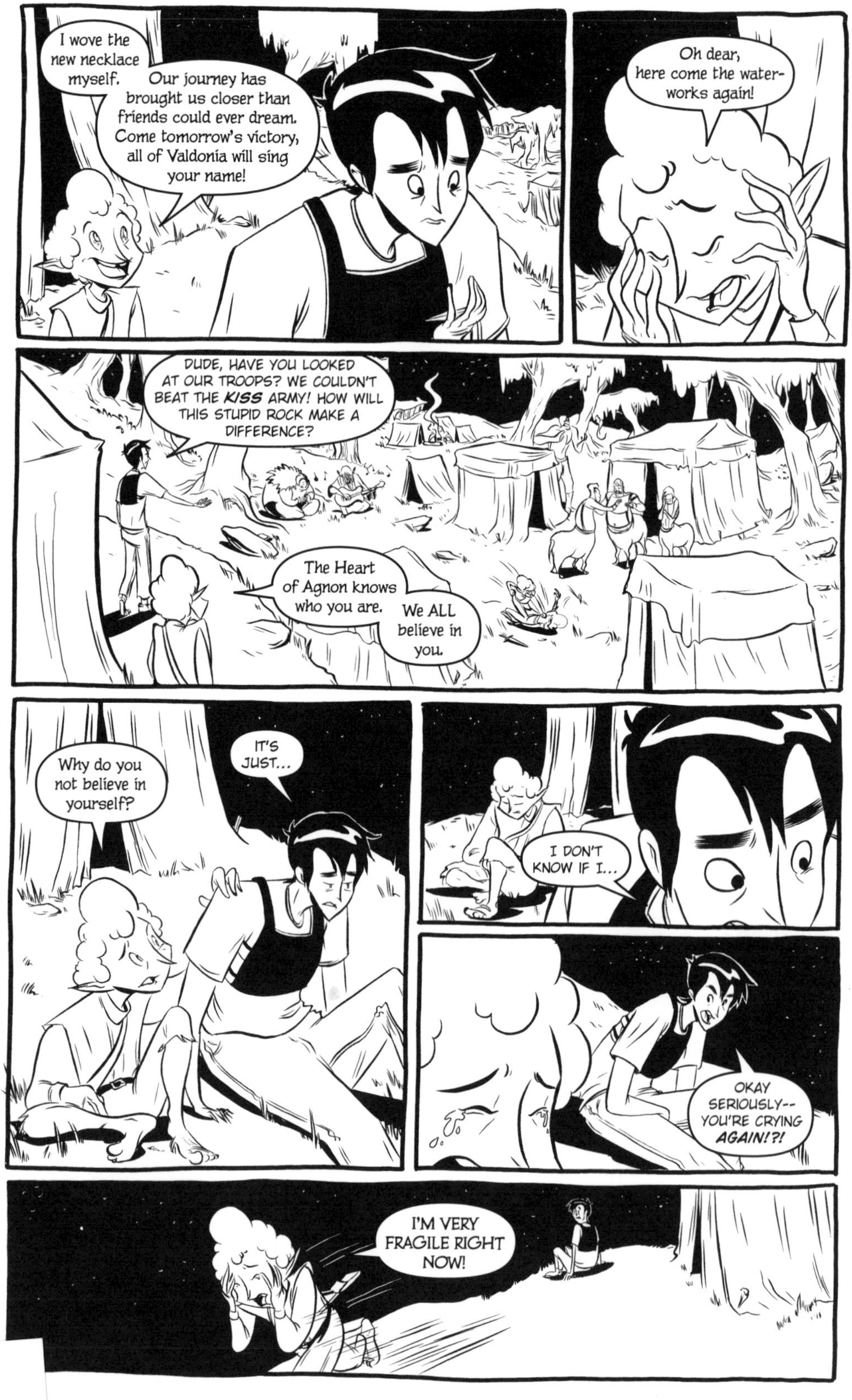
I wove the new necklace myself.
Our journey has brought us closer than friends could ever dream. Come tomorrow's victory, all of Valdonia will sing your name!
Oh dear, here come the water-works again!
DUDE, HAVE YOU LOOKED AT OUR TROOPS? WE COULDN'T BEAT THE KISS ARMY! HOW WILL THIS STUPID ROCK MAKE A DIFFERENCE?
The Heart of Agnon knows who you are.
We ALL believe in you.
Why do you not believe in yourself?
IT'S JUST...
I DON'T KNOW IF I...
OKAY SERIOUSLY-- YOU'RE CRYING AGAIN!?!
I'M VERY FRAGILE RIGHT NOW!

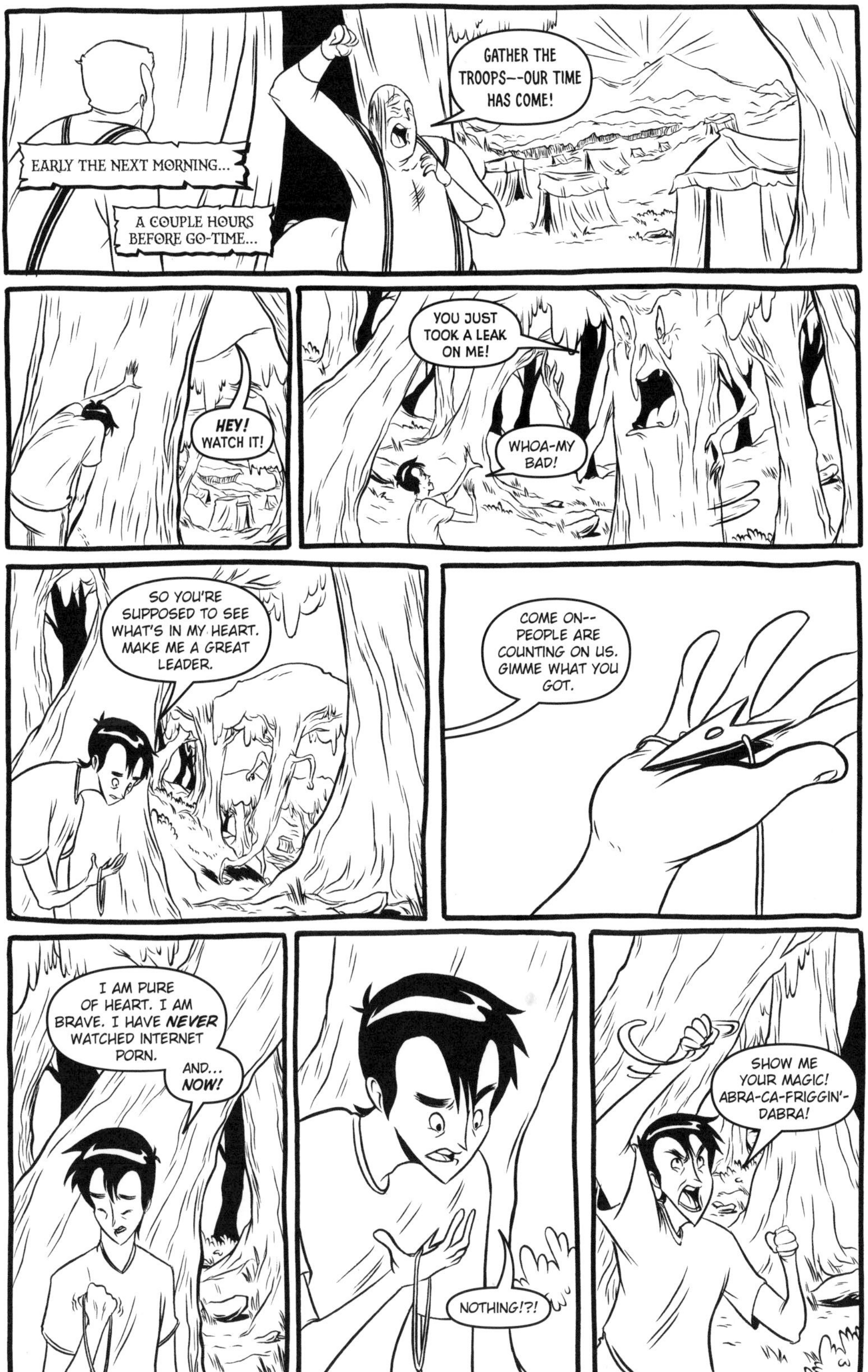
EARLY THE NEXT MORNING...
A COUPLE HOURS BEFORE GO-TIME...
GATHER THE TROOPS--OUR TIME HAS COME!
HEY! WATCH IT!
YOU JUST TOOK A LEAK ON ME!
WHOA-MY BAD!
SO YOU'RE SUPPOSED TO SEE WHAT'S IN MY HEART. MAKE ME A GREAT LEADER.
COME ON-- PEOPLE ARE COUNTING ON US. GIMME WHAT YOU GOT.
I AM PURE OF HEART. I AM BRAVE. I HAVE NEVER WATCHED INTERNET PORN.
AND... NOW!
NOTHING!?!
SHOW ME YOUR MAGIC! ABRA-CA-FRIGGIN'-DABRA!

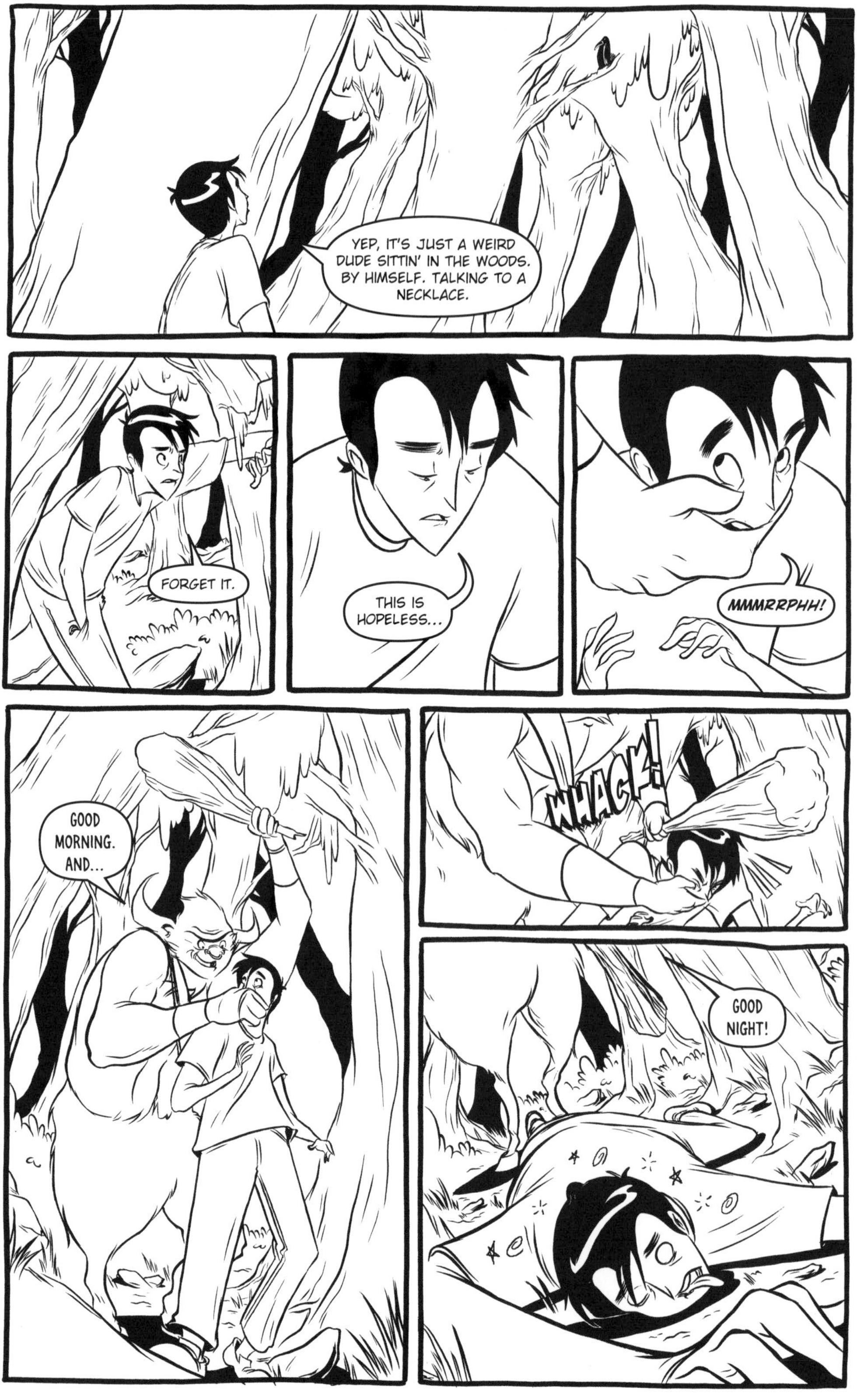
YEP, IT'S JUST A WEIRD DUDE SITTIN' IN THE WOODS. BY HIMSELF. TALKING TO A NECKLACE.
FORGET IT.
THIS IS HOPELESS...
MMMRRPHH!
GOOD MORNING. AND...
WHACK!
GOOD NIGHT!

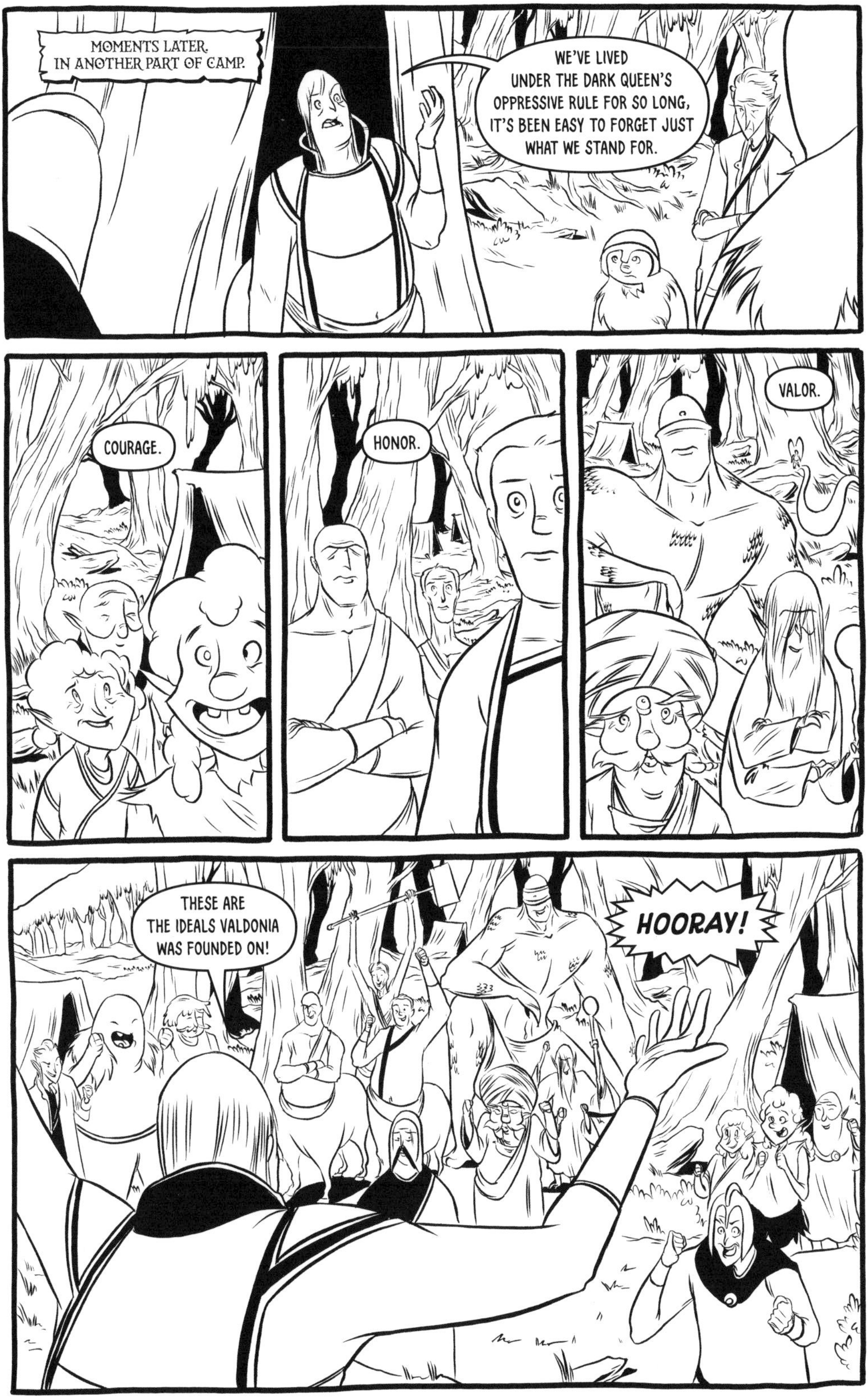
MOMENTS LATER. IN ANOTHER PART OF CAMP.
WE'VE LIVED UNDER THE DARK QUEEN'S OPPRESSIVE RULE FOR SO LONG, IT'S BEEN EASY TO FORGET JUST WHAT WE STAND FOR.
COURAGE.
HONOR.
VALOR.
THESE ARE THE IDEALS VALDONIA WAS FOUNDED ON!
HOORAY!

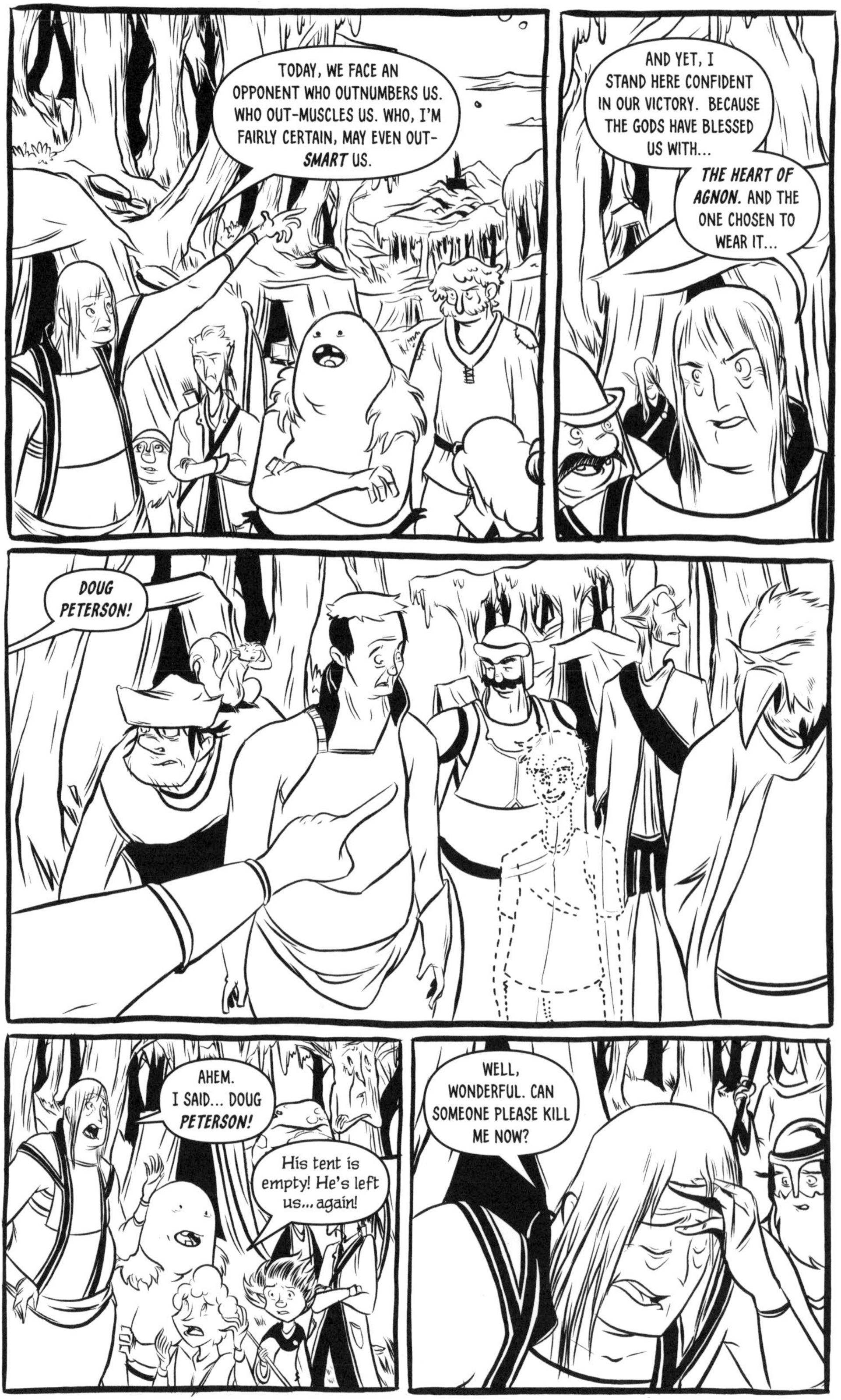
TODAY, WE FACE AN OPPONENT WHO OUTNUMBERS US. WHO OUT-MUSCLES US. WHO, I'M FAIRLY CERTAIN, MAY EVEN OUT-*SMART* US.
AND YET, I STAND HERE CONFIDENT IN OUR VICTORY. BECAUSE THE GODS HAVE BLESSED US WITH...
THE HEART OF AGNON. AND THE ONE CHOSEN TO WEAR IT...
DOUG PETERSON!
AHEM. I SAID... DOUG *PETERSON!*
His tent is empty! He's left us... again!
WELL, WONDERFUL. CAN SOMEONE PLEASE KILL ME NOW?

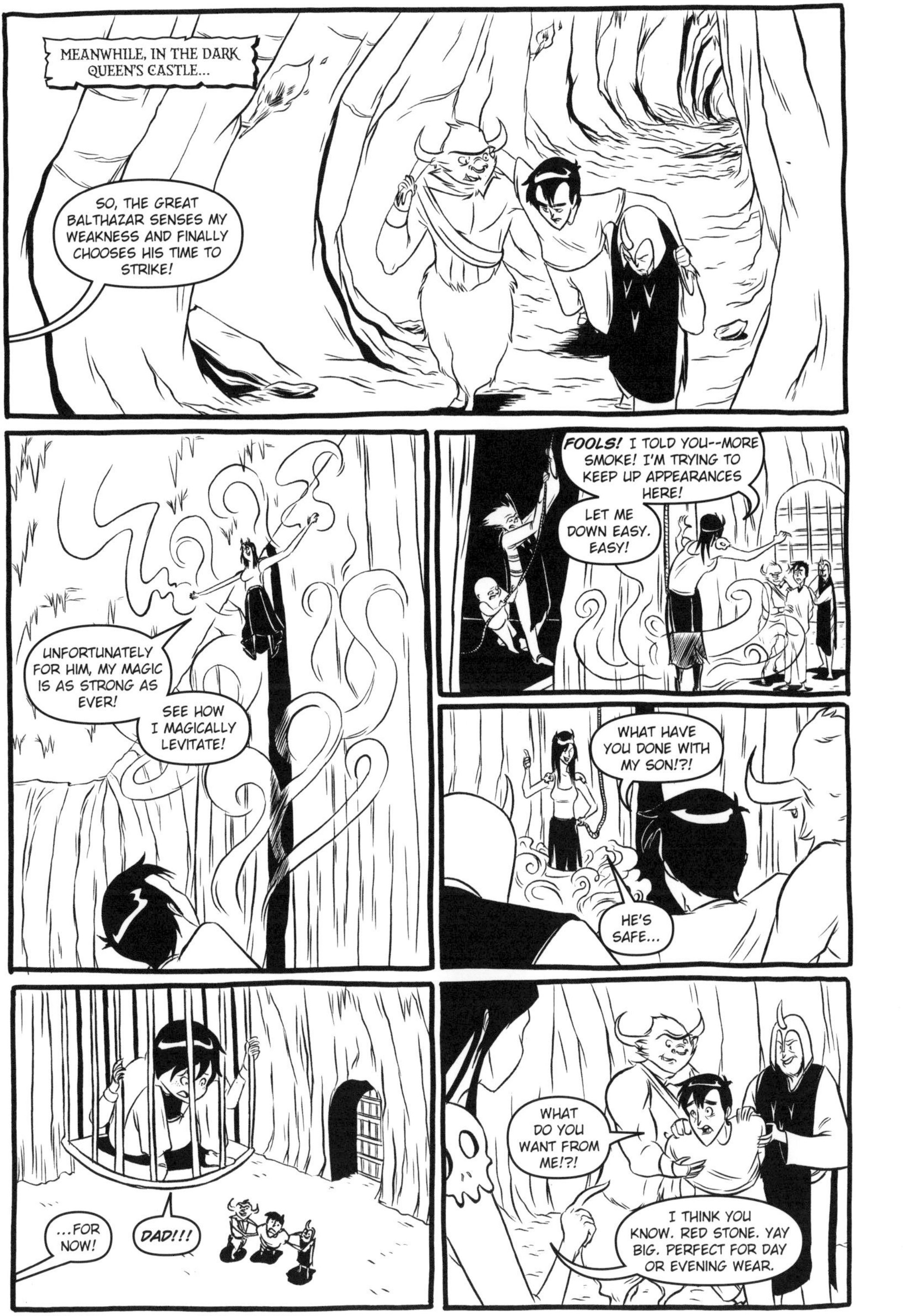
MEANWHILE, IN THE DARK QUEEN'S CASTLE...
SO, THE GREAT BALTHAZAR SENSES MY WEAKNESS AND FINALLY CHOOSES HIS TIME TO STRIKE!
UNFORTUNATELY FOR HIM, MY MAGIC IS AS STRONG AS EVER!
SEE HOW I MAGICALLY LEVITATE!
FOOLS! I TOLD YOU--MORE SMOKE! I'M TRYING TO KEEP UP APPEARANCES HERE!
LET ME DOWN EASY. EASY!
WHAT HAVE YOU DONE WITH MY SON!?!
HE'S SAFE...
...FOR NOW!
DAD!!!
WHAT DO YOU WANT FROM ME!?!
I THINK YOU KNOW. RED STONE. YAY BIG. PERFECT FOR DAY OR EVENING WEAR.

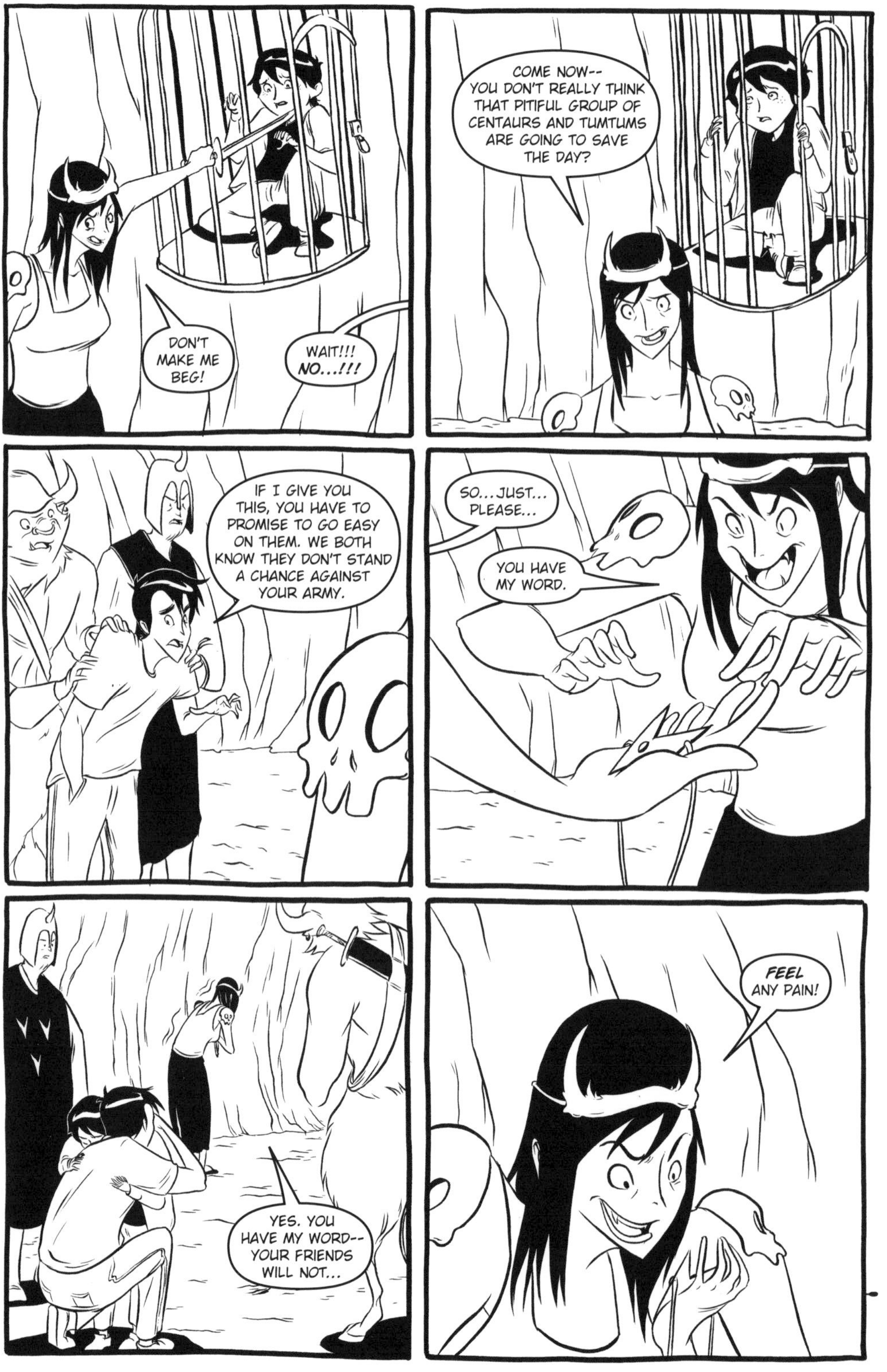
DON'T MAKE ME BEG!
WAIT!!! NO...!!!
COME NOW-- YOU DON'T REALLY THINK THAT PITIFUL GROUP OF CENTAURS AND TUMTUMS ARE GOING TO SAVE THE DAY?
IF I GIVE YOU THIS, YOU HAVE TO PROMISE TO GO EASY ON THEM. WE BOTH KNOW THEY DON'T STAND A CHANCE AGAINST YOUR ARMY.
SO... JUST... PLEASE...
YOU HAVE MY WORD.
YES. YOU HAVE MY WORD-- YOUR FRIENDS WILL NOT...
FEEL ANY PAIN!

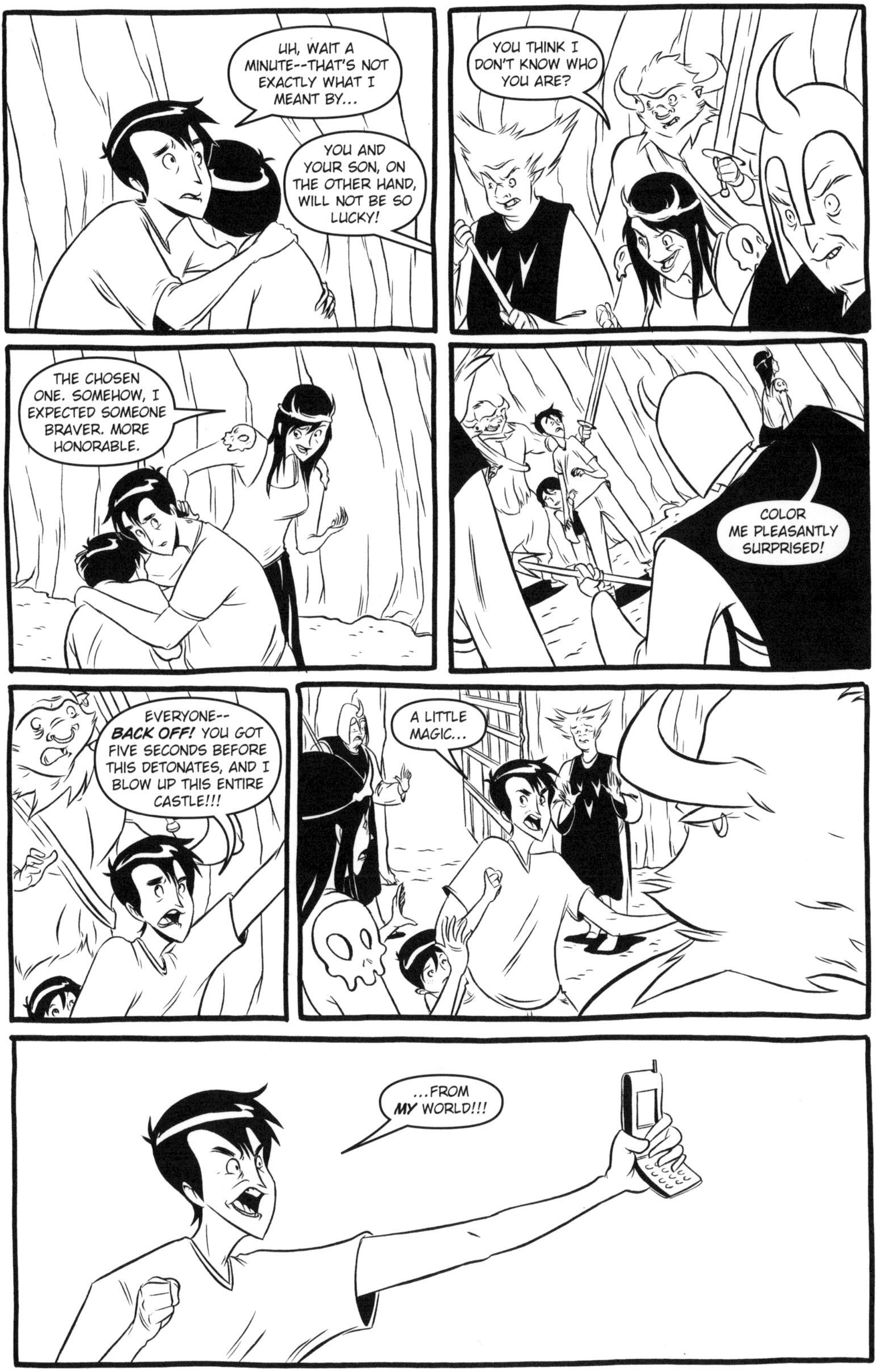
UH, WAIT A MINUTE--THAT'S NOT EXACTLY WHAT I MEANT BY...
YOU AND YOUR SON, ON THE OTHER HAND, WILL NOT BE SO LUCKY!
YOU THINK I DON'T KNOW WHO YOU ARE?
THE CHOSEN ONE. SOMEHOW, I EXPECTED SOMEONE BRAVER. MORE HONORABLE.
COLOR ME PLEASANTLY SURPRISED!
EVERYONE-- **BACK OFF!** YOU GOT FIVE SECONDS BEFORE THIS DETONATES, AND I BLOW UP THIS ENTIRE CASTLE!!!
A LITTLE MAGIC...
...FROM ***MY*** WORLD!!!

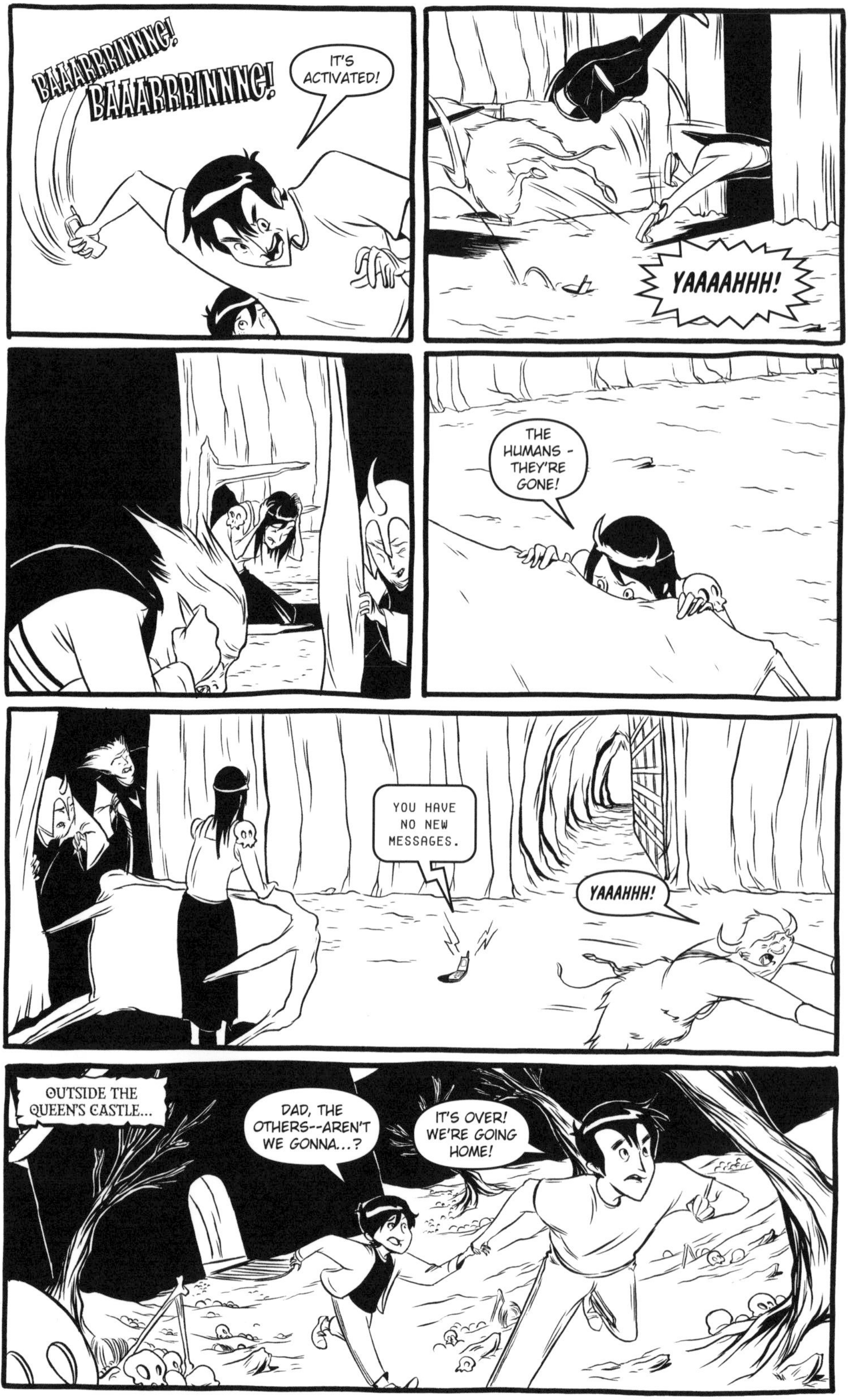
BAAARRRINNNG! BAAARRRINNNG!
IT'S ACTIVATED!
YAAAAHHH!
THE HUMANS - THEY'RE GONE!
YOU HAVE NO NEW MESSAGES.
YAAAHHH!
OUTSIDE THE QUEEN'S CASTLE...
DAD, THE OTHERS--AREN'T WE GONNA...?
IT'S OVER! WE'RE GOING HOME!

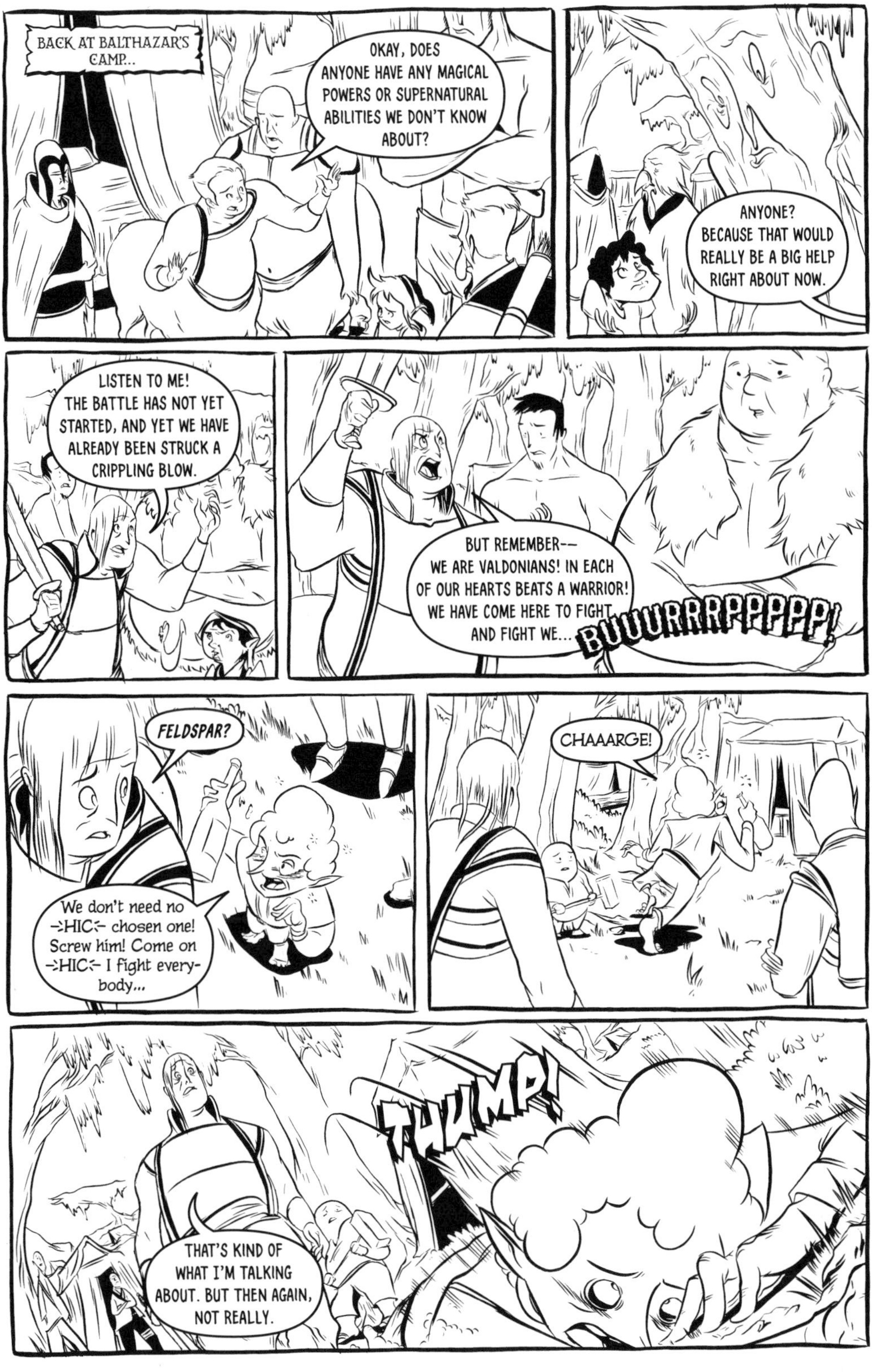
BACK AT BALTHAZAR'S CAMP...
OKAY, DOES ANYONE HAVE ANY MAGICAL POWERS OR SUPERNATURAL ABILITIES WE DON'T KNOW ABOUT?
ANYONE? BECAUSE THAT WOULD REALLY BE A BIG HELP RIGHT ABOUT NOW.
LISTEN TO ME! THE BATTLE HAS NOT YET STARTED, AND YET WE HAVE ALREADY BEEN STRUCK A CRIPPLING BLOW.
BUT REMEMBER-- WE ARE VALDONIANS! IN EACH OF OUR HEARTS BEATS A WARRIOR! WE HAVE COME HERE TO FIGHT AND FIGHT WE...
BUUURRRPPPPP!
FELDSPAR?
We don't need no -HIC- chosen one! Screw him! Come on -HIC- I fight every-body...
CHAAARGE!
THUMP!
THAT'S KIND OF WHAT I'M TALKING ABOUT. BUT THEN AGAIN, NOT REALLY.

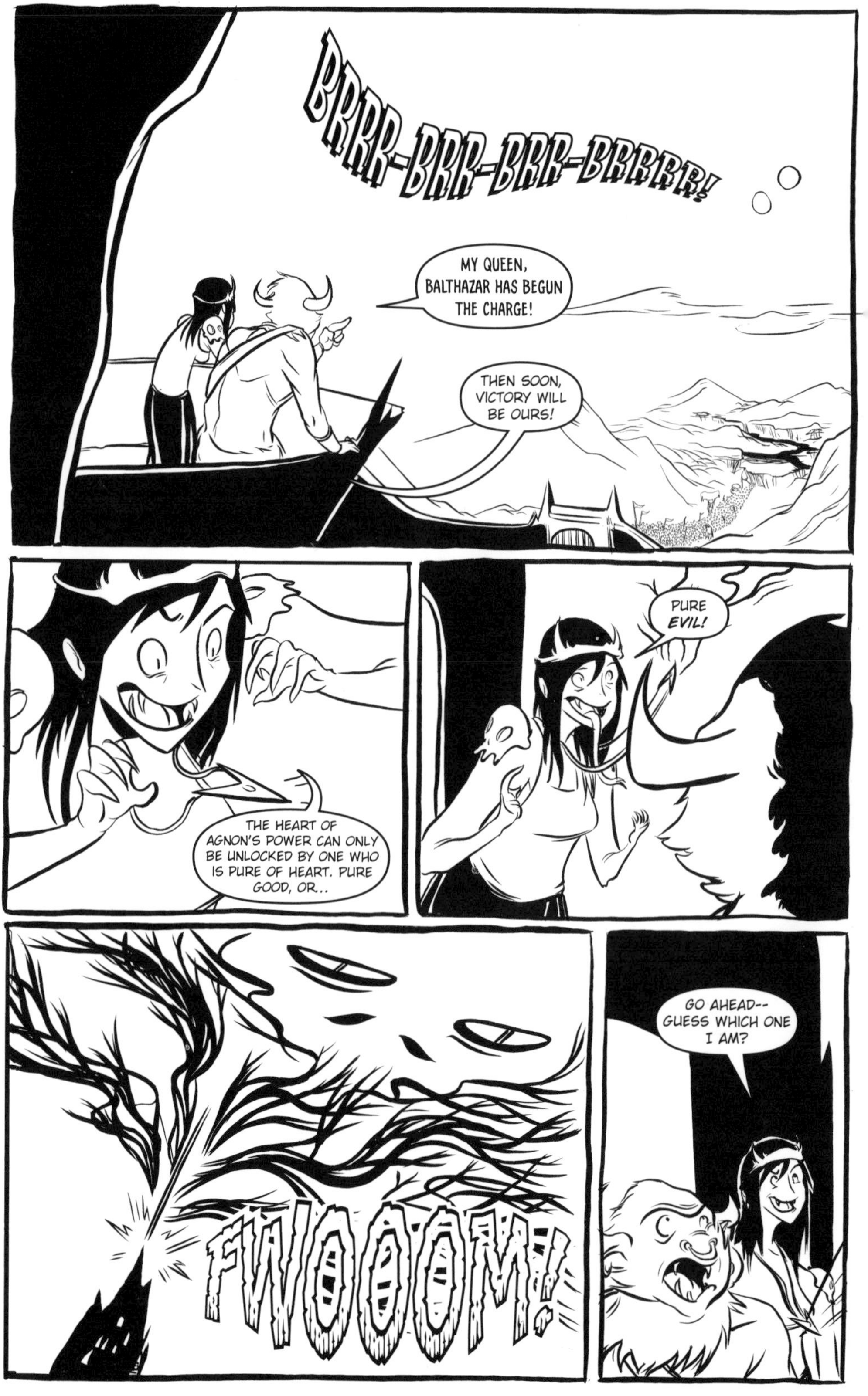
BRRR-BRR-BRR-BRRRR!
MY QUEEN, BALTHAZAR HAS BEGUN THE CHARGE!
THEN SOON, VICTORY WILL BE OURS!
THE HEART OF AGNON'S POWER CAN ONLY BE UNLOCKED BY ONE WHO IS PURE OF HEART. PURE GOOD, OR..
PURE *EVIL!*
FWOOOM!
GO AHEAD-- GUESS WHICH ONE I AM?

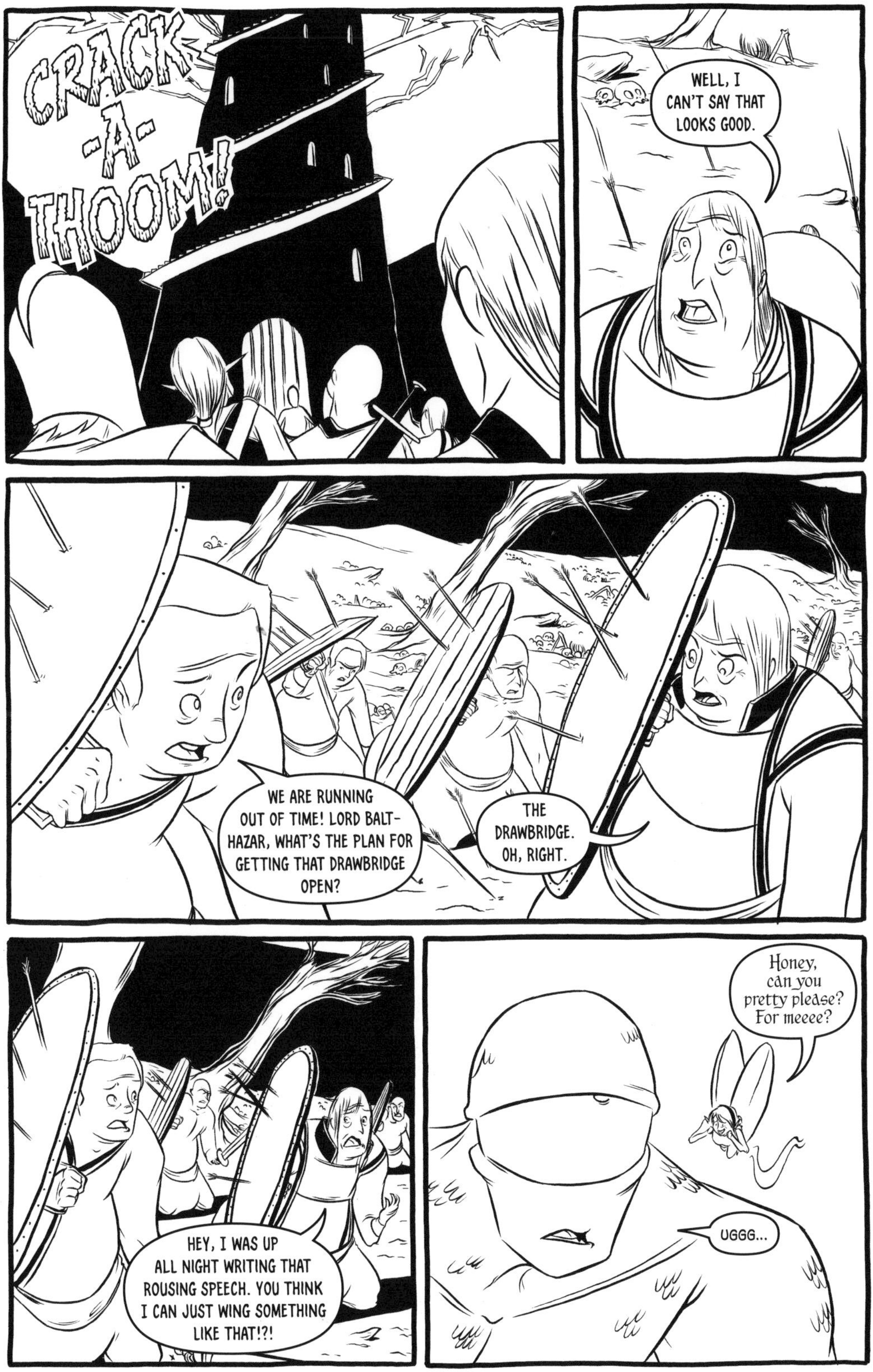
CRACK-A-THOOM!
WELL, I CAN'T SAY THAT LOOKS GOOD.
WE ARE RUNNING OUT OF TIME! LORD BALT-HAZAR, WHAT'S THE PLAN FOR GETTING THAT DRAWBRIDGE OPEN?
THE DRAWBRIDGE. OH, RIGHT.
HEY, I WAS UP ALL NIGHT WRITING THAT ROUSING SPEECH. YOU THINK I CAN JUST WING SOMETHING LIKE THAT!?!
Honey, can you pretty please? For meeee?
UGGG...

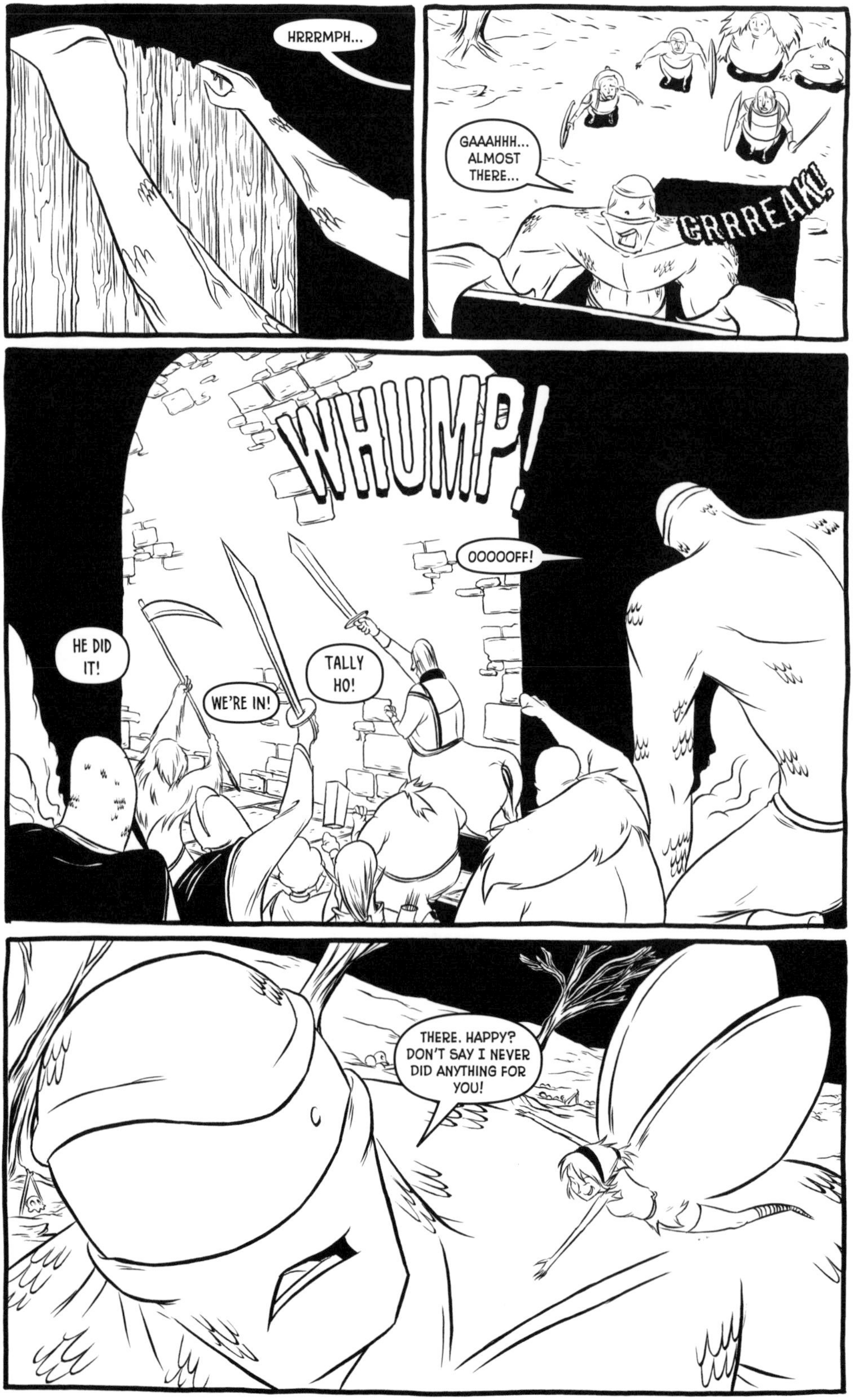
HRRRMPH...
GAAAHHH... ALMOST THERE...
GRRREAK!
WHUMP!
OOOOOFF!
HE DID IT!
WE'RE IN!
TALLY HO!
THERE. HAPPY? DON'T SAY I NEVER DID ANYTHING FOR YOU!

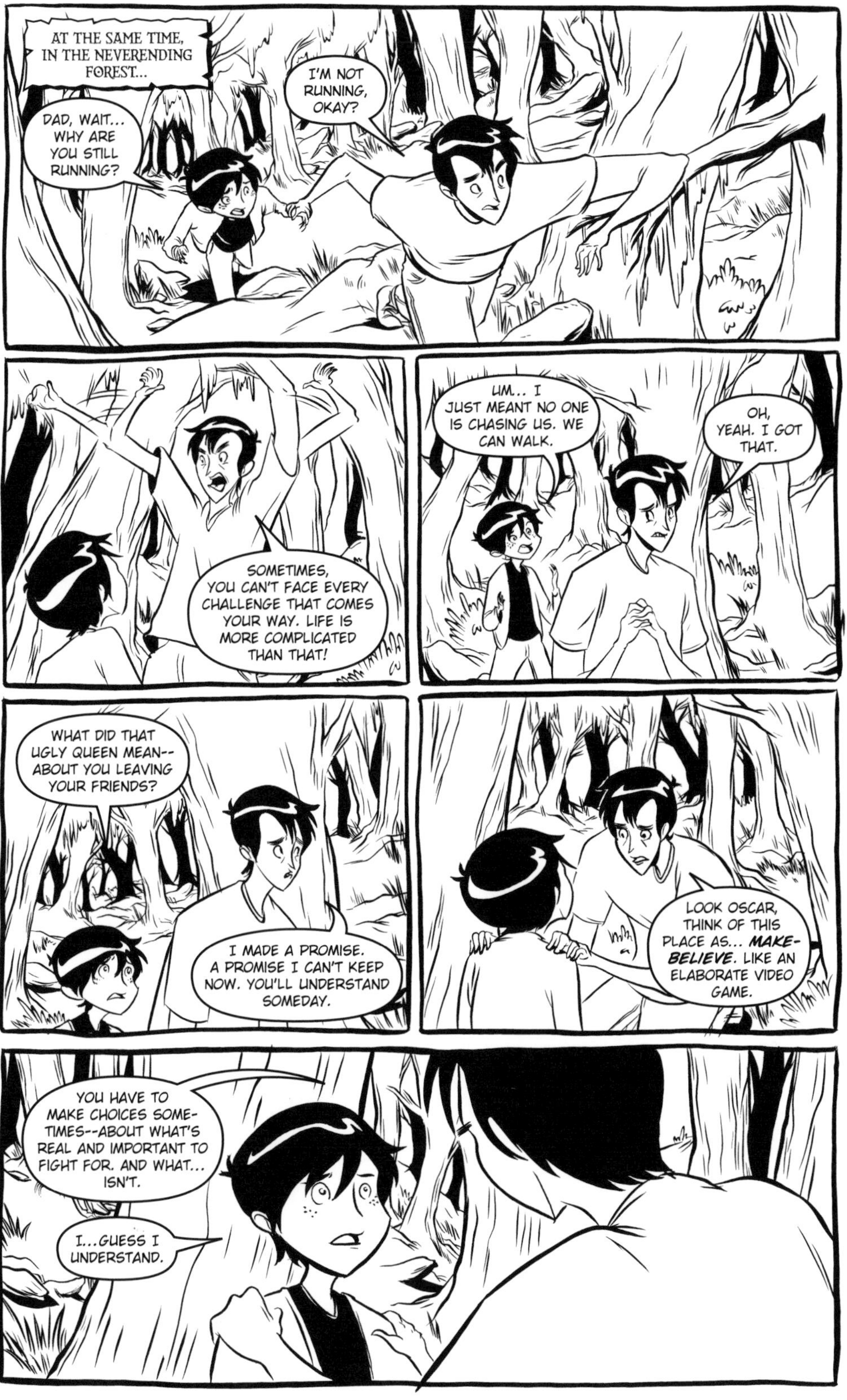
AT THE SAME TIME, IN THE NEVERENDING FOREST...
DAD, WAIT... WHY ARE YOU STILL RUNNING?
I'M NOT RUNNING, OKAY?
SOMETIMES, YOU CAN'T FACE EVERY CHALLENGE THAT COMES YOUR WAY. LIFE IS MORE COMPLICATED THAN THAT!
UM... I JUST MEANT NO ONE IS CHASING US. WE CAN WALK.
OH, YEAH. I GOT THAT.
WHAT DID THAT UGLY QUEEN MEAN--ABOUT YOU LEAVING YOUR FRIENDS?
I MADE A PROMISE. A PROMISE I CAN'T KEEP NOW. YOU'LL UNDERSTAND SOMEDAY.
LOOK OSCAR, THINK OF THIS PLACE AS... ***MAKE-BELIEVE***. LIKE AN ELABORATE VIDEO GAME.
YOU HAVE TO MAKE CHOICES SOME-TIMES--ABOUT WHAT'S REAL AND IMPORTANT TO FIGHT FOR. AND WHAT... ISN'T.
I...GUESS I UNDERSTAND.

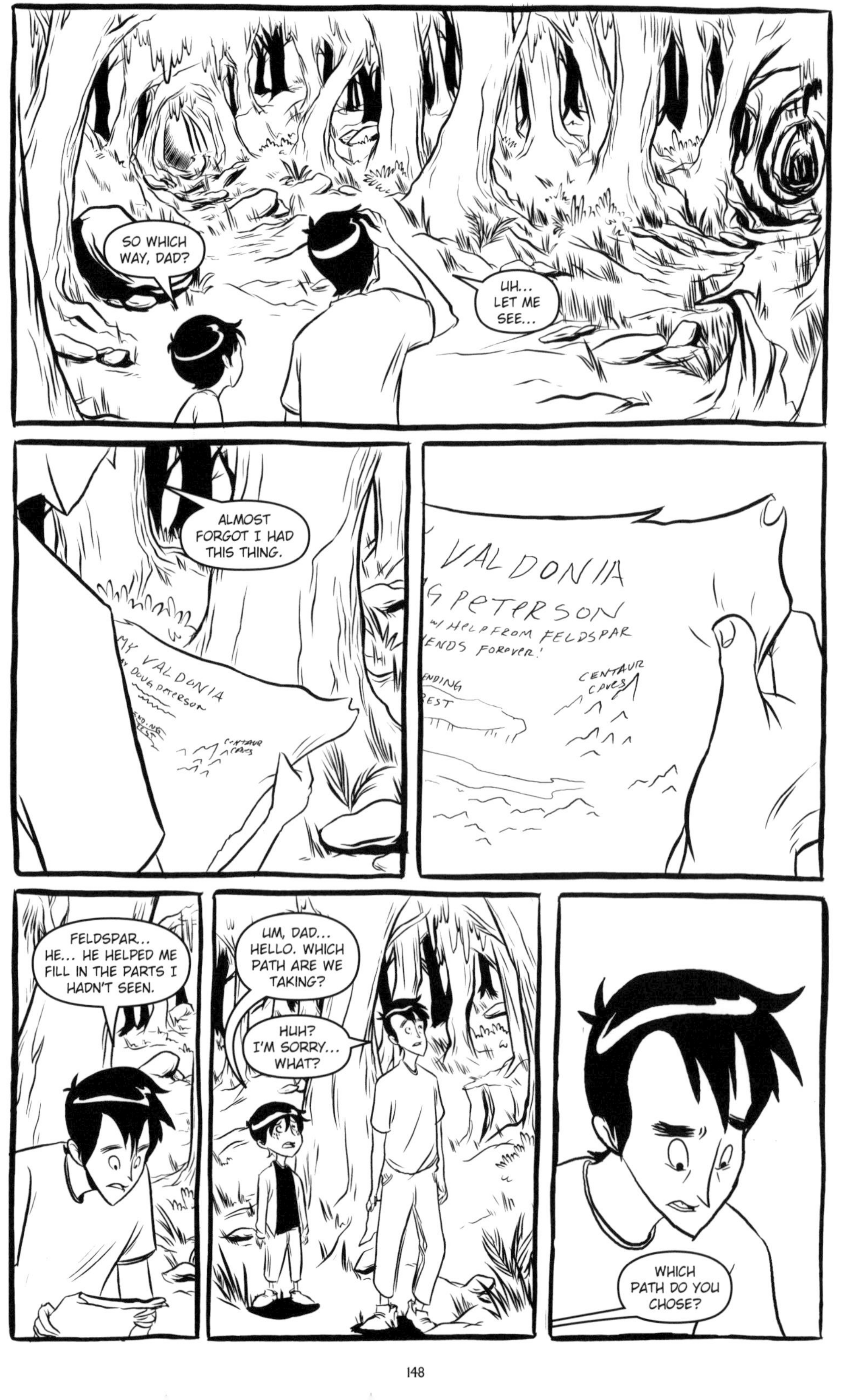
SO WHICH WAY, DAD?
UH... LET ME SEE...
ALMOST FORGOT I HAD THIS THING.
MY VALDONIA
BY DOUG PETERSON
CENTAUR CAVES
VALDONIA
G PETERSON
W/ HELP FROM FELDSPAR
ENDS FOREVER!
CENTAUR CAVES
FELDSPAR... HE... HE HELPED ME FILL IN THE PARTS I HADN'T SEEN.
UM, DAD... HELLO. WHICH PATH ARE WE TAKING?
HUH? I'M SORRY... WHAT?
WHICH PATH DO YOU CHOSE?

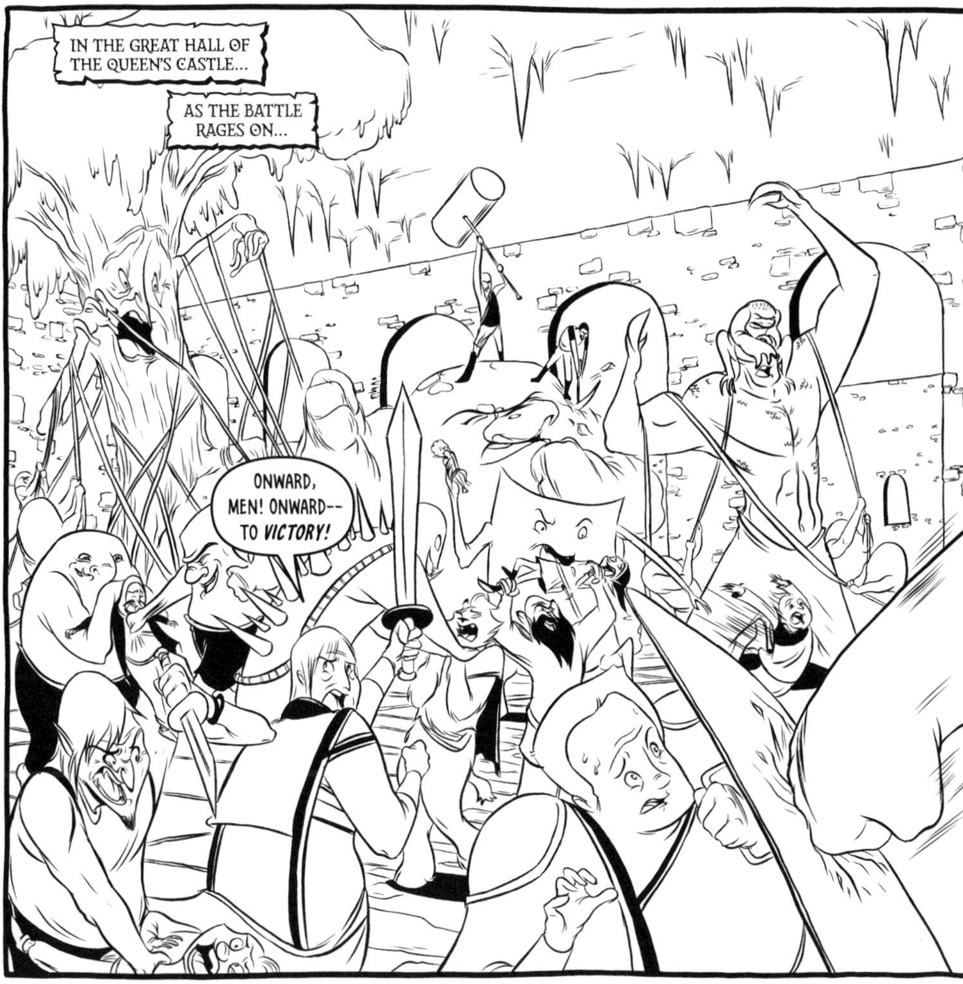
IN THE GREAT HALL OF THE QUEEN'S CASTLE...
AS THE BATTLE RAGES ON...
ONWARD, MEN! ONWARD-- TO VICTORY!
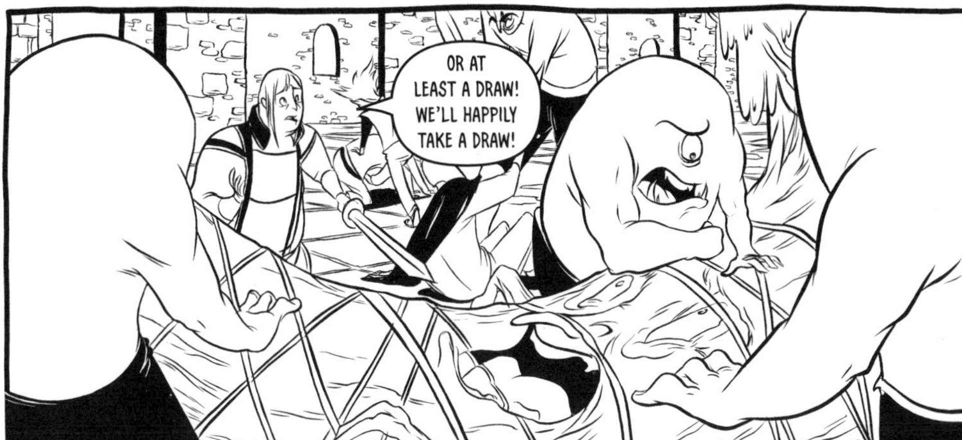
OR AT LEAST A DRAW! WE'LL HAPPILY TAKE A DRAW!

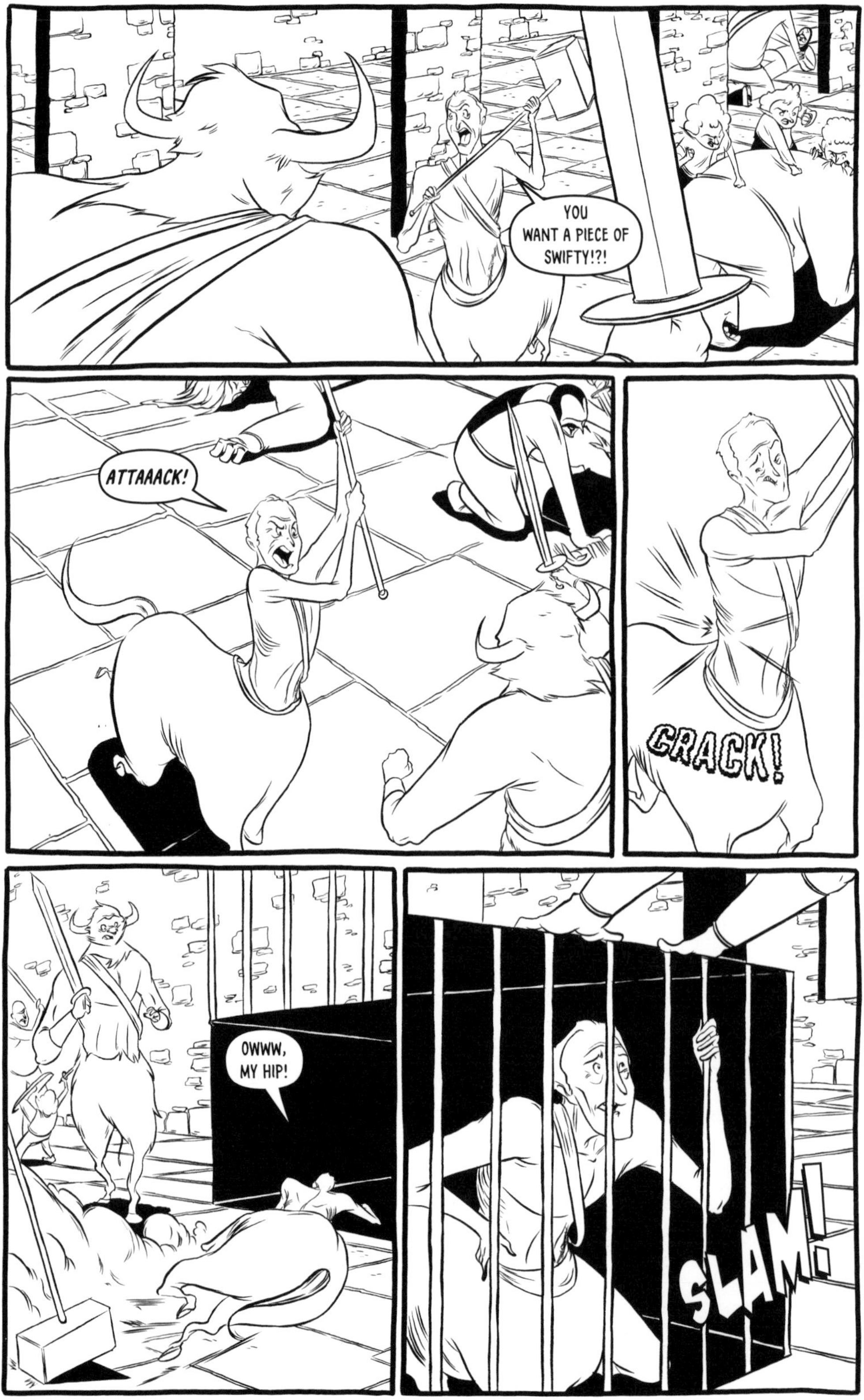
YOU WANT A PIECE OF SWIFTY!?!
ATTAAACK!
CRACK!
OWWW, MY HIP!
SLAM!

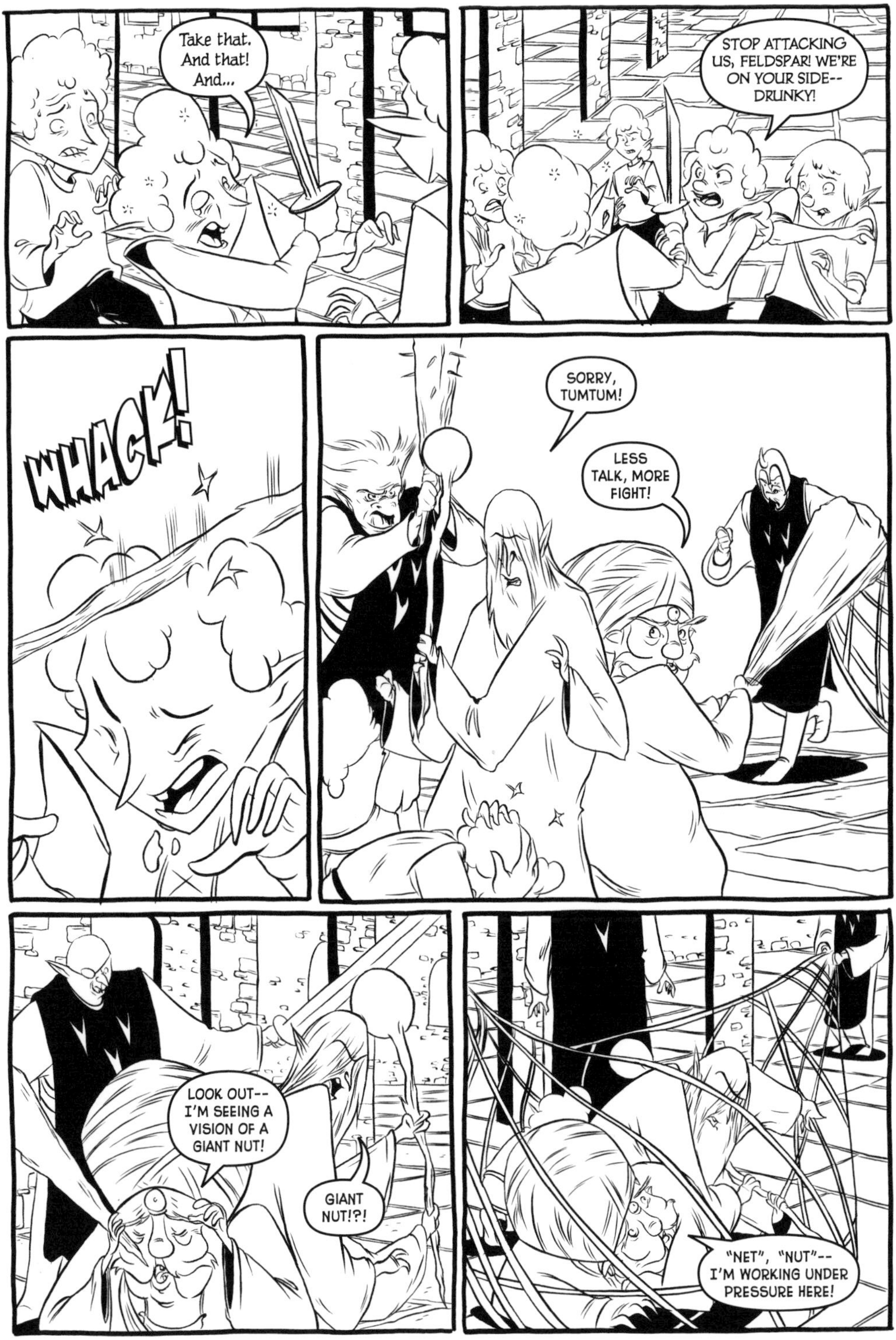
Take that. And that! And...
STOP ATTACKING US, FELDSPAR! WE'RE ON YOUR SIDE--DRUNKY!
WHACK!
SORRY, TUMTUM!
LESS TALK, MORE FIGHT!
LOOK OUT--I'M SEEING A VISION OF A GIANT NUT!
GIANT NUT!?!
"NET", "NUT"--I'M WORKING UNDER PRESSURE HERE!

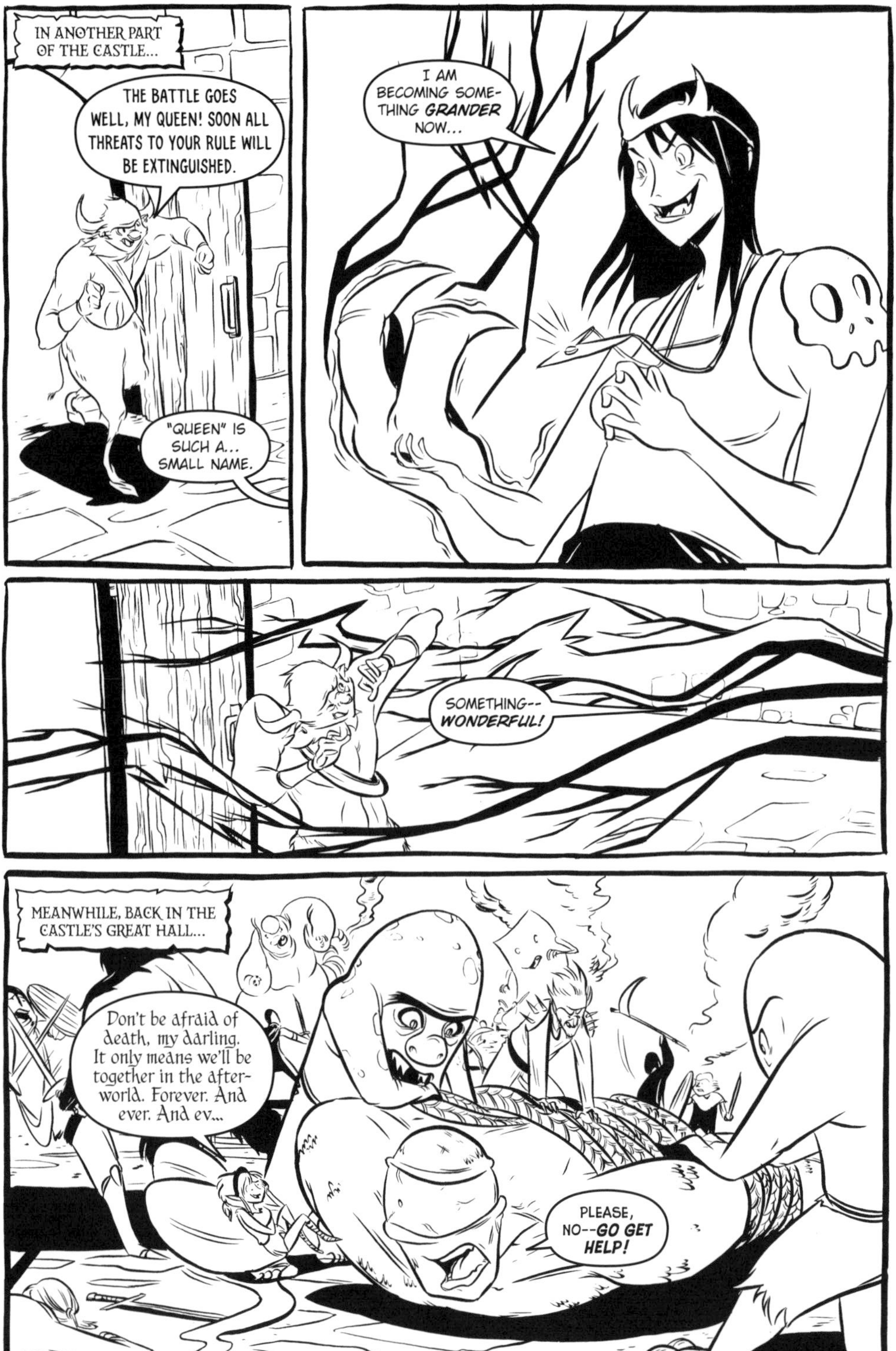
IN ANOTHER PART OF THE CASTLE...
THE BATTLE GOES WELL, MY QUEEN! SOON ALL THREATS TO YOUR RULE WILL BE EXTINGUISHED.
"QUEEN" IS SUCH A... SMALL NAME.
I AM BECOMING SOMETHING GRANDER NOW...
SOMETHING--WONDERFUL!
MEANWHILE, BACK IN THE CASTLE'S GREAT HALL...
Don't be afraid of death, my darling. It only means we'll be together in the afterworld. Forever. And ever. And ev...
PLEASE, NO--GO GET HELP!

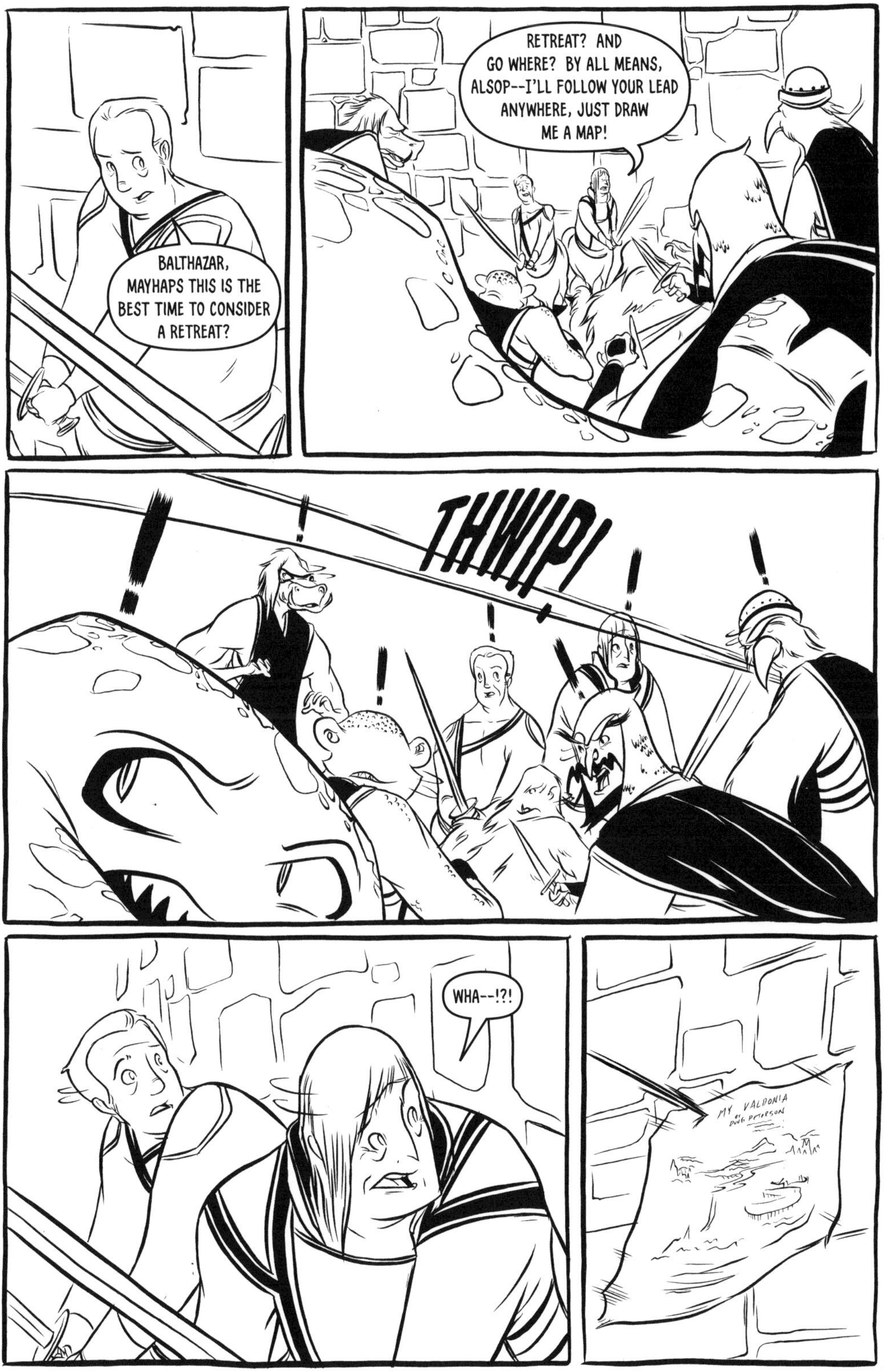
BALTHAZAR, MAYHAPS THIS IS THE BEST TIME TO CONSIDER A RETREAT?
RETREAT? AND GO WHERE? BY ALL MEANS, ALSOP--I'LL FOLLOW YOUR LEAD ANYWHERE, JUST DRAW ME A MAP!
THWIP!
WHA--!?!
MY VALDONIA BY DOUG PETERSON

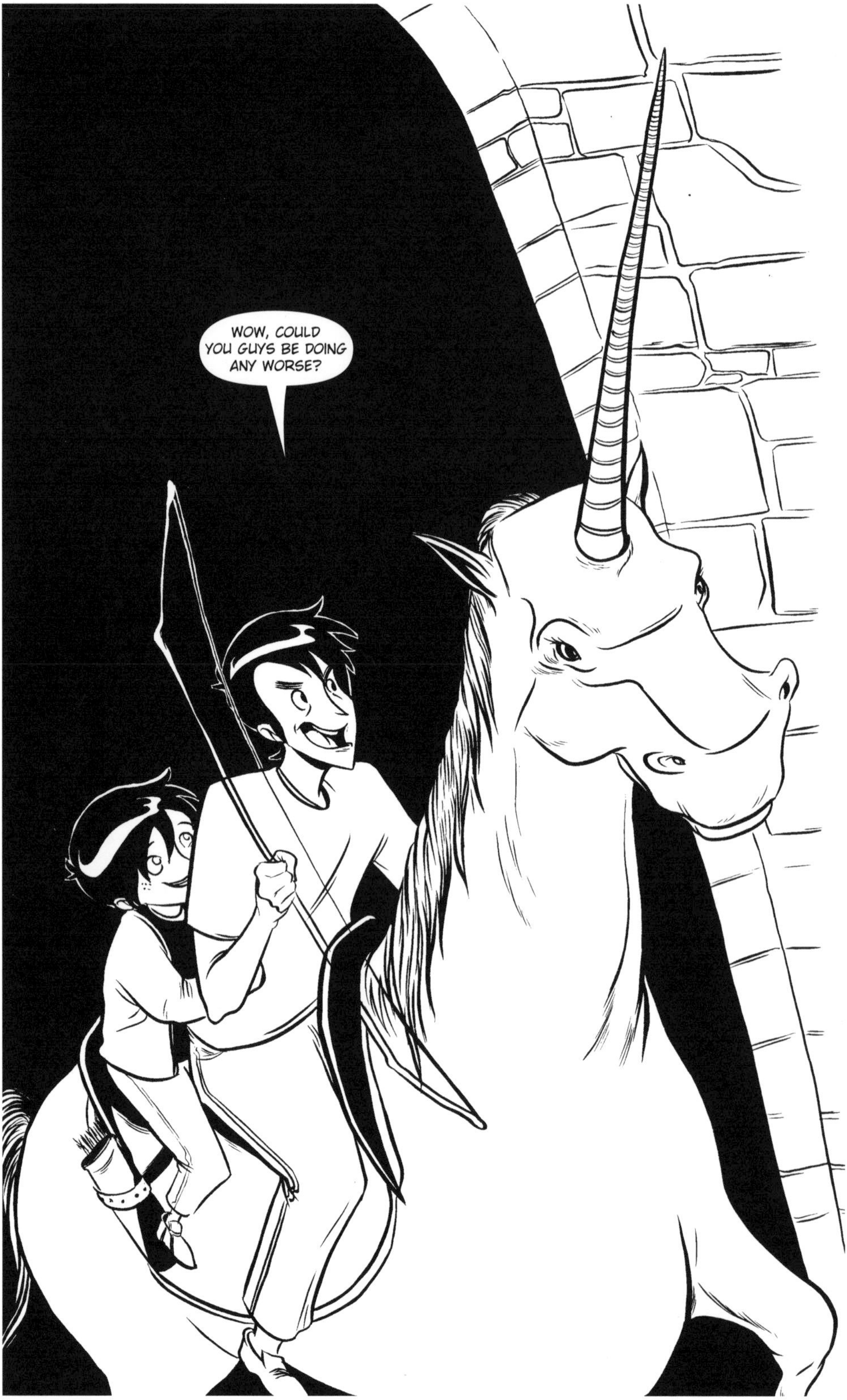
WOW, COULD YOU GUYS BE DOING ANY WORSE?

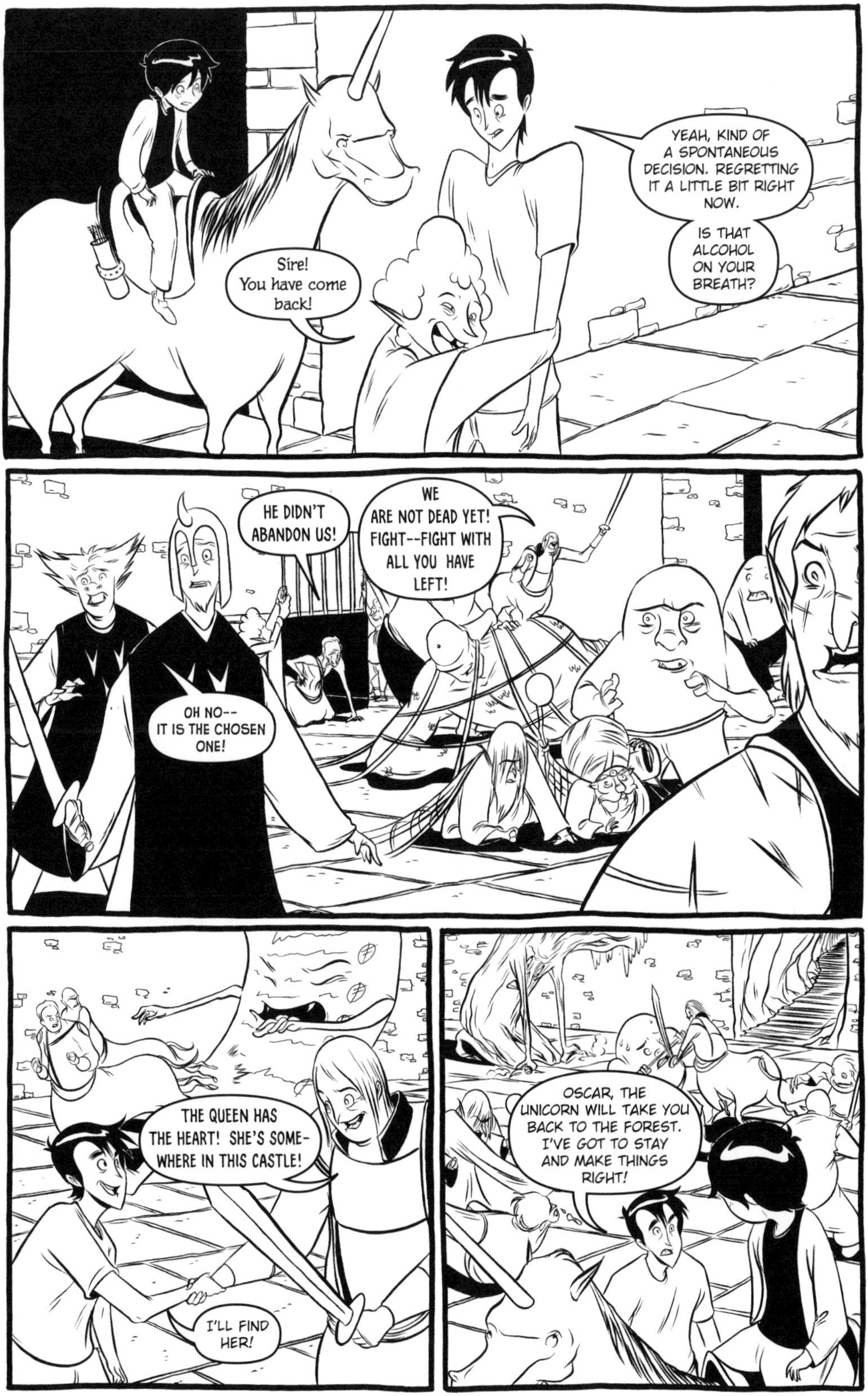
Sire! You have come back!
YEAH, KIND OF A SPONTANEOUS DECISION. REGRETTING IT A LITTLE BIT RIGHT NOW.
IS THAT ALCOHOL ON YOUR BREATH?
HE DIDN'T ABANDON US!
OH NO-- IT IS THE CHOSEN ONE!
WE ARE NOT DEAD YET! FIGHT--FIGHT WITH ALL YOU HAVE LEFT!
THE QUEEN HAS THE HEART! SHE'S SOME-WHERE IN THIS CASTLE!
I'LL FIND HER!
OSCAR, THE UNICORN WILL TAKE YOU BACK TO THE FOREST. I'VE GOT TO STAY AND MAKE THINGS RIGHT!

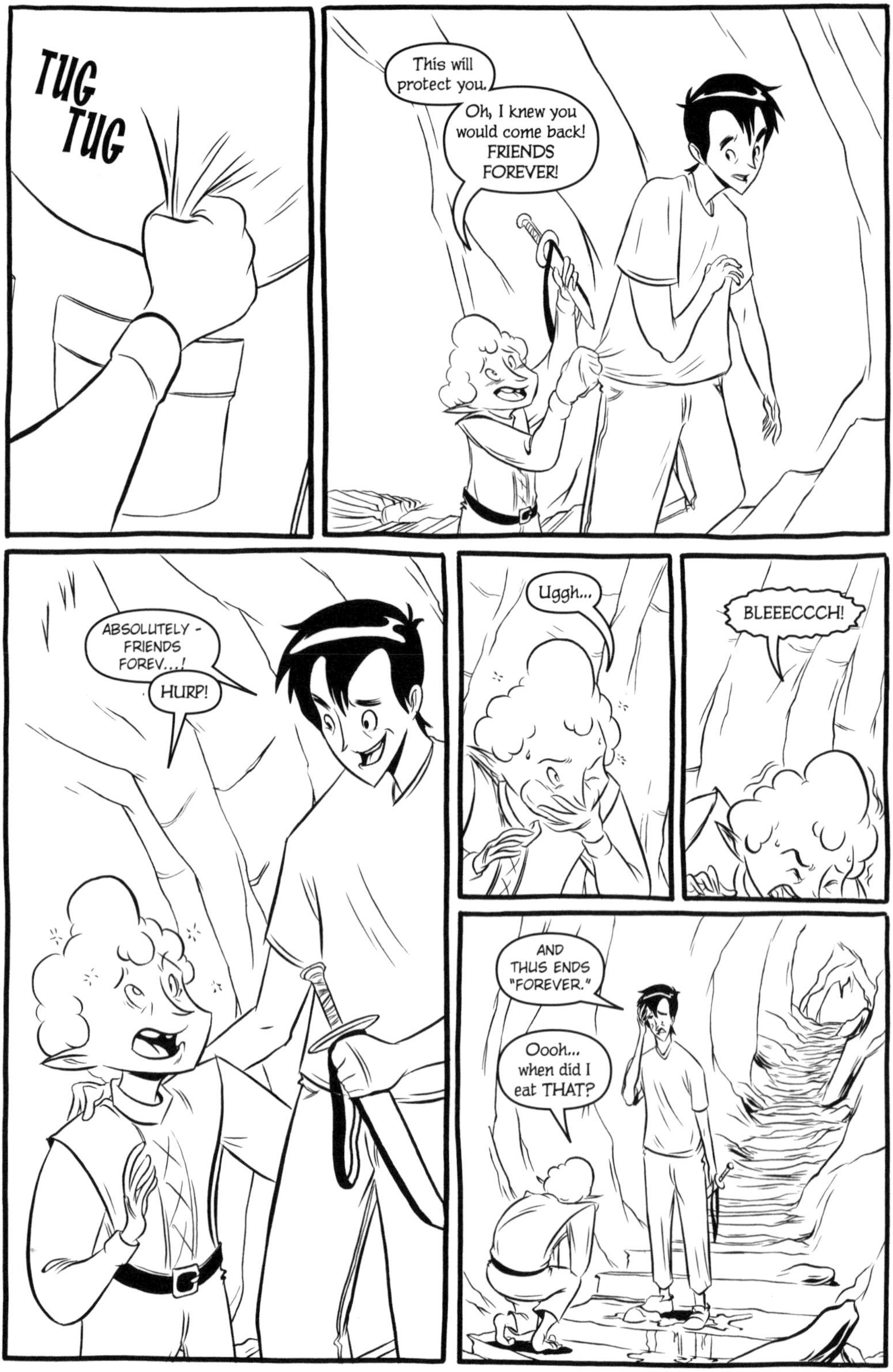
TUG
TUG
This will protect you.
Oh, I knew you would come back! FRIENDS FOREVER!
ABSOLUTELY - FRIENDS FOREV...!
HURP!
Uggh...
BLEEECCCH!
AND THUS ENDS "FOREVER."
Oooh... when did I eat THAT?

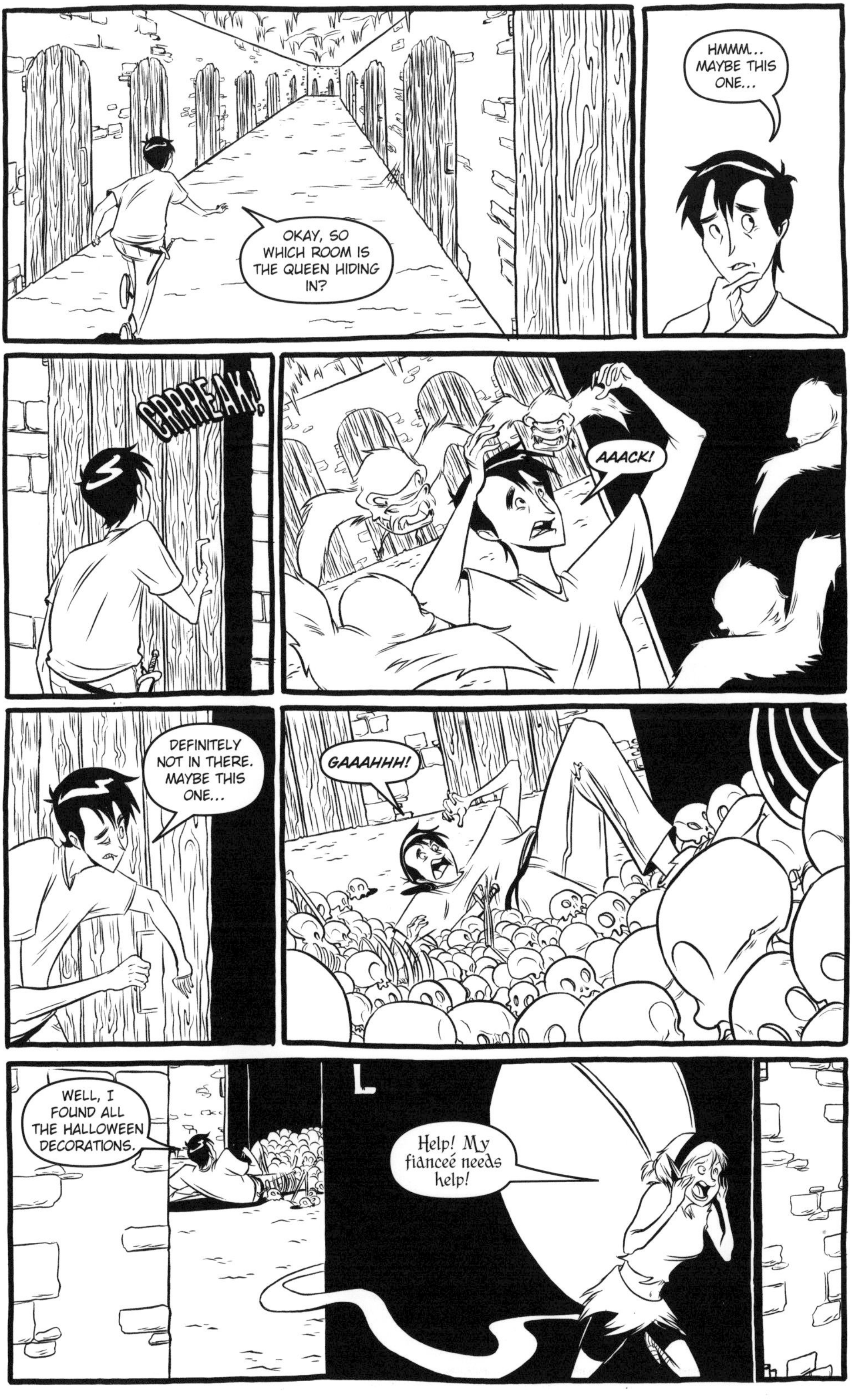
OKAY, SO WHICH ROOM IS THE QUEEN HIDING IN?
HMMM... MAYBE THIS ONE...
CRRREAK!
AAACK!
DEFINITELY NOT IN THERE. MAYBE THIS ONE...
GAAAHHH!
WELL, I FOUND ALL THE HALLOWEEN DECORATIONS.
Help! My fianceé needs help!

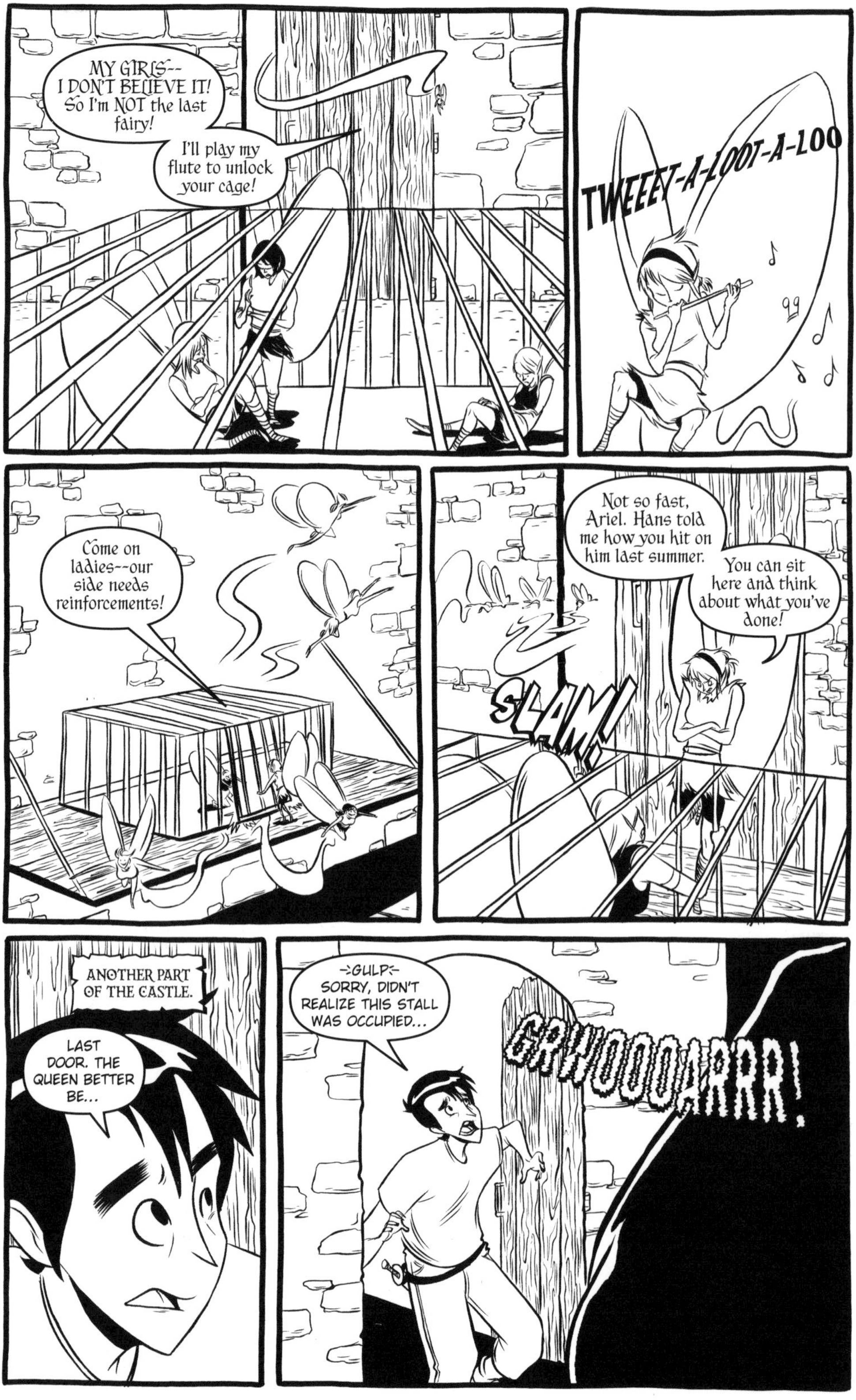
MY GIRLS-- I DON'T BELIEVE IT! So I'm NOT the last fairy!
I'll play my flute to unlock your cage!
TWEEEET-A-LOOT-A-LOO
Come on ladies--our side needs reinforcements!
Not so fast, Ariel. Hans told me how you hit on him last summer.
You can sit here and think about what you've done!
SLAM!
ANOTHER PART OF THE CASTLE.
LAST DOOR. THE QUEEN BETTER BE...
-GULP-
SORRY, DIDN'T REALIZE THIS STALL WAS OCCUPIED...
GRHOOOOARRR!

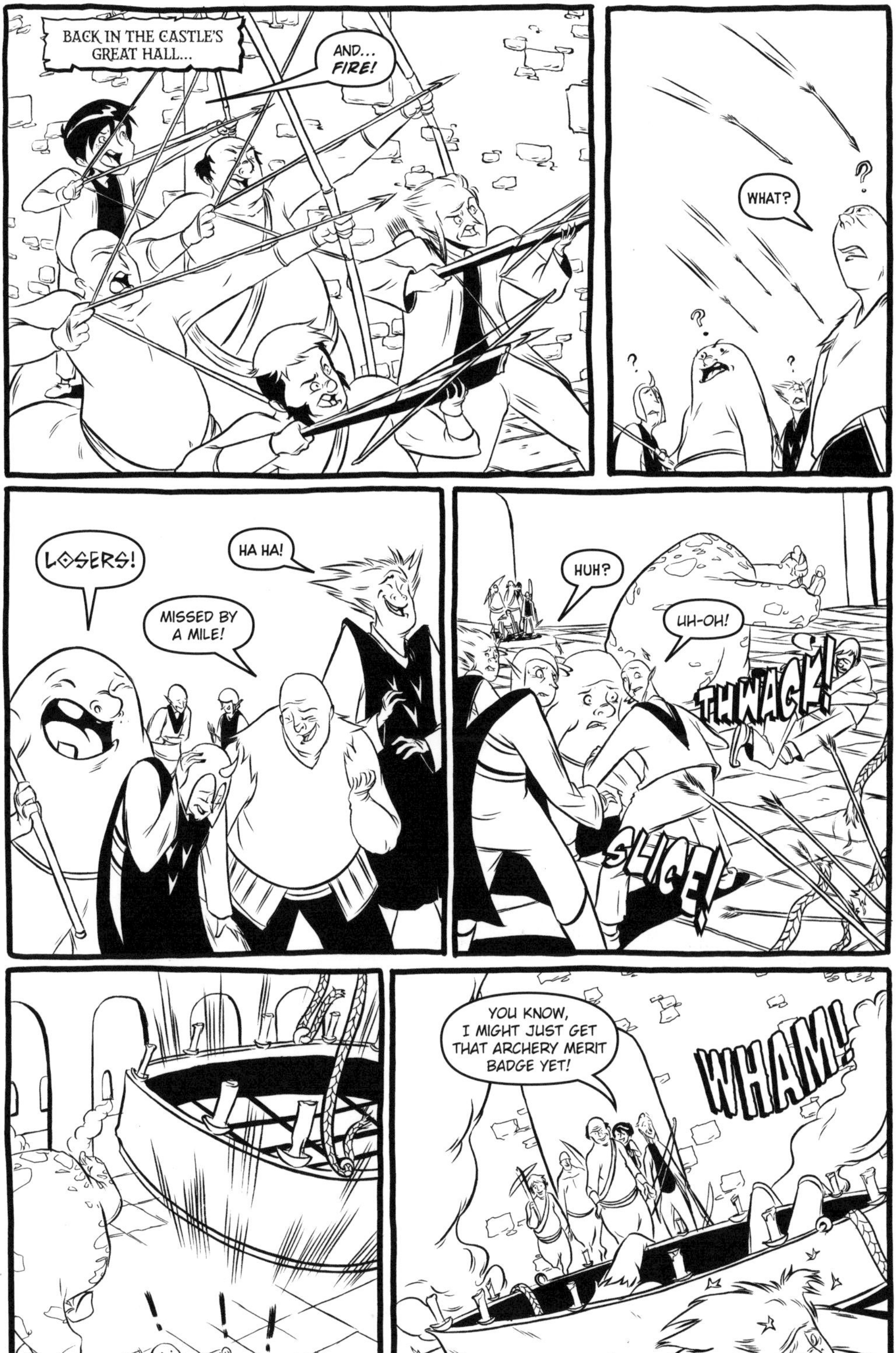
BACK IN THE CASTLE'S GREAT HALL...
AND... FIRE!
WHAT?
?
?
?
?
LOSERS!
HA HA!
MISSED BY A MILE!
HUH?
UH-OH!
THWACK!
SLICE!
!
!
!
YOU KNOW, I MIGHT JUST GET THAT ARCHERY MERIT BADGE YET!
WHAM!

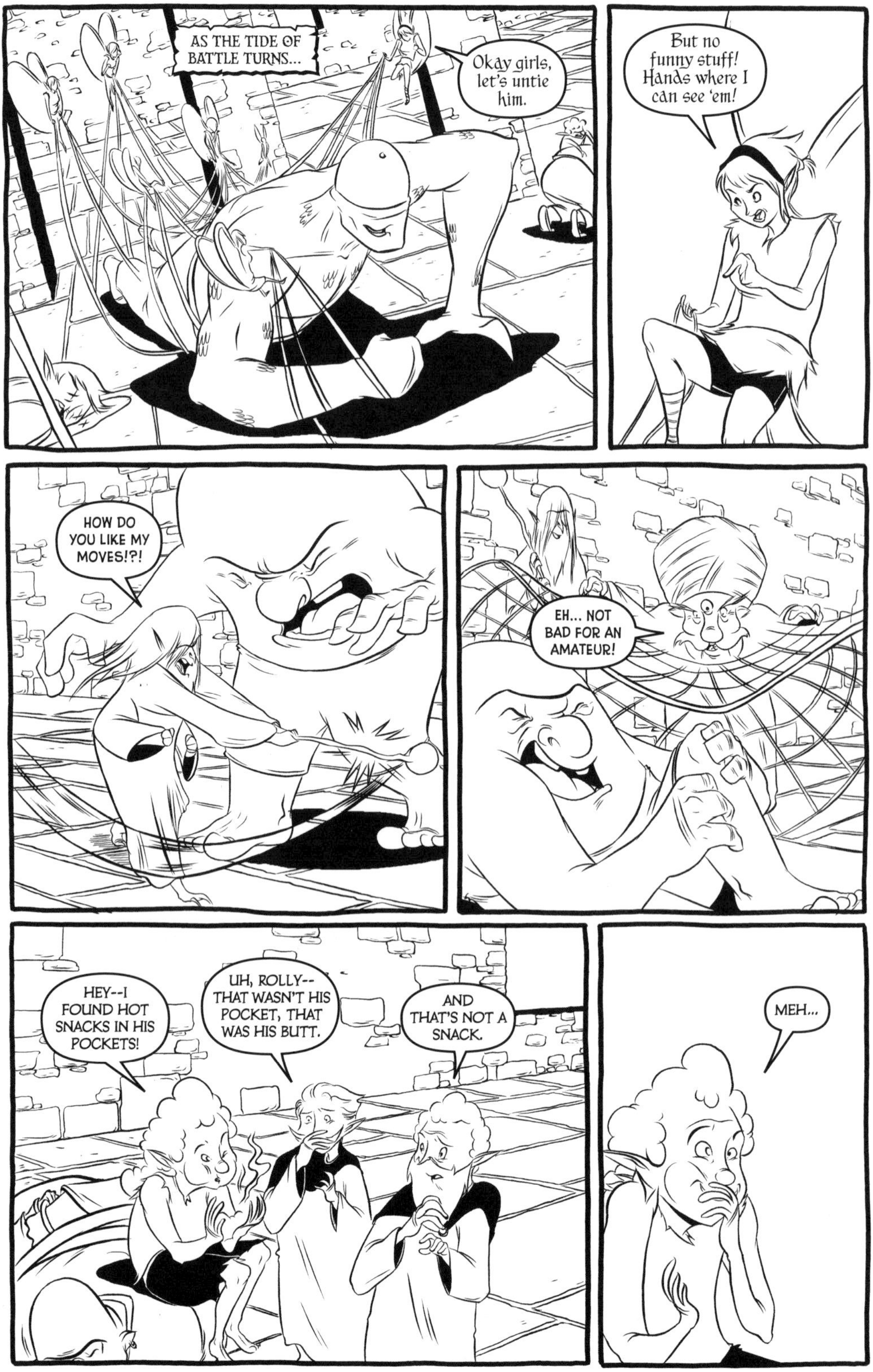
AS THE TIDE OF BATTLE TURNS...
Okay girls, let's untie him.
But no funny stuff! Hands where I can see 'em!
HOW DO YOU LIKE MY MOVES!?!
EH... NOT BAD FOR AN AMATEUR!
HEY--I FOUND HOT SNACKS IN HIS POCKETS!
UH, ROLLY--THAT WASN'T HIS POCKET, THAT WAS HIS BUTT.
AND THAT'S NOT A SNACK.
MEH...

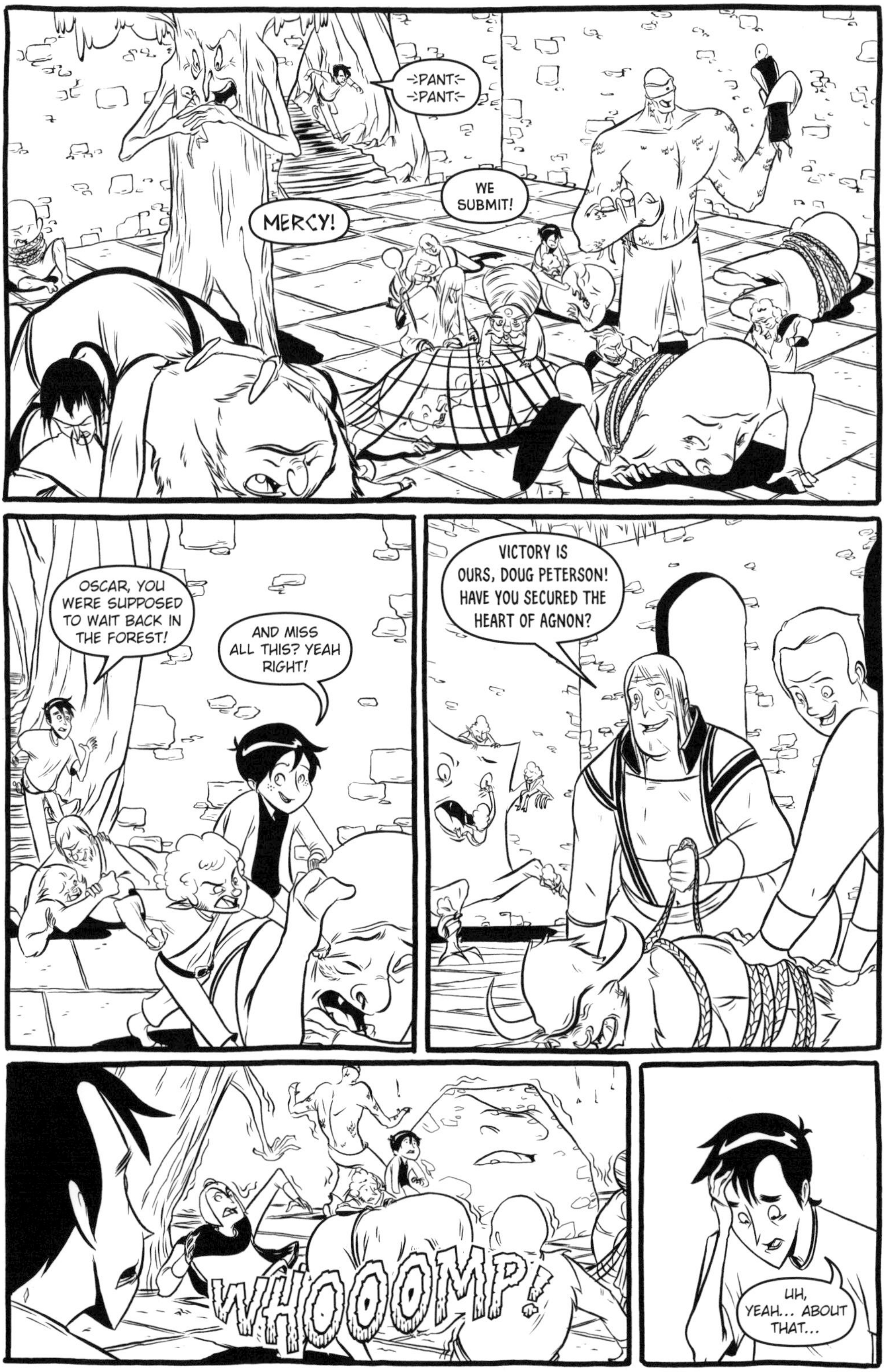

PANT
PANT
MERCY!
WE SUBMIT!
OSCAR, YOU WERE SUPPOSED TO WAIT BACK IN THE FOREST!
AND MISS ALL THIS? YEAH RIGHT!
VICTORY IS OURS, DOUG PETERSON! HAVE YOU SECURED THE HEART OF AGNON?
!
WHOOOMP!
UH, YEAH... ABOUT THAT...

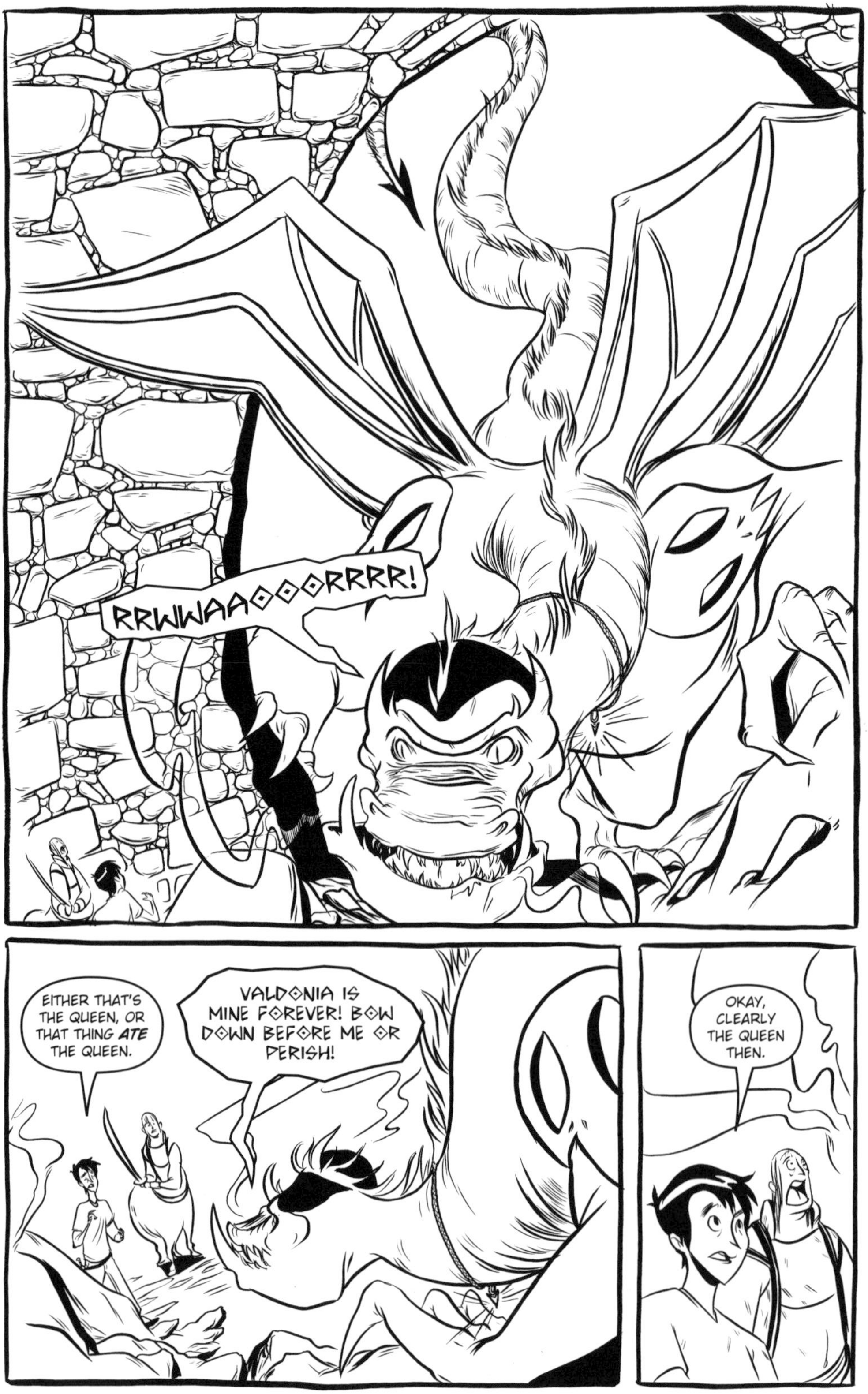
RRWWAAOOORRRR!
EITHER THAT'S THE QUEEN, OR THAT THING *ATE* THE QUEEN.
VALDONIA IS MINE FOREVER! BOW DOWN BEFORE ME OR PERISH!
OKAY, CLEARLY THE QUEEN THEN.

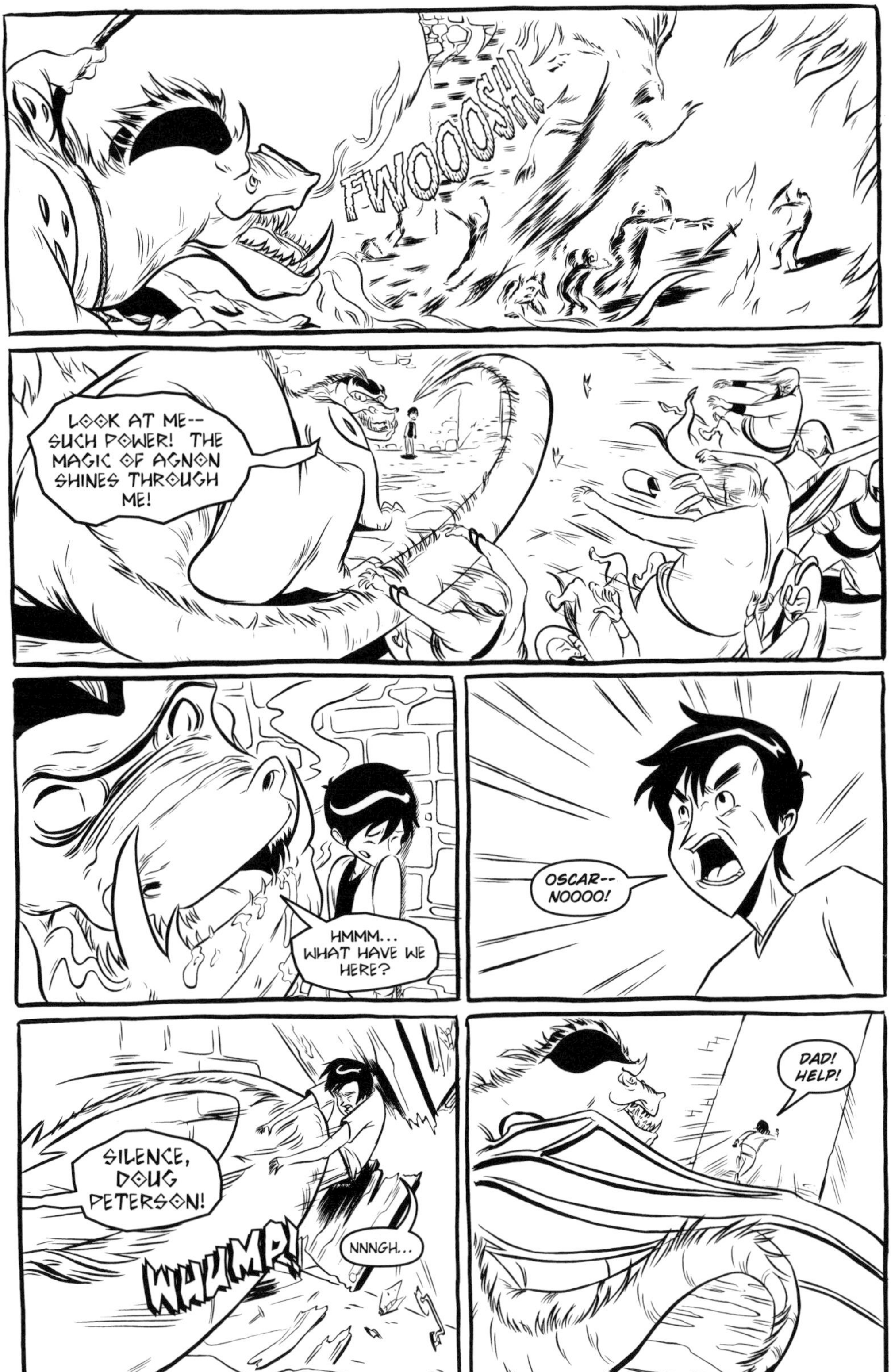
FWOOOSH!
LOOK AT ME-- SUCH POWER! THE MAGIC OF AGNON SHINES THROUGH ME!
HMMM... WHAT HAVE WE HERE?
OSCAR-- NOOOO!
SILENCE, DOUG PETERSON!
WHUMP!
NNNGH...
DAD! HELP!

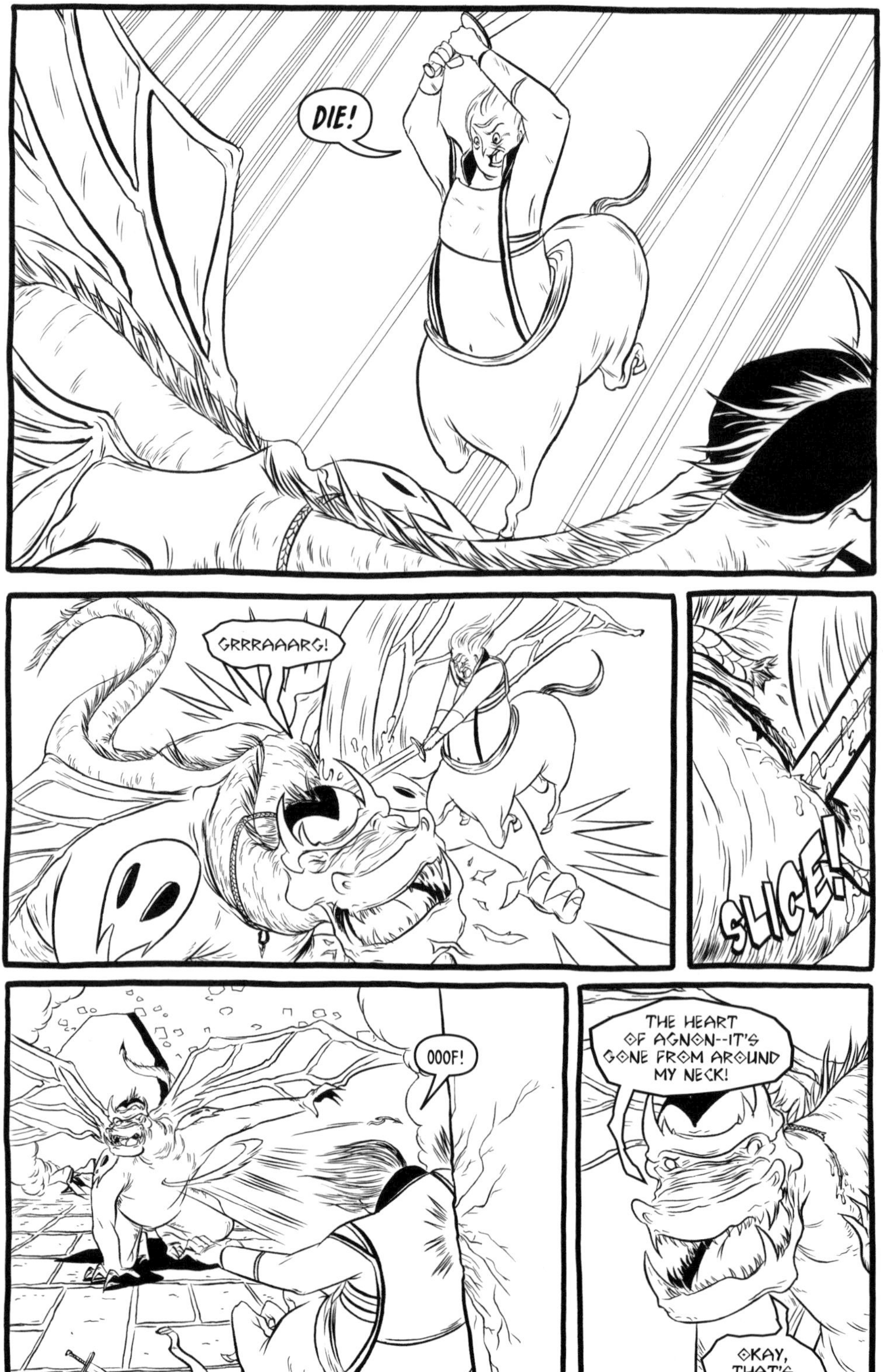
DIE!
GRRRAAARG!
SLICE!
OOOF!
THE HEART OF AGNON--IT'S GONE FROM AROUND MY NECK!
OKAY, THAT'S ANNOYING!

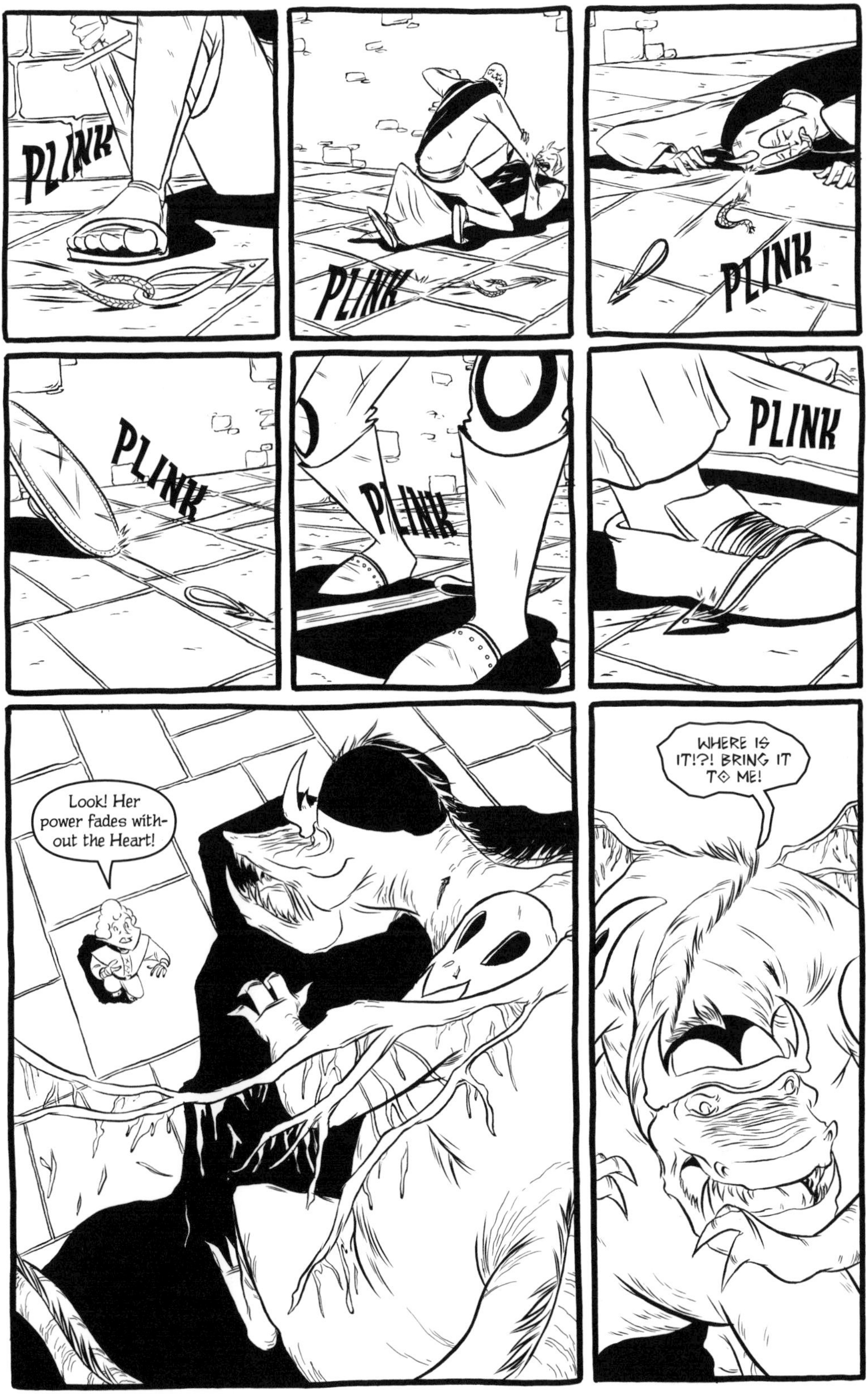
PLINK
PLINK
PLINK
PLINK
PLINK
PLINK
Look! Her power fades without the Heart!
WHERE IS IT!?! BRING IT TO ME!

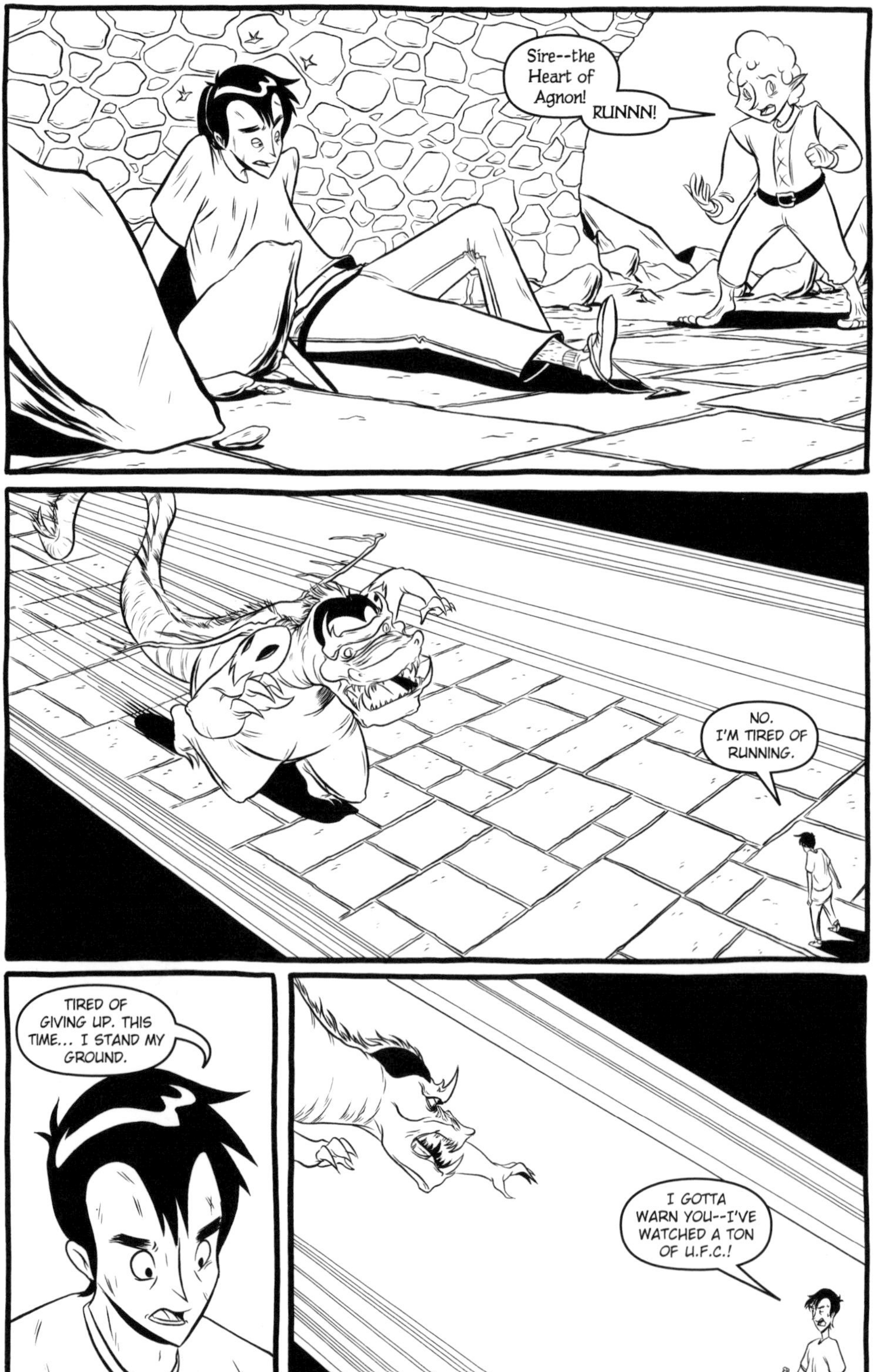
Sire--the Heart of Agnon! RUNNN!
NO. I'M TIRED OF RUNNING.
TIRED OF GIVING UP. THIS TIME... I STAND MY GROUND.
I GOTTA WARN YOU--I'VE WATCHED A TON OF U.F.C.!

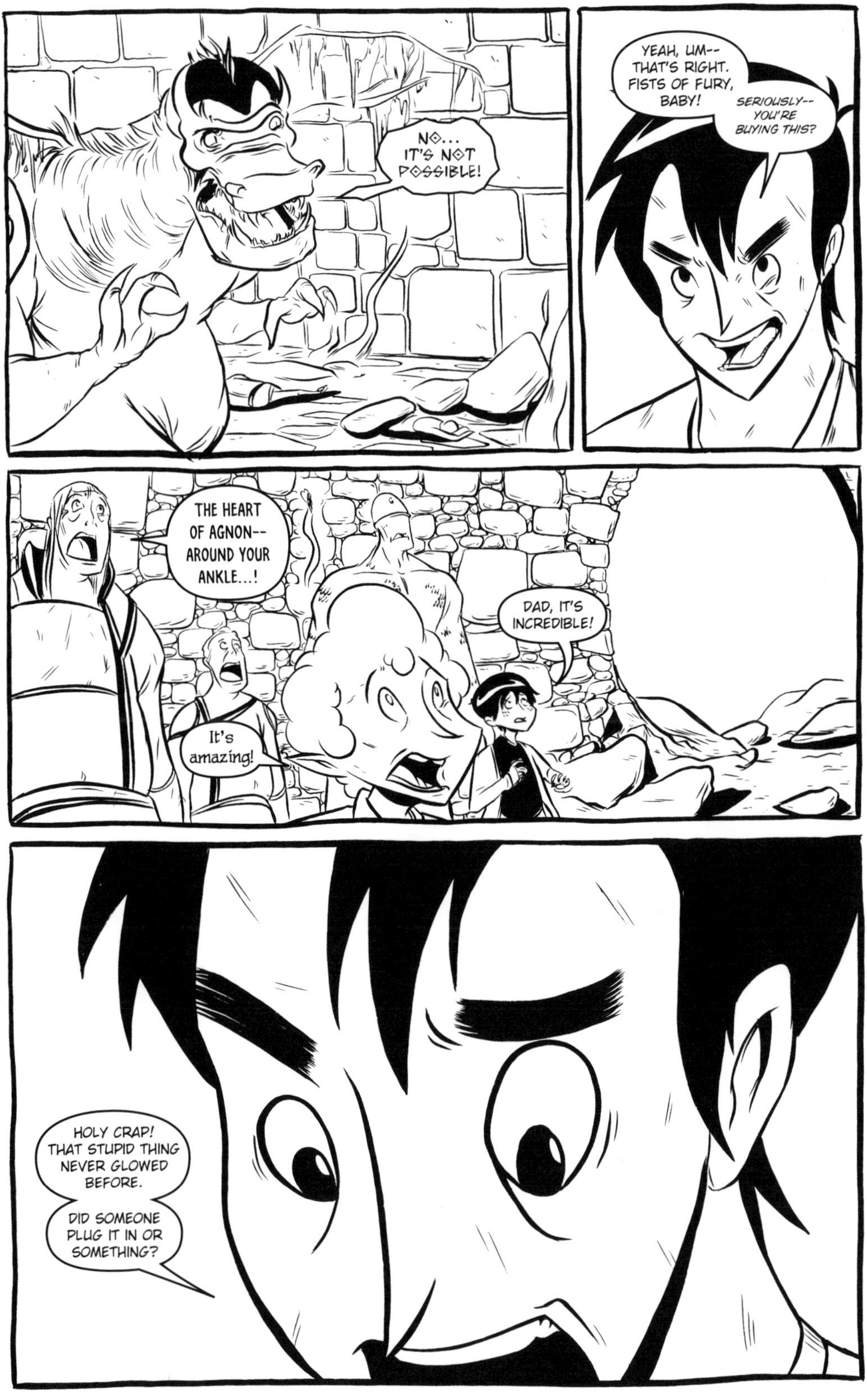
NO... IT'S NOT POSSIBLE!
YEAH, UM-- THAT'S RIGHT. FISTS OF FURY, BABY!
SERIOUSLY-- YOU'RE BUYING THIS?
THE HEART OF AGNON-- AROUND YOUR ANKLE...!
DAD, IT'S INCREDIBLE!
It's amazing!
HOLY CRAP! THAT STUPID THING NEVER GLOWED BEFORE.
DID SOMEONE PLUG IT IN OR SOMETHING?

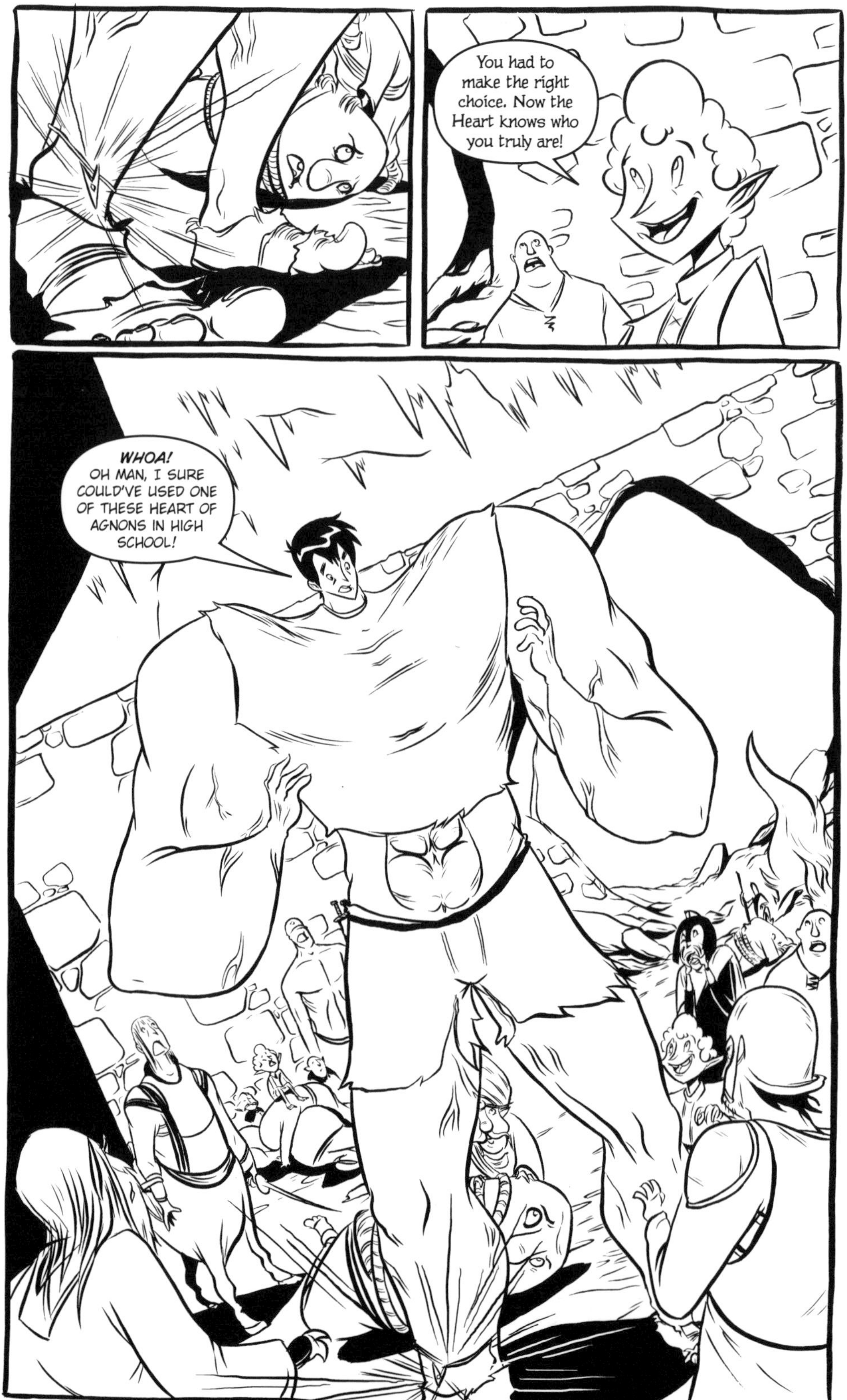
You had to make the right choice. Now the Heart knows who you truly are!
WHOA! OH MAN, I SURE COULD'VE USED ONE OF THESE HEART OF AGNONS IN HIGH SCHOOL!

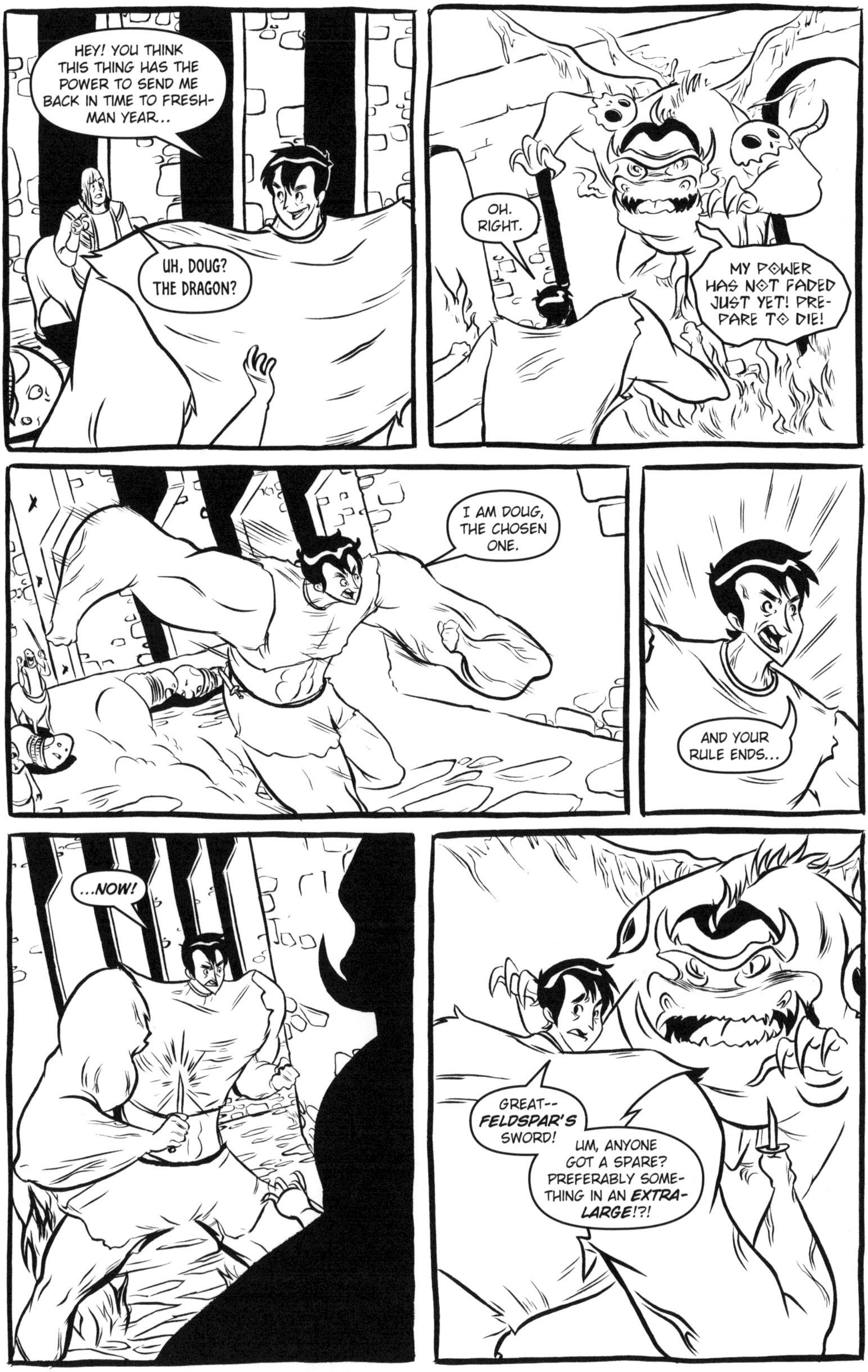
HEY! YOU THINK THIS THING HAS THE POWER TO SEND ME BACK IN TIME TO FRESH-MAN YEAR...
UH, DOUG? THE DRAGON?
OH. RIGHT.
MY POWER HAS NOT FADED JUST YET! PRE-PARE TO DIE!
I AM DOUG, THE CHOSEN ONE.
AND YOUR RULE ENDS...
...NOW!
GREAT-- FELDSPAR'S SWORD!
UM, ANYONE GOT A SPARE? PREFERABLY SOME-THING IN AN EXTRA-LARGE!?!

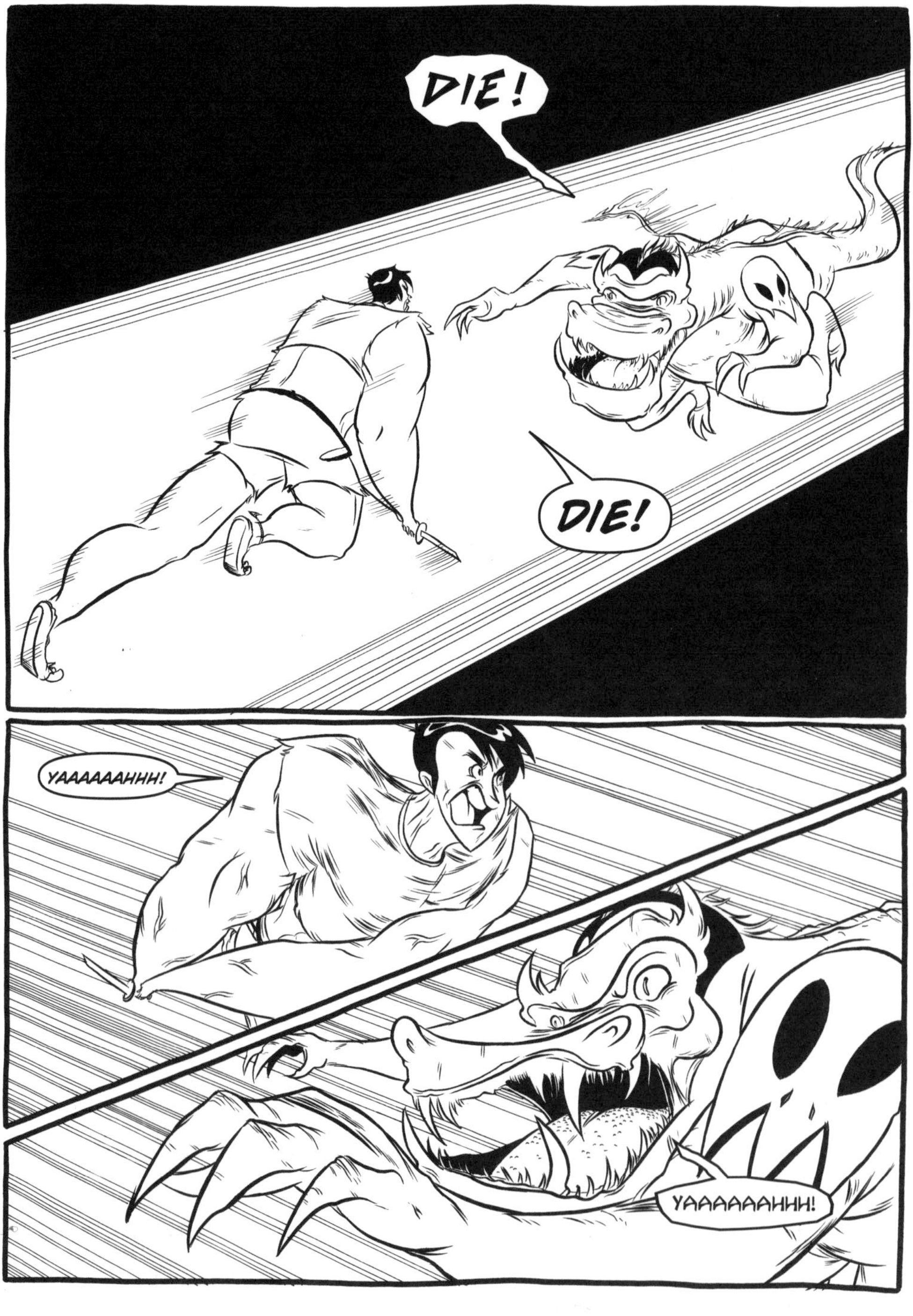
DIE!
DIE!
YAAAAAAHHH!
YAAAAAAHHH!

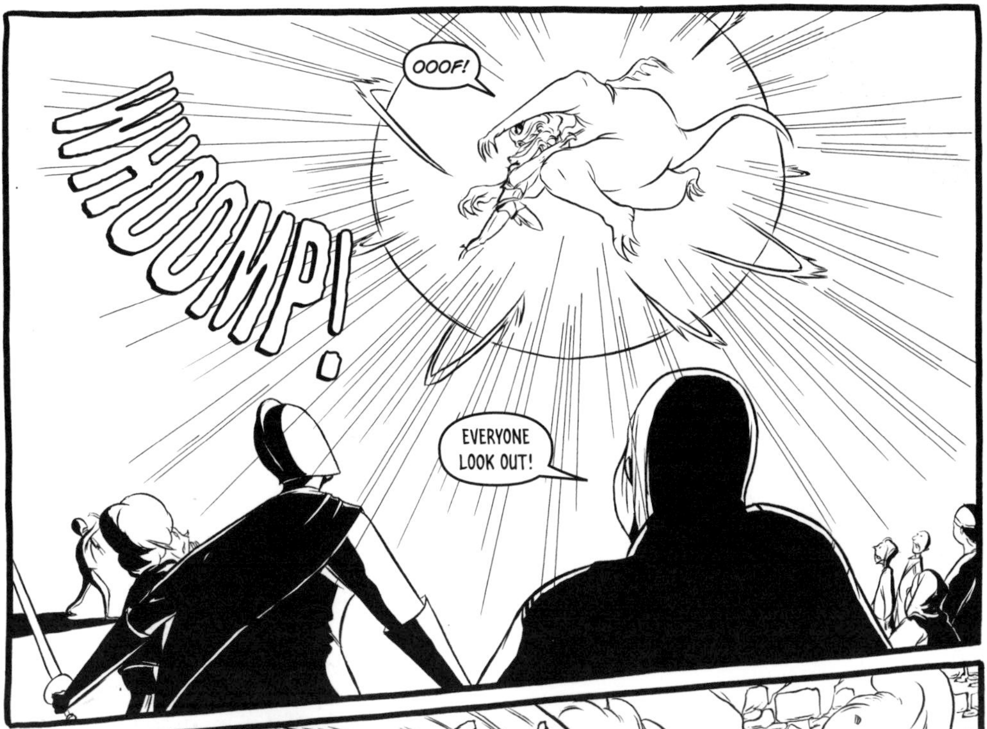
WHOOMP!
OOOF!
EVERYONE LOOK OUT!

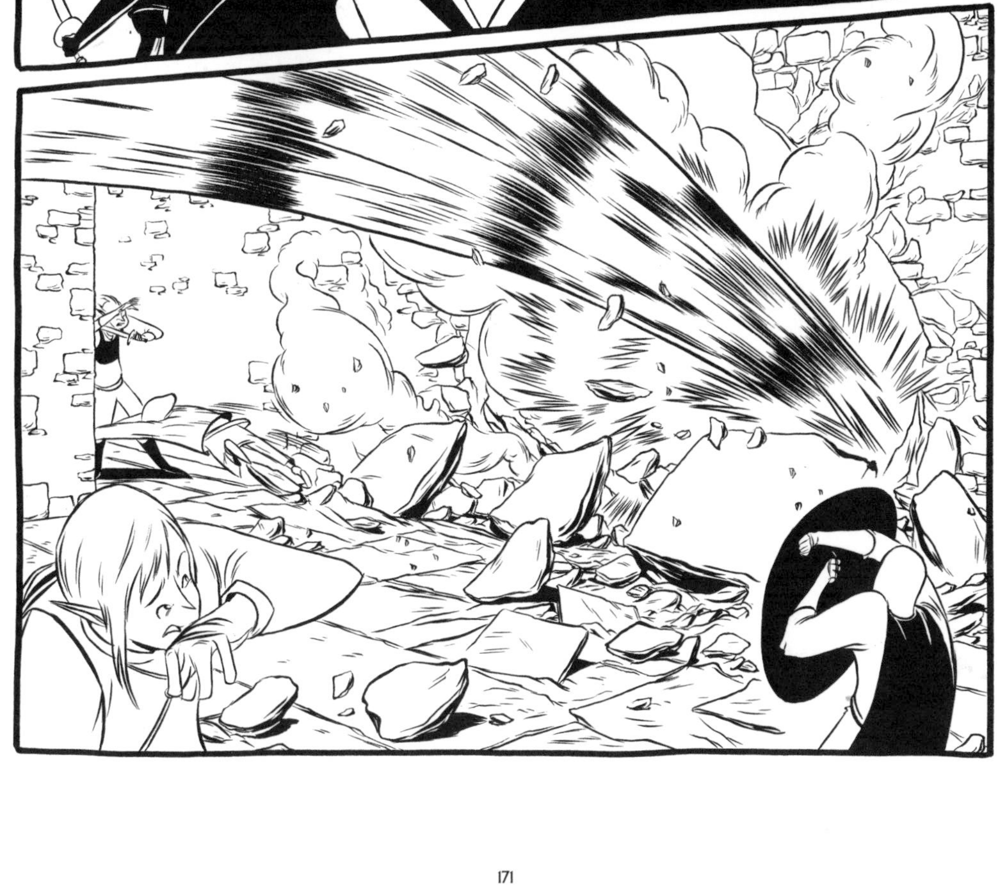

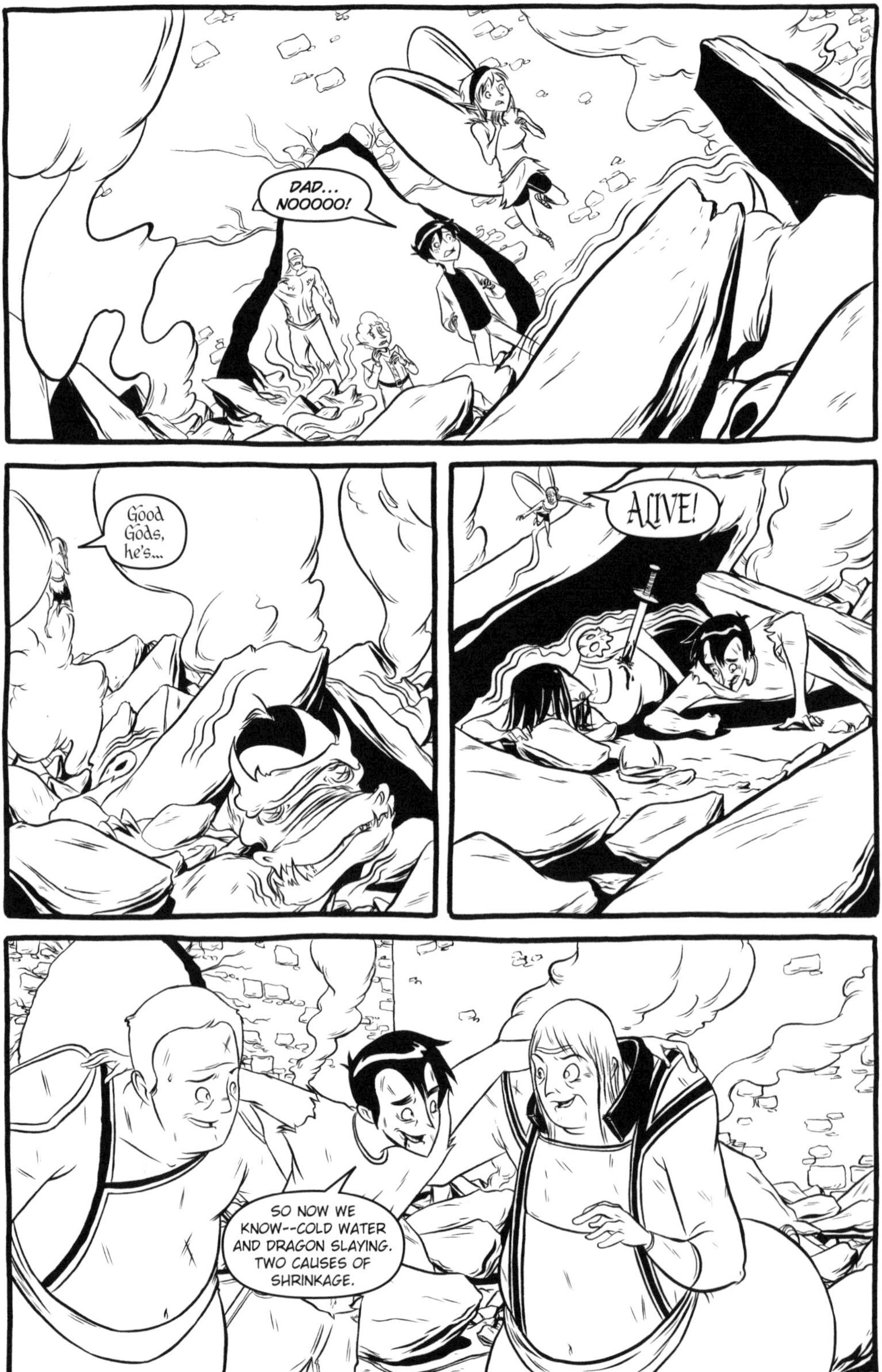
DAD... NOOOOO!
Good Gods, he's...
ALIVE!
SO NOW WE KNOW--COLD WATER AND DRAGON SLAYING. TWO CAUSES OF SHRINKAGE.

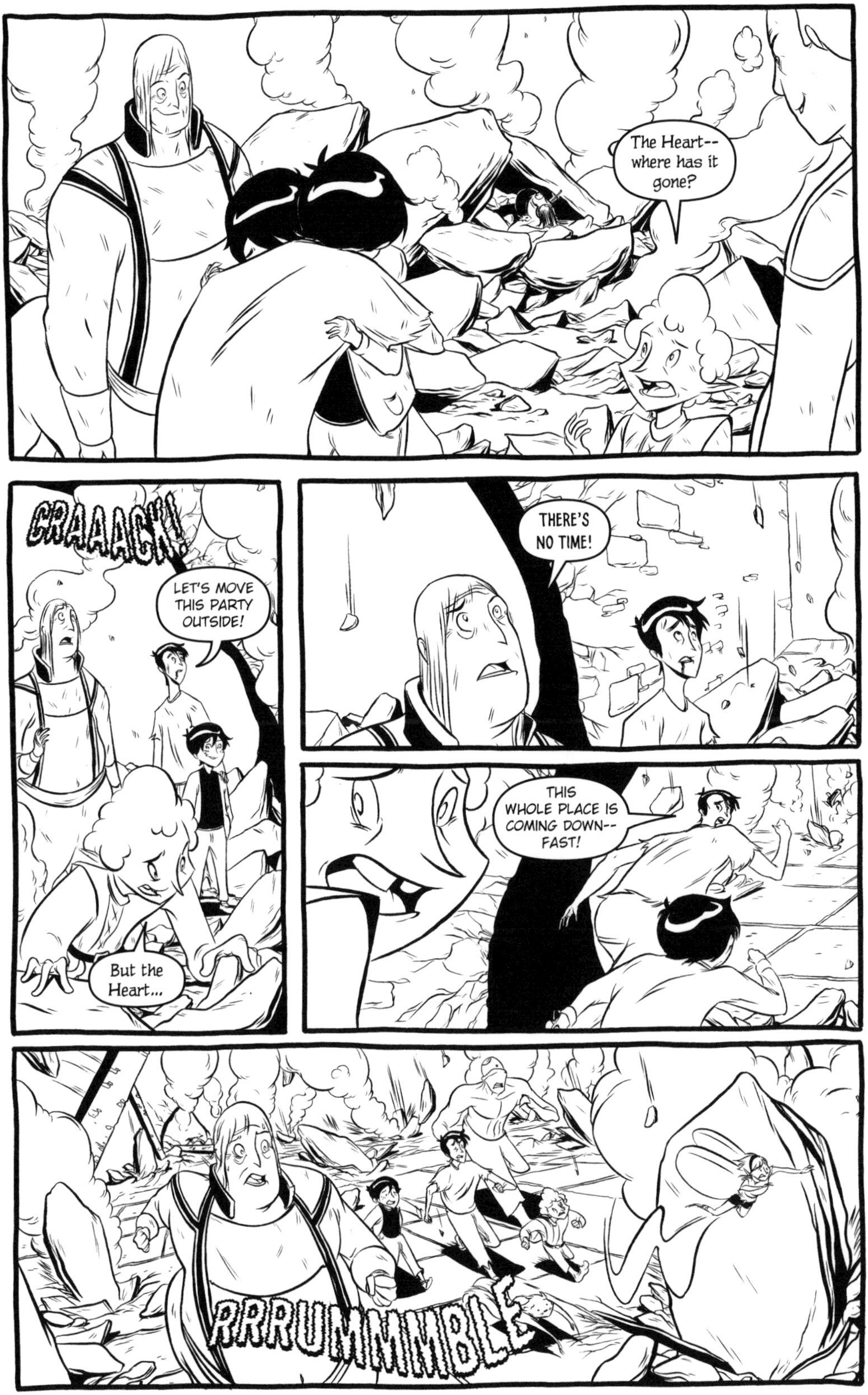
The Heart--
where has it
gone?
CRAAACK!
LET'S MOVE
THIS PARTY
OUTSIDE!
But the
Heart...
THERE'S
NO TIME!
THIS
WHOLE PLACE IS
COMING DOWN--
FAST!
RRRUMMMBLE

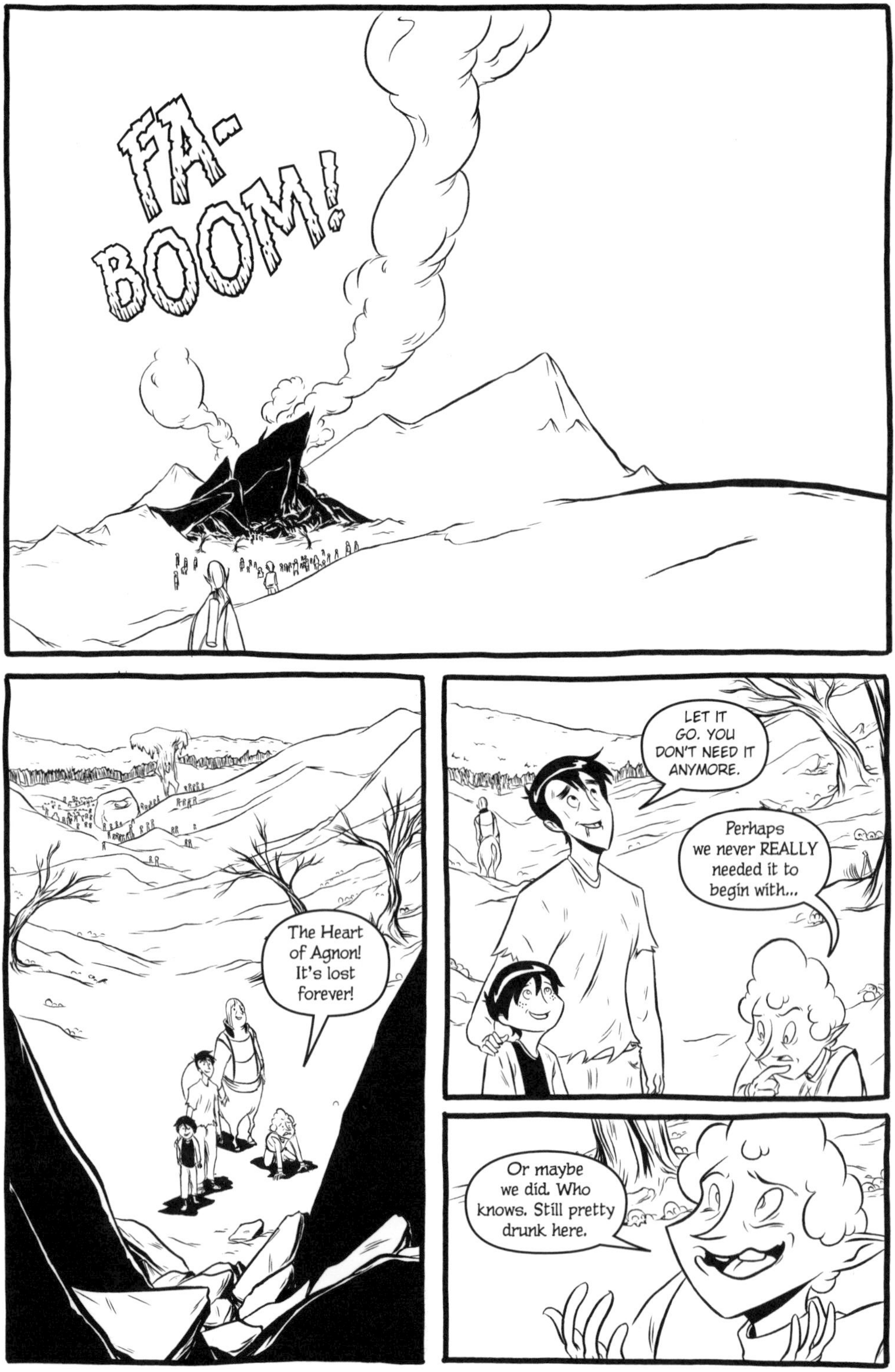
FA-BOOM!
The Heart of Agnon! It's lost forever!
LET IT GO. YOU DON'T NEED IT ANYMORE.
Perhaps we never REALLY needed it to begin with...
Or maybe we did. Who knows. Still pretty drunk here.

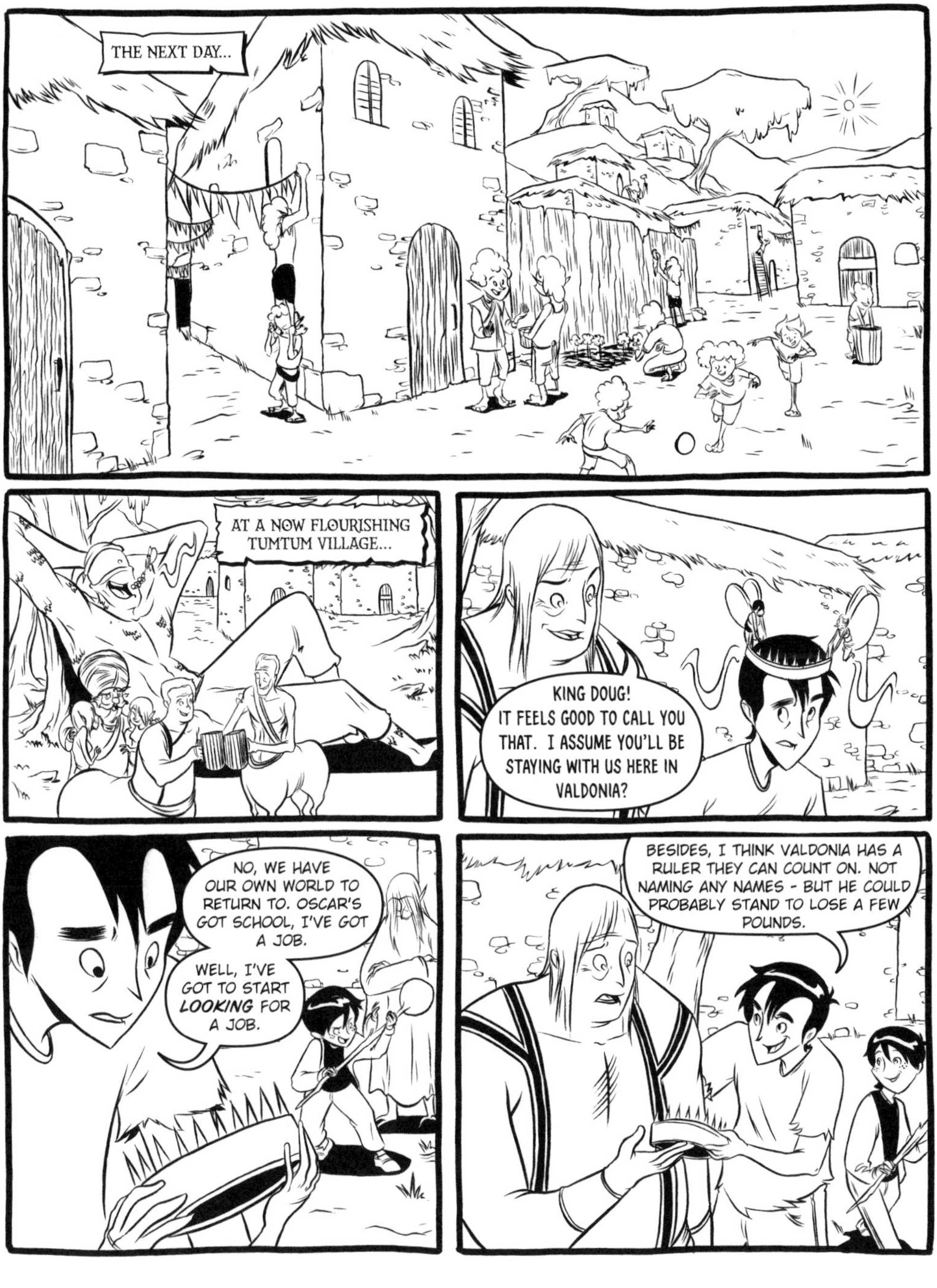

THE NEXT DAY...
AT A NOW FLOURISHING TUMTUM VILLAGE...
KING DOUG! IT FEELS GOOD TO CALL YOU THAT. I ASSUME YOU'LL BE STAYING WITH US HERE IN VALDONIA?
NO, WE HAVE OUR OWN WORLD TO RETURN TO. OSCAR'S GOT SCHOOL, I'VE GOT A JOB.
WELL, I'VE GOT TO START ***LOOKING*** FOR A JOB.
BESIDES, I THINK VALDONIA HAS A RULER THEY CAN COUNT ON. NOT NAMING ANY NAMES - BUT HE COULD PROBABLY STAND TO LOSE A FEW POUNDS.

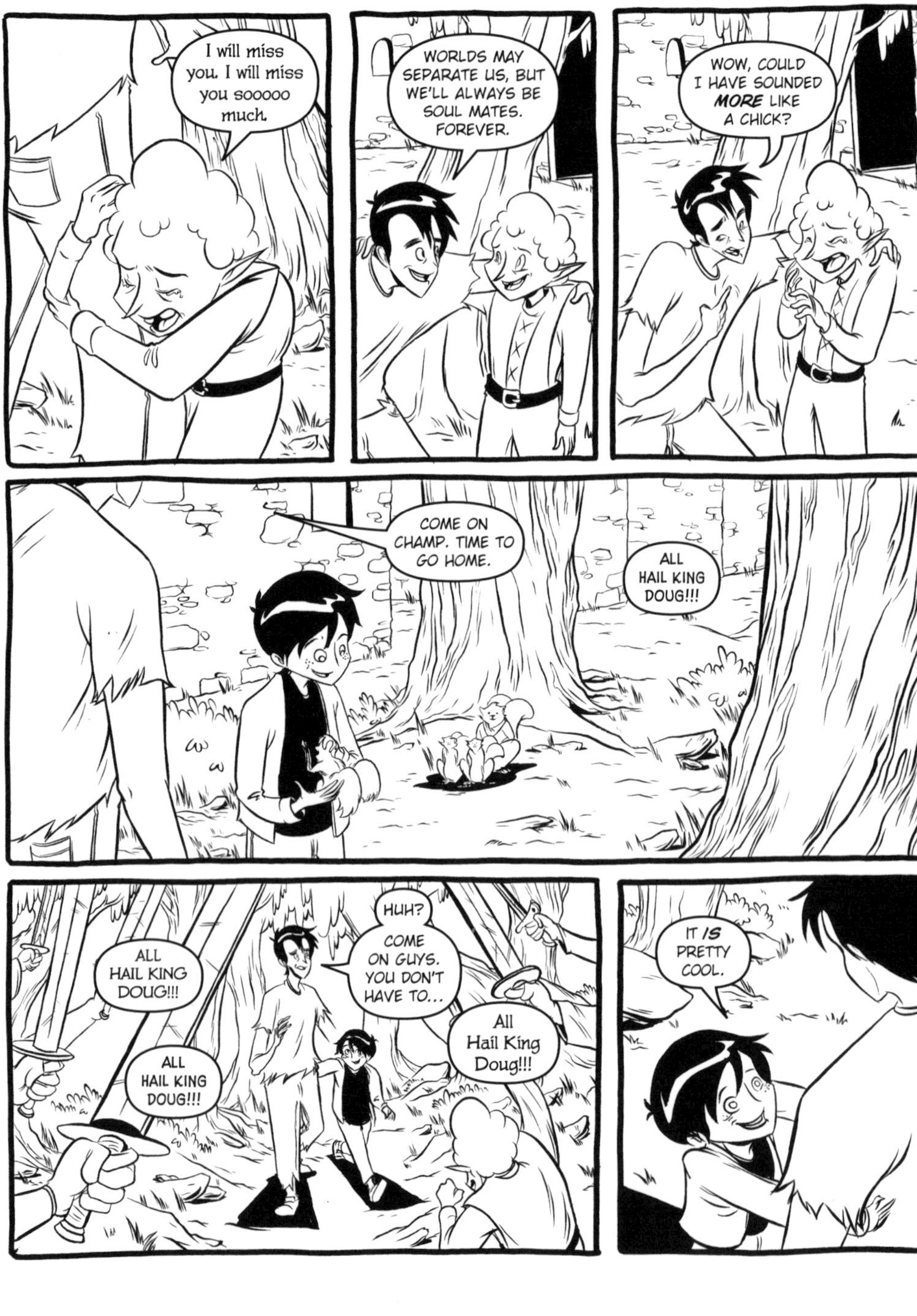
I will miss you. I will miss you sooooo much.
WORLDS MAY SEPARATE US, BUT WE'LL ALWAYS BE SOUL MATES. FOREVER.
WOW, COULD I HAVE SOUNDED **MORE** LIKE A CHICK?
COME ON CHAMP. TIME TO GO HOME.
ALL HAIL KING DOUG!!!
ALL HAIL KING DOUG!!!
ALL HAIL KING DOUG!!!
HUH?
COME ON GUYS. YOU DON'T HAVE TO...
All Hail King Doug!!!
IT ***IS*** PRETTY COOL.

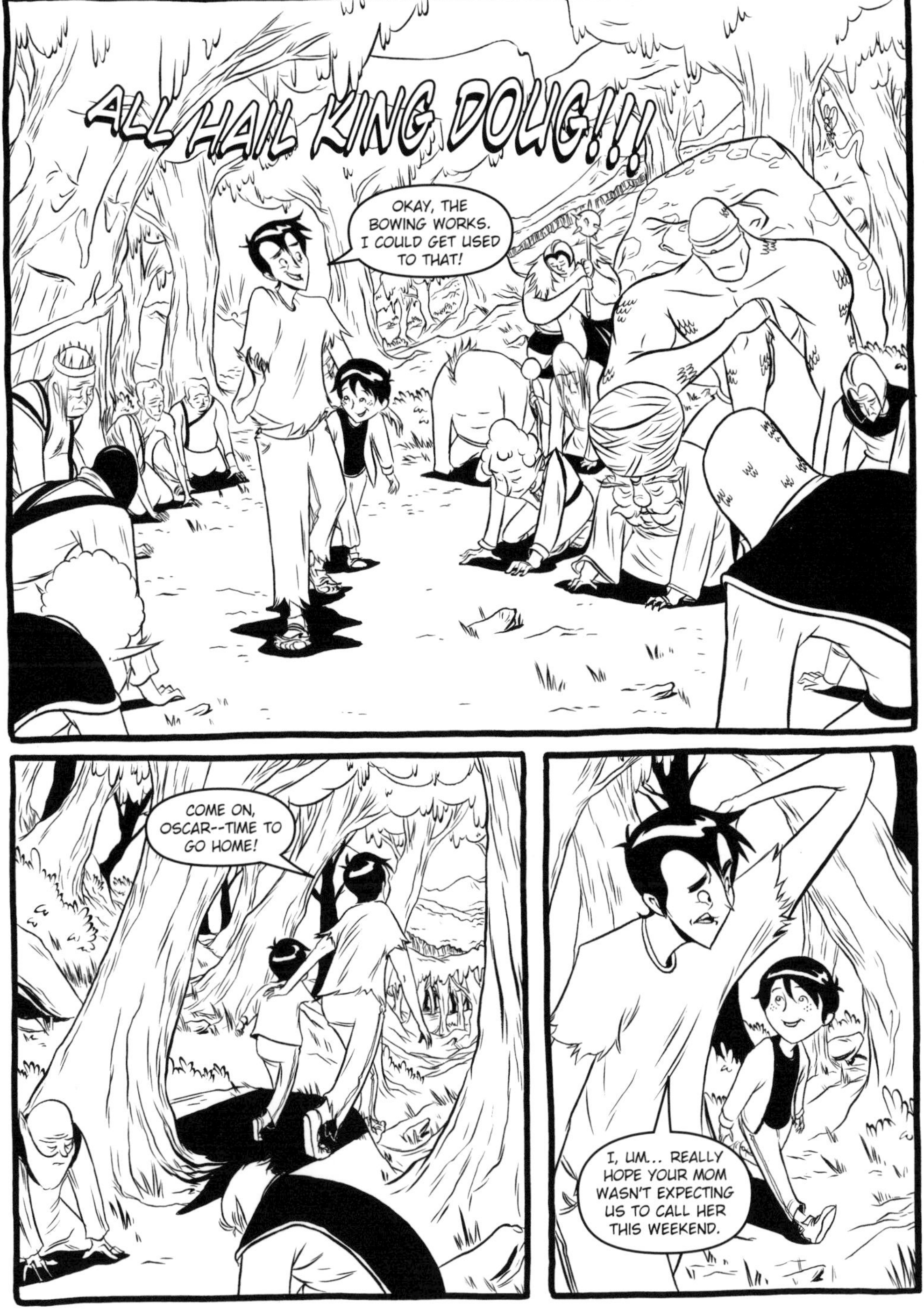
ALL HAIL KING DOUG!!!
OKAY, THE BOWING WORKS. I COULD GET USED TO THAT!
COME ON, OSCAR--TIME TO GO HOME!
I, UM... REALLY HOPE YOUR MOM WASN'T EXPECTING US TO CALL HER THIS WEEKEND.

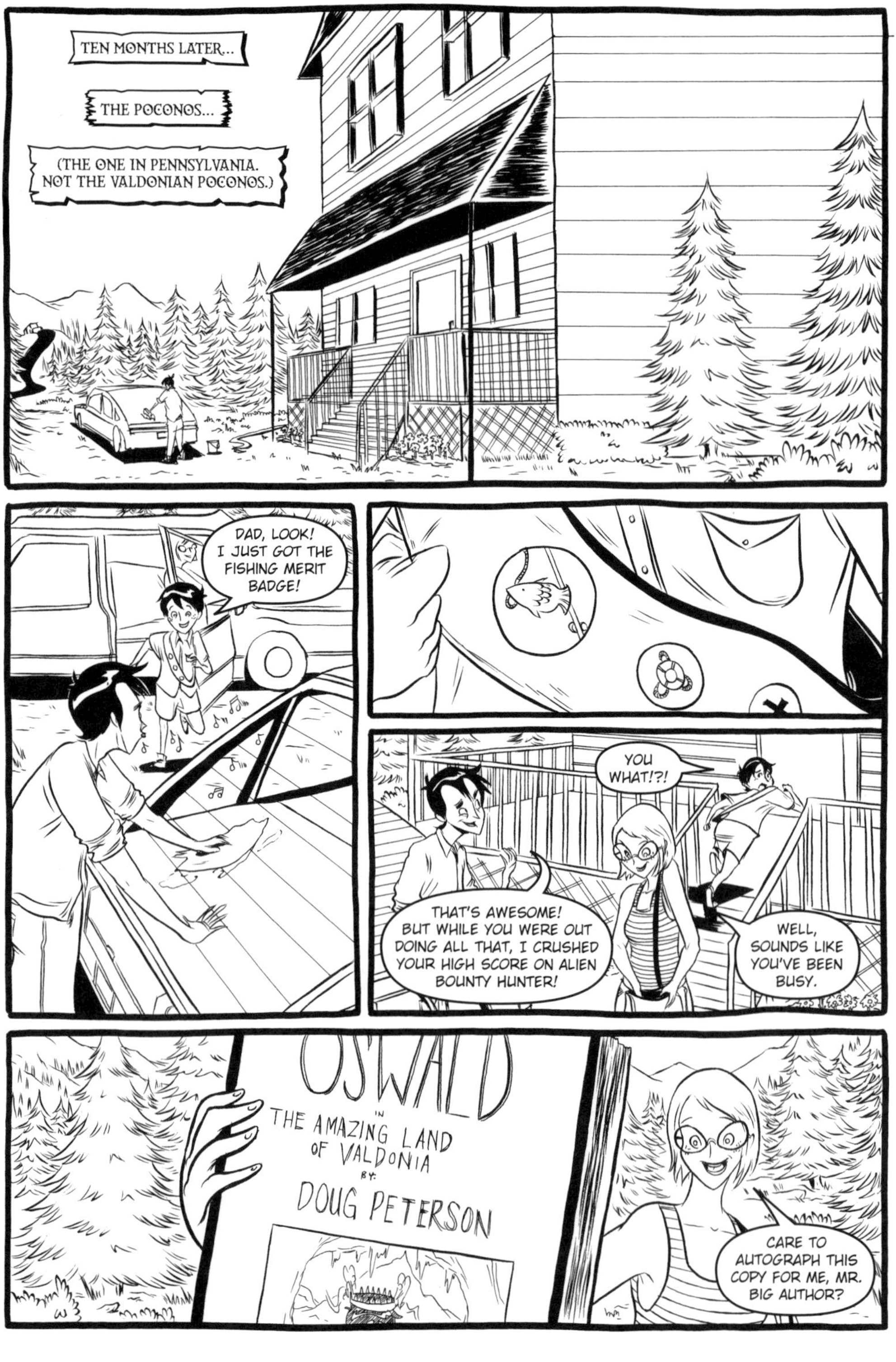
TEN MONTHS LATER...
THE POCONOS...
(THE ONE IN PENNSYLVANIA. NOT THE VALDONIAN POCONOS.)
DAD, LOOK! I JUST GOT THE FISHING MERIT BADGE!
YOU WHAT!?!
THAT'S AWESOME! BUT WHILE YOU WERE OUT DOING ALL THAT, I CRUSHED YOUR HIGH SCORE ON ALIEN BOUNTY HUNTER!
WELL, SOUNDS LIKE YOU'VE BEEN BUSY.
OSWALD
IN
THE AMAZING LAND OF VALDONIA
BY:
DOUG PETERSON
CARE TO AUTOGRAPH THIS COPY FOR ME, MR. BIG AUTHOR?

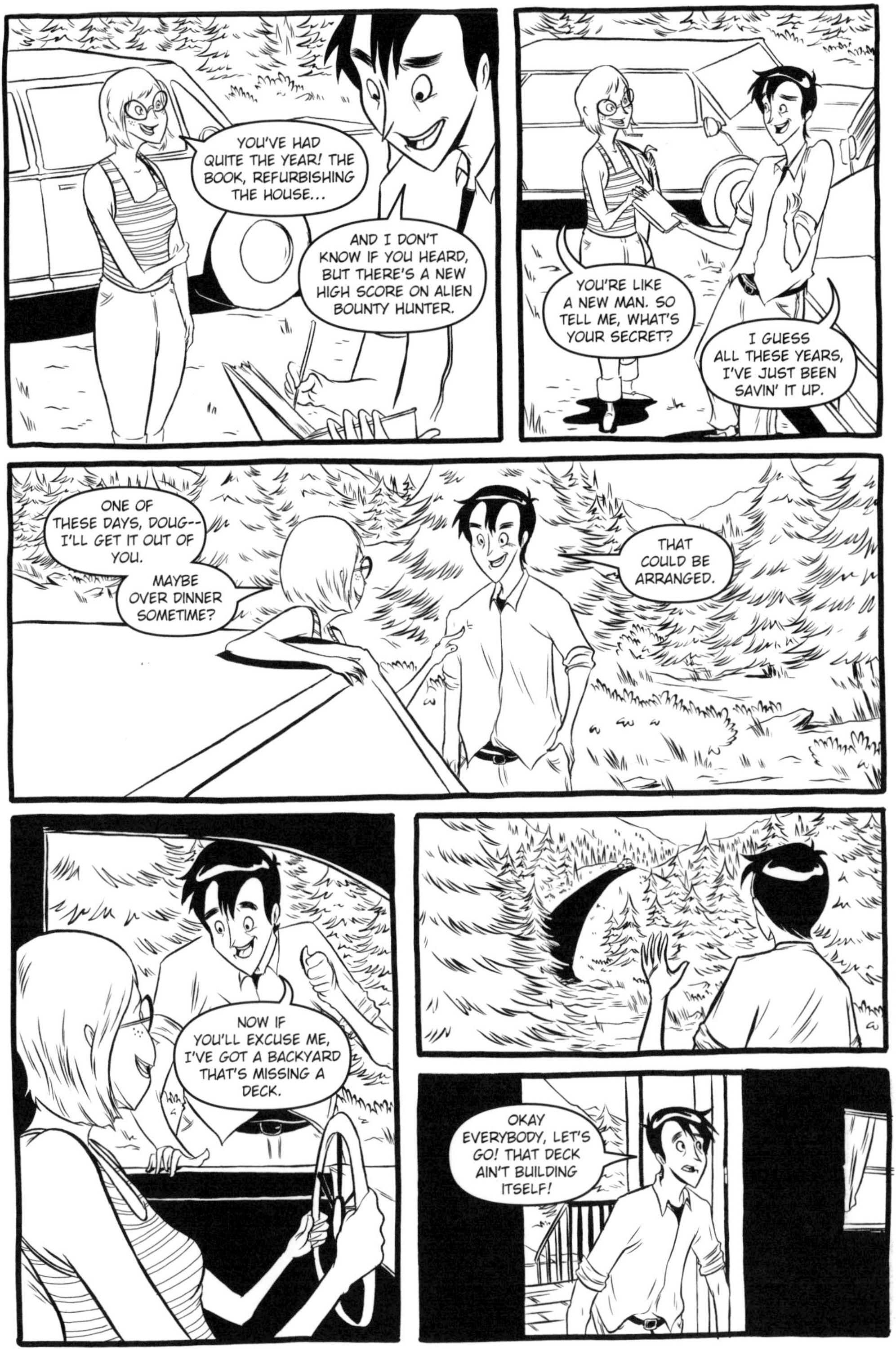
YOU'VE HAD QUITE THE YEAR! THE BOOK, REFURBISHING THE HOUSE...
AND I DON'T KNOW IF YOU HEARD, BUT THERE'S A NEW HIGH SCORE ON ALIEN BOUNTY HUNTER.
YOU'RE LIKE A NEW MAN. SO TELL ME, WHAT'S YOUR SECRET?
I GUESS ALL THESE YEARS, I'VE JUST BEEN SAVIN' IT UP.
ONE OF THESE DAYS, DOUG-- I'LL GET IT OUT OF YOU.
MAYBE OVER DINNER SOMETIME?
THAT COULD BE ARRANGED.
NOW IF YOU'LL EXCUSE ME, I'VE GOT A BACKYARD THAT'S MISSING A DECK.
OKAY EVERYBODY, LET'S GO! THAT DECK AIN'T BUILDING ITSELF!

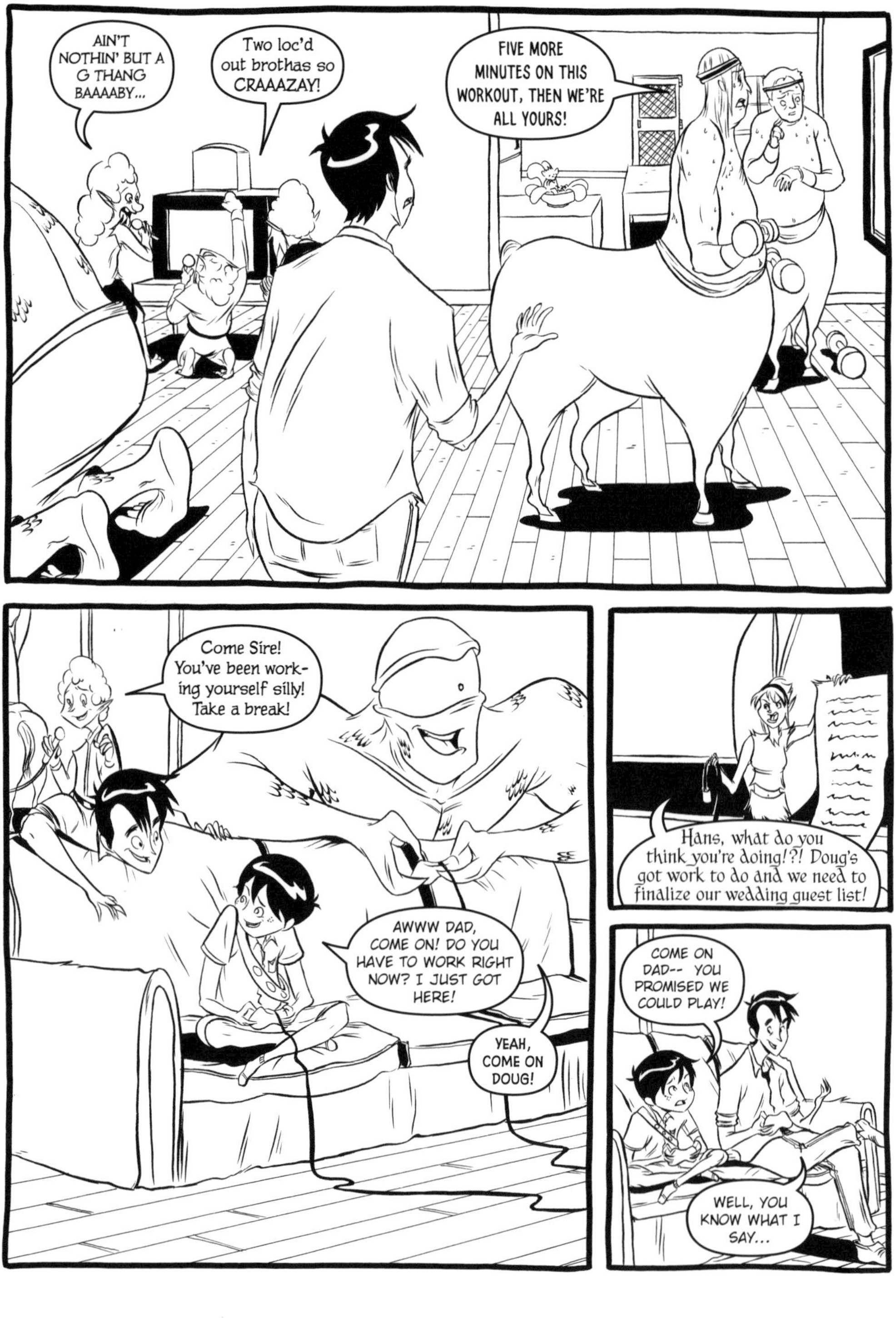
AIN'T NOTHIN' BUT A G THANG BAAAABY...
Two loc'd out brothas so CRAAAZAY!
FIVE MORE MINUTES ON THIS WORKOUT, THEN WE'RE ALL YOURS!
Come Sire! You've been work-ing yourself silly! Take a break!
AWWW DAD, COME ON! DO YOU HAVE TO WORK RIGHT NOW? I JUST GOT HERE!
YEAH, COME ON DOUG!
Hans, what do you think you're doing!?! Doug's got work to do and we need to finalize our wedding guest list!
COME ON DAD-- YOU PROMISED WE COULD PLAY!
WELL, YOU KNOW WHAT I SAY...

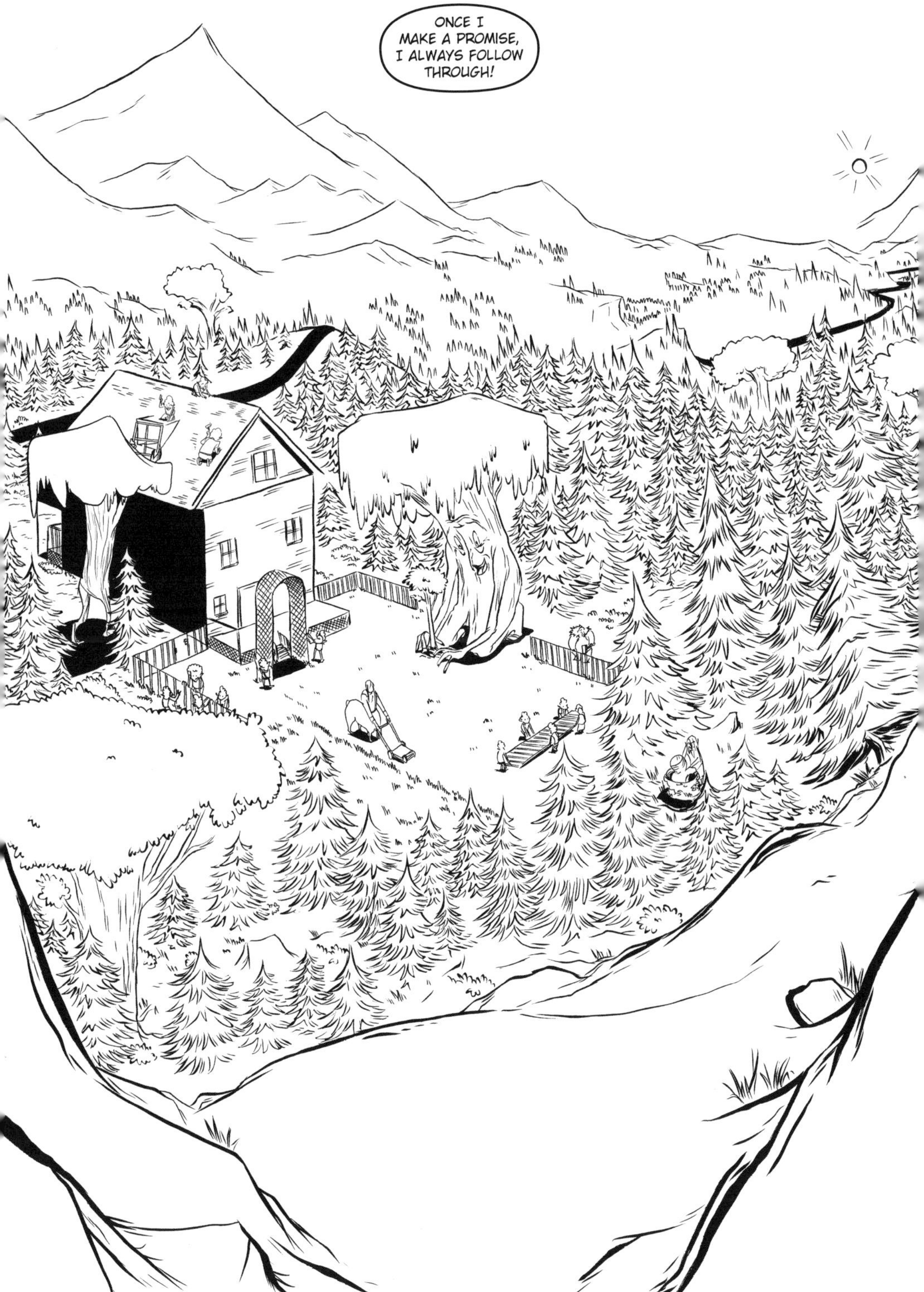
ONCE I MAKE A PROMISE, I ALWAYS FOLLOW THROUGH!

ABOUT THE AUTHORS

Photo by Charlie Chu

⬌ GREG ERB was born ON THE MOON. Now he lives AT THE CENTER OF THE EARTH. His hobbies include EATING PICKLES and dancing to THE JONAS BROTHERS.

Greg Erb also enjoys Mad Libs. Perhaps a little too much.

⬌ JASON OREMLAND was born in the sleepy hamlet of McLean, VA. He currently resides in Sherman Oaks, CA with his wife, son and dog. In addition to co-writing *The Return of King Doug*, Jason has spent his time tracking down and arresting dozens of criminals under the nickname Dog the Bounty Hunter. But he's not the one with the TV show. It's just a coincidence.

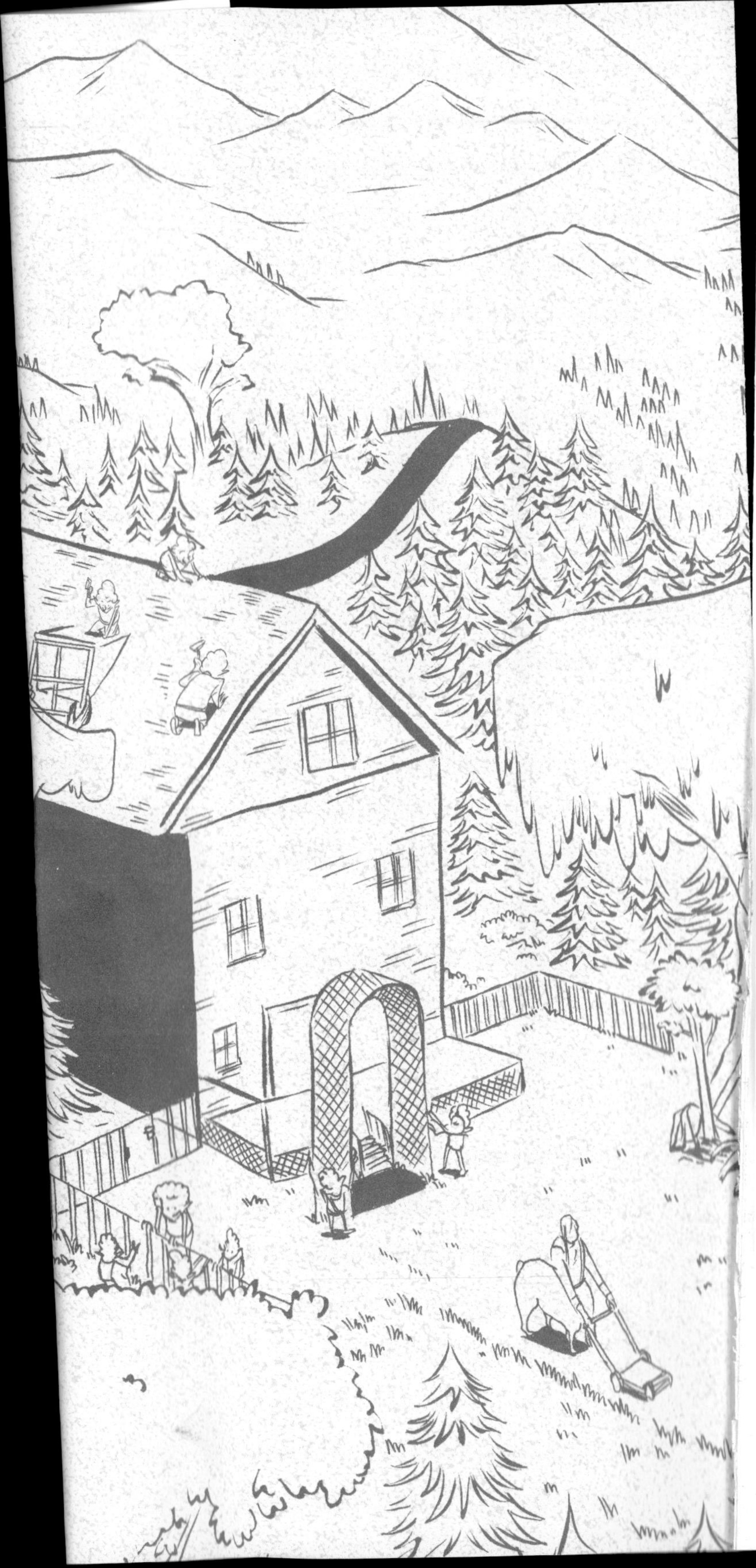

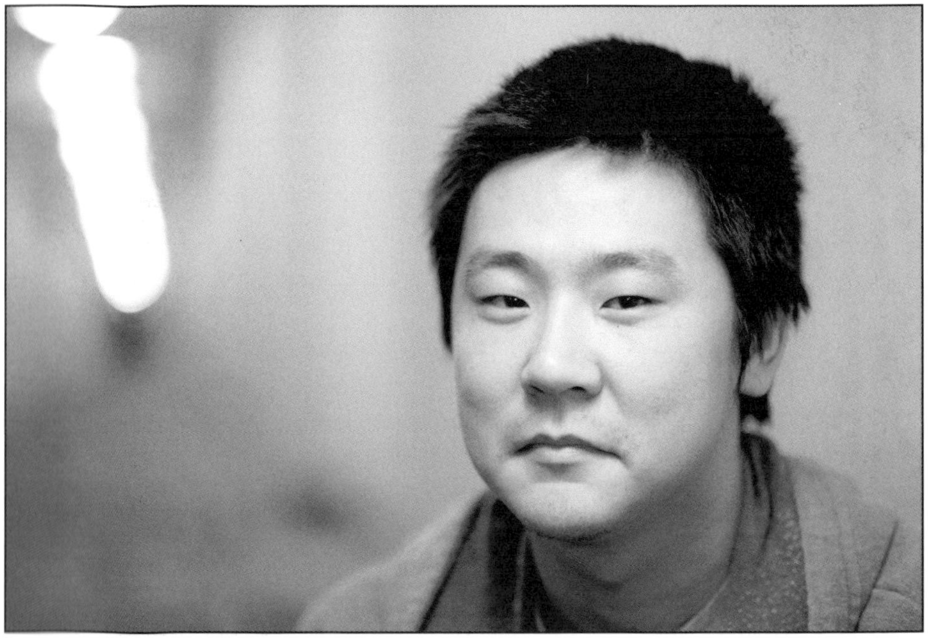

Photo by Charlie Chu

WOOK-JIN CLARK is a Southern Korean. He was born in Seoul, but was raised in South Carolina and Georgia. He's a sucker for sweet tea and chicken biscuits.

He'd really like to thank, his mom, dad, and sister for all their support, as well as Shawn Crystal, Chris Schweizer, Justin Wagner, Kevin Burkhalter, Jarrett Williams, Brad Holderfield, Rich Tommaso, Joey Weiser, Eleanor Davis, Drew Weing, Michele Chidester, and the rest of his Atlanta, Savannah, and Athens friends!

OTHER BOOKS FROM ONI PRESS

THE APOCALIPSTIX
RAY FAWKES
CAMERON STEWART

THE BIG BOOK OF
BARRY
WEEN
BOY GENIUS
JUDD WINICK

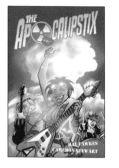

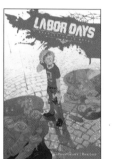

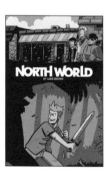

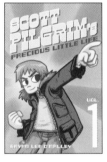

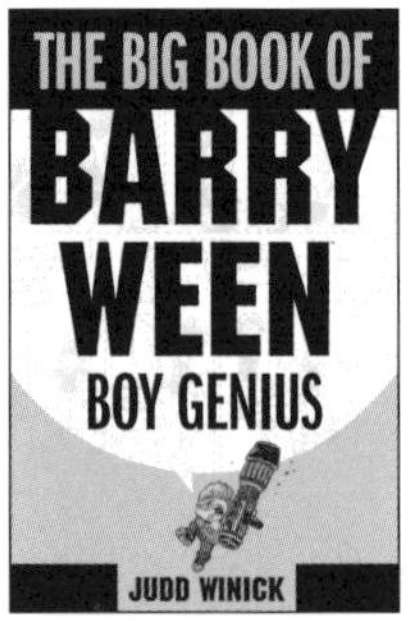

APOCALIPSTIX, VOL. 1
By Ray Fawkes & Cameron Stewart
144 pages • digest
B&W • $11.95 US
ISBN 978-1-932664-45-4

BIG BOOK OF BARRY WEEN, BOY GENIUS
By Judd Winick
360 pages • 6"x9" trade paperback
B&W • $19.95 US
ISBN 978-1-934964-03-3

LABOR DAYS

Jim Massey • Robbi Rodriguez
MAINTENANCE
IT'S A DIRTY JOB...

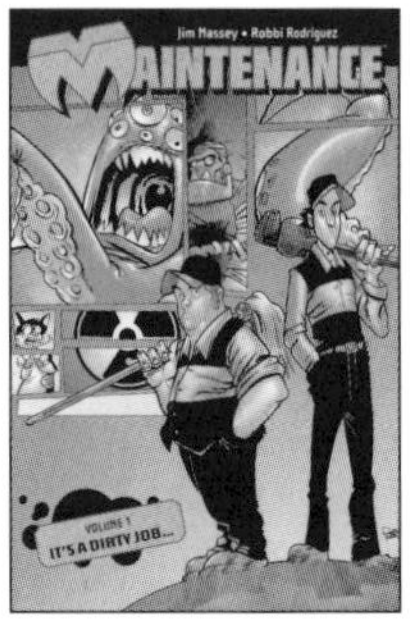

LABOR DAYS, VOL. 1
By Philip Gelatt and Rick Lacy
144 pages • 6"x9" trade paperback
B&W • $11.95 US
ISBN 978-1-932664-92-8

MAINTENANCE VOL. 1:
IT'S A DIRTY JOB...
By Jim Massey and Robbi Rodriguez
96 pages • 6"x9" trade paperback
B&W • $9.95 US
ISBN 978-1-932664-62-1

NORTH WORLD

SCOTT PILGRIM'S
PRECIOUS LITTLE LIFE
VOL. 1
BRYAN LEE O'MALLEY

NORTH WORLD VOL. 1:
THE EPIC OF CONRAD
By Lars Brown
152 pages • digest
B&W • $11.95 US
ISBN 978-1-932664-91-1

SCOTT PILGRIM, VOL. 1:
SCOTT PILGRIM'S PRECIOUS LITTLE LIFE
By Bryan Lee O'Malley
168 pages • digest
B&W • $11.95
ISBN 978-1-932664-08-9

SIDESCROLLERS
MATTHEW LOUX

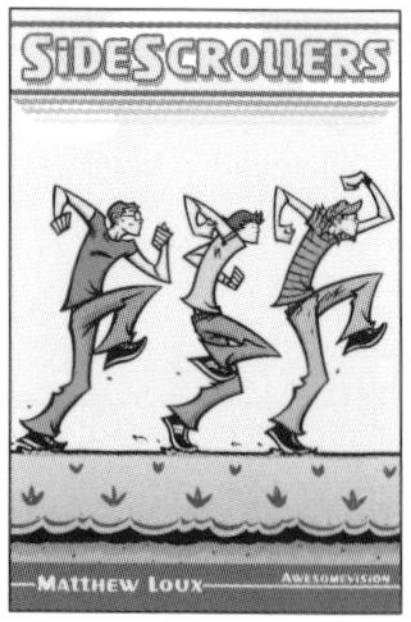

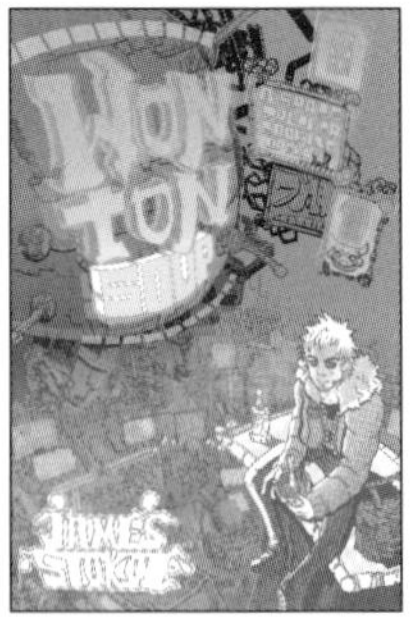

SIDESCROLLERS
By Matthew Loux
216 pages • digest
B&W • $11.95
ISBN 978-1-932664-50-8

WONTON SOUP
By James Stokoe
200 pages • digest
B&W • $11.95 US
ISBN 978-1-932664-60-7

For more information on these and other fine Oni Press comic books and graphic novels, visit www.onipress.com. To find a comic specialty store in your area, call 1-888-COMICBOOK or visit www.comicshops.us.

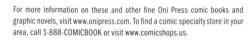

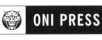

ONI PRESS www.onipress.com

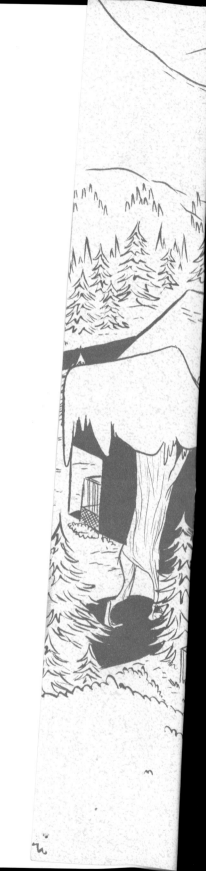

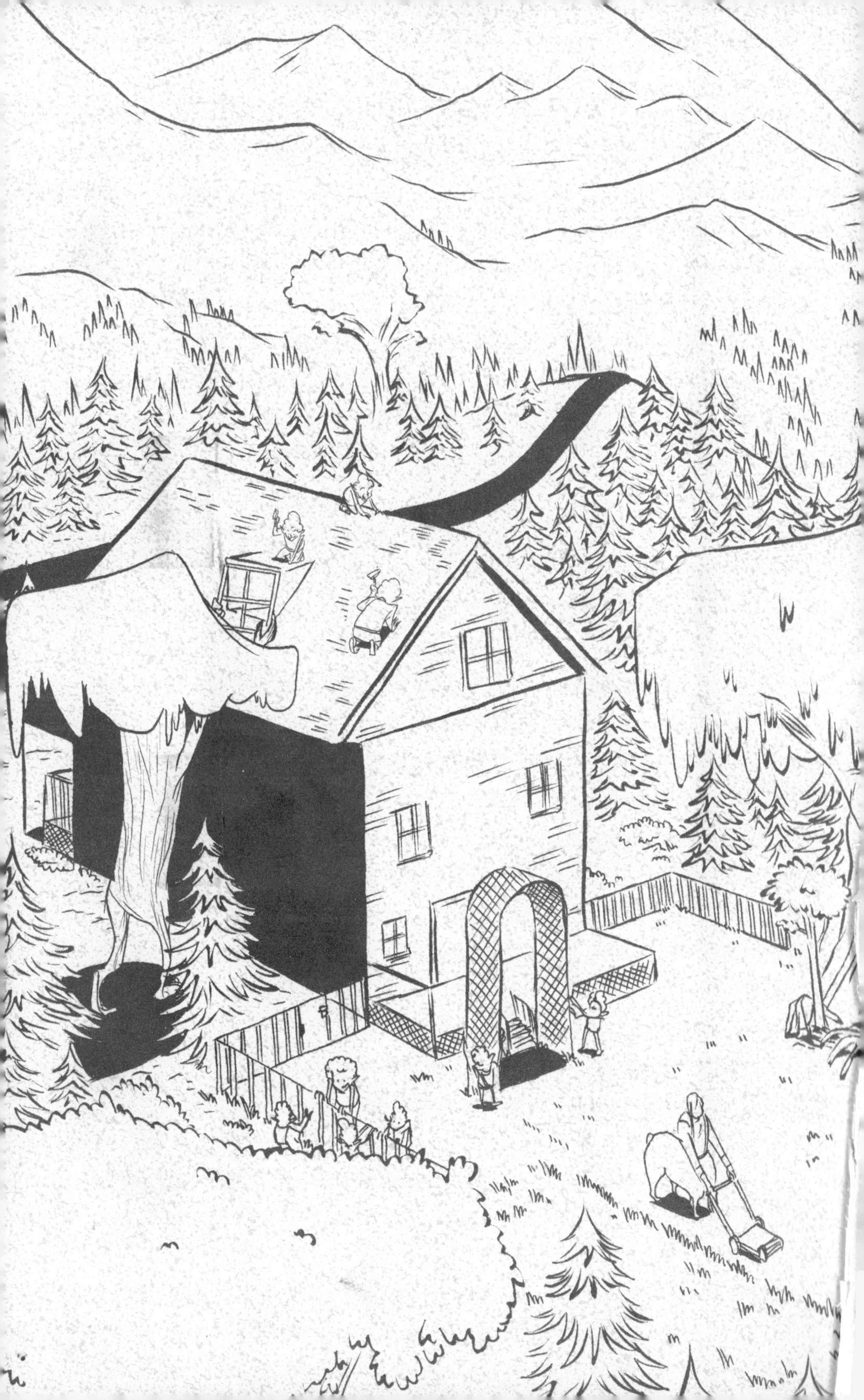